CCNP ONT Official
Exam Certification Guide

Amir S. Ranjbar, CCIE No. 8669

ISBN 978-81-317-1406-5

First Impression, 2007
Second Impression, 2008

This edition is manufactured in India and is authorized for sale only in India, Bangladesh, Bhutan, Pakistan, Nepal, Sri Lanka and the Maldives. Circulation of this edition outside of these territories is UNAUTHORIZED.

Published by Dorling Kindersley (India) Pvt. Ltd., licensees of Pearson Education in South Asia.

Head Office: 482, F.I.E., Patparganj, Delhi 110 092, India.
Registered Office: 14 Local Shopping Centre, Panchsheel Park, New Delhi 110 017, India.

Printed in India by Sheel Print N Pack.

About the Author

Amir S. Ranjbar, CCIE No. 8669, is an internetworking trainer and consultant. Born in Tehran, Iran, he moved to Canada in 1983. He received his bachelor's degree in computer science (1989) and master of science degree in knowledge-based systems (1991) from the University of Guelph in Guelph, Ontario, Canada. After graduation, Amir worked as a programmer/analyst for Statistics Canada until 1995 when he was hired by Digital Equipment Corporation as a certified Microsoft trainer. After performing training on Microsoft Backoffice products such as Windows NT, Exchange Server, and Systems Management Server for three years, he shifted his focus to Cisco Systems. In 1998, he joined GEOTRAIN Corporation, which was later acquired by Global Knowledge Network, and worked for them as a full-time Certified Cisco Systems Instructor until 2005. In October 2005, Amir started his own business (AMIRACAN Inc.) in the field of internetwork consulting, but his major activity is still conducting training for Global Knowledge Network on a contractual basis. His areas of specialty are MPLS, BGP, QoS, VoIP, and advanced routing and switching. Amir's e-mail address is aranjbar@rogers.com

About the Contributing Author

Troy Houston, CCNP, CCDP, and CCIE-written, independently provides contracted business and knowledge solutions to enterprise customers in the Mid-Atlantic area. The first half of his career was in the Aerospace industry where he gained extensive RF knowledge making him the WLAN SME today. Over the past 10 years, Troy has planned, designed, implemented, operated, and troubleshot LANs, WANs, MANs, and WLANs. He attained his bachelor of science degree in management of information systems from Eastern University. Additionally, he is an inventor and holds a patent for one of his many ideas. Formerly in the military, Troy returned to the military on a reserve basis after 9/11. He provides the Air Force Reserves his skills and knowledge as a Computers-Communications Systems Specialist (3C0). He can be contacted at troy@houstonshome.com.

About the Technical Reviewers

Dave Minutella (CCNP, CCDP, CCSP, INFOSEC, CISSP, MCSA, MCDST, CTP, Security+, Network +, A+) has been working in the IT and telecom industry for more than 12 years. He currently serves as vice president of educational services for TechTrain/The Training Camp. Prior to that, he was the lead Cisco instructor, primarily teaching CCNA, CCDA, and CCNP courses. Dave is also the technical author of *CSVPN Exam Cram 2* and coauthor of *CCNA Exam Prep 2* from Que Publishing, and he is the present Cisco certifications expert for SearchNetworking.com's *Ask the Networking Expert* panel.

Mike Valentine has 12 years of experience in the IT field, specializing in network design and installation. His projects include the installation of network services and infrastructure at the largest private aircraft maintenance facility in Canada, Cisco Unified CallManager implementations for small business clients in southwest Florida, and implementation of network mergers and development for Prospera Credit Union in British Columbia. He now heads up his own network consulting company near Vancouver, BC, providing contract Cisco certification instruction and network infrastructure consulting services to clients throughout North America.

Mike is the senior Cisco instructor for The Training Camp. His diverse background and exceptional instructional skills make him a consistent favorite with students. In addition to providing training and developing courseware for The Training Camp, he is the senior network engineer for The Client Server, Inc. in Bonita Springs, Florida, responsible for network infrastructure, security, and VoIP projects. Mike holds a Bachelor of Arts in anthropology, in addition to the following certifications: MCP+i, MCSA, MCSE (Security, Sec+, Net+), CCDA, CCNP, IPTX, CIEH, and CTP.

Mike coauthored the popular *CCNA Exam Cram 2*, published in December 2005.

Dedications

This book is dedicated to my wife, Elke Haugen-Ranjbar, whose love, hard work, understanding, and support have made my home a dream come true. Should my children Thalia, Ariana, and Armando choose a life partner when they grow up, I wish they will make as good of a choice as I did.

—Amir Ranjbar

Acknowledgments

I would like to thank the technical editors, Dave and Mike, for their valuable comments and feedback.

Special thanks to Mary Beth Ray for her patience and understanding, and to Andrew Cupp for a well-done job.

This book is the product of the hard work of a team and not just a few individuals. Managers, editors, coordinators, and designers: All of you, please accept my most sincere appreciation for your efforts and professional input.

This Book Is Safari Enabled

The Safari® Enabled icon on the cover of your favorite technology book means the book is available through Safari Bookshelf. When you buy this book, you get free access to the online edition for 45 days.

Safari Bookshelf is an electronic reference library that lets you easily search thousands of technical books, find code samples, download chapters, and access technical information whenever and wherever you need it.

To gain 45-day Safari Enabled access to this book:

- Go to www.ciscopress.com/safarienabled
- Complete the brief registration form
- Enter the coupon code 73CA-7AVE-SIZ3-46EN-LGGK

If you have difficulty registering on Safari Bookshelf or accessing the online edition, please e-mail customer-service@safaribooksonline.com.

Contents at a Glance

Contents

Icons Used in This Book

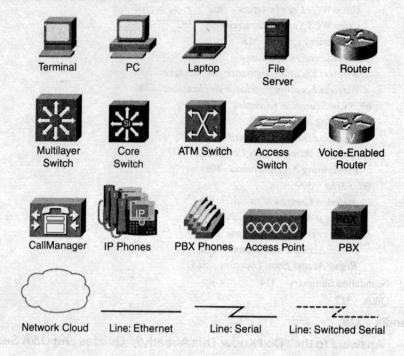

Terminal   PC   Laptop   File Server   Router

Multilayer Switch   Core Switch   ATM Switch   Access Switch   Voice-Enabled Router

CallManager   IP Phones   PBX Phones   Access Point   PBX

Network Cloud   Line: Ethernet   Line: Serial   Line: Switched Serial

Command Syntax Conventions

The conventions used to present command syntax in this book are the same ones used in the *IOS Command Reference*. The *Command Reference* describes these conventions as follows:

- **Boldface** indicates commands and keywords that are entered literally as shown. In actual configuration examples and output (not general command syntax), boldface indicates commands that are manually input by the user (such as a **show** command).
- *Italics* indicate arguments for which you supply actual values.
- Vertical bars (|) separate alternative, mutually exclusive elements.
- Square brackets [ ] indicate optional elements.
- Braces { } indicate a required choice.
- Braces within brackets [{ }] indicate a required choice within an optional element.

Foreword

CCNP ONT Official Exam Certification Guide is an excellent self-study resource for the 642-845 ONT exam. Passing the exam certifies that the successful candidate has important knowledge and skills in optimizing and providing effective QoS techniques for converged networks. Passing the exam is one of the requirements for the Cisco Certified Network Professional (CCNP) certification.

Gaining certification in Cisco technology is key to the continuing educational development of today's networking professional. Through certification programs, Cisco validates the skills and expertise required to effectively manage the modern enterprise network.

Cisco Press exam certification guides and preparation materials offer exceptional—and flexible—access to the knowledge and information required to stay current in your field of expertise, or to gain new skills. Whether used as a supplement to more traditional training or as a primary source of learning, these materials offer users the information and knowledge validation required to gain new understanding and proficiencies.

Developed in conjunction with the Cisco certifications and training team, Cisco Press books are the only self-study books authorized by Cisco and offer students a series of exam practice tools and resource materials to help ensure that learners fully grasp the concepts and information presented.

Additional authorized Cisco instructor-led courses, e-learning, labs, and simulations are available exclusively from Cisco Learning Solutions Partners worldwide. To learn more, visit http://www.cisco.com/go/training.

I hope that you find these materials to be an enriching and useful part of your exam preparation.

Erik Ullanderson
Manager, Global Certifications
Learning@Cisco
March 2007

Introduction

Professional certifications have been an important part of the computing industry for many years and will continue to become more important. There are many reasons for these certifications, but the most popularly cited reason is that of credibility. All other considerations held equal, the certified employee/consultant/job candidate is considered more valuable than one who is not.

Goals and Methods

The most important and somewhat obvious goal of this book is to help you pass the Optimizing Converged Cisco Networks (ONT) exam 642-845. In fact, if the primary objective of this book were different, the book title would be misleading; however, the methods used in this book to help you pass the ONT exam are also designed to make you much more knowledgeable about how to do your job. Although this book and the accompanying CD-ROM together have more than enough questions to help you prepare for the actual exam, the method in which they are used is not to simply make you memorize as many questions and answers as you possibly can.

One key methodology used in this book and on the CD-ROM is to help you discover the exam topics that you need to review in more depth, to help you fully understand and remember those details, and to help you prove to yourself that you have retained your knowledge of those topics. Therefore, this book does not try to help you pass by memorization; it helps you truly learn and understand the topics. The ONT exam is just one of the foundation topics in the CCNP certification, and the knowledge contained within is vitally important to considering yourself a truly skilled routing/switching engineer or specialist. This book would do you a disservice if it did not attempt to help you learn the material. To that end, this book will help you pass the ONT exam by using the following methods:

- Helping you discover which test topics you have not mastered
- Providing explanations and information to fill in your knowledge gaps
- Supplying exercises and scenarios that enhance your ability to recall and deduce the answers to test questions
- Providing practice exercises on the topics and the testing process via test questions on the CD-ROM

Who Should Read This Book?

This book is not designed to be a general networking topics book, although you can use it for that purpose. This book is intended to tremendously increase your chances of passing the CCNP ONT exam. Although you can achieve other objectives from using this book, the book was written with one goal in mind: to help you pass the exam.

Why should you want to pass the CCNP ONT exam? Because it is one of the milestones toward getting the CCNP certification—no small feat in itself. What would achieving CCNP mean to you? A raise, a promotion, or recognition? How about to enhance your résumé? Maybe it is to demonstrate that you are serious about continuing the learning process and not content to rest on your laurels. Or perhaps it is to please your reseller-employer, who needs more certified employees for a higher discount from Cisco. Or it could be for one of many other reasons.

Strategies for Exam Preparation

The strategy that you use for CCNP ONT might be slightly different from strategies that other readers use, mainly based on the skills, knowledge, and experience you already have obtained. For instance, if you have attended the ONT course, you might take a different approach than someone who learned VoIP or QoS via on-the-job training. Regardless of the strategy you use or the background you have, this book is designed to help you get to the point where you can pass the exam with the least amount of time required. For instance, it is unnecessary for you to read a chapter if you fully understand it already. However, many people like to make sure that they truly know a topic and thus read over material that they already know. Several book features, such as the "Do I Know This Already?" quizzes, will help you gain the confidence you need to be convinced that you know some material already and to help you know what topics you need to study more.

The following are some additional suggestions for using this book and preparing for the exam:

■ Familiarize yourself with the exam objectives in Table I-1 and thoroughly read the chapters on topics that you are not familiar with. Use the assessment tools provided in this book to identify areas where you need additional study. The assessment tools include the "Do I Know This Already?" quizzes, the "Q&A" questions, and the sample exam questions on the CD-ROM.

■ Take all quizzes in this book and review the answers and the answer explanations. It is not enough to know the correct answer; you also need to understand why it is correct and why the others are incorrect. Retake the chapter quizzes until you pass with 100 percent.

■ Take the CD-ROM test in this book and review the answers. Use your results to identify areas where you need additional preparation.

■ Review other documents, RFCs, and the Cisco website for additional information. If this book references an outside source, it's a good idea to spend some time looking at it.

■ Review the chapter questions and CD-ROM questions the day before your scheduled test. Review each chapter's "Foundation Summary" when you make your final preparations.

■ On the test date, arrive at least 20 minutes before your test time. This plan gives you time to register and glance through your notes before the test without feeling rushed or anxious.

■ If you are not sure of an answer to a question, attempt to eliminate incorrect answers.

■ You might need to spend more time on some questions than others. Remember, you have an average of 1 minute to answer each question.

How This Book Is Organized

Although you can read this book cover to cover if you want to, it is designed to be flexible and allow you to easily move between chapters and sections of chapters to cover just the material that you need more work with. Chapter 1 of this book matches the "Cisco VoIP Implementations" module of the Cisco ONT official training curriculum. Chapter 2 of this book matches the "Introduction to IP QoS" module of the Cisco ONT official training curriculum. Chapters 3, 4, 5, and 6 of this book match the "Implement the DiffServ QoS Model" module of the Cisco ONT official training curriculum. Chapter 7 of this book matches the "Implementing AutoQoS" module of the Cisco ONT official training curriculum. Finally, Chapters 8, 9, and 10 of this book match the "Implement Wireless Scalability" module of the Cisco ONT official training curriculum.

Following is a short description of the topics covered in this book:

- **Chapter 1, "Cisco VoIP Implementations"**—This chapter describes the benefits of, and the basic components of, VoIP networks. Conversion of analog voice signal to digital voice signal and vice versa, plus encapsulation of voice for transport across an IP network, and calculating bandwidth requirements for VoIP are also discussed in this chapter. The final section of this chapter identifies the components necessary for VoIP support in an enterprise, describes the main IP telephony deployment models, and defines call admission control.

- **Chapter 2, "IP Quality of Service"**—This chapter provides the essential background, definitions, and concepts for learning IP Quality of Service. First, QoS is defined, the main issues that must be addressed in a converged network are presented, and the key steps in implementing a QoS policy in a network are described. The three main QoS models and the key features, merits, and drawbacks of each model are discussed next. The last part of this chapter explains the legacy Command Line Interface (CLI), Modular Quality of Service Command Line Interface (MQC), Cisco AutoQoS, and Cisco Router and Security Device Manager (SDM) QoS Wizard. The advantages and disadvantages of each of these QoS implementation methods are compared.

- **Chapter 3, "Classification, Marking, and NBAR"**—This chapter defines classification and marking, and presents the markings that are available at data link and network layers. QoS service classes and how they can be used to create a service policy throughout a network are described next, followed by a discussion on Network trust boundaries. Network Based Application Recognition (NBAR), as well as Packet Description Language Modules (PDLM), are described next. The chapter concludes by presenting the IOS commands required to configure NBAR.

- **Chapter 4, "Congestion Management and Queuing"**—This chapter starts by defining what congestion is and why congestion happens. Next, the need for queuing or congestion management is explained and the router queuing components are listed and described. The rest if this chapter is dedicated to explaining and providing configuration and monitoring commands for queuing methods, namely FIFO, PQ, RR, WRR, WFQ, Class-Based WFQ, and LLQ.

- **Chapter 5, "Congestion Avoidance, Policing, Shaping, and Link Efficiency Mechanisms"**—This chapter provides an overview of three main QoS concepts: congestion avoidance, traffic shaping and policing, and link efficiency mechanisms. WRED and class-based WRED are the main mechanisms covered. Traffic shaping and policing concepts are explained in the next section; you will learn the purpose of these mechanisms and where it is appropriate to use them. Different compression techniques, plus the concept of link fragmentation and interleaving are the topics of discussion in the third and final section of this chapter.

- **Chapter 6, "Implementing QoS Pre-Classify and Deploying End-to-End QoS"**—This chapter describes the concept of QoS pre-classify, and how it is used to ensure that IOS QoS features work in conjunction with tunneling and encryption. The second part of this chapter deals with the topics related to deploying end-to-end QoS. The final part of this chapter discusses the concept of control plane policing.

- **Chapter 7, "Implementing AutoQoS"**—This chapter explains AutoQoS, including discussions on AutoQoS VoIP and AutoQoS Enterprise. It also presents the key elements of QoS deployment, protocol discovery with NBAR, and AutoQoS deployment restrictions. Configuring and verifying AutoQoS on routers and switches is another major topic of this chapter. A discussion on common AutoQoS problems and suggestions on mitigating those problems by modifying the active AutoQoS configuration completes this chapter.

- **Chapter 8, "WLAN QoS Implementation"**—This chapter starts by explaining the need for QoS in wireless LANs and describing WLAN QoS, which is work in progress. WLAN QoS implementation between client and wireless access point, between access point and controller, and between controller and Ethernet switch are described next. Configuring WLAN QoS through defining QoS profiles and WLAN IDs on wireless controllers is the last topic of this chapter.

- **Chapter 9, "Introducing 802.1x and Configuring Encryption and Authentication on Lightweight Access Points"**—The focus of this chapter is wireless security. It starts by explaining the need for wireless security and describing WLAN security. Next, 802.11x, LEAP, EAP (FAST and TLS), and PEAP are briefly introduced, and the concept of WiFi protected access (WPA) is explained. The final section of this chapter discusses how encryption and authentication on lightweight access points is configured.

- **Chapter 10, "WLAN Management"**—This chapter begins by describing the Cisco unified wireless networks: the business drivers, the elements and, of course, the Cisco implementation model and its components. The second part of this chapter describes Cisco Wireless LAN Solution Engine (WLSE) and WLSE Express and their features and benefits; it also presents a quick lesson on WLSE Express setup. The final parts of this chapter discuss Cisco Wireless Control Systems (WCS base and location software and system features), Cisco Wireless Location Appliance (architecture and applications), and rogue access point detection.

- **Appendix A, "Answers to the "Do I Know This Already?" Quizzes and Q&A Sections"**—This appendix provides the answers and explanations to all of the questions in the book.

Features of This Book

This book features the following:

- **"Do I Know This Already?" Quizzes**—Each chapter begins with a quiz that helps you determine the amount of time you need to spend studying that chapter. If you follow the directions at the beginning of the chapter, the "Do I Know This Already?" quiz directs you to study all or particular parts of the chapter.

- **Foundation Topics**—These are the core sections of each chapter. They explain the protocols, concepts, and configuration for the topics in that chapter. If you need to learn about the topics in a chapter, read the "Foundation Topics" section.

- **Foundation Summaries**—Near the end of each chapter, a summary collects the most important information from the chapter. The "Foundation Summary" section is designed to help you review the key concepts in the chapter if you scored well on the "Do I Know This Already?" quiz. This section is an excellent tool for last-minute review.

- **Q&A**—Each chapter ends with a "Q&A" section that forces you to exercise your recall of the facts and processes described inside that chapter. The questions are generally harder than the actual exam. These questions are a great way to increase the accuracy of your recollection of the facts.

- **CD-ROM Test Questions**—Using the test engine on the CD-ROM, you can take simulated exams. You can also choose to be presented with several questions on an objective that you need more work on. This testing tool gives you practice to make you more comfortable when you actually take the CCNP exam.

ONT Exam Topics

Cisco lists the topics of the ONT exam on its website at www.cisco.com/web/learning/le3/current_exams/642-845.html. The list provides key information about what the test covers. Table I-1 lists the ONT exam topics and the corresponding parts in this book that cover those topics. Each part begins with a list of the topics covered. Use these references as a road map to find the exact materials you need to study to master the ONT exam topics. Note, however, that because all exam information is managed by Cisco Systems and is therefore subject to change, candidates should continually monitor the Cisco Systems site for course and exam updates at www.cisco.com.

Table I-1 *ONT Topics and the Parts of the book Where They Are Covered*

Topic	Part
Describe Cisco VoIP implementations.	
Describe the functions and operations of a VoIP network (e.g., packetization, bandwidth considerations, CAC, etc.).	I
Describe and identify basic voice components in an enterprise network (e.g. Gatekeepers, Gateways, etc.).	I
Describe QoS considerations.	
Explain the necessity of QoS in converged networks (e.g., bandwidth, delay, loss, etc.).	II
Describe strategies for QoS implementations (e.g. QoS Policy, QoS Models, etc.).	II
Describe DiffServ QoS implementations.	
Describe classification and marking (e.g., CoS, ToS, IP Precedence, DSCP, etc.).	II
Describe and configure NBAR for classification.	II
Explain congestion management and avoidance mechanisms (e.g., FIFO, PQ, WRR, WRED, etc.).	II
Describe traffic policing and traffic shaping (i.e., traffic conditioners).	II
Describe Control Plane Policing.	II
Describe WAN link efficiency mechanisms (e.g., Payload/Header Compression, MLP with interleaving, etc.).	II
Describe and configure QoS Pre-Classify.	II
Implement AutoQoS.	
Explain the functions and operations of AutoQoS.	II
Describe the SDM QoS Wizard.	II
Configure, verify, and troubleshoot AutoQoS implementations (i.e., MQC).	II
Implement WLAN security and management.	
Describe and configure wireless security on Cisco Clients and APs (e.g., SSID, WEP, LEAP, etc.).	III
Describe basic wireless management (e.g., WLSE and WCS). Configure and verify basic WCS configuration (i.e., login, add/review controller/AP status, security, and import/review maps).	III
Describe and configure WLAN QoS.	III

This part covers the following ONT exam topics. (To view the ONT exam overview, visit http://www.cisco.com/web/learning/le3/current_exams/642-845.html.)

- Describe the functions and operations of a VoIP network (e.g., packetization, bandwidth considerations, CAC, etc.).

- Describe and identify basic voice components in an enterprise network (e.g., Gatekeepers, Gateways, etc.).

Part I: Voice over IP

Chapter 1   Cisco VoIP Implementations

Part I: Voice over IP

This chapter covers the following subjects:

- Introduction to VoIP Networks

- Digitizing and Packetizing Voice

- Encapsulating Voice Packets

- Bandwidth Calculation

- Implementing VoIP Support in an Enterprise Network

Cisco VoIP Implementations

This chapter describes Cisco Voice over IP (VoIP) implementations. Expect to see several exam questions based on the material in this chapter.

This chapter has five major topics. The first topic helps you understand the basic components of VoIP networks and the benefits of VoIP networks. The second topic is about converting an analog voice signal to a digital voice signal and the concepts of sampling, quantization, compression, and digital signal processors (DSP). The third section discusses encapsulating voice for transport across an IP network using Real-Time Transport Protocol. The fourth focuses on calculating bandwidth requirements for VoIP, considering different data link layer possibilities. The fifth section identifies the components necessary for VoIP support in an enterprise, describes the main IP Telephony deployment models, and briefly defines call admission control.

"Do I Know This Already?" Quiz

The purpose of the "Do I Know This Already?" quiz is to help you decide whether you really need to read this entire chapter. The 20-question quiz, derived from the major sections of this chapter, helps you determine how to spend your limited study time.

Table 1-1 outlines the major topics discussed in this chapter and the "Do I Know This Already?" quiz questions that correspond to those topics. You can keep track of your score here, too.

Table 1-1 *"Do I Know This Already?" Foundation Topics Section-to-Question Mapping*

Foundation Topics Section Covering These Questions	Questions	Score
"Introduction to VoIP Networks"	1–5	
"Digitizing and Packetizing Voice"	6–10	
"Encapsulating Voice Packets"	11–12	
"Bandwidth Calculation"	13–17	
"Implementing VoIP Support in an Enterprise Network"	18–20	
Total Score	**(20 possible)**	

CAUTION   The goal of self-assessment is to gauge your mastery of the topics in this chapter. If you do not know the answer to a question or are only partially sure of the answer, mark this question wrong for purposes of the self-assessment. Giving yourself credit for an answer you correctly guess skews your self-assessment results and might provide you with a false sense of security.

You can find the answers to the "Do I Know This Already?" quiz in Appendix A, "Answers to the 'Do I Know This Already?' Quizzes and Q&A Sections." The suggested choices for your next step are as follows:

- **15 or less overall score**—Read the entire chapter. This includes the "Foundation Topics," "Foundation Summary," and "Q&A" sections.

- **16–17 overall score**—Begin with the "Foundation Summary" section and then follow up with the "Q&A" section at the end of the chapter.

- **18 or more overall score**—If you want more review on this topic, skip to the "Foundation Summary" section and then go to the "Q&A" section. Otherwise, proceed to the next chapter.

1. Which one of the following is *not* a benefit of VoIP compared to traditional circuit-switched telephony?

    a. Consolidated network expenses

    b. Improved employee productivity

    c. Access to new communication devices

    d. Higher voice quality

2. Which one of the following is not considered a packet telephony device?

    a. IP phone

    b. Call agent

    c. PBX

    d. Gateway

3. Which one of the following is *not* an analog interface?

    a. FXO

    b. BRI

    c. FXS

    d. E&M

4. Which one of the following digital interface descriptions is incorrect?

   a. T1 CAS with 30 voice channels

   b. T1 CCS with 23 voice channels

   c. BRI with 2 voice channels

   d. E1 with 30 voice channels

5. Which one of the following is *not* one of the three stages of a phone call?

   a. Call setup

   b. Call maintenance

   c. Call teardown

   d. Call processing

6. Which one of the following is *not* a step in analog-to-digital signal conversion?

   a. Sampling

   b. Quantization

   c. Encoding

   d. Decompression

7. Based on the Nyquist theorem, what is the appropriate sampling rate for an analog voice signal with a maximum frequency of 4000 Hz?

   a. 8800

   b. 8000

   c. 4000

   d. 4400

8. Which of the following accurately describes the 8-bit encoding?

   a. 1 polarity bit, 3 segment bits, 4 step bits

   b. 1 polarity bit, 4 segment bits, 3 step bits

   c. 4 polarity bits, 3 segment bits, 1 step bit

   d. 3 polarity bits, 4 segment bits, 1 step bit

9. Which of the following codec descriptions is incorrect?

   a. G.711 PCM 64 Kbps

   b. G.726 ADPCM 8 Kbps

   c. G.728 LD-CELP 16 Kbps

   d. G.729 CS-ACELP 8 Kbps

10. Which of the following is *not* a telephony application that requires usage of a DSP?

   a. Voice termination

   b. Conferencing

   c. Packetization

   d. Transcoding

11. Which of the following is a false statement?

   a. Voice needs the reliability that TCP provides.

   b. Voice needs the reordering that RTP provides.

   c. Voice needs the time-stamping that RTP provides.

   d. Voice needs the multiplexing that UDP provides.

12. Which of the following correctly specifies the header sizes for RTP, UDP, and IP?

   a. 8 bytes of RTP, 12 bytes of UDP, and 20 bytes of IP

   b. 20 bytes of RTP, 12 bytes of UDP, and 8 bytes of IP

   c. 8 bytes of RTP, 20 bytes of UDP, and 12 bytes of IP

   d. 12 bytes of RTP, 8 bytes of UDP, and 20 bytes of IP

13. Which of the following is *not* a factor influencing VoIP media bandwidth?

   a. Packet rate

   b. Packetization size

   c. TCP overhead

   d. Tunneling or security overhead

14. If 30 ms of voice is packetized, what will the packet rate be?

   a. 50 packets per second

   b. 60 packets per second

   c. 30 packets per second

   d. 33.33 packets per second

15. With G.711 and a 20-ms packetization period, what will be the bandwidth requirement over Ethernet (basic Ethernet with no 802.1Q or any tunneling)?

   a. 87.2 kbps

   b. 80 kbps

   c. 64 Kbps

   d. 128 Kbps

16. With G.729 and 20 ms packetization period, what will be the bandwidth requirement over PPP if cRTP is used with no checksum?

    a. 8 Kbps

    b. 26.4 Kbps

    c. 11.2 Kbps

    d. 12 Kbps

17. Which of the following is *not* a factor in determining the amount of bandwidth that can be saved with VAD?

    a. Type of audio (one-way or two-way)

    b. Codec used

    c. Level of background noise

    d. Language and character of the speaker

18. Which of the following is *not* a voice gateway function on a Cisco router (ISR)?

    a. Connect traditional telephony devices

    b. Survivable Remote Site Telephony (SRST)

    c. CallManager Express

    d. Complete phone feature administration

19. Which of the following is *not* a Cisco Unified CallManager function?

    a. Converting analog signal to digital format

    b. Dial plan administration

    c. Signaling and device control

    d. Phone feature administration

20. Which of the following is *not* an enterprise IP Telephony deployment model?

    a. Single site

    b. Single site with clustering over WAN

    c. Multisite with either centralized or distributed call processing

    d. Clustering over WAN

Foundation Topics

Introduction to VoIP Networks

Upon completion of this section, you will know the primary advantages and benefits of packet telephony networks, the main components of packet telephony networks, the definition of analog and digital interfaces, and the stages of a phone call. The final part of this section helps you understand the meaning of distributed and centralized call control and the differences between these two types of call control.

Benefits of Packet Telephony Networks

Many believe that the biggest benefit of packet telephony is toll bypass, or simply long-distance cost savings. However, because the cost of a long-distance call to most parts of the world has decreased substantially, this is not even one of the top three reasons for migrating to packet telephony networks in the North American market.

The main benefits of packet telephony networks are as follows:

■   **More efficient use of bandwidth and equipment, and lower transmission costs**—Packet telephony networks do not use a dedicated 64-kbps channel (DS0) for each VoIP phone call. VoIP calls share the network bandwidth with other applications, and each voice call can use less bandwidth than 64 kbps. Packet telephony networks do not use expensive circuit-switching equipment such as T1 multiplexers, which helps to reduce equipment and operation costs.

■   **Consolidated network expenses**—In a converged network, the data applications, voice, video, and conferencing applications do not have separate and distinct hardware, software, and supporting personnel. They all operate over a common infrastructure and use a single group of employees for configuration and support. This introduces a significant cost saving.

■   **Improved employee productivity**—Cisco IP phones are more than just simple phones. With IP phones, you can access user directories. Furthermore, you can access databases through extensible markup language (XML). Therefore, you can utilize the Cisco IP phone as a sophisticated communication device that allows users to run applications from their IP phones. In short, Cisco IP Phones enhance the user experience by bringing informational resources to the end user.

■   **Access to new communications devices**—Unlike the traditional analog and PBX phones, IP phones can communicate with a number of devices such as computers (computer telephony applications), networking devices, personal digital assistants, and so on, through IP connectivity.

Despite the stated benefits of packet telephony networks, when an organization decides to migrate to packet telephony, it will have to make an initial investment, which will probably not have an attractive short-term return on investment (ROI). Also, if the existing telephony equipment is not fully depreciated, there will be more reluctance to migrating to packet telephony at this time. Finally, it is not easy to consolidate and train the different groups of personnel who used to separately support the data and telephone equipment and networks.

Packet Telephony Components

A packet telephony network must perform several mandatory functions, and it can perform many optional ones. This requires existence and proper operation of various components. Some devices can perform multiple functions simultaneously; for example, for a small deployment a gateway can also act as a gatekeeper. The following is a list of the major components of a packet telephony network, but not all of the components are always present and utilized:

■ **Phones**—There might be analog phones, PBX phones, IP phones, Cisco IP Communicator, and so on. Please note that non-IP phones require the existence of IP gateway(s).

■ **Gateways**—Gateways interconnect and allow communication among devices that are not all necessarily accessible from within the IP network. For instance, a call from inside an IP network to a friend or relative's residential analog phone line must go through at least one gateway. If a call from an analog phone, on a router's FXS port for example, must go through a Wide Area Network (WAN) connection such as a Frame-Relay virtual circuit to get to a remote office, it will also have to go through a gateway. Connectivity of IP networks to Private Branch Exchange (PBX) systems is also accomplished through gateways.

■ **Multipoint control units (MCU)**—An MCU is a conference hardware component. MCU is comprised of a Multipoint Controller and an optional Multipoint Processor that combines the received streams from conference participants and returns the result to all the conference participants.

■ **Application and database servers**—These servers are available for each of the required and optional applications within the IP/packet telephony network. For instance, TFTP servers save and serve IP phone operating systems and configuration files, and certain application servers provide XML-based services to IP phones.

■ **Gatekeepers**—You can obtain two distinct and independent services from gatekeepers:
1. Call routing, which is essentially resolving a name or phone number to an IP address, and
2. CAC, which grants permission for a call setup attempt.

■ **Call agents**—In a centralized call control model, call routing, address translation, call setup, and so on are handled by call agents (CA) rather than the end devices or gateways. For example, Media Gateway Control Protocol (MGCP) is a centralized model that requires the existence of CAs. Outside the context of MGCP, the Call Agents are often referred to as Common Components.

■ **Video end points**—To make video calls or conferences, you must have video end points. Naturally, for video conferencing, the MCU must also have video capabilities.

■ **DSP**—Devices that convert analog signals to digital signals and vice versa use DSPs. Through utilization of different coding and decoding (codec) algorithms such as G.729, DSPs also allow you to compress voice signals and perhaps perform *transcoding* (converting one type of signal to another, such as G.711 to G.729). IP Phones, Gateways, and conference equipment such as MCUs use DSPs.

At this point, it is important to clarify the difference between two concepts: digital signal and VoIP. Today, in almost all cases, one of the early tasks performed in voice communication is digitizing analog voice. This is true regardless of whether the call stays within the PBX system, goes through the PSTN, or traverses through an IP network. Figure 1-1 shows a company that has two branches. The local (main) branch has IP phones, but the remote branch has only PBX phones. Even though all voice calls need digitization, calls that remain within the remote branch are not VoIP calls and need not be encapsulated in IP packets.

Figure 1-1   *Packet Telephony Components*

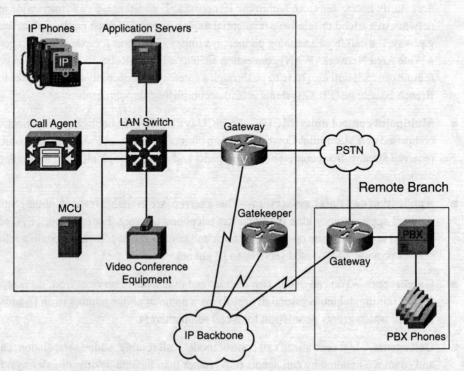

VoIP, on the other hand, in addition to digitizing voice, requires IP-based signaling (for call routing, admission control, setup, maintenance, status, teardown, and so on). Also, VoIP requires conversion of analog voice into IP packets and transport using IP-based protocols such as Real-time Transport Protocol (RTP). Many organizations might not be using VoIP (packet telephony) but have been enjoying the benefits of voice digitization technologies such as PBX and T1 lines. Converting analog voice signals to digital voice signals and back is almost always done. But VoIP signaling and VoIP encapsulation and transport happen only in packet telephony networks. In Figure 1-1, all phone calls made with the IP phones from the main local branch are IP dependent and need IP signaling, IP encapsulation, and transportation in addition to the initial digitization.

You might ask if a packet telephony network always includes and needs a gateway. The answer is this: If the IP phones need to make calls and receive them from PBX phones or the phones on the PSTN network, or if certain calls have to leave the LAN and go through a WAN to reach non-IP phones (such as analog or PBX phones) at remote locations, a gateway is definitely necessary. In Figure 1-1, a phone call made from an IP phone in the local branch to another IP phone within the local branch does not require the services of a voice gateway.

Analog Interfaces

A gateway can have many types of analog interfaces: FXS (Foreign Exchange Station), FXO (Foreign Exchange Office), and E&M (Earth and Magneto or Ear and Mouth).

An FX connection has a station and an office end. The office end (FXO) provides services such as battery, dial tone, digit collection, and ringing to the other end, namely the station (FXS).

The FXS interface of a gateway is meant for analog phones, fax machines, and modems. To those devices, the gateway acts like the PSTN central office (CO) switch.

The FXO interface of a gateway can connect to a regular phone jack to be connected to the PSTN CO switch. The FXO interface acts as a regular analog device such as a legacy analog phone, and it expects to receive battery, dial tone, digit collection, ringing, and other services from the other side, namely the PSTN CO switch. In many small branch offices, at least one FXO interface on a gateway is dedicated to and connected to the PSTN for emergency 911 call purposes.

The E&M connections traditionally provided PBX-to-PBX analog trunk connectivity. However, any two of gateways, PBX switches, or PSTN CO switches may be connected using an E&M connection with E&M interfaces present. Five different types of E&M types exist based on the circuitry, battery present, wiring, and signaling used.

Figure 1-2 shows a gateway with a fax machine plugged into its FXS interface. Its FXO interface is connected to the PSTN CO switch, and its E&M interface is connected to a PBX switch. The gateway has connectivity to the IP phones through the LAN switch, and it provides connectivity to the other branches through the IP backbone (WAN).

Figure 1-2 *Gateway Analog Interfaces*

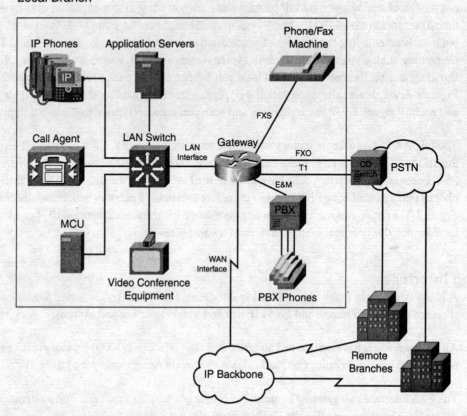

Digital Interfaces

Gateways can also connect to telco and PBX switches using digital interfaces. A gateway can have BRI or T1/E1 digital interfaces. Using a T1 connection is common in North America, whereas E1 lines are more common in Europe. You can configure the T1/E1 interface controller as an ISDN PRI or as Channelized T1/E1 and use channel associated signaling (CAS).

BRI and PRI interfaces use common channel signaling (CCS), where a D (Delta) channel is dedicated to a messaging style of signaling, such as Q931 (or QSIG). You can configure a T1 controller to perform channel associated signaling (CAS) instead. T1 CAS does not dedicate a D channel to signaling. Each T1 CAS channel gives up a few data bits to perform signaling; therefore, T1 CAS is also referred to as robbed bit signaling. You can also configure an E1 interface to perform CAS, but because E1 CAS still dedicates a channel to signaling, data channels do not lose bits to signaling.

Table 1-2 lists and compares the BRI, PRI, and CT1/CE1 digital interfaces.

Table 1-2 *Summary of Digital Interfaces*

Interface	64 Kbps Data/ Voice Channels	Signaling	Framing Overhead	Total Bandwidth
BRI	2	16 kbps (D channel)	48 kbps	192 kbps
T1 CAS	24	In-band (robbed bits)	8 kbps	1544 kbps
T1 CCS	23	64 kbps (D Channel)	8 kbps	1544 kbps
E1 CAS	30	64 kbps	64 kbps	2048 kbps
E1 CCS	30	64 kbps (D Channel)	64 kbps	2048 kbps

Stages of a Phone Call

The three most popular VoIP signaling and control protocols are H.323, which is an ITU standard; Media Gateway Control Protocol (MGCP), which is an Internet Engineering Task Force (IETF) standard; and Session Initiation Protocol (SIP), also an IETF standard. Regardless of the signaling protocol used, a phone call has three main stages: call setup, call maintenance, and call teardown.

During call setup, the destination telephone number must be resolved to an IP address, where the call request message must be sent; this is called *call routing*. Call admission control (CAC) is an optional step that determines whether the network has sufficient bandwidth for the call. If bandwidth is inadequate, CAC sends a message to the initiator indicating that the call cannot get through because of insufficient resources. (The caller usually hears a fast busy tone.)

If call routing and CAC succeed, a call request message is sent toward the destination. If the destination is not busy and it accepts the call, some parameters for the call must be negotiated before voice communication begins. Following are a few of the important parameters that must be negotiated:

- The IP addresses to be used as the destination and source of the VoIP packets between the call end points

- The destination and source User Datagram Protocol (UDP) port numbers that the RTP uses at each call end point

- The compression algorithm (codec) to be used for the call; for example, whether G.729, G.711, or another standard will be used

Call maintenance collects statistics such as packets exchanged, packets lost, end-to-end delay, and jitter during the VoIP call. The end points (devices such as IP phones) that collect this information can locally analyze this data and display the call quality information upon request, or they can submit the results to another device for centralized data analysis. Call teardown, which is usually due to either end point terminating the call, or to put it simply, hanging up, sends appropriate notification to the other end point and any control devices so that the resources can be made free for other calls and purposes.

Distributed Versus Centralized Call Control

Two major call control models exist: distributed call control and centralized call control. The H.323 and SIP protocols are classified as distributed, whereas the MGCP protocol is considered as a centralized call control VoIP signaling protocol.

In the distributed model, multiple devices are involved in setup, maintenance, teardown, and other aspects of call control. The voice-capable devices that perform these tasks have the intelligence and proper configuration to do so.

Figure 1-3 shows a simple case in which two analog phones are plugged into the FXS interfaces of two Cisco voice gateways that have connectivity over an IP network and use the H.323 signaling protocol (distributed model). From the time that the calling device goes off-hook to the time that the called device receives the ring, seven steps are illustrated within this distributed call control model:

1. The calling phone goes off-hook, and its voice gateway (R1) provides a dial tone and waits for digits.

2. The calling phone sends digits, and its voice gateway (R1) collects them.

3. The voice gateway (R1) determines whether it can route the call, or whether it has an IP destination configured for the collected digits. In this case, the voice gateway (R1) determines the other voice gateway (R2) as the destination. This is called *call routing*; the R1 is capable of doing that in the distributed model.

4. R1 sends a call setup message to R2 along with information such as the dialed number.

5. R2 receives the call setup message from R1 along with the information sent.

6. R2 determines whether it has a destination mapped to the called number. In this case, the called number maps to a local FXS interface. R2 takes care of this call routing in the distributed model.

7. If the determined FXS port on R2 is not busy and it is not configured to reject this call, R2 sends an AC ringing voltage to the FXS port, and the phone plugged into that interface rings. If the ringing phone on the FXS of R2 goes off-hook, the call is considered answered, and voice traffic starts flowing between the calling and called parties.

Figure 1-3   *Call Setup Example for Distributed Call Control*

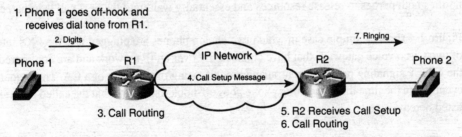

1. Phone 1 goes off-hook and
   receives dial tone from R1.

2. Digits

7. Ringing

Phone 1   R1   IP Network   R2   Phone 2

4. Call Setup Message

3. Call Routing   5. R2 Receives Call Setup
                       6. Call Routing

While the call is in progress, endpoints can monitor the quality of the call based on the number of packets sent, received, and dropped, and the amount of delay and jitter experienced. In the distributed model, the end points might have the intelligence and configuration to terminate a call if its quality is not acceptable.

If either phone on R1 or R2 hangs up (goes on-hook), the corresponding router sends a call termination message to its counterpart. Both routers release all resources that are dedicated to the call. Notice that in this distributed model example, the end-point gateways handled the call teardown in addition to the other tasks.

In the example used here, no call routing, call setup, call maintenance, or call teardown tasks depended on a centralized intelligent agent. The gateways at both ends had the intelligence and configuration to handle all the tasks involved in the end-to-end call. You must note, though, that if there were thousands of end devices, each would need the intelligence and configuration to be able to make and maintain calls to all other destinations (not necessarily at the same time). Naturally, a fully distributed model is not scalable; imagine if the telephone in your home needed the intelligence and configuration to be able to call every other phone number in the world, without the services of telco switches!

For large-scale deployments of H.323 or SIP, which are distributed call control protocols, special devices are added to offer a scalable and manageable solution. For example, the H.323 gatekeeper can be utilized to assist H.323 terminals or gateways with call routing. In SIP environments, special SIP servers such as Registrar, Location, Proxy, and Redirect can be utilized to facilitate scalability and manageability, among other benefits.

Centralized call control relieves the gateways and end points from being responsible for tasks such as call routing, call setup, CAC, and call teardown. MGCP end points do not have the intelligence and configuration to perform those tasks, and they are expected to receive those services from CAs. Analog voice digitization, encapsulation of digitized voice in IP packets, and transporting (sending) the IP packets from one end to the other remain the responsibility of the DSPs of the MGCP gateways and end points. Therefore, when the call is set up, VoIP packet flow does not involve the CA. When either end point terminates the call, the CA is notified, and the CA in turn notifies both parties to release resources and essentially wait until the next call is initiated.

Figure 1-4 shows a simple case in which two analog phones are plugged into the FXS interfaces of two Cisco voice gateways that have connectivity over an IP network and are configured to use the MGCP signaling protocol (centralized model), using the services of a CA. The sequence of events from the time that the calling phone goes off-hook to the time that the called phone rings is listed here:

1. The phone plugged into the FXS port of R1 goes off-hook. R1 detects this event (service request) and notifies the CA.

2. The CA instructs R1 to provide a dial tone on that FXS port, collect digits one at a time, and send them to the CA.

3. R1 provides a dial tone, collects dialed digits, and sends them to the CA one at a time.

4. The CA, using its call routing table and other information, determines that the call is for an FXS port on R2. It is assumed that R2 is also under the control of this CA, and that is why the CA had such detailed information about the R2 port and associated numbers. The CA must also determine if that FXS interface is free and whether the call is allowed. Note that the call routing capability of the CA not only determines that R2 is the destination end device, but it also informs which interface on R2 the call is for. In other words, neither R1 nor R2 have to know how to perform call routing tasks.

5. Upon successful call routing, availability, and restrictions checks, the CA notifies R2 of the incoming call for its FXS interface. R2 then sends an AC ringing voltage to the appropriate FXS port.

Figure 1-4 *Call Setup Example for Centralized Call Control*

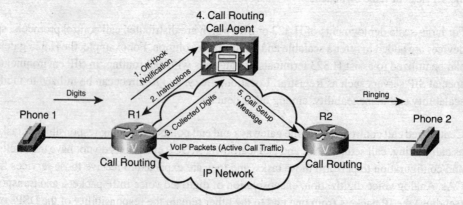

While the call is in progress, the end points (R1 and R2 in this example) collect and analyze the call statistics, such as packets sent and lost, and delay and jitter incurred (Theoretically, if the quality of the call is unacceptable, the CA is notified, and the CA instructs both parties to terminate the call.) If either phone hangs up, the gateway it is connected to (R1 or R2) notifies the CA of this event. The CA instructs both parties that call termination procedures must be performed and call resources must be released.

In the centralized call control model, the end points are not responsible for call control functions; therefore, they are simpler devices to build, configure, and maintain. On the other hand, the CA is a critical component within the centralized model and, to avoid a single point of failure, it requires deployment of fault-tolerance technologies. It is easier to manage a centralized model than to manage the distributed model, because only the CAs need to be configured and maintained. Implementing new services, features, and policies is also easier in the centralized model.

Digitizing and Packetizing Voice

Upon completion of this section, you will be able to identify the steps involved in converting an analog voice signal to a digital voice signal, explain the Nyquist theorem, the reason for taking 8000 voice samples per second; and explain the method for quantization of voice samples. Furthermore, you will be familiar with standard voice compression algorithms, their bandwidth requirements, and the quality of the results they yield. Knowing the purpose of DSP in voice gateways is the last objective of this section.

Basic Voice Encoding: Converting Analog to Digital

Converting analog voice signal to digital format and transmitting it over digital facilities (such as T1/E1) had been created and put into use before Bell (a North American telco) invented VoIP technology in 1950s. If you use digital PBX phones in your office, you must realize that one of the first actions that these phones perform is converting the analog voice signal to a digital format. When you use your regular analog phone at home, the phone sends analog voice signal to the telco CO. The Telco CO converts the analog voice signal to digital format and transmits it over the public switched telephone network (PSTN). If you connect an analog phone to the FXS interface of a router, the phone sends an analog voice signal to the router, and the router converts the analog signal to a digital format. Voice interface cards (VIC) require DSPs, which convert analog voice signals to digital signals, and vice versa.

Analog-to-digital conversion involves four major steps:

1. Sampling
2. Quantization
3. Encoding
4. Compression (optional)

Sampling is the process of periodic capturing and recording of voice. The result of sampling is called a *pulse amplitude modulation* (PAM) signal. *Quantization* is the process of assigning numeric values to the amplitude (height or voltage) of each of the samples on the PAM signal using a scaling methodology. *Encoding* is the process of representing the quantization result for each PAM sample in binary format. For example, each sample can be expressed using an 8-bit binary number, which can have 256 possible values.

One common method of converting analog voice signal to digital voice signal is *pulse code modulation* (PCM), which is based on taking 8000 samples per second and encoding each sample with an 8-bit binary number. PCM, therefore, generates 64,000 bits per second (64 Kbps); it does not perform compression. Each basic digital channel that is dedicated to transmitting a voice call within PSTN (DS0) has a 64-kbps capacity, which is ideal for transmitting a PCM signal.

Compression, the last step in converting an analog voice signal to digital, is optional. The purpose of compression is to reduce the number of bits (digitized voice) that must be transmitted per second with the least possible amount of voice-quality degradation. Depending on the compression standard used, the number of bits per second that is produced after the compression algorithm is applied varies, but it is definitely less than 64 Kbps.

Basic Voice Encoding: Converting Digital to Analog

When a switch or router that has an analog device such as a telephone, fax, or modem connected to it receives a digital voice signal, it must convert the analog signal to digital or VoIP before transmitting it to the other device. Figure 1-5 shows that router R1 receives an analog signal and converts it to digital, encapsulates the digital voice signal in IP packets, and sends the packets to router R2. On R2, the digital voice signal must be de-encapsulated from the received packets. Next, the switch or router must convert the digital voice signal back to analog voice signal and send it out of the FXS port where the phone is connected.

Figure 1-5   *Converting Analog Signal to Digital and Digital Signal to Analog*

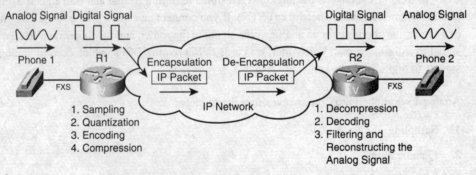

Converting digital signal back to analog signal involves the following steps:

1. Decompression (optional)

2. Decoding and filtering

3. Reconstructing the analog signal

If the digitally transmitted voice signal was compressed at the source, at the receiving end, the signal must first be decompressed. After decompression, the received binary expressions are decoded back to numbers, which regenerate the PAM signal. Finally, a filtering mechanism attempts to remove some of the noise that the digitization and compression might have introduced and regenerates an analog signal from the PAM signal. The regenerated analog signal is hopefully very similar to the analog signal that the speaker at the sending end had produced. Do not forget that DPS perform digital-to-analog conversion, similar to analog to digital conversion.

The Nyquist Theorem

The number of samples taken per second during the sampling stage, also called the *sampling rate*, has a significant impact on the quality of digitized signal. The higher the sampling rate is, the better quality it yields; however, a higher sampling rate also generates higher bits per second that must be transmitted. Based on the Nyquist theorem, a signal that is sampled at a rate at least twice the highest frequency of that signal yields enough samples for accurate reconstruction of the signal at the receiving end.

Figure 1-6 shows the same analog signal on the left side (top and bottom) but with two sampling rates applied: the bottom sampling rate is twice as much as the top sampling rate. On the right side of Figure 1-6, the samples received must be used to reconstruct the original analog signal. As you can see, with twice as many samples received on the bottom-right side as those received on the top-right side, a more accurate reconstruction of the original analog signal is possible.

Human speech has a frequency range of 200 to 9000 Hz. Hz stands for Hertz, which specifies the number of cycles per second in a waveform signal. The human ear can sense sounds within a frequency range of 20 to 20,000 Hz. Telephone lines were designed to transmit analog signals within the frequency range of 300 to 3400 Hz. The top and bottom frequency levels produced by a human speaker cannot be transmitted over a phone line. However, the frequencies that are transmitted allow the human on the receiving end to recognize the speaker and sense his/her tone of voice and inflection. Nyquist proposed that the sampling rate must be twice as much as the highest frequency of the signal to be digitized. At 4000 Hz, which is higher than 3400 Hz (the maximum frequency that a phone line was designed to transmit), based on the Nyquist theorem, the required sampling rate is 8000 samples per second.

Figure 1-6 *Effect of Higher Sampling Rate*

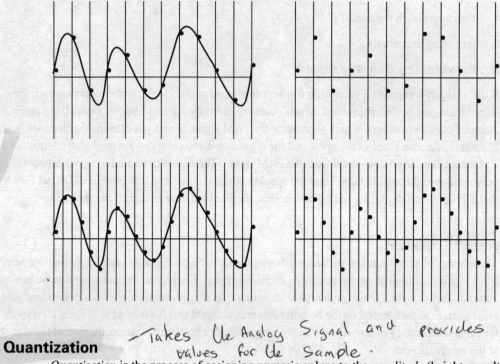

Quantization

— Takes the Analog Signal and provides values for the Sample.

Quantization is the process of assigning numeric values to the *amplitude* (height or voltage) of each of the samples on the PAM signal using a scaling methodology. A common scaling method is made of eight major divisions called *segments* on each *polarity* (positive and negative) side. Each segment is subdivided into 16 steps. As a result, 256 discrete steps ($2 \times 8 \times 16$) are possible.

The 256 steps in the quantization scale are encoded using 8-bit binary numbers. From the 8 bits, 1 bit represents polarity (+ or −), 3 represent segment number (1 through 8), and 4 bits represent the step number within the segment (1 through 16). At a sampling rate of 8000 samples per second, if each sample is represented using an 8-bit binary number, 64,000 bits per second are generated for an analog voice signal. It must now be clear to you why traditional circuit-switched telephone networks dedicated 64 Kbps channels, also called DS0s (Digital Signal Level 0), to each telephone call.

Because the samples from PAM do not always match one of the discrete values defined by quantization scaling, the process of sampling and quantization involves some rounding. This rounding creates a difference between the original signal and the signal that will ultimately be reproduced at the receiver end; this difference is called *quantization error*. Quantization error or quantization noise, is one of the sources of noise or distortion imposed on digitally transmitted voice signals.

Figure 1-7 shows two scaling models for quantization. If you look at the graph on the top, you will notice that the spaces between the segments of that graph are equal. However, the spaces between the segments on the bottom graph are not equal: the segments closer to the x-axis are closer to each other than the segments that are further away from the x-axis. Linear quantization uses graphs with segments evenly spread, whereas logarithmic quantization uses graphs that have unevenly spread segments. Logarithmic quantization yields smaller signal-to-noise quantization ratio (SQR), because it encounters less rounding (quantization) error on the samples (frequencies) that human ears are more sensitive to (very high and very low frequencies).

Figure 1-7   *Linear Quantization and Logarithmic Quantization*

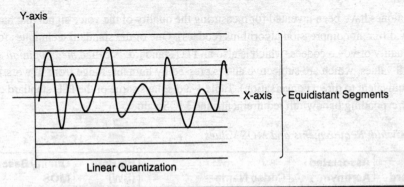

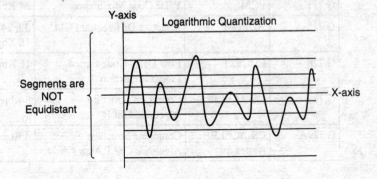

 Two variations of logarithmic quantization exist: A-Law and μ-Law. Bell developed μ-Law (pronounced me-you-law) and it is the method that is most common in North America and Japan. ITU modified μ-Law and introduced A-Law, which is common in countries outside North America (except Japan). When signals have to be exchanged between a μ-Law country and an A-Law country in the PSTN, the μ-Law country must change its signaling to accommodate the A-Law country.

Compression Bandwidth Requirements and Their Comparative Qualities

Several ITU compression standards exist. Voice compression standards (algorithms) differ based on the following factors:

- Bandwidth requirement

- Quality degradation they cause

- Delay they introduce

- CPU overhead due to their complexity

Several techniques have been invented for measuring the quality of the voice signal that has been processed by different compression algorithms (codecs). One of the standard techniques for measuring quality of voice codecs, which is also an ITU standard, is called *mean opinion score* (MOS). MOS values, which are subjective and expressed by humans, range from 1 (worst) to 5 (perfect or equivalent to direct conversation). Table 1-3 displays some of the ITU standard codecs and their corresponding bandwidth requirements and MOS values.

Table 1-3 *Codec Bandwidth Requirements and MOS Values*   mean of Score

Codec Standard	Associated Acronym	Codec Name	Bit Rate (BW)	Quality Based on MOS
G.711	PCM	Pulse Code Modulation	64 Kbps	4.10
G.726	ADPCM	Adaptive Differential PCM	32, 24, 16 Kbps	3.85 (for 32 Kbps)
G.728	LDCELP	Low Delay Code Exited Linear Prediction	16 Kbps	3.61
G.729	CS-ACELP	Conjugate Structure Algebraic CELP	8 Kbps	3.92
G.729A	CS-ACELP Annex a	Conjugate Structure Algebraic CELP Annex A	8 Kbps	3.90

MOS is an ITU standard method of measuring voice quality based on the judgment of several participants; therefore, it is a subjective method. Table 1-4 displays each of the MOS ratings along with its corresponding interpretation, and a description for its distortion level. It is noteworthy that an MOS of 4.0 is deemed to be Toll Quality.

SNR Signal to noise ratio is the ratio of transmitted signal to background noise of medium

Table 1-4 *Mean Opinion Score*

Rating	Speech Quality	Level of Distortion
5	Excellent	Imperceptible
4	Good	Just perceptible but not annoying
3	Fair	Perceptible but slightly annoying
2	Poor	Annoying but not objectionable
1	Unsatisfactory	Very annoying and objectionable

Perceptual speech quality measurement (PSQM), ITU's P.861 standard, is another voice quality measurement technique implemented in test equipment systems offered by many vendors. PSQM is based on comparing the original input voice signal at the sending end to the transmitted voice signal at the receiving end and rating the quality of the codec using a 0 through 6.5 scale, where 0 is the best and 6.5 is the worst.

Perceptual analysis measurement system (PAMS) was developed in the late 1990s by British Telecom. PAMS is a predictive voice quality measurement system. In other words, it can predict subjective speech quality measurement methods such as MOS.

Perceptual evaluation of speech quality (PESQ), the ITU P.862 standard, is based on work done by KPN Research in the Netherlands and British Telecommunications (developers of PAMS). PESQ combines PSQM and PAMS. It is an objective measuring system that predicts the results of subjective measurement systems such as MOS. Various vendors offer PESQ-based test equipment.

Digital Signal Processors

Voice-enabled devices such as voice gateways have special processors called DSPs. DSPs are usually on packet voice DSP modules (PVDM). Certain voice-enabled devices such as voice network modules (VNM) have special slots for plugging PVDMs into them. Figure 1-8 shows a network module high density voice (NM-HDV) that has five slots for PVDMs. The NM in Figure 1-8 has four PVDMs plugged into it . Different types of PVDMs have different numbers of DSPs, and each DSP handles a certain number of voice terminations. For example, one type of DSP can handle tasks such as codec and transcoding for up to 16 voice channels if a low-complexity codec is used, or up to 8 voice channels if a high-complexity codec is used.

Handwritten notes:

Voice Signal most be Converted from Analog to digital and it uses this process.
1. Samplong
2. Quantization
3. Companding (Compression and expanding)

Once the Signal arrives at the destination it is to be Converted from digital to Analog
1. Reconstrion (Reconstruction of Analog Signal)
2. Decoding - from PAM value to voltage.
3. decompression - decompress the signal.

Figure 1-8 *Network Module with PVDMs*

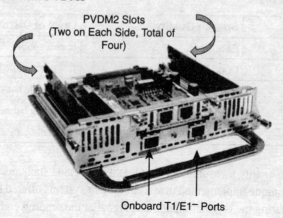

PVDM2 Slots
(Two on Each Side, Total of
Four)

Onboard T1/E1⁻ Ports

DSPs provide three major services:

- Voice termination

- Transcoding

- Conferencing

Calls to or from voice interfaces of a voice gateway are terminated by DSPs. DSP performs analog-to-digital and digital-to-analog signal conversion. It also performs compression (codec), echo cancellation, voice activity detection (VAD), comfort noise generation (CNG), jitter handling, and some other functions.

When the two parties in an audio call use different codecs, a DSP resource is needed to perform codec conversion; this is called *transcoding*. Figure 1-9 shows a company with a main branch and a remote branch with an IP connection over WAN. The voice mail system is in the main branch, and it uses the G.711 codec. However, the branch devices are configured to use G.729 for VoIP communication with the main branch. In this case, the edge voice router at the main branch needs to perform transcoding using its DSP resources so that the people in the remote branch can retrieve their voice mail from the voice mail system at the main branch.

DSPs can act as a conference bridge: they can receive voice (audio) streams from the participants of a conference, mix the streams, and send the mix back to the conference participants. If all the conference participants use the same codec, it is called a *single-mode conference*, and the DSP does not have to perform codec translation (called *transcoding*). If conference participants use different codecs, the conference is called a *mixed-mode conference*, and the DSP must perform transcoding. Because mixed-mode conferences are more complex, the number of simultaneous mixed-mode conferences that a DSP can handle is less than the number of simultaneous single-mode conferences it can support.

Figure 1-9 *DSP Transcoding Example*

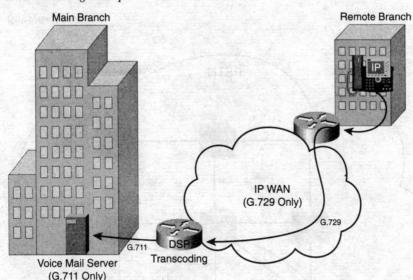

Encapsulating Voice Packets

This section explains the protocols and processes involved in delivering VoIP packets as opposed to delivering digitized voice over circuit-switched networks. It also explains the RTP as the transport protocol of choice for voice and discusses the benefits of RTP header compression (cRTP).

End-to-End Delivery of Voice

To review the traditional model of voice communication over the PSTN, imagine a residential phone that connects to the telco CO switch using an analog telephone line. After the phone goes off-hook and digits are dialed and sent to the CO switch, the CO switch, using a special signaling protocol, finds and sends call setup signaling messages to the CO that connects to the line of the destination number. The switches within the PSTN are connected using digital trunks such as T1/E1 or T3/E3. If the call is successful, a single channel (DS0) from each of the trunks on the path that connects the CO switches of the caller and called number is dedicated to this phone call. Figure 1-10 shows a path from the calling party CO switch on the left to the called party CO switch on the right.

Figure 1-10   *Voice Call over Traditional Circuit-Switched PSTN*

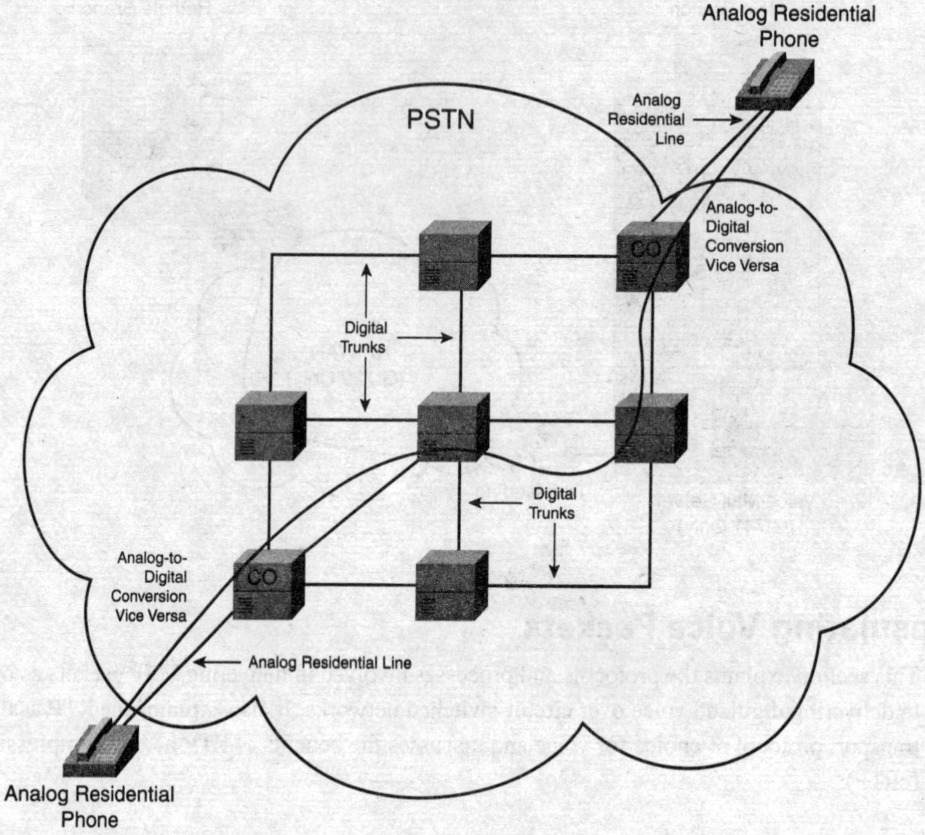

After the path between the CO switches at each end is set up, while the call is active, analog voice signals received from the analog lines must be converted to digital format, such as G.711 PCM, and transmitted over the DS0 that is dedicated to this call. The digital signal received at each CO must be converted back to analog before it is transmitted over the residential line. The bit transmission over DS0 is a synchronous transmission with guaranteed bandwidth, low and constant end-to-end delay, plus no chance for reordering. When the call is complete, all resources and the DS0 channel that is dedicated to this call are released and are available to another call.

If two analog phones were to make a phone call over an IP network, they would each need to be plugged into the FXS interface of a voice gateway. Figure 1-11 displays two such gateways (R1 and R2) connected over an IP network, each of which has an analog phone connected to its FXS interface.

Figure 1-11 *Voice Call over IP Networks*

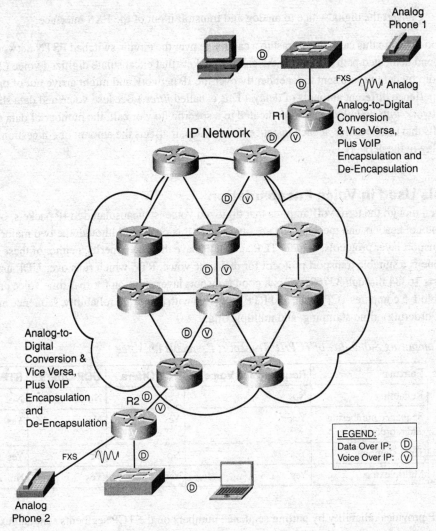

Assume that phone 1 on R1 goes off-hook and dials a number that R1 maps to R2. R1 will send a VoIP signaling call setup message to R2. If the call is accepted and it is set up, each of R1 and R2 will have to do the following:

■ Convert the analog signal received from the phone on the FXS interface to digital (using a codec such as G.711).

■ Encapsulate the digital voice signal into IP packets.

■ Route the IP packets toward the other router.

■ De-encapsulate the digital voice from the received IP packets.

■ Convert the digital voice to analog and transmit it out of the FXS interface.

Notice that in this case, in contrast to a call made over the circuit-switched PSTN network, no end-to-end dedicated path is built for the call. IP packets that encapsulate digitized voice (20 ms of audio by default) are sent independently over the IP network and might arrive out of order and experience different amounts of delay. (This is called *jitter*.) Because voice and data share the IP network with no link or circuit dedicated to a specific flow or call, the number of data and voice calls that can be active at each instance varies. Also, it affects the amount of congestion, loss, and delay in the network.

Protocols Used in Voice Encapsulation

Even though the term VoIP implies that digitized voice is encapsulated in IP packets, other protocol headers and mechanisms are involved in this process. Although the two major TCP/IP transport layer protocols, namely TCP and UDP, have their own merits, neither of these protocols alone is a suitable transport protocol for real-time voice. RTP, which runs over UDP using UDP ports 16384 through 32767, offers a good transport layer solution for real-time voice and video. Table 1-5 compares TCP, UDP, and RTP protocols with respect to reliability, sequence numbering (re-ordering), time-stamping, and multiplexing.

Table 1-5   *Comparing Suitability of TCP/IP Transport Protocols for Voice*

Feature	Required for Voice	TCP Offers	UDP Offers	RTP Offers
Reliability	No	Yes	No	No
Sequence numbering and reordering	Yes	Yes	No	Yes
Time-stamping	Yes	No	No	Yes
Multiplexing	Yes	Yes	Yes	No

TCP provides reliability by putting sequence numbers on the TCP segments sent and expecting acknowledgements for the TCP segment numbers arriving at the receiver device. If a TCP segment is not acknowledged before a retransmission timer expires, the TCP segment is resent. This model is not suitable for real-time applications such as voice, because the resent voice arrives too late for it to be useful. Therefore, reliability is not a necessary feature for a voice transport protocol. UDP and RTP do not offer reliable transport. Please note, however, that if the infrastructure capacity, configuration, and behavior are such that there are too many delayed or lost packets, the quality of voice and other real-time applications will deteriorate and become unacceptable.

Data segmentation, sequence numbering, reordering, and reassembly of data are services that the transport protocol must offer, if the application does not or cannot perform those tasks. The protocol to transport voice must offer these services. TCP and RTP offer those services, but pure UDP does not.

Voice or audio signal is released at a certain rate from its source. The receiver of the voice or audio signal must receive it at the same rate that the source has released it; otherwise, it will sound different or annoying, or it might even become incomprehensible. Putting timestamps on the segments encapsulating voice, at source, enables the receiving end to release the voice at the same rate that it was released at the source. RTP adds timestamps in the segments at source, but TCP and UDP do not.

Both TCP and UDP allow multiple applications to simultaneously use their services to transport application data, even if all the active flows and sessions originate and terminate on the same pair of IP devices. The data from different applications is distinguished based on the TCP or UDP port number that is assigned to the application while it is active. This capability of the TCP and UDP protocols is called *multiplexing*. On the other hand, RTP flows are differentiated based on the unique UDP port number that is assigned to each of the RTP flows. UDP numbers 16384 through 32767 are reserved for RTP. RTP does not have a multiplexing capability.

Knowing that RTP runs over UDP, considering the fact that neither UDP nor RTP offers the unneeded reliability and overhead offered by TCP, and that RTP uses sequence numbers and time-stamping, you can conclude that RTP is the best transport protocol for voice, video, and other real-time applications. Please note that even though the reliability that TCP offers might not be useful for voice applications, it is desirable for certain other applications.

RTP runs over UDP; therefore, a VoIP packet has IP (20 bytes), UDP (8 bytes), and RTP (12 bytes) headers added to the encapsulated voice payload. DSPs usually make a package out of 10-ms worth of analog voice, and two of those packages are usually transported within one IP packet. (A total of 20-ms worth of voice in one IP packet is common.) The number of bytes resulting from 20 ms (2×10 ms) worth of analog voice directly depends on the codec used. For instance, G.711, which generates 64 Kbps, produces 160 bytes from 20 ms of analog voice, whereas G.729, which generates 8 Kbps, produces 20 bytes for 20 ms of analog voice signal. The RTP, UDP, and IP headers, which total 40 bytes, are added to the voice bytes (160 bytes for G.711 and 20 bytes for G.729) before the whole group is encapsulated in the Layer 2 frame and transmitted.

Figure 1-12 displays two VoIP packets. One packet is the result of the G.711 codec, and the other is the result of the G.729 codec. Both have the RTP, UDP, and IP headers. The Layer 2 header is not considered here. The total number of bytes resulting from IP, UDP, and RTP is 40. Compare this 40-byte overhead to the size of the G.711 payload (160 bytes) and of the G.729 payload (20 bytes). The ratio of overhead to payload is 40/160, or 25 percent, when G.711 is used; however, the overhead-to-payload ratio is 40/20, or 200 percent, when G.729 is used!

Figure 1-12 *Voice Encapsulation Utilizing G.711 and G.729*

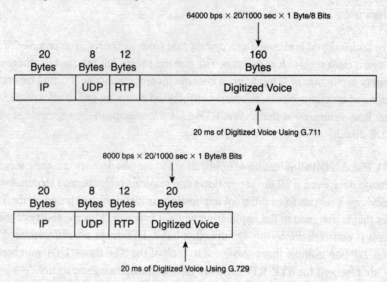

If you ignore the Layer 2 overhead for a moment, just based on the overhead imposed by RTP, UDP, and IP, you can recognize that the required bandwidth is more than the bandwidth that is needed for the voice payload. For instance, when the G.711 codec is used, the required bandwidth for voice only is 64 Kbps, but with 25 percent added overhead of IP, UDP, and RTP, the required bandwidth increases to 80 Kbps. If G.729 is used, the bandwidth required for pure voice is only 8 Kbps, but with the added 200 percent overhead imposed by IP, UDP, and RTP, the required bandwidth jumps to 24 Kbps. Again, note that the overhead imposed by the Layer 2 protocol and any other technologies such as tunneling or security has not even been considered.

Reducing Header Overhead

An effective way of reducing the overhead imposed by IP, UDP, and RTP is Compressed RTP (cRTP). cRTP is also called RTP header compression. Even though its name implies that cRTP compresses the RTP header only, the cRTP technique actually significantly reduces the overhead imposed by all IP, UDP, and RTP protocol headers. cRTP must be applied on both sides of a link, and essentially the sender and receiver agree to a hash (number) that is associated with the 40 bytes of IP, UDP, and TCP headers. Note that cRTP is applied on a link-by-link basis.

The premise of cRTP is that most of the fields in the IP, UDP, and RTP headers do not change among the elements (packets) of a common packet flow. After the initial packet with all the headers is submitted, the following packets that are part of the same packet flow do not carry the 40 bytes of headers. Instead, the packets carry the hash number that is associated with those 40 bytes (sequence number is built in the hash). The main difference among the headers of a packet flow is the header checksum (UDP checksum). If cRTP does not use this checksum, the size of the overhead is reduced from 40 bytes to only 2 bytes. If the checksum is used, the 40 bytes overhead is reduced to 4 bytes. If, during transmission of packets, a cRTP sender notices that a packet header has changed from the normal pattern, the entire header instead of the hash is submitted.

Figure 1-13 displays two packets. The top packet has a 160-byte voice payload because of usage of the G.711 codec, and a 2-byte cRTP header (without checksum). The cRTP overhead-to-voice payload ratio in this case is 2/160, or 1.25 percent. Ignoring Layer 2 header overhead, because G.711 requires 64 Kbps for the voice payload, the bandwidth needed for voice and the cRTP overhead together would be 64.8 Kbps (without header checksum). The bottom packet has a 20-byte voice payload because of usage of the G.729 codec and a 2-byte cRTP header (without checksum). The cRTP overhead-to-voice payload ratio in this case is 2/20, or 10 percent. Ignoring Layer 2 header overhead, because G.729 requires 8 Kbps for the voice payload, the bandwidth needed for voice and the cRTP overhead together would be 8.8 Kbps (without header checksum).

Figure 1-13 *RTP Header Compression (cRTP)*

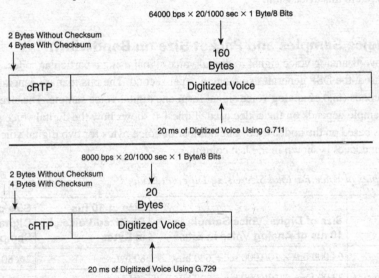

The benefit of using cRTP with smaller payloads (such as digitized voice) is more noticeable than it is for large payloads. Notice that with cRTP, the total bandwidth requirement (without Layer 2 overhead considered) dropped from 80 Kbps to 64.8 Kbps for G.711, and it dropped from 24 Kbps to 8.8 Kbps for G.729. The relative gain is more noticeable for G.729. You must, however, consider factors before enabling cRTP on a link:

■ cRTP does offer bandwidth saving, but it is only recommended for use on slow links (links with less than 2 Mbps bandwidth). More accurately, Cisco recommends cRTP on 2 Mbps links only if the cRTP is performed in hardware. cRTP is only recommended on the main processor if the link speed is below 768 kbps.

■ cRTP has a processing overhead, so make sure the device where you enable cRTP has enough resources.

■ The cRTP process introduces a delay due to the extra computations and header replacements.

■ You can limit the number of cRTP sessions on a link. By default, Cisco IOS allows up to only 16 concurrent cRTP sessions. If enough resources are available on a device, you can increase this value.

Bandwidth Calculation

Computing the exact amount of bandwidth needed for each VoIP call is necessary for planning and provisioning sufficient bandwidth in LANs and WANs. The previous section referenced parts of this computation, but this section thoroughly covers the subject of VoIP bandwidth calculation. The impact of packet size, Layer 2 overhead, tunneling, security, and voice activity detection are considered in this discussion.

Impact of Voice Samples and Packet Size on Bandwidth

DSP coverts analog voice signal to digital voice signal using a particular codec. Based on the codec used, the DSP generates so many bits per second. The bits that are generated for 10 milliseconds (ms) of analog voice signal form one digital voice sample. The size of the digital voice sample depends on the codec used. Table 1-6 shows how the digital voice sample size changes based on the codec used. The number of voice bytes for two digital voice samples using different codecs is shown in the last column.

Table 1-6   *Examples of Voice Payload Size Using Different Codecs*

Codec: Bandwidth	Size of Digital Voice Sample for 10 ms of Analog Voice in Bits	Size of 10 ms Digitized Voice in Bytes	Size of Two Digital Voice Samples (20 ms)
G.711: 64 Kbps	64,000 bps × 10/1000 sec = 640 bits	80 bytes	2 × 80 = 160 bytes
G.726 r32: 32 Kbps	32,000 bps × 10/1000 sec = 320 bits	40 bytes	2 × 40 = 80 bytes
G.726 r24: 24 Kbps	24,000 bps × 10/1000 sec = 240 bits	30 bytes	2 × 30 = 60 bytes
G.726 r16: 16 Kbps	16,000 bps × 10/1000 sec = 160 bits	20 bytes	2 × 20 = 40 bytes
G.728: 16 Kbps	16,000 bps × 10/1000 sec = 160 bits	20 bytes	2 × 20 = 40 bytes
G.729: 8 Kbps	8000 bps × 10/1000 sec = 80 bits	10 bytes	2 × 10 = 20 bytes

The total size of a Layer 2 frame encapsulating a VoIP packet depends on the following factors:

- **Packet rate and packetization size**—Packet rate, specified in packets per seconds (pps), is inversely proportional to packetization size, which is the amount of voice that is digitized and encapsulated in each IP packet. Packetization size is expressed in bytes and depends on the codec used and the amount of voice that is digitized. For example, if two 10-ms digitized voice samples (total of 20 ms voice) are encapsulated in each IP packet, the packet rate will be 1 over 0.020, or 50 packets per second (pps), and if G.711 is used, the packetization size will be 160 bytes. (See Table 1-6.)

- **IP overhead**—*IP overhead* refers to the total number of bytes in the RTP, UDP, and IP headers. With no RTP header compression, the IP overhead is 40 bytes. If cRTP with no header checksum is applied to a link, the IP overhead drops to 2 bytes, and with header checksum, the IP header checksum is 4 bytes.

- **Data link overhead**—Data link layer overhead is always present, but its size depends on the type of encapsulation (frame type) and whether link compression applied. For instance, the data link layer overhead of Ethernet is 18 bytes (it is 22 bytes with 802.1Q).

- **Tunneling overhead**—Tunneling overhead is only present if some type of tunneling is used. Generic routing encapsulation (GRE), Layer 2 Tunneling Protocol (L2TP), IP security (IPsec), QinQ (802.1Q), and Multiprotocol Label Switching (MPLS) are common tunneling techniques with their own usage reasons and benefits. Each tunneling approach adds a specific number of overhead bytes to the frame.

Codecs are of various types. The size of each VoIP packet depends on the codec type used and the number of voice samples encapsulated in each IP packet. The number of bits per second that each codec generates is referred to as *codec bandwidth*. The following is a list of some ITU codec standards, along with a brief description for each:

- **G.711 is PCM**—Based on the 8000 samples per second rate and 8 bits per sample, PCM generates 64,000 bits per second, or 64 Kbps. No compression is performed.

- **G.726 is adaptive differential pulse code modulation (ADPCM)**—Instead of constantly sending 8 bits per sample, fewer bits per sample, which only describe the change from the previous sample, are sent. If the number of bits (that describe the change) sent is 4, 3, or 2, G.726 generates 32 Kbps, 24 Kbps, or 16 Kbps respectively, and it is correspondingly called G.726 r32, G.726 r24, or G.726 r16.

- **G.722 is wideband speech encoding standard**—G.722 divides the input signal into two subbands and encodes each subband using a modified version of ADPCM. G.722 supports a bit rate of 64 Kbps, 56 Kbps, or 48 Kbps.

- **G.728 is low delay code exited linear prediction (LDCELP)**—G.728 uses codes that describe voice samples generated by human vocal cords, and it utilizes a prediction technique. Wave shapes of five samples (equivalent of 40 bits in PCM) are expressed with 10-bit codes; therefore, the G.728 bandwidth drops to 16 Kbps.

- **G.729 is conjugate structure algebraic code exited linear prediction (CS-ACELP)**— G.729 also uses codes from a code book; however, 10 samples (equivalent of 80 PCM bits) are expressed with 10-bit codes. Therefore, the G.729 is only 8 Kbps.

DSPs produce one digital voice sample for 10 milliseconds (ms) of analog voice signal. It is common among Cisco voice-enabled devices to put two digital voice samples in one IP packet, but it is possible to put three or four samples in one IP packet if desired. The *packetization period* is the amount of analog voice signal (expressed in milliseconds) that is encapsulated in each IP packet (in digitized format). The merit of more voice samples in a packet—longer packetization period, in other words—is reduction in the overhead-to-payload ratio.

The problem, though, with putting too many digital voice samples in one IP packet is that when a packet is dropped, too much voice is lost. That loss has a more noticeable negative effect on the quality of the call when packets are dropped. The other drawback of a longer packetization period (more than two or three digital voice samples in one IP packet) is the extra packetization delay it introduces. More voice bits means a larger IP packet, and a larger IP packet means a longer packetization period.

Table 1-7 shows a few examples to demonstrate the combined effect of codec used and packetization period (number of digitized 10-ms voice samples per packet) on the voice encapsulating IP packet (VoIP) size and on the packet rate. The examples in Table 1-7 do not use compressed RTP and make no reference to the effects of Layer 2 and tunneling overheads.

Table 1-7 *Packet Size and Packet Rate Variation Examples*

Codec and Packetization Period (Number of Encapsulated Digital Voice Samples)	Codec Bandwidth	Voice Payload (Packetization) Size	IP Overhead	Total IP (VoIP) Packet Size	Packet Rate (pps)
G.711 with 20-ms packetization period (two 10-ms samples)	64 Kbps	160 bytes	40 bytes	200 bytes	50 pps
G.711 with 30-ms packetization period (three 10-ms samples)	64 Kbps	240 bytes	40 bytes	280 bytes	33.33 pps
G.729 with 20 ms packetization period (two 10-ms samples)	8 Kbps	20 bytes	40 bytes	60 bytes	50 pps
G.729 with 40 ms packetization period (four 10-ms samples)	8 Kbps	40 bytes	40 bytes	80 bytes	25 pps

Data Link Overhead

Transmitting an IP packet over a link requires encapsulation of the IP packet in a frame that is appropriate for the data link layer protocol provisioned on that link. For instance, if the data link layer protocol used on a link is PPP, the interface connected to that link must be configured for PPP encapsulation. In other words, any packet to be transmitted out of that interface must be encapsulated in a PPP frame. When a router routes a packet, the packet can enter the router via an interface with a certain encapsulation type such as Ethernet, and it can leave the router through another interface with a different encapsulation such as PPP. After the Ethernet frame enters the router via the ingress interface, the IP packet is de-encapsulated. Next, the routing decision directs the packet to the egress interface. The packet has to be encapsulated in the frame proper for the egress interface data link protocol before it is transmitted.

Different data link layer protocols have a different number of bytes on the frame header; for VoIP purposes, these are referred to as data link overhead bytes. Data link overhead bytes for Ethernet, Frame Relay, Multilink PPP (MLP), and Dot1Q (802.1Q) are 18, 6, 6, and 22 bytes in that order, to name a few. During calculation of the total bandwidth required for a VoIP call, for each link type (data link layer protocol or encapsulation), you must consider the appropriate data link layer overhead.

Security and Tunneling Overhead

IPsec is an IETF protocol suite for secure transmission of IP packets. IPsec can operate in two modes: Transport mode or Tunnel mode. In Transport mode, encryption is applied only to the payload of the IP packet, whereas in Tunnel mode, encryption is applied to the whole IP packet, including the header. When the IP header is encrypted, the intermediate routers can no longer analyze and route the IP packet. Therefore, in Tunnel mode, the encrypted IP packet must be encapsulated in another IP packet, whose header is used for routing purposes. The new and extra header added in Transport mode means 20 extra bytes in overhead. In both Transport mode and Tunnel mode, either an Authentication Header (AH) or an Encapsulating Security Payload (ESP) header is added to the IP header. AH provides authentication only, whereas ESP provides authentication and encryption. As a result, ESP is used more often. AH, ESP, and the extra IP header of the Tunnel mode are the IPsec overheads to consider during VoIP bandwidth calculation. IPsec also adds extra delay to the packetization process at the sending and receiving ends.

Other common tunneling methods and protocols are not focused on security. IP packets or data link layer frames can be tunneled over a variety of protocols; the following is a short list of common tunneling protocols:

- **GRE**—GRE transports Layer 3 (network layer) packets, such as IP packets, or Layer 2 (data link) frames, over IP.

- **Layer 2 Forwarding (L2F) and L2TP**—L2F and L2TP transport PPP frames over IP.

■ **PPP over Ethernet (PPPoE)**—PPPoE transports PPP frames over Ethernet frames.

■ **802.1Q tunneling (QinQ)**—An 802.1Q frame with multiple 802.1Q headers is called QinQ. Layer 2 switching engines forward the QinQ frame based on the VLAN number in the top 802.1Q header. When the top header is removed, forwarding of the frame based on the VLAN number in the lower 802.1Q header begins.

Whether one of the preceding tunneling protocols, IPsec in Tunnel mode, or any other tunneling protocol is used, the tunnel header is always present and is referred to as *tunneling overhead*. If any tunneling protocol is used, the tunneling overhead must be considered in VoIP bandwidth calculation. Table 1-8 shows the tunneling overhead—in other words, the tunnel header size—for a variety of tunneling options.

Table 1-8 *IPsec and Main Tunneling Protocols Overheads*

Protocol	Header Size
IPsec Transport Mode With ESP header utilizing DES or 3DES for encryption and MD5 or SHA-1 for authentication. (DES and 3DES require the payload size to be multiples of 8 bytes; therefore, 0 to 7 bytes padding may be necessary.)	30 to 37 bytes
IPsec Transport Mode With ESP header utilizing AES for encryption and AES-XCBC for authentication. (AES requires the payload size to be multiples of 16 bytes; therefore, 0 to 15 bytes of padding might be necessary.)	38 to 53 bytes
IPsec Tunnel Mode Extra 20 bytes must be added to the IPsec transport mode header size for the extra IP header in Tunnel mode	50 to 57 bytes or 58 to 73 bytes
L2TP	24 bytes
GRE	24 bytes
MPLS	4 bytes
PPPoE	8 bytes

If a company connects two of its sites over the public Internet using IPsec in Tunnel mode (also called IPsec VPN), you must be able to calculate the total size of the IP packet encapsulating voice (VoIP). To do that, you need to know the codec used, the packetization period, and whether compressed RTP is used. The fictitious company under discussion uses the G.729 codec for site-to-site IP Telephony and a 20-ms packetization period (two 10-ms equivalent digital voice samples per packet); it does not utilize cRTP. For IPsec, assume tunnel mode with ESP header utilizing 3DES for encryption and SHA-1 for authentication. The voice payload size with G.729 and 20-ms packetization period will be 20 bytes. IP, UDP, and RTP headers add 40 bytes to the voice payload, bringing the total to 60 bytes. Because 60 is not a multiple of 8, 4 bytes of padding are added to bring the total to 64 bytes. Finally, the ESP header of 30 bytes and the extra IP header of 20 bytes bring the total packet size to 114 byes. The ratio of total IP packet size to the size of the voice payload is 114 over 20—more than 500 percent! Notice that without IPsec (in Tunnel mode), the total size of the IP packet (VoIP) would have been 60 bytes.

Calculating the Total Bandwidth for a VoIP Call

Calculating the bandwidth that a VoIP call consumes involves consideration for all the factors discussed thus far. Some fields and protocols are required, each of which might offer implementation alternatives. Other protocols and fields are optional. You use the bandwidth consumed by each VoIP call to calculate the total bandwidth required for the aggregate of simultaneous VoIP calls over LAN and WAN connections. This information is required for the following purposes:

- Designing and planning link capacities

- Deployment of CAC

- Deployment of quality of service (QoS)

QoS can be defined as the ability of a network to provide services to different applications as per their particular requirements. Those services can include guarantees to control end-to-end delay, packet loss, jitter, and guaranteed bandwidth based on the needs of each application. CAC is used to control the number of concurrent calls to prevent oversubscription of the resources guaranteed for VoIP calls.

Computing the bandwidth consumed by a VoIP call involves six major steps:

Step 1   Determine the codec and the packetization period. Different codecs generate different numbers of bits per second (also called codec bandwidth), and they generally range from 5.3 Kbps to 64 Kbps. The number of digital voice samples (each of which is equivalent to 10 ms of analog voice) encapsulated in each IP packet determines the packetization period. A packetization period of 20 ms, which is the default in Cisco voice-enabled devices, means that each VoIP packet will encapsulate two 10-ms digital voice samples.

Step 2   Determine the link-specific information; this includes discovering whether cRTP is used and what the data link layer protocol (encapsulation type) is. You must also find out if any security or tunneling protocols and features are used on the link.

Step 3   Calculate the packetization size or, in other words, calculate the size of voice payload based on the information gathered in Step 1. Multiplying the codec bandwidth by the packetization period and dividing the result by 8 results in the size of voice payload in bytes. Please note that the packetization period is usually expressed in milliseconds, so you first must divide this number by 1000 to convert it to seconds. If G.729 with the codec bandwidth of 8 Kbps is used and the packetization period is 20 ms, the voice payload size will equal 20 bytes. 8000 (bps) multiplied by 0.020 (seconds) and divided by 8 (bits per byte) yields 20 bytes.

Step 4   Calculate the total frame size. Add the size of IP, UDP, and RTP headers, or cRTP header if applied, plus the optional tunneling headers and the data link layer header determined in Step 2, to the size of voice payload (packetization size) determined in Step 3. The result is the total frame size. If the voice payload size is 20 bytes, adding 40 bytes for RTP, UDP, and IP, and adding 6 bytes for PPP will result in a frame size of 66 bytes (without usage of cRTP and any tunneling or security features).

Step 5   Calculate the packet rate. The packet rate is inversed packetization period (converted to seconds). For example, if the packetization period is 20 ms, which is equivalent to 0.020 seconds, the packet rate is equal to 1 divided by 0.020, resulting in a packet rate of 50 packets per second (pps).

Step 6   Calculate the total bandwidth. The total bandwidth consumed by one VoIP call is computed by multiplying the total frame size (from step 4) converted to bits multiplied by the packet rate (from step 5). For instance, if the total frame size is 66 bytes, which is equivalent to 528 bits, and the packet rate is 50 pps, multiplying 528 by 50 results in a total bandwidth of 26400 bits per second, or 26.4 Kbps.

Figure 1-14 shows VoIP framing and two methods for computing the bandwidth required for a VoIP call. Method 1 displayed in Figure 1-14 is based on the six-step process just discussed.

The second method for calculating voice bandwidth is shown as Method 2 in Figure 1-14. This method is based on the ratio shown on the bottom of Figure 1-14: The ratio of total bandwidth over voice payload is equal to the ratio of total frame size over voice payload size. If G.729 is used and the packetization period is 20 milliseconds, the voice payload size will be 20 bytes. With PPP encapsulation and no cRTP, security, or tunneling, the total frame size adds up to 66 bytes. The ratio of total frame size to voice payload size is 66 over 20, which is equal to the ratio of voice bandwidth over codec bandwidth (8 Kbps for G.729). This 66 multiplied by 8 Kbps and divided by 20 results in voice bandwidth of 26.4 Kbps.

[Handwritten notes at top: "Remember — How many Concurrent Calls Can be made per Link. Total Packet Size / Payload Size = Total bandwidth Per Call / nominal bandwidth Per CALL."]

Figure 1-14 *Computing the VoIP Bandwidth Requirement*

[Handwritten note: "Can be"]

E Bytes	D Bytes	C Bytes	B Bytes	A Bytes
Layer 2 Header	Possible Tunnel Header	Possible Security Header	Either IP+UDP+RTP Header or cRTP Header	Digitized Voice — The size of this section depends on the codec type and the amount (msec) of analog voice that is digitized and encapsulated in each IP packet.

[Handwritten note: "VI"]

VoIP Bandwidth Calculation Method 1:

```
A = Amount of digitized voice per packet (Bytes)
  = CODEC Bandwidth (bps) x Packetization Period (in Sec) / 8 (bytes)
F = Total Frame Size (bits) = 8 x (E + D + C + B + A)
R = Packet Rate = 1/(Packetization Period in Seconds)
Bandwidth per call (kbps) = F x R divided by 1000
```

VoIP Bandwidth Calculation Method 2:

```
A = Amount of digitized voice per packet (bytes)
  = CODEC Bandwidth (bps) x Packetization Period (in Sec) / 8 (bytes)
F = Total Frame Size (bytes) = E + D + C + B + A
Bandwidth per call = codec bandwidth multiplied by F divided by A

Total Frame Size       Total Bandwidth Requirement
------------------  =  ---------------------------------
Voice Payload Size     codec Bandwidth (also called Nominal
                       Bandwidth Requirement)
```

After you compute the bandwidth for one voice call, you can base the total bandwidth for VoIP on the maximum number of concurrent VoIP calls you expect or are willing to allow using CAC. The bandwidth required by VoIP and other applications (non-VoIP) added together generally should not exceed 75 percent of any bandwidth link. VoIP signaling also consumes bandwidth, but it takes much less bandwidth than actual VoIP talk (audio) packets. QoS tools and techniques treat VoIP signaling and VoIP data (audio) packets differently, so VoIP signaling bandwidth and QoS considerations need special attention.

Effects of VAD on Bandwidth

VAD is a feature that is available in voice-enabled networks. VAD detects silence (speech pauses) and one-way audio and does not generate data; as a result, it produces bandwidth savings. This does not happen in circuit-switched voice networks such as the PSTN, where a channel (usually a 64 Kbps DS0) is dedicated to a call regardless of the amount of activity on that circuit.

It is common for about one-third of a regular voice call to be silence; therefore, the concept of VAD for bandwidth saving is promising. One instance of a modern-day situation is when a caller is put on hold and listens to music on hold (MOH); in this situation, audio flows in one direction only, and it is not necessary to send data from the person on hold to anywhere.

[Handwritten note: "VAD Gets rid of Speech Pauses Audio"]

The amount of bandwidth savings experienced based on VAD depends on the following factors:

- **Type of audio**—During a regular telephone call, only one person speaks at a time (usually!); therefore, no data needs to be sent from the silent party toward the speaking party. The same argument applies when a caller is put on hold or when the person gets MOH.

- **Background noise level**—If the background noise is too loud, VAD does not detect silence and offers no savings. In other words, the background noise is transmitted as regular audio.

- **Other factors**—Differences in language and culture and the type of communication might vary the amount of bandwidth savings due to VAD. During a conference, or when one person is lecturing other(s), the listeners remain silent, and VAD certainly takes advantage of that.

Studies have shown that even though VAD can produce about 35 percent bandwidth savings, its results depend heavily on the fore-mentioned factors. The 35 percent bandwidth savings is based on distribution of different call types; this is only realized if at least 24 active voice calls are on a link. If you expect fewer than 24 calls, the bandwidth savings due of VAD should not be included in the bandwidth calculations. Most conservative people do not count on the VAD savings; in other words, even though they use the VAD feature, they do not include the VAD bandwidth savings in their calculations.

Implementing VoIP Support in an Enterprise Network

This section is intended to give you an overview of telephony deployment models and their necessary elements and components in an enterprise network. It briefly introduces Cisco Unified CallManager, and it discusses a few different implementation options for CallManager clusters. The last part of this section includes a simple configuration for a Cisco voice gateway and concludes with a brief discussion of CAC.

Enterprise Voice Implementations

The main telephony elements of an enterprise Cisco VoIP implementation are gateway, gatekeeper, Cisco Unified CallManager, and Cisco IP phones. Cisco IP phones need CallManager, because it acts as an IP PBX for the Cisco IP phones. The gateways provide connectivity between analog, digital, and IP-based telephony devices and circuits. Gatekeeper is an H.323 device that provides call routing or CAC services.

Enterprise voice implementations can vary based on many factors. One of those factors is the number of sites, and the preferred method of data and voice connectivity (primary and backup) between the sites. Some sites might not have VoIP implemented; other sites might have VoIP connectivity but no IP phones or other IP Telephony services. The sites with IP phones and services might have the control components, such as Cisco Unified CallManager cluster, locally present, or they might have to communicate with the control devices that reside at another branch or site. Figure 1-15 displays an enterprise with three branches: Branch A, Branch B, and Branch C.

Figure 1-15 *VoIP Implementation Within an Enterprise*

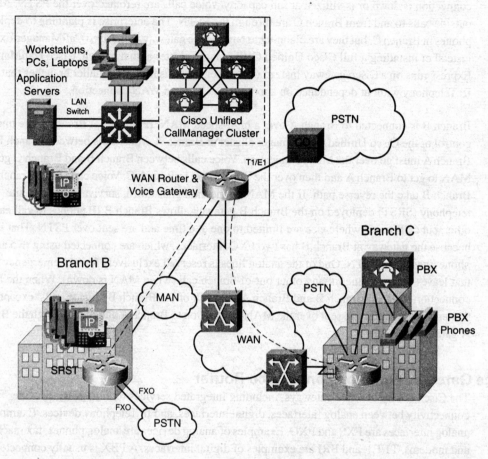

At Branch A, IP Telephony services and IP phones have been deployed. Branch A has a Cisco Unified CallManager cluster, and all employees use IP phones. Branch A is connected to Branch B using a metropolitan-area network (MAN) connection such as Metro Ethernet; voice calls between Branch A and Branch B must use this path. The Branch A connection to Branch C is over a WAN, such as legacy Frame Relay or ATM (a modern connection would be an MPLS VPN connection); voice calls between Branch A and Branch C must use this path. If WAN or MAN connections are down, voice calls must be rerouted via PSTN; if there is congestion, using the automated alternate routing (AAR) feature, voice calls are again rerouted via PSTN. Note that at Branch A, voice calls to and from people outside the enterprise are naturally through PSTN.

At Branch C, on the other hand, the old PBX system and phones are still in use. A voice gateway at Branch C provides connectivity between the Branch C PBX system (and phones) to the PSTN and all other branch phones over the WAN connection. Again, the preferred path for voice calls between Branch C and the other branches is over the WAN connection; however, when the WAN connection is down or is utilized at full capacity, voice calls are rerouted over the PSTN. All outside calls to and from Branch C are through the PSTN. The enterprise is planning to deploy IP phones in Branch C, but they are planning to buy a voice gateway with Cisco CallManager Express instead of installing a full Cisco Unified CallManager cluster at that branch. Cisco CallManager Express runs on a Cisco gateway instead of a server, and it is ideal for smaller branches that want IP Telephony without dependence on another branch over a WAN connection.

Branch B is connected to Branch A over a high-speed MAN. IP phones at Branch B are under control of the Cisco Unified CallManager cluster at Branch A. Voice calls between Branch B and Branch A must go over the MAN connection. Voice calls between Branch B and Branch C go over MAN to get to Branch A and then over the WAN to get to Branch C. Voice calls from Branch C to Branch B take the reverse path. If the MAN connection goes down, survivable remote site telephony (SRST) deployed on the Branch B gateway allows Branch B IP phones to call each other, but calls to anywhere else are limited to one at a time and are sent over PSTN. That is because the gateway at Branch B has two FXO interfaces, which are connected using two analog phone lines to the PSTN. One of the analog lines is reserved exclusively for 911 emergency calls; that leaves only one line for any other out-of-branch call (when MAN is down). When the MAN connection between Branch B and Branch A is up, all of the Branch B outside calls, except the 911 emergency calls, are sent over the MAN connection to Branch A and then through the Branch A gateway to PSTN.

Voice Gateway Functions on a Cisco Router

The Cisco family of voice gateways, including integrated services routers (ISR), provide connectivity between analog interfaces, digital interfaces, and IP Telephony devices. Examples of analog interfaces are FXS and FXO. Examples of analog devices are analog phones, fax machines, and modems. T1/E1 and BRI are examples of digital interfaces. A PBX is usually connected to a gateway using T1/E1 interfaces, even though using an E&M interface is also possible. You can set up a gateway connection to the PSTN CO switch over a T1/E1 or an E&M connection. You can configure a gateway T1/E1 for CCS, where one channel is dedicated to signaling such as ISDN Q.931 or QSIG, and the rest of the channels are available for data or digital voice signals. You can also configure a gateway T1/E1 as CAS. When configured for CAS, a T1 interface can have all 24 channels available for data/digital voice, but each channel loses a few bits to signaling; for this reason, CAS is also referred to as robbed bit signaling (RBS). A gateway can have one or more LAN and WAN interfaces, such as Fast Ethernet, synchronous Serial interface, and ATM.

Gateways convert analog signals to digital and digital signals to analog. They might also be able to handle several different types of codecs. These capabilities depend on the DSPs installed in that gateway and its IOS feature set. DSPs also allow gateways to provide transcoding and conferencing services. Cisco IOS routers (gateways) support the most common VoIP gateway signaling protocols, namely H.323, SIP, and MGCP.

SRST is a useful IOS feature on gateways at remote sites with no CallManager servers. The IP phones at these types of sites communicate with and receive services from CallManager servers at another branch, such as a central branch. If the IP connectivity between the central and remote branch is lost, the IP phones at the remote branch are dysfunctional, unless the gateway of the remote site has the SRST feature. With SRST, the IP phones at the remote site survive, can call among themselves, and have limited features such as hold and transfer. However, the gateway with SRST has to route all other calls to the PSTN.

The IOS on certain Cisco routers and switches has the Cisco Unified CallManager Express feature. This feature allows the gateway to act as a complete CA (CallManager) for the IP phones at a branch. This is not disaster recovery, but a permanent solution or option for smaller branches.

In addition to the features listed, the Cisco gateways offer fax relay, modem relay, and DTMF relay services. Other features such as Hot Standby Routing Protocol (HSRP), Virtual Router Redundancy Protocol (VRRP), and Gateway Load Balancing Protocol (GLBP) provide fault tolerance and load sharing among redundant gateways.

Cisco Unified CallManager Functions — V N

Cisco CallManager (CCM) is call processing software; it is the main component of the Cisco Unified Communication System. CCM supports the MGCP, H.323, SIP, and SCCP IP Telephony signaling protocols. Within the MGCP context, CCM acts as the CA and controls MGCP gateways, and within the SCCP context, it controls the IP phones (Skinny Clients). CCM interacts with H.323 and SIP devices. Cisco CallManager version 5.0 supports SIP clients, such as SIP-based IP phones. CallManager servers form a cluster that provides the means for load sharing and fault tolerance through redundancy. Some of the important services and functions that Cisco Unified CallManager provides are these:

- **Call processing**—CCM performs call routing, signaling, and accounting; furthermore, it has bandwidth management and class of service (CoS) capabilities. (Class of service in this context means enforcing call restrictions.)

- **Dial plan administration**—CCM acts as the CA for MGCP gateways and IP phones; therefore, the dial plan is administered, implemented, and enforced on CCM, and its clients do not and need not have that information or capability.

- **Signaling and device control**—Acting as the CA for MGCP gateways and IP phones, CCM performs signaling for these devices and fully controls their configuration and behavior. When an event occurs, the device informs CCM (the CA), and CCM in turn instructs the device as to the action it should take in response to that event.

- **Phone feature administration**—IP phone configuration files are stored on the Cisco CallManager server; therefore, IP phone administration is centralized. At the time of bootup or when it is manually reset, an IP phone loads its configuration file from its own CallManager server.

- **Directory and XML services**—Directory services can be made available on Cisco CallManager; IP phones can then perform lookup on the available directories. XML applications can be administered as IP phone services on CCM.

- **Programming interface to external applications**—Cisco Systems provides an application programming interface (API) so that applications software can be written to work and communicate with Cisco Unified CallManager. Examples of such applications already developed are Cisco IP Communicator (a computer-based soft IP phone), Cisco Interactive Voice Response System (IVR), Cisco Attendant Console, and Cisco Personal Assistant.

Enterprise IP Telephony Deployment Models

Many IP Telephony deployment options, utilizing Cisco Unified CallManager, are available. The option that is suitable for an enterprise depends on the organization of that enterprise, its business strategy, budget, and objectives. You can deploy the options presented here in combination (hybrid models) or slightly differently. The four main options are as follows:

- Single site

- Multisite with centralized call processing

- Multisite with distributed call processing

- Clustering over WAN

Single-Site Model

In the single-site model, as the name implies, the enterprise has one site, and within that site it has a Cisco CallManager cluster deployed. The local IP phones and perhaps MGCP gateways are under the control of CCM, and CCM can communicate with H.323 and SIP devices. Calls that are external to and from the site are routed through a gateway to the PSTN. The gateway DSPs can provide codec, compression, transcoding, or conferencing resources. If the site has a WAN connection to another place, the WAN connection is not used for IP Telephony purposes in this model.

Multisite with Centralized Call Processing Model

In the multisite with centralized call processing model, the Cisco Unified CallManager (CCM) cluster and application servers are placed at one of the sites—usually a main or central site. This

IP Telephony solution spans multiple sites; in other words, all devices such as IP phones and MGCP gateways at all sites are under the control of the CCM cluster at the central site. Notice that even though call processing is centralized, DSP resources can be distributed.

If network connectivity, such as IP WAN, exists between sites, it carries signaling messages to and from remote sites. Even if a device in a remote site calls another device within the same site, signaling traffic must go through the WAN connection. However, VoIP packets (not signaling) go through the WAN connection only for intersite calls.

Usually, each site has a PSTN connection that serves two purposes: It allows the site to make outside calls, and it can act as an alternate route for when the WAN is down or is utilized to its limit. CAC is used to prohibit too many active intersite calls from hindering data communications or making the quality of calls drop. Administrators decide how many concurrent intersite calls over the WAN connection are viable and configure CAC to deny permission to any new calls over the WAN when the number of active intersite calls reaches that level. In those situations, a new intersite call can either fail (reorder tone or annunciator message), or it can be transparently rerouted through PSTN by means of automated alternate routing (AAR).

If a remote site temporarily loses its WAN connection to the central site, rendering its IP phones useless, SRST is utilized on the gateway of that site. SRST is a feature available on Cisco gateways that allows the IP phones at the remote site to stay active (in the absence of a path to their CCM server) and be able to call each other within the site. SRST routes all calls through the PSTN when the WAN connection is down.

Multisite with Distributed Call Processing Model

In the multisite with distributed call processing model, each site has its own Cisco Unified CallManager cluster controlling all call processing aspects of that site—hence the term *distributed call processing*. Application servers and DSP resources are also distributed at all sites. Sites, in this case, do not depend on the call processing offered at another site. In distributed call processing, each site has a CallManager cluster. Please note that the other resources (voice mail, IPCC, IVR, DSP resources, etc.) can be centralized or distributed; while they're normally distributed, they do not have to be.

The WAN connection between the sites carries intersite data exchange, signaling, and VoIP packets. However, when a device calls another device within its own site, no traffic is sent over the WAN. CAC is still necessary to prohibit too many calls from going through the WAN connection. Each site has PSTN connectivity, which serves two purposes: it allows outside enterprise calls for each site, and it allows rerouting of intersite calls that cannot go through the WAN connection (either due to CAC denial or WAN outage).

This model is comparable to a legacy telephony model, where an enterprise would have a PBX system at each site and, using telco services, the enterprise would connect each pair of PBX systems at remote sites using tie-lines or trunks. In the distributed call processing model, an IP Telephony trunk must be configured between each pair of CallManager clusters (IP PBX) to make intersite calls possible. Examples of IP Telephony trunks that CCM supports are intercluster trunks, H.323 trunks, and SIP trunks.

Clustering over WAN Model

This model uses only one Cisco CallManager cluster for all sites. However, not all servers of the cluster are put in a single site together. Instead, the CCM servers, application servers, and DSP resources are distributed to different locations to provide local service to their clients (such as IP phones and gateways). The CCM servers need to communicate over the intersite IP WAN connection to perform database synchronization and replication. For clustering over WAN to work properly, the maximum round trip delay between each pair of servers within the cluster must be less than 40 ms.

In this model, IP phones acquire services and are controlled by servers in the same site. IP WAN carries signaling and voice packets only for intersite calls. CAC is needed to control the number of calls utilizing the WAN connection. PSTN connection at each site is necessary for outside calls and for AAR purposes.

Identifying Voice Commands in IOS Configurations

Cisco routers that have proper interfaces can be configured to provide connectivity between analog or digital telephony devices over an IP network; they are called *voice gateways* in those circumstances. Figure 1-16 shows two voice gateways, R1 and R2, each with an analog phone connected to its FXS interface. To provide connectivity between the two phones over the IP network, in addition to basic configurations, each of the routers (gateways) needs one plain old telephone service (POTS) and one VoIP dial peer configured.

Figure 1-16 *Two Sample Voice Gateways with Analog Phones Connected to Their FXS Interfaces*

A *dial peer* is a Cisco IOS configuration that links or binds a telephone number to a local POTS interface such as FXS or to a remote IP address; therefore, one POTS dial peer and one VoIP dial peer exist. The series of dial peers configured on a gateway together form its VoIP call routing table. The configurations of R1 and R2 shown in Example 1-1 and Example 1-2 take advantage of the default VoIP signaling protocol on Cisco gateways (H.323). If the phone on R1 goes off-hook and, after receiving the dial tone, number 22 is dialed, R1 sends H.323 signaling (call setup) messages to the R2 IP address 192.168.2.2. After the message from R1 is received and processed, based on the dialed number 22, R2 sends a ring signal to interface 2/0/0 (the FXS port), and the phone on R2 rings.

Example 1-1 *R1 VoIP Configuration*

```
Dial-peer voice 1 pots
 destination-pattern 11
 port 1/1/1

Dial-peer voice 2 voip
 destination-pattern 22
 session target ipv4:192.168.2.2
```

Example 1-2 *R2 VoIP Configuration*

```
Dial-peer voice 1 pots
 destination-pattern 22
 port 2/0/0

Dial-peer voice 2 voip
 destination-pattern 11
 session target ipv4:192.168.1.1
```

Call Admission Control (CAC)

Call admission control is a feature that is configured to limit the number of concurrent calls. Usually, because the bandwidth of the WAN link is much less than LAN links, CAC is configured so that WAN bandwidth does not get oversubscribed by VoIP calls. CAC complements QoS configurations. For instance, if a strict priority queue with enough bandwidth for three voice calls is configured on all routers between two phones, although there are fewer than four concurrent calls, all will be good quality. What would happen if ten calls went active concurrently? If all the VoIP traffic packets (RTP) must share the strict priority queue that is provisioned with enough bandwidth for three calls, routers will drop many VoIP packets when there are ten active calls. The packets that will be dropped belong to any or all active calls, indiscriminately. It is wrong to believe that only packets associated to the calls beyond the third one will be dropped. As a result, all calls can and probably will experience packet drops and, naturally, poor call quality. When there are available and reserved resources for a certain number of concurrent calls, CAC must be configured so that no more calls than the limit can go active. QoS features such as classification, marking, congestion avoidance, congestion management, and so on provide priority services to voice packets (RTP) but do not prevent their volume from exceeding the limit; for that, you need CAC.

Foundation Summary

The "Foundation Summary" is a collection of information that provides a convenient review of many key concepts in this chapter. If you are already comfortable with the topics in this chapter, this summary can help you recall a few details. If you just read this chapter, this review should help solidify some key facts. If you are doing your final preparation before the exam, the information in this section is a convenient way to review the day before the exam.

Benefits of packet telephony networks include usage of common infrastructure for voice and data, lower transmission costs, more efficient usage of bandwidth, higher employee productivity, and access to new communication devices. Main packet telephony components are phones, video end points, gateways, MCUs, application servers, gatekeepers, and call agents. Voice gateways can have analog interfaces such as FXS, FXO, and E&M; they may have digital interfaces such as BRI, CT1/PRI, or CE1/PRI.

The main stages of a phone call are call setup, call maintenance, and call teardown. Call control has two main types: centralized call control and distributed call control. H.323 and SIP are examples of distributed VoIP call control protocol, whereas MGCP is an example of a centralized VoIP call control protocol.

The steps involved in analog-to-digital voice conversion are sampling, quantization, encoding, and compression. Digital-to-analog voice conversion steps include decompression, decoding, and reconstruction of analog signal from pulse amplitude modulation (PAM) signal. Based on the Nyquist theorem, the sampling rate must be at least twice the maximum analog audio signal frequency. *Quantization* is the process of expressing the amplitude of a sampled signal by a binary number. Several different ITU coding, decoding, and compression standards (called codecs) exist, each of which requires a specific amount of bandwidth per call and yields a different quality. Digital signal processors (DSP) convert analog voice signal to digital and vice versa; DSPs are also voice termination points on voice gateways and are responsible for transcoding and conferencing. Digitized voice is encapsulated in IP packets, which are routed and transported over IP networks. RTP, UDP, and IP headers are added to digitized voice, and the data link layer header is added to form a frame that is ready for transmission over media. Compressed RTP (cRTP) can reduce or compress the RTP/UDP/IP headers when configured on the router interfaces on both sides of a link; the reduction in overhead produced by cRTP is mainly beneficial and recommended on links with less than 2 Mbps bandwidth.

The factors that influence the bandwidth requirement of each VoIP call over a link are packet rate, packetization size, IP overhead, data link overhead, and tunneling overhead. The amount of voice that is encapsulated in an IP packet affects the packet size and the packet rate. Smaller IP packets mean more of them will be present, so the IP overhead elevates. Different data link layer protocols have varying amounts of header size and hence overhead. Tunneling and Security (IPsec) also add overhead and hence increase the bandwidth demand for VoIP. Computing the total bandwidth required on a link for each VoIP flow includes knowledge of the codec used, packetization period, and all the overheads that will be present. Voice activity detection (VAD) can reduce bandwidth requirements of VoIP calls and produce bandwidth savings of up to 35 percent.

The main components of enterprise voice implementations are IP phones, gateways, gatekeepers, and Cisco Unified CallManager (CCM). Gateway, call agent, and DSP are among the capabilities offered by Cisco integrated services routers (ISRs). CCM provides call processing, dial plan administration, signaling and device control, phone feature administration, and access to applications from IP phones. Enterprise IP Telephony deployment models are single site, multisite with centralized call processing, multisite with distributed call processing, and clustering over WAN. Dial peers are created with Cisco IOS commands configured on gateways to implement a local dial plan. Call admission control (CAC) is configured to limit the number of concurrent VoIP calls. It is required even in the presence of good QoS configurations so that WAN resources (bandwidth) do not become oversubscribed.

Q&A

Some of the questions that follow challenge you more than the exam by using an open-ended question format. By reviewing now with this more difficult question format, you can exercise your memory better and prove your conceptual and factual knowledge of this chapter. The answers to these questions appear in Appendix A.

1. List at least three benefits of packet telephony networks.

2. List at least three important components of a packet telephony (VoIP) network.

3. List three types of analog interfaces through which legacy analog devices can connect to a VoIP network.

4. List at least two digital interface options to connect VoIP equipment to PBXs or the PSTN.

5. List the three stages of a phone call.

6. What are the two main models of call control?

7. List the steps for converting analog signals to digital signals.

8. List the steps for converting digital signals to analog signals.

9. Based on the Nyquist theorem, what should be the minimum sampling rate of analog signals?

10. What are the two main quantization techniques?

11. Name and explain the quantization methods used in North America and in other countries.

12. Name at least three main codec/compression standards, and specify their bandwidth requirements.

13. What is MOS?

14. What is a DSP?

15. Which TCP/IP protocols are responsible for transporting voice? What are the sizes of those protocol headers?

16. What features does RTP provide to complement UDP?

17. What is cRTP?

18. List at least three factors that influence bandwidth requirements of VoIP.

19. What is the relationship between the packet rate and the packetization period?

20. What are the sizes of Ethernet, 802.1Q, Frame Relay, and Multilink PPP (MLP) overheads?

21. Name at least three tunneling and security protocols and their associated overheads.

22. Briefly list the steps necessary to compute the total bandwidth for a VoIP call.

23. What is VAD?

24. List at least three important components of enterprise voice implementations.

25. List at least three voice gateway functions on a Cisco router.

26. List the main functions of Cisco Unified CallManager.

27. List the four main enterprise IP Telephony deployment models.

28. What is CAC?

29. With QoS features in place, there can be up to ten concurrent VoIP calls over a company WAN link. Is there a need for CAC? With no CAC, what will happen when there are more than ten concurrent calls?

This part covers the following ONT exam topics. (To view the ONT exam overview, visit http://www.cisco.com/web/learning/le3/current_exams/ 642-845.html.)

- Explain the necessity of QoS in converged networks (e.g., bandwidth, delay, loss, etc.).

- Describe strategies for QoS implementations (e.g. QoS Policy, QoS Models, etc.).

- Describe classification and marking (e.g., CoS, ToS, IP Precedence, DSCP, etc.).

- Describe and configure NBAR for classification.

- Explain congestion management and avoidance mechanisms (e.g., FIFO, PQ, WRR, WRED, etc.).

- Describe traffic policing and traffic shaping (i.e., traffic conditioners).

- Describe Control Plane Policing.

- Describe WAN link efficiency mechanisms (e.g., Payload/Header Compression, MLP with interleaving, etc.).

- Describe and configure QoS Pre-Classify.

- Explain the functions and operations of AutoQoS.

- Describe the SDM QoS Wizard.

- Configure, verify, and troubleshoot AutoQoS implementations (i.e., MQC).

Part II: Quality of Service

Part II: Quality of Service

This chapter covers the following subjects:

- Introduction to QoS

- Identifying and Comparing QoS Models

- QoS Implementation Methods

CHAPTER 2

IP Quality of Service

This chapter provides the essential background, definitions, and concepts for you to start learning IP quality of service (QoS). The following two chapters complement this one and provide more coverage of this topic. It is probably safe to expect about 20 percent of the ONT exam questions from this chapter.

"Do I Know This Already?" Quiz

The purpose of the "Do I Know This Already?" quiz is to help you decide whether you really need to read the entire chapter. The 20-question quiz, derived from the major sections of this chapter, helps you determine how to spend your limited study time.

Table 2-1 outlines the major topics discussed in this chapter and the "Do I Know This Already?" quiz questions that correspond to those topics. You can keep track of your score here, too.

Table 2-1 *"Do I Know This Already?" Foundation Topics Section-to-Question Mapping*

Foundation Topics Section Covering These Questions	Questions	Score
"Introduction to QoS"	1–7	
"Identifying and Comparing QoS Models"	8–13	
"QoS Implementation Methods"	14–20	
Total Score	**(20 possible)**	

CAUTION The goal of self-assessment is to gauge your mastery of the topics in this chapter. If you do not know the answer to a question or are only partially sure of the answer, mark this question wrong for purposes of the self-assessment. Giving yourself credit for an answer you correctly guess skews your self-assessment results and might provide you with a false sense of security.

You can find the answers to the "Do I Know This Already?" quiz in Appendix A, "Answers to the 'Do I Know This Already?' Quizzes and Q&A Sections." The suggested choices for your next step are as follows:

- **15 or less overall score**—Read the entire chapter. This includes the "Foundation Topics," "Foundation Summary," and "Q&A" sections.

- **16–17 overall score**—Begin with the "Foundation Summary" section and then follow up with the "Q&A" section at the end of the chapter.

- **18 or more overall score**—If you want more review on this topic, skip to the "Foundation Summary" section and then go to the "Q&A" section. Otherwise, proceed to the next chapter.

1. Which of the following items is *not* considered one of four major issues and challenges facing converged enterprise networks?

   a. Available bandwidth

   b. End-to-end delay

   c. Delay variation (jitter)

   d. Packet size

2. Which of the following is defined as the maximum bandwidth of a path?

   a. The bandwidth of the link within the path that has the largest bandwidth

   b. The bandwidth of the link within the path that has the smallest bandwidth

   c. The total of all link bandwidths within the path

   d. The average of all the link bandwidths within the path

3. Which of the following is *not* considered one of the main methods to tackle the bandwidth availability problem?

   a. Increase (upgrade) the link bandwidth.

   b. Classify and mark traffic and deploy proper queuing mechanisms.

   c. Forward large packets first.

   d. Use compression techniques.

4. Which of the following is *not* considered a major delay type?

   a. Queuing delay

   b. CEF (Cisco Express Forwarding) delay

   c. Serialization delay

   d. Propagation delay

5. Which of the following does *not* reduce delay for delay-sensitive application traffic?

   a. Increasing (upgrade) the link bandwidth

   b. Prioritizing delay-sensitive packets and forwarding important packets first

   c. Layer 2 payload encryption

   d. Header compression

6. Which of the following approaches does *not* tackle packet loss?

   a. Increase (upgrade) the link bandwidth.

   b. Increase the buffer space.

   c. Provide guaranteed bandwidth.

   d. Eliminate congestion avoidance.

7. Which of the following is *not* a major step in implementing QoS?

   a. Apply access lists to all interfaces that process sensitive traffic

   b. Identify traffic types and their requirements

   c. Classify traffic based on the requirements identified

   d. Define policies for each traffic class

8. Which of following is *not* one of the three main QoS models?

   a. MPLS QoS

   b. Differentiated services

   c. Best effort

   d. Integrated services

9. Which two of the following items are considered drawbacks of the best-effort model?

   a. Inability to scale

   b. Lack of service guarantee

   c. Lack of service differentiation

   d. Difficulty in implementing (complexity)

10. Which of the following is *not* a function that IntServ requires to be implemented on the routers along the traffic path?

    a. Admission control and policing

    b. Classification

    c. Queuing and scheduling

    d. Fast switching

11. Which of the following is the role of RSVP within the IntServ model?

 a. Routing

 b. Switching

 c. Signaling/Bandwidth Reservation

 d. Caching

12. Which of the following is *not* considered a benefit of the IntServ model?

 a. Explicit end-to-end resource admission control

 b. Continuous signaling per active flow

 c. Per-request policy admission control

 d. Signaling of dynamic port numbers

13. Which of the following is *not* true about the DiffServ model?

 a. Within the DiffServ model, QoS policies (are deployed to) enforce differentiated treatment of the defined traffic classes.

 b. Within the DiffServ model, classes of traffic and the policies are defined based on business requirements; you choose the service level for each traffic class.

 c. Pure DiffServ makes extensive use of signaling; therefore, it is called *hard QoS*.

 d. DiffServ is a scalable model.

14. Which of the following is *not* a QoS implementation method?

 a. Cisco IOS CLI

 b. MQC

 c. Cisco AVVID (VoIP and Enterprise)

 d. Cisco SDM QoS Wizard

15. Which of the following is *not* a major step in implementing QoS with MQC?

 a. Define traffic classes using the class map.

 b. Define QoS policies for the defined traffic classes using the policy map.

 c. Apply the defined policies to each intended interface using the **service-policy** command.

 d. Enable AutoQoS.

16. Which of the following is the simplest QoS implementation method with an option specifically for VoIP?

   a. AutoQoS (VoIP)

   b. CLI

   c. MQC

   d. Cisco SDM QoS Wizard

17. Select the most time-consuming and the least time-consuming QoS implementation methods.

   a. CLI

   b. MQC

   c. AutoQoS

   d. Cisco SDM QoS Wizard

18. What is the most significant advantage of MQC over CLI?

   a. It requires little time to implement.

   b. It requires little expertise to implement.

   c. It has a GUI and interactive wizard.

   d. It separates traffic classification from policy definition.

19. Before you enable AutoQoS on an interface, which two of the following must you ensure have been configured on that interface?

   a. Cisco modular QoS is configured.

   b. CEF is enabled.

   c. The SDM has been enabled.

   d. The correct bandwidth on the interface is configured.

20. Select the item that is *not* a main service obtained from SDM QoS.

   a. It enables you to implement QoS on the network.

   b. It enables you to fine-tune QoS on the network.

   c. It enables you to monitor QoS on the network.

   d. It enables you to troubleshoot QoS on the network.

Foundation Topics

Introduction to QoS

This section introduces the concept of QoS and discusses the four main issues in a converged network that have QoS implications, as well as the Cisco IP QoS mechanisms and best practices to deal with those issues. This section also introduces the three steps in implementing a QoS policy on a network.

Converged Network Issues Related to QoS

A converged network supports different types of applications, such as voice, video, and data, simultaneously over a common infrastructure. Accommodating these applications that have different sensitivities and requirements is a challenging task on the hands of network engineers.

The acceptable end-to-end delay for the Voice over IP (VoIP) packets is 150 to 200 milliseconds (ms). Also, the delay variation or jitter among the VoIP packets must be limited so that the buffers at the receiving end do not become exhausted, causing breakup in the audio flow. In contrast, a data application such as a file download from an FTP site does not have such a stringent delay requirement, and jitter does not impose a problem for this type of application either. When numerous active VoIP and data applications exist, mechanisms must be put in place so that while critical applications function properly, a reasonable number of voice applications can remain active and function with good quality (with low delay and jitter) as well.

Many data applications are TCP-based. If a TCP segment is dropped, the source retransmits it after a timeout period is passed and no acknowledgement for that segment is received. Therefore, TCP-based applications have some tolerance to packet drops. The tolerance of video and voice applications toward data loss is minimal. As a result, the network must have mechanisms in place so that at times of congestion, packets encapsulating video and voice receive priority treatment and are not dropped.

Network outages affect all applications and render them disabled. However, well-designed networks have redundancy built in, so that when a failure occurs, the network can reroute packets through alternate (redundant) paths until the failed components are repaired. The total time it takes to notice the failure, compute alternate paths, and start rerouting the packets must be short enough for the voice and video applications not to suffer and not to annoy the users. Again, data applications usually do not expect the network recovery to be as fast as video and voice applications expect it to be. Without redundancy and fast recovery, network outage is unacceptable, and mechanisms must be put in place to avoid it.

Based on the preceding information, you can conclude that four major issues and challenges face converged enterprise networks:

- **Available bandwidth**—Many simultaneous data, voice, and video applications compete over the limited bandwidth of the links within enterprise networks.

- **End-to-end delay**—Many actions and factors contribute to the total time it takes for data or voice packets to reach their destination. For example, compression, packetization, queuing, serialization, propagation, processing (switching), and decompression all contribute to the total delay in VoIP transmission.

- **Delay variation (jitter)**—Based on the amount of concurrent traffic and activity, plus the condition of the network, packets from the same flow might experience a different amount of delay as they travel through the network.

- **Packet loss**—If volume of traffic exhausts the capacity of an interface, link, or device, packets might be dropped. Sudden bursts or failures are usually responsible for this situation.

The sections that follow explore these challenges in detail.

Available Bandwidth

Packets usually flow through the best path from source to destination. The maximum bandwidth of that path is equal to the bandwidth of the link with the smallest bandwidth. Figure 2-1 shows that R1-R2-R3-R4 is the best path between the client and the server. On this path, the maximum bandwidth is 10 Mbps because that is the bandwidth of the link with the smallest bandwidth on that path. The average available bandwidth is the maximum bandwidth divided by the number of flows.

Figure 2-1 *Maximum Bandwidth and Average Available Bandwidth Along the Best Path (R1-R2-R3-R4) Between the Client and Server*

$\text{Bandwidth}_{(Max)} = \text{Min}(10 \text{ Mbps}, 10 \text{ Mbps}, 100 \text{ Mbps}) = 10 \text{ Mbps}$

$\text{Bandwidth}_{(Avail)} = \text{Bandwidth}_{(Max)}/\text{Flows}$

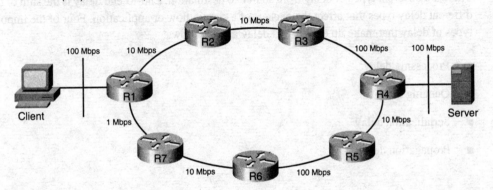

Lack of sufficient bandwidth causes delay, packet loss, and poor performance for applications. The users of real-time applications (voice and video) detect this right away. You can tackle the bandwidth availability problem in numerous ways:

- **Increase (upgrade) link bandwidth**—This is effective, but it is costly.

- **Classify and mark traffic and deploy proper queuing mechanisms**—Forward important packets first.

- **Use compression techniques**—Layer 2 payload compression, TCP header compression, and cRTP are some examples.

Increasing link bandwidth is undoubtedly beneficial, but it cannot always be done quickly, and it has cost implications. Those who just increase bandwidth when necessary notice that their solution is not very effective at times of heavy traffic bursts. However, in certain scenarios, increasing link bandwidth might be the first action necessary (but not the last).

Classification and marking of the traffic, combined with congestion management, is an effective approach to providing adequate bandwidth for enterprise applications.

Link compression, TCP header compression, and RTP header compression are all different compression techniques that can reduce the bandwidth consumed on certain links, and therefore increase throughput. Cisco IOS supports the Stacker and Predictor Layer 2 compression algorithms that compress the payload of the packet. Usage of hardware compression is always preferred over software-based compression. Because compression is CPU intensive and imposes yet another delay, it is usually recommended only on slow links.

> **NOTE**   Most compression mechanisms must be configured on a link-by-link basis—in other words, on both ends of each link. Classification, marking, compression, and advanced queuing mechanisms are discussed in Chapters 3, 4, and 5 in detail.

End-to-End Delay

There are different types of delay from source to destination. End-to-end delay is the sum of those different delay types that affect the packets of a certain flow or application. Four of the important types of delay that make up end-to-end delay are as follows:

- Processing delay

- Queuing delay

- Serialization delay

- Propagation delay

Processing delay is the time it takes for a device such as a router or Layer 3 switch to perform all the tasks necessary to move a packet from the input (ingress) interface to the output (egress) interface. The CPU type, CPU utilization, switching mode, router architecture, and configured features on the device affect the processing delay. For example, packets that are distributed-CEF switched on a versatile interface processor (VIP) card cause no CPU interrupts.

Queuing delay is the amount of time that a packet spends in the output queue of a router interface. The busyness of the router, the number of packets waiting in the queue, the queuing discipline, and the interface bandwidth all affect the queuing delay.

Serialization delay is the time it takes to send all the bits of a frame to the physical medium for transmission across the physical layer. The time it takes for the bits of that frame to cross the physical link is called the *propagation delay*. Naturally, the propagation delay across different media can be significantly different. For instance, the propagation delay on a high-speed optical connection such as OC-192 is significantly lower than the propagation delay on a satellite-based link.

> **NOTE**   In best-effort networks, while serialization and propagation delays are fixed, the processing and queuing delays are variable and unpredictable.
>
> Other types of delay exist, such as WAN delay, compression and decompression delay, and de-jitter delay.

Delay Variation

The variation in delays experienced by the packets of the same flow is called *delay variation* or *jitter*. Packets of the same flow might not arrive at the destination at the same rate that they were released. These packets, individually and independent from each other, are processed, queued, de-queued, and so on. Therefore, they might arrive out of sequence, and their end-to-end delays might vary. For voice and video packets, it is essential that at the destination point, the packets are released to the application in the correct order and at the same rate that they were released at the source. The de-jitter buffer serves that purpose. As long as the delay variation is not too much, at the destination point, the de-jitter buffer holds packets, sorts them, and releases them to the application based on the Real-Time Transport Protocol (RTP) time stamp on the packets. Because the buffer compensates the jitter introduced by the network, it is called the *de-jitter buffer*.

Average queue length, packet size, and link bandwidth contribute to serialization and propagation delay. You can reduce delay by doing some or all of the following:

- **Increase (upgrade) link bandwidth**—This is effective as the queue sizes drop and queuing delays soar. However, upgrading link capacity (bandwidth) takes time and has cost implications, rendering this approach unrealistic at times.

- **Prioritize delay-sensitive packets and forward important packets first**—This might require packet classification or marking, but it certainly requires deployment of a queuing mechanism such as weighted fair queuing (WFQ), class-based weighted fair queuing (CBWFQ), or low-latency queuing (LLQ). This approach is not as costly as the previous approach, which is a bandwidth upgrade.

- **Reprioritize packets**—In certain cases, the packet priority (marking) has to change as the packet enters or leaves a device. When packets leave one domain and enter another, this priority change might have to happen. For instance, the packets that leave an enterprise network with critical marking and enter a provider network might have to be reprioritized (remarked) to best effort if the enterprise is only paying for best effort service.

- **Layer 2 payload compression**—Layer 2 compression reduces the size of the IP packet (or any other packet type that is the frame's payload), and it frees up available bandwidth on that link. Because complexity and delay are associated with performing the compression, you must ensure that the delay reduced because of compression is more than the delay introduced by the compression complexity. Note that payload compression leaves the frame header in tact; this is required in cases such as frame relay connections.

- **Use header compression**—RTP header compression (cRTP) is effective for VoIP packets, because it greatly improves the overhead-to-payload ratio. cRTP is recommended on slow (less than 2 Mbps) links. Header compression is less CPU-intensive than Layer 2 payload compression.

Packet Loss

Packet loss occurs when a network device such as a router has no more buffer space on an interface (output queue) to hold the new incoming packets and it ends up dropping them. A router may drop some packets to make room for higher priority ones. Sometimes an interface reset causes packets to be flushed and dropped. Packets are dropped for other reasons, too, including interface overrun.

TCP resends the dropped packets; meanwhile, it reduces the size of the send window and slows down at times of congestion and high network traffic volume. If a packet belonging to a UDP-based file transfer (such as TFTP) is dropped, the whole file might have to be resent. This creates even more traffic on the network, and it might annoy the user. Application flows that do not use TCP, and therefore are more drop-sensitive, are called *fragile flows*.

During a VoIP call, packet loss results in audio breakup. A video conference will have jerky pictures and its audio will be out of synch with the video if packet drops or extended delays occur. When network traffic volume and congestion are heavy, applications experience packet drops, extended delays, and jitter. Only with proper QoS configuration can you avoid these problems or at least limit them to low-priority packets.

On a Cisco router, at times of congestion and packet drops, you can enter the **show interface** command and observe that on some or all interfaces, certain counters such as those in the following list have incremented more than usual (baseline):

- **Output drop**—This counter shows the number of packets dropped, because the output queue of the interface was full at the time of their arrival. This is also called *tail drop*.

- **Input queue drop**—If the CPU is overutilized and cannot process incoming packets, the input queue of an interface might become full, and the number of packets dropped in this scenario will be reported as input queue drops.

- **Ignore**—This is the number of frames ignored due to lack of buffer space.

- **Overrun**—The CPU must allocate buffer space so that incoming packets can be stored and processed in turn. If the CPU becomes too busy, it might not allocate buffer space quickly enough and end up dropping packets. The number of packets dropped for this reason is called *overruns*.

- **Frame error**—Frames with cyclic redundancy check (CRC) error, runt frames (smaller than minimum standard), and giant frames (larger than the maximum standard) are usually dropped, and their total is reported as frame errors.

You can use many methods, all components of QoS, to tackle packet loss. Some methods protect packet loss from all applications, whereas others protect specific classes of packets from packet loss only. The following are examples of approaches that packet loss can merit from:

- **Increase (upgrade) link bandwidth**—Higher bandwidth results in faster packet departures from interface queues. If full queue scenarios are prevented, so are tail drops and random drops (discussed later).

- **Increase buffer space**—Network engineers must examine the buffer settings on the interfaces of network devices such as routers to see if their sizes and settings are appropriate. When dealing with packet drop issues, it is worth considering an increase of interface buffer space (size). A larger buffer space allows better handling of traffic bursts.

- **Provide guaranteed bandwidth**—Certain tools and features such as CBWFQ and LLQ allow the network engineers to reserve certain amounts of bandwidth for a specific class of traffic. As long as enough bandwidth is reserved for a class of traffic, packets of such a class will not become victims of packet drop.

- **Perform congestion avoidance**—To prevent a queue from becoming full and starting tail drop, you can deploy random early detection (RED) or weighted random early detection (WRED) to drop packets from the queue before it becomes full. You might wonder what the merit of that deployment would be. When packets are dropped before a queue becomes full, the packets can be dropped from certain flows only; tail drop loses packets from all flows.

With WRED, the flows that lose packets first are the lowest priority ones. It is hoped that the highest priority packet flows will not have drops. Drops due to deployment of RED/WRED slow TCP-based flows, but they have no effect on UDP-based flows.

Most companies that connect remote sites over a WAN connection transfer both TCP- and UDP-based application data between those sites. Figure 2-2 displays a company that sends VoIP traffic as well as file transfer and other application data over a WAN connection between its remote branch and central main branch. Note that, at times, the collection of traffic flows from the remote branch intending to cross R2 and the WAN connection (to go to the main central branch) can reach high volumes.

Figure 2-2 *Solutions for Packet Loss and Extended Delay*

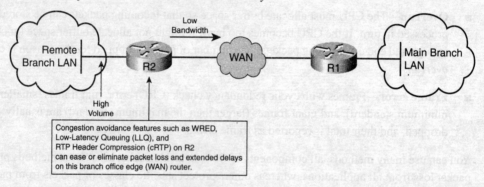

Figure 2-2 displays the stated scenario that leads to extended delay and packet loss. Congestion avoidance tools trigger TCP-based applications to throttle back before queues and buffers become full and tail drops start. Because congestion avoidance features such as WRED do not trigger UDP-based applications (such as VoIP) to slow down, for those types of applications, you must deploy other features, including compression techniques such as cRTP and advanced queuing such as LLQ.

Definition of QoS and the Three Steps to Implementing It

Following is the most recent definition that Cisco educational material provides for QoS:

QoS is the ability of the network to provide better or special service to a set of users or applications or both to the detriment of other users or applications or both.

The earliest versions of QoS tools protected data against data. For instance, priority queuing made sure packets that matched an access list always had the right of way on an egress interface. Another example is WFQ, which prevents small packets from waiting too long behind large packets on an egress interface outbound queue. When VoIP started to become a serious technology, QoS tools were created to protect voice from data. An example of such a tool is RTP priority queue.

RTP priority queue is reserved for RTP (encapsulating voice payload). RTP priority queuing ensures that voice packets receive right of way. If there are too many voice streams, data applications begin experiencing too much delay and too many drops. Strict priority queue (incorporated in LLQ) was invented to limit the bandwidth of the priority queue, which is essentially dedicated to voice packets. This technique protects data from voice; too many voice streams do not downgrade the quality of service for data applications. However, what if there are too many voice streams? All the voice calls and streams must share the bandwidth dedicated to the strict priority queue that is reserved for voice packets. If the number of voice calls exceeds the allocated resources, the quality of those calls will drop. The solution to this problem is call admission control (CAC). CAC prevents the number of concurrent voice calls from going beyond a specified limit and hurting the quality of the active calls. CAC protects voice from voice. Almost all the voice requirements apply to video applications, too; however, the video applications are more bandwidth hungry.

Enterprise networks must support a variety of applications with diverse bandwidth, drop, delay, and jitter expectations. Network engineers, by using proper devices, Cisco IOS features, and configurations, can control the behavior of the network and make it provide predictable service to those applications. The existence of voice, video, and multimedia applications in general not only adds to the bandwidth requirements in networks but also adds to the challenges involved in having to provide granular and strictly controlled delay, jitter, and loss guarantees.

Implementing QoS

Implementing QoS involves three major steps:

Step 1   Identifying traffic types and their requirements

Step 2   Classifying traffic based on the requirements identified

Step 3   Defining policies for each traffic class

Even though many common applications and protocols exist among enterprise networks, within each network, the volumes and percentages of those traffic types vary. Furthermore, each enterprise might have its own unique application types in addition to the common ones. Therefore, the first step in implementing QoS in an enterprise is to study and discover the traffic types and define the requirements of each identified traffic type. If two, three, or more traffic types have identical importance and requirements, it is unnecessary to define that many traffic classes. Traffic classification, which is the second step in implementing QoS, will define a few traffic classes, not hundreds. The applications that end up in different traffic classes have different requirements; therefore, the network must provide them with different service types. The definition of how each traffic class is serviced is called the *network policy*. Defining and deploying the network QoS policy for each class is Step 3 of implementing QoS. The three steps of implementing QoS on a network are explained next.

Step 1: Identifying Traffic Types and Their Requirements

Identifying traffic types and their requirements, the first step in implementing QoS, is composed of the following elements or substeps:

- **Perform a network audit**—It is often recommended that you perform the audit during the busy hour (BH) or congestion period, but it is also important that you run the audit at other times. Certain applications are run during slow business hours on purpose. There are scientific methods for identifying the busy network moments, for example, through statistical sampling and analysis, but the simplest method is to observe CPU and link utilizations and conduct the audit during the general peak periods.

- **Perform a business audit and determine the importance of each application**—The business model and goals dictate the business requirements. From that, you can derive the definition of traffic classes and the requirements for each class. This step considers whether delaying or dropping packets of each application is acceptable. You must determine the relative importance of different applications.

- **Define the appropriate service levels for each traffic class**—For each traffic class, within the framework of business objectives, a specific service level can define tangible resource availability or reservations. Guaranteed minimum bandwidth, maximum bandwidth, guaranteed end-to-end maximum delay, guaranteed end-to-end maximum jitter, and comparative drop preference are among the characteristics that you can define for each service level. The final service level definitions must meet business objectives and satisfy the comfort expectations of the users.

Step 2: Classifying Traffic Based on the Requirements Identified

The definition of traffic classes does not need to be general; it must include the traffic (application) types that were observed during the network audit step. You can classify tens or even hundreds of traffic variations into very few classes. The defined traffic classes must be in line with business objectives. The traffic or application types within the same class must have common requirements and business requirements. The exceptions to this rule are the applications that have not been identified or scavenger-class traffic.

Voice traffic has specific requirements, and it is almost always in its own class. With Cisco LLQ, VoIP is assigned to a single class, and that class uses a strict priority queue (a priority queue with strict maximum bandwidth) on the egress interface of each router. Many case studies have shown the merits of using some or all of the following traffic classes within an enterprise network:

- **Voice (VoIP) class**—Voice traffic has specific bandwidth requirements, and its delay and drops must be eliminated or at least minimized. Therefore, this class is the highest priority class but has limited bandwidth. VoIP packet loss should remain below 1% and the goal for its end-to-end delay must be 150 ms.

- **Mission-critical traffic class**—Critical business applications are put in one or two classes. You must identify the bandwidth requirements for them.

- **Signaling traffic class**—Signaling traffic, voice call setup and teardown for example, is often put in a separate class. This class has limited bandwidth expectations.

- **Transactional applications traffic class**—These applications, if present, include interactive, database, and similar services that need special attention. You must also identify the bandwidth requirements for them. Enterprise Resource Planning (ERP) applications such as Peoplesoft and SAP are examples of these types of applications.

- **Best-effort traffic class**—All the undefined traffic types are considered best effort and receive the remainder of bandwidth on an interface.

- **Scavenger traffic class**—This class of applications will be assigned into one class and be given limited bandwidth. This class is considered inferior to the best-effort traffic class. Peer-to-peer file sharing applications are put in this class.

Step 3: Defining Policies for Each Traffic Class

After the traffic classes have been formed based on the network audit and business objectives, the final step of implementing QoS in an enterprise is to provide a network-wide definition for the QoS service level that must be assigned to each traffic class. This is called *defining a QoS policy*, and it might include having to complete the following tasks:

- Setting a maximum bandwidth limit for a class

- Setting a minimum bandwidth guarantee for a class

- Assigning a relative priority level to a class

- Applying congestion management, congestion avoidance, and many other advanced QoS technologies to a class.

To provide an example, based on the traffic classes listed in the previous section, Table 2-2 defines a practical QoS policy.

Table 2-2 *Defining QoS Policy for Set Traffic Classes*

Class	Priority	Queue Type	Min/Max Bandwidth	Special QoS Technology
Voice	5	Priority	1 Mbps Min 1 Mbps Max	Priority queue
Business mission critical	4	CBWFQ	1 Mbps Min	CBWFQ

continues

Table 2-2   *Defining QoS Policy for Set Traffic Classes (Continued)*

Class	Priority	Queue Type	Min/Max Bandwidth	Special QoS Technology
Signaling	3	CBWFQ	400 Kbps Min	CBWFQ
Transactional	2	CBWFQ	1 Mbps Min	CBWFQ
Best-effort	1	CBWFQ	500 Kbps Max	CBWFQ CB-Policing
Scavenger	0	CBWFQ	Max 100 Kbps	CBWFQ +CB-Policing WRED

Identifying and Comparing QoS Models

This section discusses the three main QoS models, namely best-effort, Integrated Services, and Differentiated Services. The key features, and the benefits and drawbacks of each of these QoS models, are explained in turn.

Best-Effort Model

The best-effort model means that no QoS policy is implemented. It is natural to wonder why this model was not called no-effort. Within this model, packets belonging to voice calls, e-mails, file transfers, and so on are treated as equally important; indeed, these packets are not even differentiated. The basic mail delivery by the post office is often used as an example for the best-effort model, because the post office treats all letters as equally important.

The best-effort model has some benefits as well as some drawbacks. Following are the main benefits of this model:

- **Scalability**—The Internet is a best-effort network. The best-effort model has no scalability limit. The bandwidth of router interfaces dictates throughput efficiencies.

- **Ease**—The best-effort model requires no special QoS configuration, making it the easiest and quickest model to implement.

The drawbacks of the best-effort model are as follows:

- **Lack of service guarantee**—The best-effort model makes no guarantees about packet delivery/loss, delay, or available bandwidth.

- **Lack of service differentiation**—The best-effort model does not differentiate packets that belong to applications that have different levels of importance from the business perspective.

Integrated Services Model

The Integrated Services (IntServ) model, developed in the mid-1990s, was the first serious attempt to provide end-to-end QoS, which was demanded by real-time applications. IntServ is based on explicit signaling and managing/reserving network resources for the applications that need it and demand it. IntServ is often referred to as Hard-QoS, because Hard-QoS guarantees characteristics such as bandwidth, delay, and packet loss, thereby providing a predictable service level. Resource Reservation Protocol (RSVP) is the signaling protocol that IntServ uses. An application that has a specific bandwidth requirement must wait for RSVP to run along the path from source to destination, hop by hop, and request bandwidth reservation for the application flow. If the RSVP attempt to reserve bandwidth along the path succeeds, the application can begin operating. While the application is active, along its path, the routers provide the bandwidth that they have reserved for the application. If RSVP fails to successfully reserve bandwidth hop by hop all the way from source to destination, the application cannot begin operating.

IntServ mimics the PSTN model, where every call entails end-to-end signaling and securing resources along the path from source to destination. Because each application can make a unique request, IntServ is a model that can provide multiple service levels. Within the Cisco QoS framework, RSVP can act both as a signaling mechanism and as a CAC mechanism. If an RSVP attempt to secure and reserve resources for a voice call fails, the call does not get through. Controlled volume services within the Cisco IOS QoS feature set are provided by RSVP and advanced queuing mechanisms such as LLQ. The Guaranteed Rate service type is offered by deploying RSVP and LLQ. Controlled Load service is provided by RSVP and WRED.

For a successful implementation of IntServ, in addition to support for RSVP, enable the following features and functions on the routers or switches within the network:

Admission control—Admission control responds to application requests for end-to-end resources. If the resources cannot be provided without affecting the existing applications, the request is turned down.

Classification—The traffic belonging to an application that has made resource reservations must be classified and recognized by the transit routers so that they can furnish appropriate service to those packets.

Policing—It is important to measure and monitor that applications do not exceed resource utilization beyond their set profiles. Rate and burst parameters are used to measure the behavior of an application. Depending on whether an application conforms to or exceeds its agreed-upon resource utilizations, appropriate action is taken.

Queuing—It is important for network devices to be able to hold packets while processing and forwarding others. Different queuing mechanisms store and forward packets in unique ways.

Scheduling—Scheduling works in conjunction with queuing. If there are multiple queues on an interface, the amount of data that is dequeued and forwarded from each queue at each cycle, hence the relative attention that each queue gets, is called the *scheduling algorithm*. Scheduling is enforced based on the queuing mechanism configured on the router interface.

When IntServ is deployed, new application flows are admitted until requested resources can no longer be furnished. Any new application will fail to start because the RSVP request for resources will be rejected. In this model, RSVP makes the QoS request for each flow. This request includes identification for the requestor, also called the *authorized user* or *authorization object*, and the needed traffic policy, also called the *policy object*. To allow all intermediate routers between source and destination to identify each flow, RSVP provides the flow parameters such as IP addresses and port numbers. The benefits of the IntServ model can be summarized as follows:

■ Explicit end-to-end resource admission control

■ Per-request policy admission control

■ Signaling of dynamic port numbers

Some drawbacks to using IntServ exist, the most important of which are these:

■ Each active flow has a continuous signaling. This overhead can become substantially large as the number of flows grows. This is because of the stateful architecture of RSVP.

■ Because each flow is tracked and maintained, IntServ as a flow-based model is not considered scalable for large implementations such as the Internet.

Differentiated Services Model

Differentiated Services (DiffServ) is the newest of the three QoS models, and its development has aimed to overcome the limitations of its predecessors. DiffServ is not a guaranteed QoS model, but it is a highly scalable one. The Internet Engineering Task Force (IETF) description and discussion on DiffServ are included in RFCs 2474 and 2475. Whereas IntServ has been called the "Hard QoS" model, DiffServ has been called the "Soft QoS" model. IntServ, through usage of signaling and admission control, is able to either deny application of requested resources or admit it and guarantee the requested resources.

Pure DiffServ does not use signaling; it is based on per-hop behavior (PHB). PHB means that each hop in a network must be preprogrammed to provide a specific level of service for each class of traffic. PHB then does not require signaling as long as the traffic is marked to be identified as one of the expected traffic classes. This model is more scalable because signaling and status monitoring (overhead) for each flow are not necessary. Each node (hop) is prepared to deal with a limited variety of traffic classes. This means that even if thousands of flows become active, they are still categorized as one of the predefined classes, and each flow will receive the service level that is appropriate for its class. The number of classes and the service level that each traffic class should receive are decided based on business requirements.

Within the DiffServ model, traffic is first classified and marked. As the marked traffic flows through the network nodes, the type of service it receives depends on its marking. DiffServ can protect the network from oversubscription by using policing and admission control techniques as well. For example, in a typical DiffServ network, voice traffic is assigned to a priority queue that has reserved bandwidth (through LLQ) on each node. To prohibit too many voice calls from becoming active concurrently, you can deploy CAC. Note that all the voice packets that belong to the admitted calls are treated as one class.

The DiffServ model is covered in detail in Chapters 3, 4, and 5. Remember the following three points about the DiffServ model:

■ Network traffic is classified.

■ QoS policies enforce differentiated treatment of the defined traffic classes.

■ Classes of traffic and the policies are defined based on business requirements; you choose the service level for each traffic class.

The main benefit of the DiffServ model is its scalability. The second benefit of the DiffServ model is that it provides a flexible framework for you to define as many service levels as your business requirements demand. The main drawback of the DiffServ model is that it does not provide an absolute guarantee of service. That is why it is associated with the term Soft QoS. The other drawback of this model is that several complex mechanisms must be set up consistently on all the elements of the network for the model to yield the desired results.

Following are the benefits of DiffServ:

■ Scalability

■ Ability to support many different service levels

The drawbacks of DiffServ are as follows:

■ It cannot provide an absolute service guarantee.

■ It requires implementation of complex mechanisms through the network.

QoS Implementation Methods

This section explores the four main QoS implementation methods, namely CLI, MQC, Cisco AutoQoS, and SDM QoS Wizard. A high-level explanation of each QoS implementation method and the advantages and disadvantages of each are provided in turn.

Legacy Command-Line Interface (CLI)

Legacy CLI was the method used up to about six years ago to implement QoS on network devices. Legacy CLI requires configuration of few to many lines of code that for the most part would have to be applied directly at the interface level. Configuration of many interfaces required a lot of typing or cutting and pasting. Maintaining consistency, minimizing errors, and keeping the configuration neat and understandable were difficult to do using legacy CLI.

Legacy CLI configuration required the user to log into the router via console using a terminal (or a terminal emulator) or via a virtual terminal line using a Telnet application. Because it was a nonmodular method, legacy CLI did not allow users to completely separate traffic classification from policy definition and how the policy is applied. Legacy CLI was also more error prone and time consuming. Today, people still use CLI, but mostly to fine-tune the code generated by AutoQoS, which will be discussed later.

You began legacy CLI configuration by identifying, classifying, and prioritizing the traffic. Next, you had to select one of the available and appropriate QoS tools such as link compression or an available queuing mechanism such as custom or priority queuing. Finally, you had to enter from a few to several lines of code applying the selected QoS mechanisms for one or many interfaces.

Modular QoS Command-Line Interface (MQC)

Cisco introduced MQC to address the shortcomings of the legacy CLI and to allow utilization of the newer QoS tools and features available in the modern Cisco IOS. With the MQC, traffic classification and policy definition are done separately. Traffic policies are defined after traffic classes. Different policies might reference the same traffic classes, thereby taking advantage of the modular and reusable code. When one or more policies are defined, you can apply them to many interfaces, promoting code consistency and reuse.

MQC is modular, more efficient, and less time consuming than legacy CLI. Most importantly, MQC separates traffic classification from policy definition, and it is uniform across major Cisco IOS platforms. With MQC, defined policies are applied to interfaces rather than a series of raw CLI commands being applied to interfaces.

Implementing QoS with MQC involves three major steps:

Step 1   Define traffic classes using the **class-map** command. This step divides the identified network traffic into a number of named classes.

Step 2   Define QoS policies for the defined traffic classes using the **policy-map** command. This step involves QoS features being linked to traffic classes. It defines the treatment of the defined classes of traffic.

Step 3   Apply the defined policies in the inbound or outbound direction to each intended interface, subinterface, or circuit, using the **service-policy** command. This step defines where the defined policies are applied.

Each class map, which has a case-sensitive name, is composed of one or more **match** statements. One or all of the **match** statements must be matched, depending on whether class map contains the **match-any** or the **match-all** command. When neither **match-any** nor **match-all** is specified on the **class-map** statement, **match-all** applies by default.

Example 2-1 shows two class maps. The first class map is called VOIP. This class map specifies that traffic matching access list 100 is classified as VOIP. The second class map is called Business-Application. It specifies that traffic matching **access-list 101** is classified as Business-Application.

Example 2-1   *Class Maps*

```
class-map VOIP
 match access-group 100
!
class-map Business-Application
 match access-group 101
!
```

In Example 2-1, note that both of the class maps have only one **match** statement, and neither **match-all** nor **match-any** is specified, which defaults to **match-all**. When only one **match** statement exists, **match-all** and **match-any** yield the same result. However, when more than one **match** statement exists, using **match-any** or **match-all** makes a big difference. **match-any** means only one of the match statements needs to be met, and **match-all** means all the **match** statements must be met to bind the packet to the class.

> **NOTE**   The opposite of the **match** condition is the **match not** condition.

You create traffic policies by associating required QoS features to traffic classes defined by class maps; you use the **policy-map** command to do that. A policy map has a case-sensitive name and can associate QoS policies for up to 256 traffic classes (each defined by a class map). Example 2-2 exhibits a policy map called Enterprise-Policy. This policy map specifies that traffic classified as

VOIP is assigned to a priority queue that has a bandwidth guarantee of 256 Kbps. Enterprise-Policy also states that the traffic classified as Business-Application is assigned to a WFQ with a bandwidth guarantee of 256 Kbps. According to this policy map, all other traffic, classified as **class-default**, will be assigned to a queue that gets the rest of the available bandwidth, and a WFQ policy will be applied to it.

Example 2-2 *Policy Map*

```
policy-map Enterprise-Policy
 class VOIP
  priority 256
 class Business-Application
  bandwidth 256
 class class-default
  fair-queue
!
```

If you configure a policy map that includes a **class** statement followed by the name of a nonexistent class map, as long as the statement includes a condition, a class map is created and inserted into the configuration with that name automatically. If, within a policy map, you do not refer to the **class-default** (and do not configure it), any traffic that the defined classes do not match will still be treated as **class-default**. The **class-default** gets no QoS guarantees and can use a FIFO or a WFQ.

A policy map is applied on an interface (or subinterface, virtual template, or circuit) in the outbound or inbound direction using the **service-policy** command (and the direction specified using the **input** or **output** keywords). You can apply a defined and configured policy map to more than one interface. Reusing class maps and policy maps is highly encouraged because it promotes standardization and reduces the chance of errors. Example 2-3 shows that the policy map Enterprise-Policy is applied to the serial 1/0 interface of a router on the outbound direction.

Example 2-3 *Service-Policy*

```
interface serial 1/0
 service-policy output Enterprise-Policy
!
```

The following commands allow you to display and verify QoS classes and policies you have configured using the MQC:

show class-map—This command displays all the configured class maps.

show policy-map—This command displays all the configured policy maps.

show policy-map interface *interface*—This command displays the policy map that is applied to a particular interface using the **service-policy** command. This command also displays QoS interface statistics.

AutoQoS

AutoQoS is a value-added feature of Cisco IOS. After it is enabled on a device, AutoQoS automatically generates QoS configuration commands for the device. The initial release of AutoQoS (Auto QoS VoIP) focused on generating commands that made the device ready for VoIP and IP Telephony. Later, the AutoQoS Discovery feature was introduced. The next generation of AutoQoS that takes advantage of AutoQoS discovery is called AutoQoS for the Enterprise. AutoQoS Discovery, as its name implies, analyzes live network traffic for as long as you let it run and generates traffic classes based on the traffic it has processed. Next, you enable the AutoQoS feature. AutoQoS uses the traffic classes (class maps) formed by AutoQoS Discovery to generate network QoS policy (policy map), and it applies the policy. Based on the interface type, AutoQoS might also add features such as fragmentation and interleaving, multilink, and traffic shaping to the interface configuration.

The main advantage of AutoQoS is that it simplifies the task of QoS configuration. Network administrators who lack in-depth knowledge of QoS commands and features can use AutoQoS to implement those features consistently and accurately. AutoQoS participates in all the main aspects of QoS deployment:

- **Classification**—AutoQoS for the Enterprise, through AutoQoS Discovery, automatically discovers applications and protocols (using Network Based Application Recognition, or NBAR). It uses Cisco Discovery Protocol (CDP) to check whether an IP phone is attached to a switch port.

- **Policy generation**—It provides appropriate treatment of traffic by the QoS policies that it auto-generates. AutoQoS checks interface encapsulations, and accordingly, it considers usage of features such as fragmentation, compression, and traffic shaping. Access lists, class maps, and policy maps, which normally have to be entered manually, are automatically generated by AutoQoS.

- **Configuration**—It is enabled by entering only one command, **auto qos**, at the interface. In a matter of seconds, proper commands to classify, mark, prioritize, preempt packets, and so on are added to the configuration appropriately.

- **Monitoring and reporting**—It generates system logging messages, SNMP traps, and summary reports.

- **Consistency**—The commands generated on different routers, using AutoQoS, are consistent and interoperable.

AutoQoS was introduced in Cisco IOS Software Release 12.2(15)T and provides a quick and consistent way to enter the bulk of QoS commands. Network administrators can then modify those commands and policies or optimize them using CLI. Cisco SDM QoS Wizard is a newer GUI tool that generates QoS commands and policies; that tool will be discussed in the next section.

AutoQoS performs a series of functions on WAN devices and interfaces. It creates a traffic class for voice payload (RTP), and it builds another class for voice signaling (Skinny, H.323, SIP, and MGCP). Service policies for voice bearer and voice signaling are created and deployed using LLQ with bandwidth guarantees. Voice traffic is assigned to the priority queue. On Frame Relay connections, AutoQoS turns on Frame Relay traffic shaping (FRTS) and link fragmentation and interleaving (LFI); on other types of links, such as PPP links, AutoQoS might turn on multilink PPP (MLP) and compressed RTP (cRTP). AutoQoS also provides SNMP and syslog alerts for VoIP packet drops.

In LAN environments, AutoQoS trust boundaries are set and enforced on the different types of switch ports, such as access ports and uplinks. Expedited queuing (strict priority) and weighted round-robin (WRR) are also enforced where required. Traffic is assigned to the proper queue based on its marking or application recognition based on NBAR.

Using AutoQoS has some prerequisites. Before you enable AutoQoS on an interface, you must ensure that the following tasks have been completed:

- Cisco Express Forwarding (CEF) is enabled. CEF is the prerequisite for NBAR.

- NBAR is enabled. AutoQoS for the Enterprise (not Auto QoS VoIP) uses NBAR for traffic discovery and classification.

- The correct bandwidth on the interface is configured. AutoQoS configures LLQ, cRTP, and LFI based on the interface type and the interface bandwidth. On certain interfaces, such as Ethernet, the bandwidth is auto-sensed; however, on other interfaces, such as synchronous serial interface, if the bandwidth is not specified, the IOS assumes a bandwidth of 1544 Kbps.

After these tasks have been completed, AutoQoS can be configured (enabled) on the desired interface. Example 2-4 shows a serial interface that has been configured with bandwidth, IP address, CEF, and AutoQoS.

Example 2-4   *Configuring AutoQoS on an Interface*

```
ip cef
interface serial 1/0
bandwidth 256
ip address 10.1.1.1 255.255.255.252
auto qos voip
!
```

Note that in Example 2-4, the command **auto qos voip** is applied to interface serial 1/0. This command represents the first generation of AutoQoS. The focus of **auto qos voip** was to automate generation of QoS commands to get the device ready for VoIP traffic. In the second generation *AutoQoS for the Enterprise*, you must first enter the **auto discovery qos** so that the router discovers and analyzes network traffic entering the interface using NBAR. Next, you enter the **auto qos** command. When you enter the **auto qos** command on an interface, the router builds class maps (based on the results of discovery) and then creates and applies a policy map on the interface. AutoQoS will be discussed in detail in Chapter 7, "Implementing AutoQoS."

Router and Security Device Manager (SDM) QoS Wizard

Cisco SDM is a web-based device-management tool for Cisco routers. With SDM, router deployment and troubleshooting of network and VPN connectivity issues becomes simpler. Proactive management through performance monitoring is also accomplished using SDM.

Cisco SDM supports a range of Cisco IOS Software releases and is available on many Cisco router models (from Cisco 830 Series to Cisco 7301); on several router models, SDM is preinstalled. Cisco SDM offers smart wizards that provide step-by-step assistance for configuration of LAN and WAN interfaces, Network Address Translation (NAT), firewall policy, IPS, IPsec VPN, and QoS. Inexperienced users find the SDM GUI easier to use than the CLI and enjoy the comprehensive online help and tutorials for SDM.

The QoS Wizard of SDM provides you with an easy-to-use user interface to define traffic classes and configure QoS policies for your network. The SDM predefines three different application categories: real-time, business-critical, and best-effort. SDM supports and uses NBAR to validate the bandwidth consumed by different application categories. Additional features offered by the SDM QoS Wizard include QoS policing and traffic monitoring. The SDM QoS Wizard enables you to do three things:

- Implement QoS

- Monitor QoS

- Troubleshoot QoS on your network

Figure 2-3 displays the main page of Cisco SDM. This page is comprised of two sections:

- About Your Router

- Configuration Overview

Figure 2-3   *Main Page of Cisco SDM*

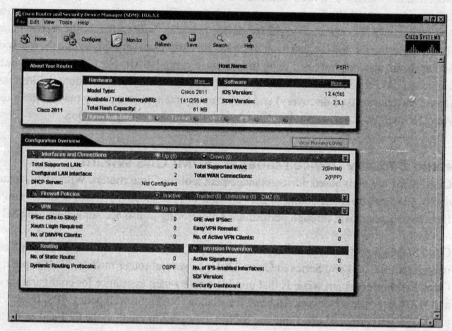

In the About Your Router section of the SDM main page you can find information about your router's hardware, software, and the available features. For example, you can see the router's total and available memory, flash capacity, IOS version, SDM version, and whether features such as IP, firewall, VPN, IPS, and NAC are available. Further information can be seen through the **More...** options in the hardware and software sections. The Configuration Overview section of the SDM main page provides information about your router's LAN and WAN interfaces, firewall policies, VPN, routing, and IPS configurations. You can also see the router's running configuration through the **View Running Config** option. You can navigate to the main page by pressing the **Home** button on the main tool bar of the Cisco SDM. The other two important buttons on the Cisco SDM main tool bar are the **Configure** and **Monitor** buttons. The tasks available on the left side of the Configure page are:

- **Interfaces and Connections**

- **Firewall and ACL**

- **VPN**

- **Security Audit**

- **Routing**

- **NAT**

- **Intrusion Prevention**

- **Quality of Service**

- **NAC**

- **Additional Tasks**

The tasks available on the left side of the Monitor page are:

- **Overview**

- **Interface Status**

- **Firewall Status**

- **VPN Status**

- **Traffic Status**

- **NAC Status**

- **Logging**

- **IPS Status**

If you select the **Traffic Status** task, you will have the option to view graphs about QoS or application/protocol traffic.

The remainder of this section takes you through the steps necessary to create a QoS policy, apply it to an interface, and monitor the QoS status using the Cisco SDM (GUI) Wizard. For each step one or more figures are provided so that you are well prepared for the exam questions that might be asked about creating QoS policy using the SDM Wizard.

To begin to create a QoS policy you must complete the following steps:

Step 1   Click the **Configure** button on the main toolbar of SDM.

Step 2   Click the **Quality of Service** button on the tasks toolbar on the left side of the SDM window (in Configuration mode; see Figure 2-4).

Step 3   Click the **Create QoS Policy** tab in the middle section of the SDM window (see Figure 2-4).

Step 4   Click the **Launch QoS Wizard** button on the bottom right side of the SDM window (see Figure 2-4).

Figure 2-4 *Four Steps to Start Creating a QoS Policy with SDM*

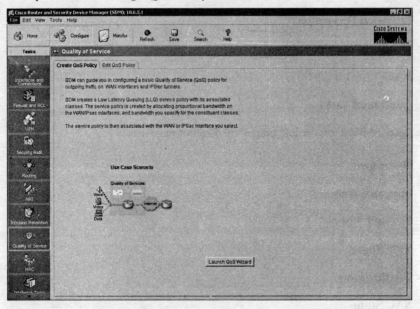

Now the SDM QoS Wizard page pops up on your computer screen (see Figure 2-5) and it informs you that SDM by default creates QoS policy to handle two main types of traffic, namely Real-Time and Business-Critical. To proceed press the **Next** button.

Figure 2-5 *SDM QoS Wizard Initial Page*

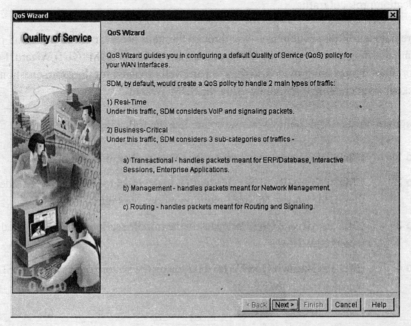

The QoS Wizard asks you to select an interface on which you want the QoS policy to be applied. Figure 2-6 shows you this screen. After making your selection press the **Next** button on that screen to proceed.

Figure 2-6 *Interface Selection Page of SDM QoS Wizard*

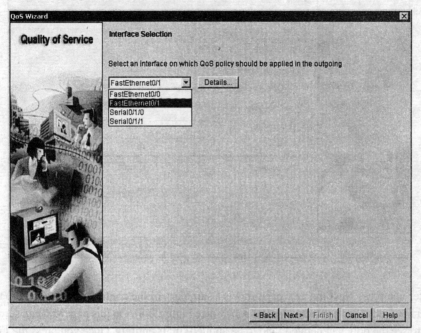

The SDM QoS Wizard asks you to enter the bandwidth percent for Real Time and Business-Critical traffic (see Figure 2-7). SDM will then automatically compute the bandwidth percent for the Best-Effort traffic and the actual bandwidth (kbps) for all three traffic classes.

Figure 2-7 *QoS Policy Generation Page of SDM QoS Wizard*

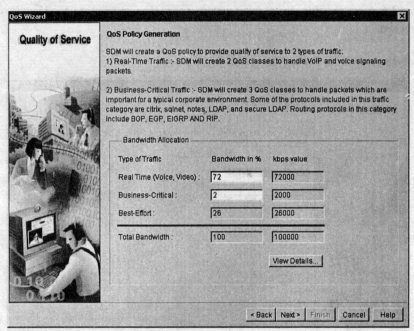

After you press **Next** the new page shows a summary of the configuration applied to the interface you have previously selected for the policy (see Figure 2-8). On this page you can scroll down and up to see the policy generated (and to be applied) in its entirety. Once you press the **Finish** button.

After you press the **Finish** button on the SDM QoS summary of the configuration screen, a Commands Delivery Status window appears (see Figure 2-9). This screen first informs you that commands are being prepared, then it tells you that the commands are being submitted, and finally it tells you that the commands have been delivered to the router. At this time, you can press the **OK** button and the job is complete.

Figure 2-8 *QoS Policy: Summary of the Configuration*

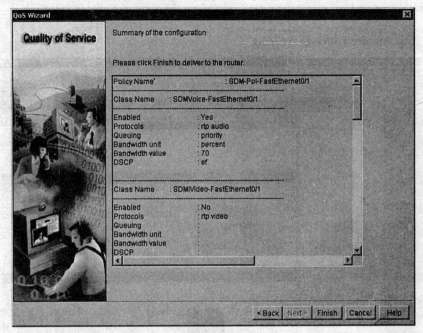

Figure 2-9 *QoS Policy: Commands Delivery Status*

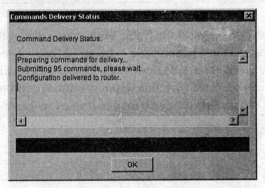

Upon completion of your QoS configuration tasks, SDM allows you to monitor the QoS status. You must first click the **Monitor** button of the SDM main tool bar. Next, from the list of available tasks you must select **Traffic Status** (see Figure 2-10). Note that in the ONT courseware, this option is shown as **QoS Status**, probably due to SDM version differences. In the middle of the Traffic Status screen, you will then notice a folder called **Top N Traffic Flows** with **QoS** and **Application/Protocol Traffic** as two options displayed below it. If you click **QoS** (effectively requesting to see the QoS status), you can then choose any of the interfaces displayed in the Traffic Status screen and see informative QoS-related graphs about the chosen interface.

Figure 2-10 *SDM Monitor Traffic/QoS Status*

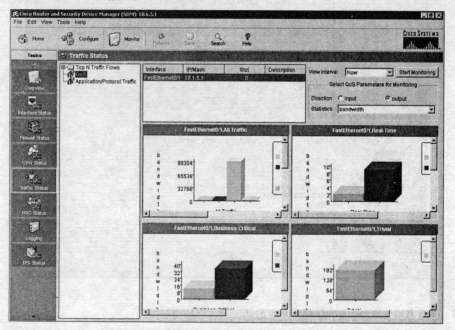

When you select the **QoS** option of the Traffic Status, notice that on the top right corner of the screen you can select the **View Interval** (**Now**, **Every 1 Minute**, **Every 5 Minutes**, **Every 1 Hour**). Furthermore, there is a small area with the "Select QoS Parameters for Monitoring" title that allows you to select the **Direction** (**input** or **output**) of the traffic, and the **Statistics** (**bandwidth**, **byte**, and **packets dropped**) for which you want to see graphs.

Foundation Summary

The "Foundation Summary" is a collection of information that provides a convenient review of many key concepts in this chapter. If you are already comfortable with the topics in this chapter, this summary can help you recall a few details. If you just read this chapter, this review should help solidify some key facts. If you are doing your final preparation before the exam, the information in this section is a convenient way to review the day before the exam.

In a converged enterprise network, four major issues affect the performance and perceived quality of applications:

- Available bandwidth

- End-to-end delay

- Variation of delay (jitter)

- Packet loss

Lack of sufficient bandwidth, high end-to-end delay, high variation in delay, and excessive packet loss lower the quality of applications.

QoS is the ability of the network to provide better or "special" service to a set of users or applications or both to the detriment of other users or applications or both. You can use several QoS features, tools, and technologies to accomplish the QoS goals. Classification, marking, congestion avoidance, congestion management, compression, shaping, and policing are examples of QoS tools available in Cisco IOS. The three steps of implementing QoS in an enterprise network are as follows:

Step 1   Identify the network traffic and its requirements

Step 2   Define traffic classes

Step 3   Define a QoS policy for each traffic class

The main QoS models of today are as follows:

- **Best-effort**—The best-effort model requires no QoS configuration and mechanisms; therefore, it is easy and scalable, but it provides no Differentiated Service to different application types.

- **IntServ**—IntServ provides guaranteed service (Hard QoS). It uses signaling to reserve and guarantee resources for each traffic flow below it. RSVP is the common signaling protocol for resource reservation signaling on IP networks. Per-flow signaling and monitoring escalate the overhead of the IntServ model and make it nonscalable.

- **DiffServ**—DiffServ is the most modern of the three models. It requires traffic classification and marking and providing differentiated service to each traffic class based on its marking. DiffServ is scalable, but its drawback is that it requires implementation of complex QoS features on network devices throughout the network.

Network administrators have four methods at their disposal to implement QoS on their network's Cisco devices:

- **Cisco IOS CLI**—Configuring QoS using Cisco IOS CLI is the most complex and time-consuming method. It requires that you learn different syntax for each QoS mechanism.

- **MQC**—MQC is a modular command-line interface that is common across different Cisco platforms, and it separates the task of defining different traffic classes from the task of defining QoS policies.

- **Cisco AutoQoS**—Because AutoQoS automatically generates QoS commands on your router or switch, it is the simplest and fastest method among the four QoS implementation methods. However, should you need to fine-tune the AutoQoS configuration results, you must use MQC (or CLI) to do so. Fine-tuning of the commands that AutoQoS generates is seldom necessary.

- **Cisco Router and Security Device Manager (SDM) QoS Wizard**—Cisco SDM offers several wizards for implementing services, such as IPsec, VPN, and proactive management through performance monitoring, in addition to the QoS Wizard. Cisco SDM QoS Wizard allows you to remotely configure and monitor your Cisco routers without using the CLI. The SDM GUI makes it simple for you to implement QoS services, features, and policies.

Table 2-3 compares Cisco IOS CLI, MQC, AutoQoS, and SDM with respect to how easy they are to use, whether they allow you to fine-tune their results, how time consuming they are, and how modular they are.

Table 2-3 *Comparing QoS Implementation Methods*

Method	CLI	MQC	AutoQoS	SDM
Ease of use	Most difficult	Easier than legacy CLI	Simple	Simple
Ability to fine-tune	Yes (OK)	Very well	Limited	Limited
Time consuming to implement	Most time consuming (longest)	Moderate time consumed (average)	Least time consuming	Very little time consumed (short)
Modularity	Weakest (poor)	Very modular (excellent)	Very modular (excellent)	Good

MQC is the recommended and the most powerful method for implementing QoS. It is modular, it promotes re-use of written code, and it facilitates consistency of QoS configurations among your Cisco devices. MQC also reduces the chances for errors and conflicts, while allowing you to take advantage of the latest features and mechanisms offered by your version of Cisco IOS.

Q&A

Some of the questions that follow challenge you more than the exam by using an open-ended question format. By reviewing now with this more difficult question format, you can exercise your memory better and prove your conceptual and factual knowledge of this chapter. The answers to these questions appear in Appendix A.

1. List the four key quality issues with converged networks.

2. Provide a definition for maximum available bandwidth and average available bandwidth per flow.

3. List at least three types of delay.

4. Provide at least three ways to reduce delay.

5. Provide at least two ways to reduce or prevent loss of important packets.

6. Provide a definition for QoS.

7. List the three key steps in implementing QoS on a network.

8. List the three main QoS models.

9. Provide a short description of the best-effort model.

10. What are the benefits and drawbacks of the best-effort model?

11. Provide a short description for the IntServ model.

12. Name the functions that the IntServ model requires on the network routers and switches.

13. What are the benefits and drawbacks of the IntServ model?

14. What are the main features of the DiffServ model?

15. What are the benefits and drawbacks of the DiffServ model?

16. What are the four QoS implementation methods?

17. Which of the four QoS implementation methods is nonmodular and the most time consuming?

18. What are the main benefits of MQC?

19. What is the most important advantage of AutoQoS?

20. What are the prerequisites for Auto QoS VoIP?

21. What are the prerequisites for Auto QoS for the enterprise?

22. Which of the four QoS implementation methods is the fastest?

23. What are the three main tasks that you can accomplish using the SDM QoS Wizard?

This chapter covers the following subjects:

- **Classification and Marking**

- **The DiffServ Model, Differentiated Services Code Point (DSCP), and Per-Hop Behavior (PHB)**

- **QoS Service Class**

- **Trust Boundaries**

- **Network Based Application Recognition (NBAR)**

- **Cisco IOS Commands to Configure NBAR**

Classification, Marking, and NBAR

Classification and marking are key IP QoS mechanisms used to implement the DiffServ QoS model. This chapter defines classification and marking and explains the markings that are available at the data link and network layers. This chapter also explains QoS service classes and how to use them to create a service policy throughout a network. It also defines network trust boundaries. Finally, it describes NBAR and PDLM and presents the IOS commands that are required to configure NBAR.

"Do I Know This Already?" Quiz

The purpose of the "Do I Know This Already?" quiz is to help you decide whether you really need to read the entire chapter. The 15-question quiz, derived from the major sections of this chapter, helps you determine how to spend your limited study time.

Table 3-1 outlines the major topics discussed in this chapter and the "Do I Know This Already?" quiz questions that correspond to those topics.

Table 3-1 *"Do I Know This Already?" Foundation Topics Section-to-Question Mapping*

Foundation Topics Section Covering These Questions	Questions	Score
"Classification and Marking"	1–5	
"The DiffServ Model, Differentiated Services Code Point (DSCP), and Per-Hop Behavior (PHB)"	6–8	
"QoS Service Class"	9	
"Trust Boundaries"	10	
"Network Based Application Recognition (NBAR)"	11–13	
"Cisco IOS Commands to Configure NBAR"	14–15	
Total Score	**(15 possible)**	

> **CAUTION** The goal of self-assessment is to gauge your mastery of the topics in this chapter. If you do not know the answer to a question or are only partially sure of the answer, mark this question wrong for purposes of the self-assessment. Giving yourself credit for an answer you correctly guess skews your self-assessment results and might provide you with a false sense of security.

You can find the answers to the "Do I Know This Already?" quiz in Appendix A, "Answers to the 'Do I Know This Already?' Quizzes and Q&A Sections." The suggested choices for your next step are as follows:

- **9 or less overall score**—Read the entire chapter. This includes the "Foundation Topics," "Foundation Summary," and "Q&A" sections.

- **10–12 overall score**—Begin with the "Foundation Summary" section and then follow up with the "Q&A" section at the end of the chapter.

- **13 or more overall score**—If you want more review on this topic, skip to the "Foundation Summary" section and then go to the "Q&A" section. Otherwise, proceed to the next chapter.

1. Which of the following is *not* a valid classification traffic descriptor?

    a. Incoming interface

    b. Traffic path

    c. IP precedence or DSCP value

    d. Source or destination address

2. Which of the following is *not* considered a data link layer QoS marking field?

    a. CoS

    b. Frame Relay DE

    c. DSCP

    d. ATM CLP

3. Which of the following CoS values is reserved for internetwork and network control?

    a. 0,1

    b. 2,3

    c. 4,5

    d. 6,7

4. Which of the following is the Frame Relay QoS marking field?

   a. DE

   b. CLP

   c. CoS

   d. EXP

5. Which of the following is true about the MPLS header and its EXP field size?

   a. The MPLS header is 2 bytes and the EXP field is 3 bits long.

   b. The MPLS header is 2 bytes and the EXP field is 6 bits long.

   c. The MPLS header is 4 bytes and the EXP field is 6 bits long.

   d. The MPLS header is 4 bytes and the EXP field is 3 bits long.

6. What is "an externally observable forwarding behavior of a network node toward a group of IP packets that have the same DSCP value"?

   a. BA

   b. Prec

   c. Service class

   d. PHB

7. Which of the following is *not* a DSCP PHB?

   a. Default PHB

   b. Class selector PHB

   c. Assured forwarding PHB

   d. Cisco Express Forwarding PHB

8. Which of the following has the higher drop probability?

   a. AF31.

   b. AF32.

   c. AF33.

   d. They all have the same drop probability.

9. Which of the following is *not* a common voice and video service class?

   a. Voice bearer (or payload)

   b. Voice and video conferencing

   c. Video payload

   d. Voice and video signaling

10. At which of the following places is the trust boundary *not* implemented?

    a. Core switch

    b. Distribution switch

    c. Access switch

    d. End system

11. Which of the following is *not* a service that NBAR provides?

    a. Protocol discovery

    b. Collection of traffic statistics

    c. Traffic classification

    d. Traffic policing

12. Which of the following is true about loading a new PDLM?

    a. You need to upgrade the IOS and reload your router.

    b. You need to upgrade the IOS, but a reload is not necessary.

    c. You do not need to upgrade the IOS, but a router reload is necessary.

    d. You do not need to upgrade the IOS and do not need to reload either.

13. Which of the following is *not* an NBAR limitation?

    a. NBAR can handle only up to 24 concurrent URLs.

    b. NBAR analyzes only the first 400 bytes of the packet.

    c. NBAR is not supported on interfaces in which tunneling or encryption is used.

    d. NBAR is dependent on CEF.

14. Which of the following commands uses the NBAR classification feature within a class map?

    a. **match protocol** *protocol-name*

    b. **match nbar protocol** *protocol-name*

    c. **match** *protocol-name*

    d. **match nbar** *protocol-name*

15. What does the * character mean in a regular expression?

    a. Match one of a choice of characters.

    b. Match any zero or more characters in this position.

    c. Match any one character in this position.

    d. It means OR.

Foundation Topics

Classification and Marking

With QoS, you intend to provide different treatments to different classes of network traffic. Therefore, it is necessary to define traffic classes by identifying and grouping network traffic. Classification does just that; it is the process or mechanism that identifies traffic and categorizes it into classes. This categorization is done using traffic descriptors. Common traffic descriptors are any of the following:

- Ingress (or incoming) interface

- CoS value on ISL or 802.1p frame

- Source or destination IP address

- IP precedence or DSCP value on the IP Packet header

- MPLS EXP value on the MPLS header

- Application type

In the past, you performed classification without marking. As a result, each QoS mechanism at each device had to classify before it could provide unique treatments to each class of traffic. For example, to perform priority queuing, you must classify the traffic using access lists so that you can assign different traffic classes to various queues (high, medium, normal, or low). On the same device or another, to perform queuing, shaping, policing, fragmentation, RTP header compression, and so on, you must perform classification again so that different classes of traffic are treated differently. Repeated classification in that fashion, using access-lists for example, is inefficient. Today, after you perform the first-time classification, mark (or color) the packets. This way, the following devices on the traffic path can provide differentiated service to packets based on packet markings (colors): after the first-time classification is performed at the edge (which is mostly based on deep packet inspection) and the packet is marked, only a simple and efficient classification based on the packet marking is performed inside the network.

Classification has traditionally been done with access lists (standard or extended), but today the Cisco IOS command **class-map** is the common classification tool. **class-map** is a component of the Cisco IOS modular QoS command-line interface (MQC). The **match** statement within a class map can refer to a traffic descriptor, an access list, or an NBAR protocol. NBAR is a classification tool that will be discussed in this chapter. Please note that **class-map** does not eliminate usage of other tools such as access lists. It simply makes the job of classification more sophisticated and powerful. For example, you can define a traffic class based on multiple conditions, one of which may be matching an access-list.

It is best to perform the initial classification (and marking) task as close to the source of traffic as possible. The network edge device such as the IP phone, and the access layer switch would be the preferable locations for traffic classification and marking.

Marking is the process of tagging or coloring traffic based on its category. Traffic is marked after you classify it. What is marked depends on whether you want to mark the Layer 2 frame or cell or the Layer 3 packet. Commonly used Layer 2 markers are CoS (on ISL or 802.1Q header), EXP (on MPLS header, which is in between layers 2 and 3), DE (on Frame Relay header), and CLP (on ATM cell header). Commonly used Layer 3 markers are IP precedence or DSCP (on IP header).

Layer 2 QoS: CoS on 802.1Q/P Ethernet Frame

The IEEE defined the 802.1Q frame for the purpose of implementing trunks between LAN devices. The 4-byte 802.1Q header field that is inserted after the source MAC address on the Ethernet header has a VLAN ID field for trunking purposes. A three-bit user priority field (PRI) is available also and is called CoS (802.1p). CoS is used for QoS purposes; it can have one of eight possible values, as shown in Table 3-2.

Table 3-2 *CoS Bits and Their Corresponding Decimal Values and Definitions*

CoS (bits)	CoS (in Decimal)	IETF RFC791	Application
000	0	Routine	Best-Effort Data
001	1	Priority	Medium Priority Data
010	2	Immediate	High Priority Data
011	3	Flash	Call Signaling
100	4	Flash-Override	Video Conferencing
101	5	Critical	Voice Bearer
110	6	Internet	Reserved (inter-network control)
111	7	Network	Reserved (network control)

Figure 3-1 shows the 4-byte 802.1Q field that is inserted into the Ethernet header after the source MAC address. In a network with IP Telephony deployed, workstations connect to the IP phone Ethernet jack (marked PC), and the IP phone connects to the access layer switch (marked Switch).

The IP phone sends 802.1Q/P frames to the workgroup switch. The frames leaving the IP phone toward the workgroup (access) switch have the voice VLAN number in the VLAN ID field, and their priority (CoS) field is usually set to 5 (decimal), which is equal to 101 binary, interpreted as critical or voice bearer.

Figure 3-1 *802.1Q/P Field*

Ethernet 802.1Q/P Frame

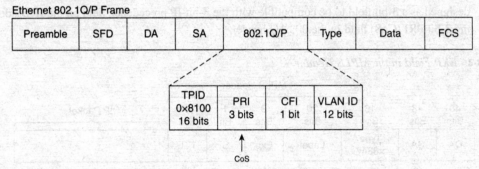

Layer 2 QoS: DE and CLP on Frame Relay and ATM (Cells)

Frame Relay and ATM QoS standards were defined and used (by ITU-T and FRF) before Internet Engineering Task Force (IETF) QoS standards were introduced and standardized. In Frame Relay, for instance, the forward explicit congestion notification (FECN), backward explicit congestion notification (BECN), and discard eligible (DE) fields in the frame header have been used to perform congestion notification and drop preference notification. Neither Frame Relay frames nor ATM cells have a field comparable to the 3-bit CoS field previously discussed on 802.1P frames. A Frame Relay frame has a 1-bit DE, and an ATM cell has a 1-bit cell loss priority (CLP) field that essentially informs the transit switches whether the data unit is not (DE or CLP equal 0) or whether it is (DE or CLP equal 1) a good candidate for dropping, should the need for dropping arise. Figure 3-2 displays the position of the DE field in the Frame Relay frame header.

Figure 3-2 *DE Field on Frame Relay Frame Header*

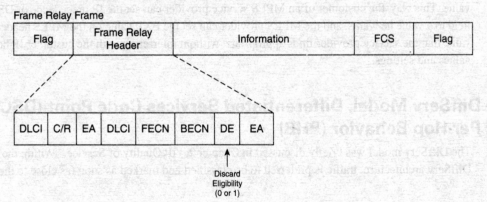
Frame Relay Frame

Layer 2 1/2 QoS: MPLS EXP Field

MPLS packets are IP packets that have one or more 4-byte MPLS headers added. The IP packet with its added MPLS header is encapsulated in a Layer 2 protocol data unit (PDU) such as Ethernet before it is transmitted. Therefore, the MPLS header is often called the SHIM or layer 2 1/2 header. Figure 3-3 displays an MPLS-IP packet encapsulated in an Ethernet frame. The EXP (experimental) field within the MPLS header is used for QoS purposes. The EXP field was designed as a 3-bit field to be compatible with the 3-bit IP precedence field on the IP header and the 3-bit PRI (CoS) field in the 802.1Q header.

Figure 3-3 *EXP Field in the MPLS Header*

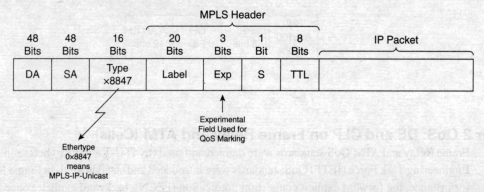

By default, as an IP packet enters an MPLS network, the edge router copies the three most significant bits of the type of service (ToS) byte of the IP header to the EXP field of the MPLS header. The three most significant bits of the ToS byte on the IP header are called the IP precedence bits. The ToS byte of the IP header is now called the DiffServ field; the six most significant bits of the DiffServ field are called the DSCP.

Instead of allowing the EXP field of MPLS to be automatically copied from IP precedence, the administrator of the MPLS edge router can configure the edge router to set the EXP to a desired value. This way, the customer of an MPLS service provider can set the IP precedence or DSCP field to a value he wants, and the MPLS provider can set the EXP value on the MPLS header to a value that the service provider finds appropriate, without interfering with the customer IP header values and settings.

The DiffServ Model, Differentiated Services Code Point (DSCP), and Per-Hop Behavior (PHB)

The DiffServ model was briefly discussed in Chapter 2, "IP Quality of Service." Within the DiffServ architecture, traffic is preferred to be classified and marked as soon (as close to the source) as possible. Marking of the IP packet was traditionally done on the three IP precedence bits, but now, marking (setting) the six DSCP bits on the IP header is considered the standard method of IP packet marking.

> **NOTE**   Some network devices cannot check or set Layer 3 header QoS fields (such as IP precedence or DSCP). For example, simple Layer 2 wiring closet LAN switches can only check and set the CoS (PRI) bits on the 802.1Q header.

Each of the different DSCP values—in other words, each of the different combinations of DSCP bits—is expected to stimulate every network device along the traffic path to behave in a certain way and to provide a particular QoS treatment to the traffic. Therefore, within the DiffServ framework, you set the DSCP value on the IP packet header to select a per-hop behavior (PHB). *PHB* is formally defined as an externally observable forwarding behavior of a network node toward a group of IP packets that have the same DSCP value. The group of packets with a common DSCP value (belonging to the same or different sources and applications), which receive similar PHB from a DiffServ node, is called a behavior aggregate (BA). The PHB toward a packet, including how it is scheduled, queued, policed, and so on, is based on the BA that the packet belongs to and the implemented service level agreement (SLA) or policy.

Scalability is a main goal of the DiffServ model. Complex traffic classification is performed as close to the source as possible. Traffic marking is performed subsequent to classification. If marking is done by a device under control of the network administration, the marking is said to be trusted. It is best if the complex classification task is not repeated, and the PHB of the transit network devices will solely depend on the trusted traffic marking. This way, the DiffServ model has a coarse level of classification, and the marking-based PHB is applied to traffic aggregates or behavior aggregates (BAs), with no per-flow state in the core.

Application-generated signaling (IntServ style) is not part of the DiffServ framework, and this boosts the scalability of the DiffServ model. Most applications do not have signaling and Resource Reservation Protocol (RSVP) capabilities. The DiffServ model provides specific services and QoS treatments to groups of packets with common DSCP values (BAs). These packets can, and in large scale do, belong to multiple flows. The services and QoS treatments that are provided to traffic aggregates based on their common DSCP values are a set of actions and guarantees such as queue insertion policy, drop preference, and bandwidth guarantee. The DiffServ model provides particular service classes to traffic aggregates by classifying and marking the traffic first, followed by PHB toward the marked traffic within the network core.

IP Precedence and DSCP

The initial efforts on IP QoS were based on the specifications provided by RFC 791 (1981), which had called the 3 most significant bits of the ToS byte on the IP header the IP precedence bits. The 3 IP precedence bits can have one of eight settings. The larger the IP precedence value, the more important the packet and the higher the probability of timely forwarding. Figure 3-4 displays an IP packet and focuses on the IP ToS byte, particularly on the IP precedence bits. The eight IP precedence combinations and their corresponding decimal values, along with the name given to each IP precedence value, are also displayed in Figure 3-4. The IP precedence values 6 and 7, called Internetwork Control and Network Control, are reserved for control protocols and are not allowed to be set by user applications; therefore, user applications have six IP precedence values available.

Figure 3-4 *IP Header ToS Byte and IP Precedence Values*

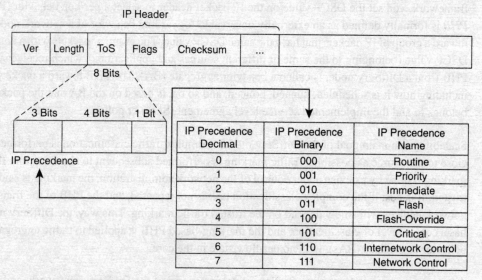

IP Precedence Decimal	IP Precedence Binary	IP Precedence Name
0	000	Routine
1	001	Priority
2	010	Immediate
3	011	Flash
4	100	Flash-Override
5	101	Critical
6	110	Internetwork Control
7	111	Network Control

Redefining the ToS byte as the Differentiated Services (DiffServ) field, with the 6 most significant bits called the DSCP, has provided much more flexibility and capability to the new IP QoS efforts. The 2 least significant bits of the DiffServ field are used for flow control and are called explicit congestion notification (ECN) bits. DSCP is backward compatible with IP Precedence (IPP), providing the opportunity for gradual deployment of DSCP-based QoS in IP networks. The current DSCP value definitions include four PHBs:

- **Class selector PHB**—With the least significant 3 bits of the DSCP set to 000, the class selector PHB provides backward compatibility with ToS-based IP Precedence. When DSCP-compliant network devices receive IP packets from non-DSCP compliant network devices, they can be configured only to process and interpret the IP precedence bits. When IP packets are sent from DSCP-compliant devices to the non-DSCP-compliant devices, only the 3 most significant bits of the DiffServ field (equivalent to IP precedence bits) are set; the rest of the bits are set to 0.

- **Default PHB**—With the 3 most significant bits of the DiffServ/DSCP field set to 000, the Default PHB is used for best effort (BE) service. If the DSCP value of a packet is not mapped to a PHB, it is consequently assigned to the default PHB.

- **Assured forwarding (AF) PHB**—With the most significant 3 bits of the DSCP field set to 001, 010, 011, or 100 (these are also called AF1, AF2, AF3, and AF4), the AF PHB is used for guaranteed bandwidth service.

- **Expedited forwarding (EF) PHB**—With the most significant 3 bits of the DSCP field set to 101 (the whole DSCP field is set to 101110, decimal value of 46), the EF PHB provides low delay service.

Figure 3-5 displays the DiffServ field and the DSCP settings for the class selector, default, AF, and EF PHBs.

Figure 3-5 *IP Header DS Field and DSCP PHBs*

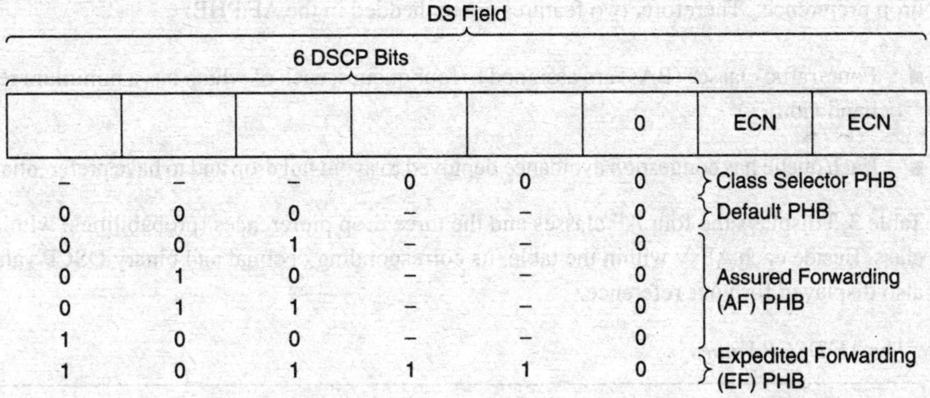

DS Field							
6 DSCP Bits							
					0	ECN	ECN
–	–	–	0	0	0	} Class Selector PHB	
0	0	0	–	–	0	} Default PHB	
0	0	1	–	–	0		
0	1	0	–	–	0	Assured Forwarding	
0	1	1	–	–	0	(AF) PHB	
1	0	0	–	–	0		
1	0	1	1	1	0	} Expedited Forwarding (EF) PHB	

The EF PHB provides low delay service and should minimize jitter and loss. The bandwidth that is dedicated to EF must be limited (capped) so that other traffic classes do not starve. The queue that is dedicated to EF must be the highest priority queue so that the traffic-assigned to it gets through fast and does not experience significant delay and loss. This can only be achieved if the volume of the traffic that is assigned to this queue keeps within its bandwidth limit/cap. Therefore, successful deployment of EF PHB is ensured by utilizing other QoS techniques such as admission control. You must remember three important facts about the EF PHB:

- It imposes minimum delay.

- It provides bandwidth guarantee.

- During congestion, EF polices bandwidth.

Older applications (non-DSCP compliant) set the IP precedence bits to 101 (decimal 5, called Critical) for delay-sensitive traffic such as voice. The most significant bits of the EF marking (101110) are 101, making it backward compatible with the binary 101 IP precedence (Critical) setting.

The AF PHB as per the standards specifications provides four queues for four classes of traffic (AFxy): AF1y, AF2y, AF3y, and AF4y. For each queue, a prespecified bandwidth is reserved. If the amount of traffic on a particular queue exceeds the reserved bandwidth for that queue, the queue builds up and eventually incurs packet drops. To avoid tail drop, congestion avoidance techniques such as weighted random early detection (WRED) are deployed on each queue. Packet drop is performed based on the marking difference of the packets. Within each AFxy class, y specifies the drop preference (or probability) of the packet. Some packets are marked with minimum probability/preference of being dropped, some with medium, and the rest with maximum probability/preference of drop. The y part of AFxy is one of 2-bit binary numbers 01, 10, and 11; this is embedded in the DSCP field of these packets and specifies high, medium, and low drop preference. Note that the bigger numbers here are not better, because they imply higher drop preference. Therefore, two features are embedded in the AF PHB:

■   Four traffic classes (BAs) are assigned to four queues, each of which has a minimum reserved bandwidth.

■   Each queue has congestion avoidance deployed to avoid tail drop and to have preferential drops.

Table 3-3 displays the four AF classes and the three drop preferences (probabilities) within each class. Beside each AFxy within the table, its corresponding decimal and binary DSCP values are also displayed for your reference.

Table 3-3   *The AF DSCP Values*

Class	Drop Probability		
	Low Drop	**Medium Drop**	**High Drop**
Class 1	AF11 DSCP 10: (001010)	AF12 DSCP 12: (001100)	AF13 DSCP 14: (001110)
Class 2	AF21 DSCP 18: (010010)	AF22 DSCP 20: (010100)	AF23 DSCP 22: (010110)
Class 3	AF31 DSCP 26: (011010)	AF32 DSCP 28: (011100)	AF33 DSCP 30: (011110)
Class 4	AF41 DSCP 34: (100010)	AF42 DSCP 36: (100100)	AF43 DSCP 38: (100110)

You must remember a few important facts about AF:

■ The AF model has four classes: AF1, AF2, AF3, and AF4; they have no advantage over each other. Different bandwidth reservations can be made for each queue; any queue can have more or less bandwidth reserved than the others.

■ On a DSCP-compliant node, the second digit (y) of the AF PHB specifies a drop preference or probability. When congestion avoidance is applied to an AF queue, packets with AFx3 marking have a higher probability of being dropped than packets with AFx2 marking, and AFx2 marked packets have a higher chance of being dropped than packets with AFx1 marking, as the queue size grows.

■ You can find the corresponding DSCP value of each AFxy in decimal using this formula:

DSCP (Decimal) = 8x + 2y.

For example, the DSCP value for AF31 is 26 = (8 * 3) + (2 * 1).

■ Each AFx class is backward compatible with a single IP precedence value x. AF1y maps to IP precedence 1, AF2y maps to IP precedence 2, AF3y maps to IP precedence 3, and AF4y maps to IP precedence 4.

■ During implementation, you must reserve enough bandwidth for each AF queue to avoid delay and drop in each queue. You can deploy some form of policing or admission control so that too much traffic that maps to each AF class does not enter the network or node. The exact congestion avoidance (and its parameters) that is applied to each AF queue is also dependent on the configuration choices.

■ If there is available bandwidth and an AF queue is not policed, it can consume more bandwidth than the amount reserved.

Most of the fields within the IP packet header in a transmission do not change from source to destination. (However, TTL, checksum, and sometimes the fragment-related fields do change.) The Layer 3 QoS marking on the packet can be preserved, but the Layer 2 QoS marking must be rewritten at every Layer 3 router because the Layer 3 router is responsible for rewriting the Layer 2 frame. The packet marking is used as a classification mechanism on each ingress interface of a subsequent device. The BA of the service class that the traffic maps to must be committed. To guarantee end-to-end QoS, every node in the transmission path must be QoS capable. QoS differentiated service in MPLS networks is provided based on the EXP bits on the MPLS header. As a result, it is important that at certain points in the network, such as at edge devices, mapping is performed between IP precedence, DSCP, CoS, MPLS, or other fields that hold QoS markings. The mapping between 802.1Q/P CoS, MPLS EXP, and IP precedence is straightforward because all of them are based on the old-fashioned 3-bit specifications of the 1980s. Mapping the DSCP PHBs to those 3-bit fields requires some administrative decisions and compromises.

QoS Service Class

Planning and implementing QoS policies entails three main steps:

Step 1   Identify network traffic and its requirements.

Step 2   Divide the identified traffic into classes.

Step 3   Define QoS policies for each class.

In Step 1, you use tools such as NBAR to identify the existing traffic in the network. You might discover many different traffic types. In Step 1, you must then recognize and document the relevance and importance of each recognized traffic type to your business.

In Step 2, you group the network traffic into traffic or service classes. Each traffic or service class, composed of one or more traffic types, receives a specific QoS treatment. Each service class is created for one or more traffic types (a single group) that is called a BA. A common model used by service providers, called the customer model, defines four service classes:

- Mission critical

- Transactional

- Best-effort

- Scavenger

A traffic class can be defined based on many factors. For example, these criteria, should they be appropriate, can also be used to define traffic classes: an organization or department, a customer (or a set of them), an application (or a group of applications, such as Telnet, FTP, SAP, Oracle), a user or group of users (by location, job description, workstation MAC address), a traffic destination, and so on.

Step 3 in planning and implementing QoS policies using QoS service classes is defining policies for each service class. This step requires an understanding of the QoS needs of the traffic and applications that are within your network. When you design the policies, be careful not to make too many classes and make the matter too complex and over-provisioned. Limiting the service classes to four or five is common. Also, do not assign too many applications and traffic to the high-priority and mission-critical classes, because assigning a large percentage of traffic to those classes will ultimately have a negative effect. Some of the existing common traffic classes are as follows:

- Voice applications (VoIP)

- Mission-critical applications, such as Oracle and SAP

- Transactional/Interactive applications, such as Telnet and SSH

- Bulk applications such as FTP and TFTP

- Best-effort applications, such as WWW and e-mail

- Scavenger applications, such as Napster and Kazaa

You can find many sources of information and recommendations on QoS design and implementation; however, each network is unique and requires special attention. It is important to implement the QoS policies throughout the network and in a consistent way. Keep in mind the following two important points:

- If you do not implement QoS policies in certain parts of the network, the QoS offering of your network will be incomplete, unpredictable, and inadequate.

- Because not all network devices have consistent and complete capabilities and features, you must map QoS techniques and features well. That way, the behavior of the diverse devices within your network will be consistent and in-line with your policies.

One required task during the QoS policy implementation stage is mapping and translating between CoS, DSCP, IP precedence, and MPLS EXP markings. Table 3-4 shows the Cisco recommended mappings between Layer 2 CoS, IP precedence, DSCP, PHB and Class Selector Name, and their corresponding traffic types.

Table 3-4 *Mapping Different Markings to Different Traffic Types*

Cisco AutoQoS Class	Layer 2 CoS or IP Precedence	DSCP Value in Decimal	DSCP Value in Binary	Code Name
Best Effort	0	0	000000	BE (Best Effort)
Scavenger	1	8	001000	CS1 (Class Selector 1)
Bulk Data	1	10	001010	AF11
		12	001100	AF12
		14	001110	AF13
Network Management	2	16	010000	CS2 (Class Selector 2)

Table 3-4 *Mapping Different Markings to Different Traffic Types (Continued)*

Cisco AutoQoS Class	Layer 2 CoS or IP Precedence	DSCP Value in Decimal	DSCP Value in Binary	Code Name
Telephony Signaling	3	26	011010	AF31
Local Mission Critical	3	28	011100	AF32
		30	011110	AF33
Streaming Media Traffic	4	32	100000	CS4 (Class Selector 4)
Interactive Video Traffic	4	34	100010	AF41
		36	100100	AF42
		38	100110	AF43
Interactive Voice Bearer Traffic	5	46	101110	EF

Trust Boundaries

End-system devices such as personal computers, IP phones, IP conference devices, and video conference gateways, plus switches and routers at different levels of the network hierarchy, can mark the IP packets or the encapsulating frames such as 802.1Q/P. One of the design and policy decisions you have to make is where to place your network trust boundary. The trust boundary forms a perimeter on your network; your network respects and trusts (does not override) the markings that the devices on or inside this perimeter (trust boundary) make. Markings that devices make outside the trust boundary are often reset, or at least checked and modified if necessary. The devices that check and reset the markings of the traffic received from the untrusted devices (devices outside the trust boundary), form the trust boundary of the network. The devices that form the trust boundary are the first set of devices that are trusted because they forward traffic toward the network core. It is considered good practice to place the trust boundary as close to the traffic source (and away from the network core) as possible.

You should certainly try to place the trust boundary as close to the network edge as possible. However, two other factors can affect your decision. First, the trusted device must be under your administration and control; at the very least, you should be confident that its marking is in-line with your QoS policies. Second, different devices have different capabilities and feature sets with respect to the ability to check and set/reset various QoS markings such as CoS and DSCP. With all facts considered, the trust boundary is implemented at one of the following network hierarchy layers:

- End system

- Access switch

- Distribution switch

Figure 3-6 depicts three scenarios with the trust boundary placed on the IP phone, the access switch, and the distribution switch. The end systems, except for telephony and conference systems, are generally recommended not to be trusted. New microcomputer operating systems such as the Linux and Microsoft operating systems make it possible to set the DSCP or CoS field on the transmitted traffic. Access switches, if they have the capability, are generally configured to (or by default do) trust the markings set by the IP phone only. If the access switch does not have any or enough QoS capabilities, you might have to shift the trust boundary to the distribution layer switch.

Figure 3-6 *Trust Boundary Placement Choices*

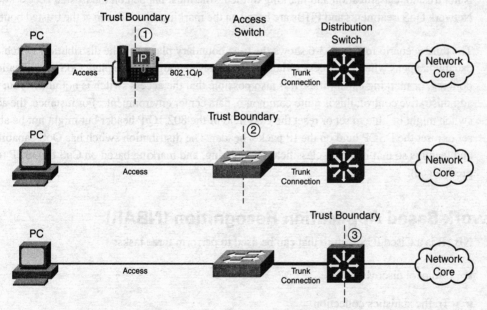

In the first scenario displayed in Figure 3-6, the trust boundary is placed on the Cisco IP phone. The phone sets/resets the CoS field to 0 (000 binary) for the frames it receives from the PC as it forwards them to the switch. The CoS value on the IP phone-generated frames that are carrying voice signaling is set to 3 (011 binary), and it is set to 5 (101 binary) for those that are carrying voice. The access switch is configured to trust the markings of the traffic received on the port that the Cisco IP phone is connected to. But how does the switch know that a Cisco IP phone, and not another IP device such as a PC, is connected to that port? The switch discovers that a Cisco IP phone is connected to its port by means of the Cisco Discovery Protocol version 2 (CDP v2) that both the switch and the IP phone are supposed to have enabled. If the switch does not discover an IP phone, it does not extend the trust boundary to the end device and dynamically shifts the trust boundary to itself (the access switch).

In the second scenario, the PC is connected to the access switch, the trusted device. The access switch must be configured to check (and reset if necessary) the CoS field in case it receives 802.1Q/P frames from the PC (rare case). Some access switches are capable of checking (and setting) the IP header QoS fields (ToS field's IP precedence or DSCP). When the traffic from the PC is forwarded toward the distribution switch, because the connection between the access switch and distribution switch is usually an 802.1Q/P trunk, the access switch can set the CoS field (and the DSCP field, if the switch has the capability) of the outgoing traffic to certain values based on QoS policies and the traffic type. For instance, the PC can run several different applications, including Cisco IP Communicator. In that case, if the marking of the traffic coming from the PC is not trusted, classification and marking of the traffic must happen on the trusted access switch. Network QoS treatments and PHBs are based on the markings that happen at the trusted boundary.

The third scenario in Figure 3-6 shows the trust boundary placed on the distribution switch. This usually happens when the access switch does not have enough or complete QoS classification, policing, or marking capabilities. It is also possible that the access switch is not under your administrative control; this is quite common in data center environments. For instance, the access switch might be able to set or reset the CoS field of the 802.1Q/P header but might not be able to set or reset the DSCP field on the IP packet header. The distribution switch has QoS capabilities and features so that it can do classification, policing, and marking based on CoS or DSCP (or IP precedence).

Network Based Application Recognition (NBAR)

NBAR is a Cisco IOS feature that can be used to perform three tasks:

- Protocol discovery

- Traffic statistics collection

- Traffic classification

Because NBAR can discover which applications and protocols are running on your network and display volume and statistics about them, you can use it as a powerful yet simple tool to form the definitions of your network traffic classes (BAs). You can also use NBAR within class-based (CB) marking or other MQC-based tools to classify packets for purposes such as marking, policing, and queuing. NBAR is a powerful protocol discovery and classification tool, but the overhead it imposes is considered small or medium. The amount of CPU utilization increase that a router running NBAR experiences depends on the amount of traffic and the router CPU type and speed.

NBAR recognizes a limited number of protocols. However, you can expand the list of recognized protocols by loading new Packet Description Language Modules (PDLMs), published by Cisco systems, into your device (flash memory) and making a reference to the new PDLM in the device configuration. PDLMs are files that Cisco Systems publishes; these files contain rules that NBAR uses to recognize protocols and applications. A new PDLM can be loaded in the flash memory of the Cisco device and then referenced within its configuration without a need to perform an IOS upgrade or reload the device. Cisco Systems makes up-to-date PDLMs available to registered users on Cisco Connection Online (CCO) at www.cisco.com/cgi-bin/tablebuild.pl/pdlm.

Before you can design a classification and marking scheme for your network, you need to identify and recognize the existing traffic for your network. The NBAR protocol-discovery feature provides a simple way to discover and report the applications and protocols that transit (in and out) a particular interface of a network device you choose. Protocol discovery discovers and reports on the protocols and applications that NBAR supports (plus those added by the loaded PDLMs). Key statistics are also reported on the discovered protocols and applications. Examples of the statistics that NBAR protocol discovery reports on each protocol are the total number of input and output packets and bytes and the input and output bit rates. The list of discovered protocols and applications, plus the associated statistics, which NBAR reports, are valuable when you want to define your traffic classes and their QoS policies.

NBAR can classify traffic by inspecting bytes beyond the network and transport layer headers. This is called *subport classification*. This means that NBAR looks into the segment (TCP or UDP) payload and classifies based on that content. For example, NBAR can classify HTTP traffic based on the URL; it can also classify based on MIME type.

NBAR has some limitations. First, it does not function on the Fast EtherChannel logical interface. Second, NBAR can only handle up to 24 concurrent URLs, hosts, or MIME types. Third, NBAR only analyzes the first 400 bytes of the packet. Fourth, it only supports CEF and does not work if another switching mode is used. It does not support multicast packets, fragmented packets, and packets that are associated with secure HTTP (URL, host, or MIME classification). NBAR does not analyze or recognize the traffic that is destined to or emanated from the router where NBAR is running.

Configuring classification without NBAR is mostly dependent on writing and maintaining access lists. Using NBAR for classification is not only simpler than using access lists, but NBAR also offers capabilities beyond those offered by access lists. NBAR can do stateful inspection of flows. This means that it can discover the dynamic TCP or UDP port numbers that are negotiated at connection establishment time by inspecting the control session packets. For example, a TFTP session is initiated using the well-known UDP port 69, but the two ends of the session negotiate other ports for the remainder of the session traffic. NBAR also supports some non-IP and non-TCP/non-UDP protocols and applications such as Internetwork Packet Exchange (IPX), IPsec, and GRE. Finally, as stated already, NBAR is able to discover and classify by deep packet inspection, too. This means that NBAR can inspect the payload of TCP and UDP segments (up to the 400th byte of the packet) and classify. HTTP sessions can be classified by URL, hostname, or MIME type.

Cisco IOS Commands to Configure NBAR

To enhance the list of protocols that NBAR recognizes through a PDLM, download the PDLM from CCO and copy it into the flash or on a TFTP server. Next, enter the following command, which refers to the PDLM name in URL format:

```
Router(config)# ip nbar pdlm pdlm-name
```

The URL, for example, can be flash://citrix.pdlm, referring to the citrix.pdlm file in flash memory. The URL can also refer to a file on a TFTP server, such as tftp://192.168.19.66/citrix.pdlm.

To modify the port number that NBAR associates to a protocol name or to add a port to the list of ports associated to a protocol name, use this command:

```
Router(config)# ip nbar port-map protocol-name [tcp | udp] port-number
```

The preceding command configures NBAR to search for a protocol or protocol name using a port number other than the well-known one. You can specify up to 16 additional port numbers.

To see the current NBAR protocol-to-port mapping, use the following **show** command:

```
Router# show ip nbar port-map [protocol-name]
```

Example 3-1 displays partial sample output of the preceding command.

Example 3-1 *Displaying NBAR Protocol-to-Port Mapping*

```
Router# show ip nbar portmap

port-map bgp tcp 179
port-map dhcp udp 67 68
port-map dns udp 53
port-map dns tcp 53
...
```

To enable NBAR protocol discovery on a router interface, first ensure that CEF is enabled on that interface. CEF is turned on using the **IP CEF** command from Cisco IOS global configuration mode. Next, enter the following command in the interface configuration mode:

```
Router(config-if)# ip nbar protocol-discovery
```

To display the discovered protocols and the statistics gathered for each discovered protocol, enter the following **show** command. Note that unless you specify an interface, the output will include the statistics gathered for all interfaces (back to back):

```
Router# show ip nbar protocol-discovery
```

Sample output of the preceding command is shown in Example 3-2.

Example 3-2 *Displaying NBAR* **protocol-discovery** *Results*

```
Router# show ip nbar protocol-discovery
Ethernet 0/0/0
               Input                     Output
               Packet Count              Packet Count
Protocol       Byte Count                Byte Count
               5 minute bit rate (bps)   5 minute bit rate (bps)
------------ ------------------------- -----------------------------
eigrp          60                        0
               3600                      0
               0                         0
bgp            0                         0
               0                         0
               0                         0
...
```

You can use NBAR to recognize and classify protocols that use static port numbers; NBAR can do the same for protocols that dynamically negotiate port numbers. If you want NBAR to classify network traffic based on protocol and subsequently apply certain QoS policies to each traffic class, use MQC class map and refer to the desired NBAR protocol with a **match** statement. The following is the syntax for the **match** statement within a class map:

```
Router(config-cmap)# match protocol protocol-name
```

The *protocol-name* that is referred by the class map **match protocol** statement is an NBAR-supported protocol such as **ip**, **arp**, **compressed tcp**, **cdp**, **dlsw**, **ipx**, and so on. Do not forget that you can specify additional ports (besides the well-known ports) for each protocol by configuring the previously introduced **ip nbar port-map** command. Also, to expand the list of NBAR-supported protocols, you can load new PDLMs in your device, as discussed earlier in this section. To use NBAR for classification and marking of traffic belonging to static-port protocols and to apply the policy to an interface, you have to perform the following tasks:

■ Enable NBAR protocol discovery.

■ Configure a traffic class using the MQC class map.

■ Configure a QOS policy using the MQC policy map.

■ Apply the policy to the interface(s).

■ Expand the NBAR protocol ports or PDLM protocols if needed.

Example 3-3 shows partial configuration of a router with a policy called www-ltd-bw (implying limited bandwidth for web browsing or HTTP protocol) applied to its serial 1/1 interface. The first line shows that TCP ports 80 and 8080 are defined for HTTP. The configured class map defines a traffic class called www, which includes all traffic classified by NBAR as http. The policy map called www-ltd-bw is applied to the outgoing traffic of the serial 1/1 interface using the **service-policy output** command. The policy map www-ltd-bw specifies that the traffic classified as www is assigned to a queue with a 512-Kbps bandwidth reservation.

Example 3-3 *Implementing QoS Policy Using NBAR for Static Protocols*

```
ip nbar port-map http tcp 80 8080
!
class-map www
  match protocol http
!
policy-map www-ltd-bw
  class www
    bandwidth 512
!
interface serial 1/1
  ip nbar protocol-discovery
  service-policy output www-ltd-bw
!
```

In Example 3-3, the command **ip nbar protocol-discovery** is applied to the serial 1/1 interface. In the past (earlier Cisco IOS releases), you had to apply this command to the interface before you could apply a service policy that used NBAR (through the **match protocol** *name* command); however, as of Cisco IOS 12.2T, this is no longer necessary. The ONT course does not mention this fact in its initial release, so for examination purposes, you might want to do it the old-fashioned way and apply the **ip nbar protocol-discovery** command to the interface.

You can also use NBAR to do traffic classification for stateful protocols, those that negotiate the data session port numbers during the initial control session. You still need to take three steps:

1. Configure a traffic class using MQC class map.

(Within the class map, the **match** statement references the stateful protocol such as TFTP).

2. Configure a QOS policy using MQC policy map.

3. Apply the policy to the interface(s).

One of the most attractive and powerful NBAR features is its ability to do deep packet inspection. Four popular uses of NBAR deep packet inspection are as follows:

- Classifying traffic based on the hostname or the URL after the hostname in the HTTP GET requests

- Classifying traffic based on the MIME type

- Classifying traffic belonging to fast-track protocols file transfers using regular expressions that match strings

- Classifying traffic based on the RTP payload type or CODEC

The **match protocol** commands required within MQC class map, to classify traffic according to the preceding criteria, are as follows:

```
Router(config-cmap)# match protocol http url url-string
Router(config-cmap)# match protocol http host host-name
Router(config-cmap)# match protocol http mime mime-type
Router(config-cmap)# match protocol fasttrack file-transfer regular-expression
Router(config-cmap)# match protocol rtp [audio | video |
    payload-type payload-type-string]
```

Example 3-4 shows three class maps: from-cisco, whats-up, and cool-jpegs. The class map from-cisco matches any HTTP GET request from hosts whose names begin with cisco. **cisco*** is a regular expression that matches any string that begins with characters cisco (followed by zero or more characters). Special characters such as *, which means zero or more characters (wildcard), make writing regular expressions a lot easier. The class map whats-up matches HTTP packets based on any URL containing the string /latest/whatsnew followed by zero or more characters. The last class map in Example 3-4, cool-jpegs, classifies packets based on the Joint Photographics Expert Group (JPEG) MIME type.

Example 3-4 *Using NBAR to Match HTTP Hostname, URL, and MIME Type*

```
!
class-map from-cisco
  match protocol http host cisco*
!
class-map whats-up
  match protocol http url /latest/whatsnew*
!
class-map cool-jpegs
  match protocol http mime "*jpeg"
!
```

For your reference only (not for the purpose of exam preparation), Table 3-5 presents a few useful special characters you can use within regular expressions of the class map **match** statement.

Table 3-5 *Special Strings and Characters for Regular Expressions*

Character or String	Description
*	Match zero or more characters in this position.
?	Match any one character in this position.
|	It means OR. Match one of a choice of characters on either side of the | symbol.
(|)	Match one of a choice of characters inside the parentheses on either side of the | symbol. For example, **xyz.(gif|jpg)** matches either xyz.gif or xyz.jpg.
[ ]	Match any character in the range specified, or one of the special characters. For example, **[0-9]** is any single digit; **[*]** matches the * character, and **[[]** matches the [character.

You can also use NBAR deep packet inspection to match traffic from FastTrack peer-to-peer protocols such as Kazaa and Grokster. To configure NBAR to match FastTrack peer-to-peer traffic, use the following command in class map configuration mode:

```
Router(config-cmap)# match protocol fasttrack file-transfer reg-exp
```

Please note that the preceding command syntax expects a regular expression to identify a specific FastTrack traffic. Gnutella traffic can be classified similarly using NBAR, by changing the keyword FastTrack to Gnutella.

Example 3-5 shows three class maps. The class map called fasttrack1 configures NBAR to match all FastTrack traffic. In the second class map, all FastTrack files that have the .mpeg extension are classified into traffic class fasttrack2. Class map fasttrack3 specifies that all FastTrack traffic that contains the string "cisco" is part of the traffic class called fasttrack3.

Example 3-5 *Using NBAR to Match FastTrack Protocol Traffic*

```
!
class-map fasttrack1
  match protocol fasttrack file-transfer "*"
!
class-map fasttrack2
  match protocol fasttrack file-transfer "*.mpeg"
!
class-map fasttrack3
  match protocol fasttrack file-transfer "*cisco*"
!
```

The Real-Time Transport Protocol (RTP) is considered the transport protocol of choice for real-time audio and video. It adds a header above the UDP header to include information such as reconstruction timestamp and sequence number, plus security and content identification. RTP has a control protocol sister called Real-Time Protocol Control Protocol (RTCP). Whereas RTP uses the UDP even-numbered ports (starting with 16384 by default), RTCP uses the UDP odd-number ports. NBAR deep packet inspection allows you to do classification based on RTP payload type (audio or video) or do a deeper classification based on audio or video CODEC type. The syntax to configure NBAR to match RTP traffic in class map configuration mode is as follows:

```
Router(config-cmap)# match protocol rtp [audio | video |
    payload-type payload-type-string]
```

In the preceding command syntax, the optional keyword **audio** specifies matching by audio payload type. (Values in the range of 0 to 23 are reserved for audio traffic.) Similarly, the optional keyword **video** specifies matching by video payload type. (Values in the range of 24 to 33 are reserved for video traffic.) If you use the optional keyword **payload-type**, you can specify (using a string) matching by a specific payload type value, providing more granularity than is available with the **audio** or **video** keywords. A payload string argument can contain commas to separate payload type values and hyphens to indicate a range of payload type values.

Example 3-6 shows two class maps. The first class map is called voice, and as the name implies, it matches the RTP audio protocol. The class map called video matches the RTP video protocol.

Example 3-6 *Using NBAR to Match RTP Protocol Traffic*

```
!
class-map voice
  match protocol RTP audio
!
class-map video
  match protocol RTP video
!
```

Foundation Summary

The "Foundation Summary" is a collection of information that provides a convenient review of many key concepts in this chapter. If you are already comfortable with the topics in this chapter, this summary can help you recall a few details. If you just read this chapter, this review should help solidify some key facts. If you are doing your final preparation before the exam, the information in this section is a convenient way to review the day before the exam.

Table 3-6 summarizes the major topics in this chapter.

Table 3-6 *Summary of Classification, Marking, and NBAR*

Topic	Summary
Purpose of packet classification	Packet classification is a QoS mechanism that distinguishes and divides network traffic into traffic classes or behavior aggregates (BAs).
Purpose of packet marking	Packets, frames, and some other protocol data units (PDUs) have a special field designed for QoS purposes. Marking is a QoS mechanism that sets this field to a common value on packets that belong to the same traffic/service class (BA) and sets them to different values on packets that belong to different classes.
Classification and marking at the data link layer	Different data link layer protocol data units (PDUs) have different fields for QoS classification and marking purposes. On 802.1Q/P or ISL frames, the 3-bit PRI (CoS) field is used for that purpose. On Frame Relay frames, the DE bit is used for that purpose, and on AMT cells, the CLP bit is used. On the MPLS header (layer 2) the 3-bit EXP field is used for QoS purposes.
PHB	A per-hop behavior (PHB) is an externally observable forwarding behavior applied at a DiffServ-compliant node to a DiffServ BA.
Class selector PHB (DSCP)	The class-selector PHB is a set of DSCP values that make DSCP backward compatible with IPP (IP precedence). The least significant bits of the class selectors (CS1 through CS7) are 000.
AF PHB	The assured forwarding (AF) PHB provides four queues for four classes of traffic. Bandwidth reservation can be made for each AF queue. Each AF has three DSCP values associated to it so that differentiated drop policy can be applied to the packets in the same AF queue.
EF PHB	The expedited forwarding (EF) PHB provides a priority queue with guaranteed but policed bandwidth. EF PHB is ideal for delay-sensitive traffic as long as this type of traffic is not oversubscribed.

Table 3-6 *Summary of Classification, Marking, and NBAR (Continued)*

Topic	Summary
QoS service class	QoS service class is a logical grouping of packets that, as per the administrative policy definitions, are required to receive the same QoS treatment.
Trust boundary	Marking is recommended to take place as close to the ingress edge of the network as possible. Marking, however, must be done by a trusted device. The ingress edge/perimeter of the network where the trusted devices reside and perform marking is called the trust boundary.
NBAR	NBAR is a protocol discovery and a classification tool/feature. Within a class map, you can configure a match statement that refers to an NBAR protocol.
NBAR Protocol Discovery	To discover the network traffic mix that transits through an interface (both input and output), apply the NBAR protocol discovery feature to that interface. NBAR protocol discovery also reports traffic statistics such as total number of input/output packets and bytes and input/output bit rates.
NBAR PDLMs	The NBAR Packet Description Language Modules (PDLM) are files provided by Cisco Systems that you can load into your network device to extend the NBAR list of supported protocols or enhance the NBAR existing protocol-recognition capability. Loading a new PDLM does not require a router reload.
NBAR application support	NBAR can discover and classify both types of applications: those that use static ports and those that use dynamically assigned ports. NBAR can do classification through deep packet inspection; for example, it can classify based on URL, MIME type, and RTP payload type. CEF must be enabled on device interfaces for NBAR to function.

Q&A

Some of the questions that follow challenge you more than the exam by using an open-ended question format. By reviewing now with this more difficult question format, you can exercise your memory better and prove your conceptual and factual knowledge of this chapter. The answers to these questions appear in Appendix A.

1. Define and explain classification.

2. Define and explain marking.

3. What is the marker field on the 802.1Q/P frame called?

4. What are the names and definitions for CoS values 0 through 7?

5. Which one of the DSCP PHBs provides backward compatibility with ToS-based IP precedence?

6. What are the four DiffServ (DSCP) PHBs?

7. How is compatibility between MPLS and network layer QoS achieved?

8. What is a QoS service class?

9. What is a trust boundary?

10. What is NBAR?

11. Name at least three limitations of NBAR.

12. List application support for NBAR.

13. What is PDLM?

14. What types of RTP payload classification does NBAR offer?

15. Which **match** command within a class map allows you to identify FastTrack peer-to-peer protocols?

This chapter covers the following subjects:

- Introduction to Congestion Management and Queuing"

- First-In-First-Out, Priority Queuing, Round-Robin, and Weighted Round-Robin Queuing"

- Weighted Fair Queuing

- Class-Based Weighted Fair Queuing

- Low-Latency Queuing

CHAPTER 4

Congestion Management and Queuing

This chapter starts by defining what congestion is and why it happens. Next, it explains the need for queuing or congestion management and describes the router queuing components. The rest of this chapter is dedicated to explaining and providing configuration and monitoring commands for queuing methods, namely FIFO, PQ, RR, WRR, WFQ, CBWFQ, and LLQ.

"Do I Know This Already?" Quiz

The purpose of the "Do I Know This Already?" quiz is to help you decide whether you really need to read the entire chapter. The 13-question quiz, derived from the major sections of this chapter, helps you determine how to spend your limited study time.

Table 4-1 outlines the major topics discussed in this chapter and the "Do I Know This Already?" quiz questions that correspond to those topics. You can keep track of your score here, too.

Table 4-1 *"Do I Know This Already?" Foundation Topics Section-to-Question Mapping*

Foundation Topics Section Covering These Questions	Questions	Score
"Introduction to Congestion Management and Queuing"	1–4	
"First-In-First-Out, Priority Queuing, Round-Robin, and Weighted Round-Robin Queuing"	5–7	
"Weighted Fair Queuing"	8–11	
"Class-Based Weighted Fair Queuing"	12	
"Low-Latency Queuing"	13	
Total Score	**(13 possible)**	

CAUTION The goal of self-assessment is to gauge your mastery of the topics in this chapter. If you do not know the answer to a question or are only partially sure of the answer, mark this question wrong for purposes of the self-assessment. Giving yourself credit for an answer you correctly guess skews your self-assessment results and might provide you with a false sense of security.

You can find the answers to the "Do I Know This Already?" quiz in Appendix A, "Answers to the 'Do I Know This Already?' Quizzes and Q&A Sections." The suggested choices for your next step are as follows:

- **9 or less overall score**—Read the entire chapter. This includes the "Foundation Topics," "Foundation Summary," and "Q&A" sections.

- **10–11 overall score**—Begin with the "Foundation Summary" section and then follow up with the "Q&A" section at the end of the chapter.

- **12 or more overall score**—If you want more review on this topic, skip to the "Foundation Summary" section and then go to the "Q&A" section. Otherwise, proceed to the next chapter.

1. Which of the following is not a common reason for congestion?

   a. Speed mismatch

   b. Aggregation

   c. Confluence

   d. Queuing

2. Which of the following is a congestion management tool?

   a. Aggregation

   b. Confluence

   c. Queuing

   d. Fast Reroute

3. Which of the following is not a function within a queuing system?

   a. Creating one or more queues

   b. CEF

   c. Assigning arriving packets to queues

   d. Scheduling departure of packets from queues

4. How many queuing subsystems exist in an interface queuing system?

   a. One

   b. Two: a software queue and a hardware queue

   c. Three: a software, a transmit, and a hardware queue

   d. Four: a software, a hold, a transmit, and a hardware queue

5. What is the default queuing discipline on all but slow serial interfaces?

   a. FIFO

   b. WFQ

   c. CQ

   d. WRR

6. How many queues does PQ have?

   a. One

   b. Two: High and Low

   c. Three: High, Medium, and Low

   d. Four: High, Medium, Normal, and Low

7. Custom queuing is a modified version of which queuing discipline?

   a. WFQ

   b. PQ

   c. FIFO

   d. WRR

8. Which of the following is not a goal or objective of WFQ?

   a. Provide high bandwidth to high-volume traffic

   b. Divide traffic into flows

   c. Provide fair bandwidth allocation to the active flows

   d. Provide faster scheduling to low-volume interactive flows

9. Which of the following is not used to recognize and differentiate flows in WFQ?

   a. Source and destination IP address

   b. Packet size

   c. Source and destination TCP/UDP port number

   d. Protocol number and type of service

10. Which of the following is an advantage of WFQ?

   a. WFQ does not starve flows and guarantees throughput to all flows.

   b. WFQ drops/punishes packets from most aggressive flows first.

   c. WFQ is a standard queuing mechanism that is supported on most Cisco platforms.

   d. All of the above.

11. Which of the following is not a disadvantage of WFQ?

a. WFQ does not offer guarantees such as bandwidth and delay guarantees to traffic flows.

b. FQ classification and scheduling are not configurable and modifiable.

c. You must configure flow-based queues for WFQ, and that is a complex task.

d. Multiple traffic flows may be assigned to the same queue within the WFQ system.

12. Which of the following is not true about CBWFQ?

a. CBWFQ allows creation of user-defined classes.

b. CBWFQ allows minimum bandwidth reservation for each queue.

c. CBWFQ addresses all of the shortcomings of WFQ.

d. Each of the queues in CBWFQ is a FIFO queue that tail drops by default.

13. Which of the following is not true about LLQ?

a. LLQ includes a strict-priority queue.

b. The LLQ strict priority queue is given priority over other queues.

c. The LLQ strict-priority queue is policed.

d. LLQ treats all traffic classes fairly.

Foundation Topics

Introduction to Congestion Management and Queuing

Congestion happens when the rate of input (incoming traffic switched) to an interface exceeds the rate of output (outgoing traffic) from an interface. Why would this happen? Sometimes traffic enters a device from a high-speed interface and it has to depart from a lower-speed interface; this can cause congestion on the egress lower-speed interface, and it is referred to as the *speed mismatch problem*. If traffic from many interfaces aggregates into a single interface that does not have enough capacity, congestion is likely; this is called the *aggregation problem*. Finally, if joining of multiple traffic streams causes congestion on an interface, it is referred to as the *confluence problem*.

Figure 4-1 shows a distribution switch that is receiving traffic destined to the core from many access switches; congestion is likely to happen on the interface Fa 0/1, which is the egress interface toward the core. Figure 4-1 also shows a router that is receiving traffic destined to a remote office from a fast Ethernet interface. Because the egress interface toward the WAN and the remote office is a low-speed serial interface, congestion is likely on the serial 0 interface of the router.

Figure 4-1 *Examples of Why Congestion Can Occur on Routers and Switches*

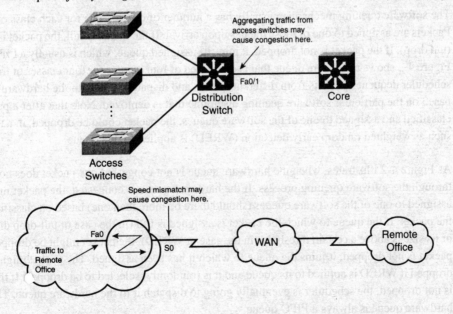

A network device can react to congestion in several ways, some of which are simple and some of which are sophisticated. Over time, several queuing methods have been invented to perform congestion management. The solution for permanent congestion is often increasing capacity rather than deploying queuing techniques. Queuing is a technique that deals with temporary congestion. If arriving packets do not depart as quickly as they arrive, they are held and released. The order in which the packets are released depends on the queuing algorithm. If the queue gets full, new arriving packets are dropped; this is called *tail drop*. To avoid tail drop, certain packets that are being held in the queue can be dropped so that others will not be; the basis for selecting the packets to be dropped depends on the queuing algorithm. Queuing, as a congestion management technique, entails creating a few queues, assigning packets to those queues, and scheduling departure of packets from those queues. The default queuing on most interfaces, except slow interfaces (2.048 Mbps and below), is FIFO. To entertain the demands of real-time, voice, and video applications with respect to delay, jitter, and loss, you must employ more sophisticated queuing techniques.

The queuing mechanism on each interface is composed of software and hardware components. If the hardware queue, also called the *transmit queue* (TxQ), is not congested (full/exhausted), the packets are not held in the software queue; they are directly switched to the hardware queue where they are quickly transmitted to the medium on the FIFO basis. If the hardware queue is congested, the packets are held in/by the software queue, processed, and released to the hardware queue based on the software queuing discipline. The software queuing discipline could be FIFO, PQ, custom queuing (CQ), WRR, or another queuing discipline.

The software queuing mechanism usually has a number of queues, one for each class of traffic. Packets are assigned to one of those queues upon arrival. If the queue is full, the packet is dropped (tail drop). If the packet is not dropped, it joins its assigned queue, which is usually a FIFO queue. Figure 4-2 shows a software queue that is composed of four queues for four classes of traffic. The scheduler dequeues packets from different queues and dispatches them to the hardware queue based on the particular software queuing discipline that is deployed. Note that after a packet is classified and assigned to one of the software queues, the packet could be dropped, if a technique such as weighted random early detection (WRED) is applied to that queue.

As Figure 4-2 illustrates, when the hardware queue is not congested, the packet does not go through the software queuing process. If the hardware queue is congested, the packet must be assigned to one of the software queues (should there be more than one) based on classification of the packet. If the queue to which the packet is assigned is full (in the case of tail-drop discipline) or its size is above a certain threshold (in the case of WRED), the packet might be dropped. If the packet is not dropped, it joins the queue to which it has been assigned. The packet might still be dropped if WRED is applied to its queue and it is (randomly) selected to be dropped. If the packet is not dropped, the scheduler is eventually going to dispatch it to the hardware queue. The hardware queue is always a FIFO queue.

Figure 4-2   *Router Queuing Components: Software and Hardware Components*

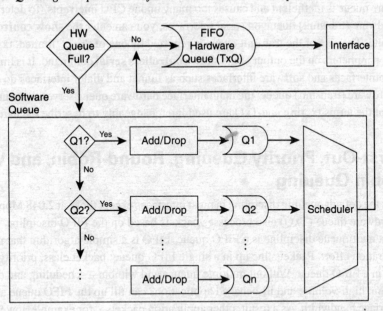

Having both software and hardware queues offers certain benefits. Without a software queue, all packets would have to be processed based on the FIFO discipline on the hardware queue. Offering discriminatory and differentiated service to different packet classes would be almost impossible; therefore, real-time applications would suffer. If you manually increase the hardware queue (FIFO) size, you will experience similar results. If the hardware queue becomes too small, packet forwarding and scheduling is entirely at the mercy of the software queuing discipline; however, there are drawbacks, too. If the hardware queue becomes so small, for example, that it can hold only one packet, when a packet is transmitted to the medium, a CPU interrupt is necessary to dispatch another packet from the software queue to the hardware queue. While the packet is being transferred from the software queue, based on its possibly complex discipline, to the hardware queue, the hardware queue is not transmitting bits to the medium, and that is wasteful. Furthermore, dispatching one packet at a time from the software queue to the hardware queue elevates CPU utilization unnecessarily.

Many factors such as the hardware platform, the software version, the Layer 2 media, and the particular software queuing applied to the interface influence the size of the hardware queue. Generally speaking, faster interfaces have longer hardware queues than slower interfaces. Also, in some platforms, certain QoS mechanisms adjust the hardware queue size automatically. The IOS effectively determines the hardware queue size based on the bandwidth configured on the interface. The determination is usually adequate. However, if needed, you can set the size of the hardware queue by using the **tx-ring-limit** command from the interface configuration mode.

Remember that a too-long hardware queue imposes a FIFO style of delay, and a too-short hardware queue is inefficient and causes too many undue CPU interrupts. To determine the size of the hardware (transmit) queue on serial interfaces, you can enter the **show controllers serial** command. The size of the transmit queue is reported by one of the tx_limited, tx_ring_limit, or tx_ring parameters on the output of the **show controllers serial** command. It is important to know that subinterfaces and software interfaces such as tunnel and dialer interfaces do not have their own hardware (transmit) queue; the main interface hardware queue serves those interfaces. Please note that the terms tx_ring and TxQ are used interchangeably to describe the hardware queue.

First-In-First-Out, Priority Queuing, Round-Robin, and Weighted Round-Robin Queuing

FIFO is the default queuing discipline in most interfaces except those at 2.048 Mbps or lower (E1). The hardware queue (TxQ) also processes packets based on the FIFO discipline. Each queue within a multiqueue discipline is a FIFO queue. FIFO is a simple algorithm that requires no configuration effort. Packets line up in a single FIFO queue; packet class, priority, and type play no role in a FIFO queue. Without multiple queues and without a scheduling and dropping algorithm, high-volume and ill-behaved applications can fill up the FIFO queue and consume all the interface bandwidth. As a result, other application packets—for example, low volume and less aggressive traffic such as voice—might be dropped or experience long delays. On fast interfaces that are unlikely to be congested, FIFO is often considered an appropriate queuing discipline.

PQ, which has been available for many years, requires configuration. PQ has four queues available: high-, medium-, normal-, and low-priority queues. You must assign packets to one of the queues, or the packets will be assigned to the normal queue. Access lists are often used to define which types of packets are assigned to which of the four queues. As long as the high-priority queue has packets, the PQ scheduler forwards packets only from the high-priority queue. If the high-priority queue is empty, one packet from the medium-priority queue is processed. If both the high- and medium-priority queues are empty, one packet from the normal-priority queue is processed, and if high-, medium-, and normal-priority queues are empty, one packet from the low-priority queue is processed. After processing/de-queuing one packet (from any queue), the scheduler always starts over again by checking if the high-priority queue has any packets waiting, before it checks the lower priority queues in order. When you use PQ, you must both understand and desire that as long as packets arrive and are assigned to the high-priority queue, no other queue gets any attention. If the high-priority queue is not too busy, however, and the medium-priority queue gets a lot of traffic, again, the normal- and low-priority packets might not get service, and so on. This phenomenon is often expressed as a PQ danger for starving lower-priority queues. Figure 4-3 shows a PQ when all four queues are holding packets.

Figure 4-3 *Priority Queuing*

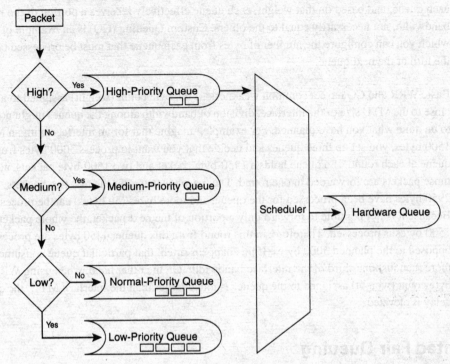

In the situation depicted in Figure 4-3, until all the packets are processed from the high-priority queue and forwarded to the hardware queue, no packets from the medium-, normal-, or low-priority queues are processed. Using the Cisco IOS command **priority-list**, you define the traffic that is assigned to each of the four queues. The priority list might be simple, or it might call an access list. In this fashion, packets, based on their protocol, source address, destination address, size, source port, or destination port, can be assigned to one of the four queues. Priority queuing is often suggested on low-bandwidth interfaces in which you want to give absolute priority to mission-critical or valued application traffic.

RR is a queuing discipline that is quite a contrast to priority queuing. In simple RR, you have a few queues, and you assign traffic to them. The RR scheduler processes one packet from one queue and then a packet from the next queue and so on. Then it starts from the first queue and repeats the process. No queue has priority over the others, and if the packet sizes from all queues are (roughly) the same, effectively the interface bandwidth is shared equally among the RR queues. If a queue consistently has larger packets than other queues, however, that queue ends up consuming more bandwidth than the other queues. With RR, no queue is in real danger of starvation, but the limitation of RR is that it has no mechanism available for traffic prioritization.

A modified version of RR, Weighted Round Robin (WRR), allows you to assign a "weight" to each queue, and based on that weight, each queue effectively receives a portion of the interface bandwidth, not necessarily equal to the others. Custom Queuing (CQ) is an example of WRR, in which you can configure the number of bytes from each queue that must be processed before it is the turn of the next queue.

Basic WRR and CQ have a common weakness: if the byte count (weight) assigned to a queue is close to the MTU size of the interface, division of bandwidth among the queues might not turn out to be quite what you have planned. For example, imagine that for an interface with an MTU of 1500 bytes, you set up three queues and decide that you want to process 3000 bytes from each queue at each round. If a queue holds a 1450-byte packet and two 1500-byte packets, all three of those packets are forwarded in one round. The reason is that after the first two packets, a total of 2950 bytes have been processed for the queue, and more bytes (50 bytes) can be processed. Because it is not possible to forward only a portion of the next packet, the whole packet that is 1500 bytes is processed. Therefore, in this round from this queue, 4450 bytes are processed as opposed to the planned 3000 bytes. If this happens often, that particular queue consumes much more than just one-third of the interface bandwidth. On the other hand, when using WRR, if the byte count (weight) assigned to the queues is much larger than the interface MTU, the queuing delay is elevated.

Weighted Fair Queuing

WFQ is a simple yet important queuing mechanism on Cisco routers for two important reasons: first, WFQ is the default queuing on serial interfaces at 2.048 Mbps (E1) or lower speeds; second, WFQ is used by CBWFQ and LLQ, which are two popular, modern and advanced queuing methods. (CBWFQ and LLQ are discussed in the following sections of this chapter.) WFQ has the following important goals and objectives:

- Divide traffic into flows

- Provide fair bandwidth allocation to the active flows

- Provide faster scheduling to low-volume interactive flows

- Provide more bandwidth to the higher-priority flows

WFQ addresses the shortcomings of both FIFO and PQ:

- FIFO might impose long delays, jitter, and possibly starvation on some packets (especially interactive traffic).

- PQ will impose starvation on packets of lower-priority queues, and within each of the four queues of PQ, which are FIFO based, dangers associated to FIFO queuing are present.

WFQ Classification and Scheduling

WFQ is a flow-based queuing algorithm. Arriving packets are classified into flows, and each flow is assigned to a FIFO queue. Flows are identified based on the following fields from IP and either TCP or UDP headers:

- Source IP address

- Destination IP address

- Protocol number

- Type of service (ToS)

- Source TCP/UDP port number

- Destination TCP/UDP port number

A hash is generated based on the preceding fields. Because packets of the same traffic flow end up with the same hash value, they are assigned to the same queue. Figure 4-4 shows that as a packet arrives, the hash based on its header fields is computed. If the packet is the first from a new flow, it is assigned to a new queue for that flow. If the packet hash matches an existing flow hash, the packet is assigned to that flow queue.

Figure 4-4 *Weighted Fair Queuing*

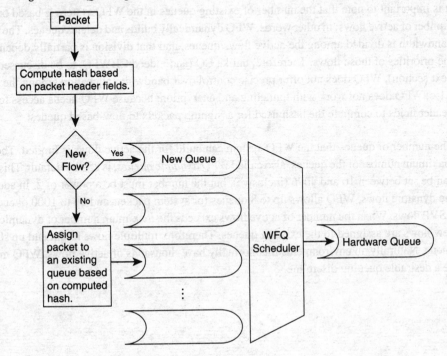

Figure 4-4 does not show that, based on how full the interface hold queue is, and based on whether the packet queue size is beyond a congestive discard threshold value, the packet might end up being dropped. It is worth mentioning that when a packet arrives, it is assigned a sequence number for scheduling purposes. The priority of a packet or flow influences its scheduling sequence number. These concepts and mechanisms are discussed next.

NOTE The sequence number assigned to an arriving packet is computed by adding the sequence number of the last packet in the flow queue to the modified size of the arriving packet. The size of the arriving packet is modified by multiplying it by the weight assigned to the packet. The weight is inversely proportional to the packet priority (from the ToS field). To illustrate this, consider two packets of the same size but of different priorities arriving at the same time. The two queues that these packets are mapped to are equally busy. The packet with the higher priority gets a smaller scheduling sequence number and will most likely be forwarded faster than the packet with the lower priority.

If all flows have the same priority (weight), WFQ effectively divides the interface bandwidth among all the existing flows. As a result, low-volume interactive flows are scheduled and forwarded to the hardware queue and do not end up with packets waiting in their corresponding queues (or at least not for long). Packets of high-volume flows build up their corresponding queues and end up waiting and delayed more and possibly dropped.

It is important to note that the number of existing queues in the WFQ system is based on the number of active flows; in other words, WFQ dynamically builds and deletes queues. The interface bandwidth is divided among the active flows/queues, and that division is partially dependent on the priorities of those flows. Therefore, unlike CQ (and indeed CBWFQ, to be discussed in the next section), WFQ does not offer precise control over bandwidth allocation among the flows. Also, WFQ does not work with tunneling and encryption, because WFQ needs access to packet header fields to compute the hash used for assigning packets to flow-based queues.

The number of queues that the WFQ system can build for the active flows is limited. The maximum number of the queues, also called *WFQ dynamic queues*, is 256 by default. This number can be set between 16 and 4096 (inclusive), but the number must be a power of 2. In addition to the dynamic flows, WFQ allows up to 8 queues for system packets and up to 1000 queues for RSVP flows. When the number of active flows exceeds the maximum number of dynamic queues, new flows are assigned to the existing queues. Therefore, multiple flows might end up sharing a queue. Naturally, in environments that normally have thousands of active flows, WFQ might not be a desirable queuing discipline.

WFQ Insertion and Drop Policy

WFQ has a hold queue for all the packets of all flows (queues within the WFQ system). The hold queue is the sum of all the memory taken by the packets present in the WFQ system. If a packet arrives while the hold queue is full, the packet is dropped. This is called *WFQ aggressive dropping*. Aggressive dropping has one exception: if a packet is assigned to an empty queue, it is not dropped.

Each flow-based queue within WFQ has a congestive discard threshold (CDT). If a packet arrives and the hold queue is not full but the CDT of that packet flow queue is reached, the packet is dropped. This is called *WFQ early dropping*. Early dropping has an exception: if a packet in another queue has a higher (larger) sequence number than the arriving packet, the packet with the higher sequence number is dropped instead. The dropped packet is assumed to belong to an aggressive flow. It can be concluded that the early drop of WFQ punishes packets from aggressive flows more severely and that packet precedence does not affect WFQ drop decisions.

Benefits and Drawbacks of WFQ

The main benefits of WFQ are as follows:

- Configuring WFQ is simple and requires no explicit classification.

- WFQ does not starve flows and guarantees throughput to all flows.

- WFQ drops packets from the most aggressive flows and provides faster service to nonaggressive flows.

- WFQ is a standard and simple queuing mechanism that is supported on most Cisco platforms and IOS versions.

WFQ has some limitations and drawbacks:

- WFQ classification and scheduling are not configurable and modifiable.

- WFQ is supported only on slow links (2.048 Mbps and less).

- WFQ does not offer guarantees such as bandwidth and delay guarantees to traffic flows.

- Multiple traffic flows may be assigned to the same queue within the WFQ system.

Configuring and Monitoring WFQ

WFQ is enabled by default on all serial interfaces that are slower than or equal to 2.048 Mbps. If WFQ is disabled on an interface and you want to enable it or if you want to change its configurable parameters, you can use the **fair-queue** command in the interface configuration mode. The following shows the optional parameters that can be configured while you enter the **fair-queue** command:

```
Router(config-if)# fair-queue [cdt [dynamic-queues [reservable-queues]]]
Router(config-if)# hold-queue max-limit out
```

This syntax also shows how the overall size of the WFQ system can be modified: the number of packets an interface can hold in its outbound software queue can be set using the **hold-queue** *max-limit* **out** command.

As you can see in this command syntax, configuring WFQ on an interface is simple. The *cdt* parameter (congestive discard threshold) sets the number of packets allowed in each queue. The default is 64, but you can change it to any power of 2 in the range from 16 to 4096. If a queue size exceeds its CDT limit, new packets that are assigned to this queue are discarded. The *dynamic-queues* parameter allows you to set the maximum number of flow queues allowed within the WFQ system. This number can be between 16 and 4096 (inclusive) and must be a power of 2. (The default is 256.) The parameter *reservable-queues* sets the number of allowed reserved conversations. This number must be between 0 and 1000 (inclusive). (The default is 0.) Reservable queues are used for interfaces that are configured for features such as Resource Reservation Protocol (RSVP).

You can check the settings for the WFQ configurable parameters by using the output of the **show interface** *interface* command. Example 4-1 displays sample output of this command. The queuing strategy is stated to be weighted fair queuing. For the output queue, the current size, maximum size (hold-queue max-limit), congestive discard threshold (per queue), and number of drops are stated to be 0, 1000, 64, and 0, respectively. The current number of conversations is stated to be 0, while it shows that a maximum of 10 conversations has been active during the measurement interval. The maximum allowed number of concurrent conversations is shown to be 256, which is the default value.

Example 4-1 *Sample Output of the* **show interface** *Command*

```
Router#show interfaces serial 1/0
Serial1/0 is up, line protocol is up
  Hardware is CD2430 in sync mode
  MTU 1500 bytes, BW 128000 Kbit, DLY 20000 usec,
      reliability 255/255, txload 1/255, rxload 1/255
  Encapsulation FRAME-RELAY, loopback not set
  Keepalive not set
  LMI DLCI 1023  LMI type is CISCO  frame relay DTE
  FR SVC disabled, LAPF state down
  Broadcast queue 0/64, broadcasts sent/dropped 105260/0, interface broadcasts 9 2894
  Last input 00:00:00, output 00:00:02, output hang never
  Last clearing of "show interface" counters 2d20h
  Input queue: 0/75/0/0 (size/max/drops/flushes); Total output drops: 0
  Queueing strategy: weighted fair
```

Example 4-1 *Sample Output of the* **show interface** *Command (Continued)*

```
    Output queue: 0/1000/64/0 (size/max total/threshold/drops)
       Conversations  0/10/256 (active/max active/max total)
       Reserved Conversations 0/0 (allocated/max allocated)
       Available Bandwidth 96000 kilobits/sec
    5 minute input rate 2000 bits/sec, 1 packets/sec
    5 minute output rate 2000 bits/sec, 0 packets/sec
       228008 packets input, 64184886 bytes, 0 no buffer
       Received 0 broadcasts, 0 runts, 0 giants, 0 throttles
       0 input errors, 0 CRC, 0 frame, 0 overrun, 0 ignored, 0 abort
       218326 packets output, 62389216 bytes, 0 underruns
       0 output errors, 0 collisions, 3 interface resets
       0 output buffer failures, 0 output buffers swapped out
       0 carrier transitions
       DCD=up  DSR=up  DTR=up  RTS=up  CTS=up
    !
```

You can obtain detailed information about the WFQ system on a particular interface (including a particular virtual circuit) by using the **show queue** *interface* command. Example 4-2 shows sample output of this command for your review. Observe that the output of this command for each queue (conversation) displays the IP packet header fields that distinguish one flow from another. Furthermore, for each conversation (queue), its depth (size), weight (related to distribution of bandwidth), and other statistics are displayed individually.

Example 4-2 *Sample Output of the* **show queue interface** *Command*

```
    Router# show queue atm2/0.33 vc 33
    Interface ATM2/0.33 VC 0/33
      Queueing strategy: weighted fair
      Total output drops per VC: 18149
      Output queue: 57/512/64/18149 (size/max total/threshold/drops)
         Conversations  2/2/256 (active/max active/max total)
         Reserved Conversations 3/3 (allocated/max allocated)

      (depth/weight/discards/tail drops/interleaves) 29/4096/7908/0/0
      Conversation 264, linktype: ip, length: 254
      source: 10.1.1.1, destination: 10.0.2.20, id: 0x0000, ttl: 59,
      TOS: 0 prot: 17, source port 1, destination port 1

      (depth/weight/discards/tail drops/interleaves) 28/4096/10369/0/0
      Conversation 265, linktype: ip, length: 254
      source: 10.1.1.1, destination: 10.0.2.20, id: 0x0000, ttl: 59,
      TOS: 32 prot: 17, source port 1, destination port 2
    !
```

Class-Based Weighted Fair Queuing

CBWFQ addresses some of the limitations of PQ, CQ, and WFQ. CBWFQ allows creation of user-defined classes, each of which is assigned to its own queue. Each queue receives a user-defined (minimum) bandwidth guarantee, but it can use more bandwidth if it is available. In contrast to PQ, no queue in CBWFQ is starved. Unlike PQ and CQ, you do not have to define classes of traffic to different queues using complex access lists. WFQ does not allow creation of user-defined classes, but CBWFQ does; moreover, defining the classes for CBWFQ is done with class maps, which are flexible and user friendly, unlike access lists. Similar to WFQ and CQ, CBWFQ does not address the low-delay requirements of real-time applications such as VoIP. The next section discusses LLQ, which through the use of a strict priority queue provides a minimum but policed bandwidth, plus a low-delay guarantee to real-time applications.

Figure 4-5 shows a CBWFQ with three user-defined classes. As each packet arrives, it is assigned to one of the queues based on the class to which the packet belongs. Each queue has a reserved bandwidth, which is a bandwidth guarantee.

Figure 4-5 *CBWFQ*

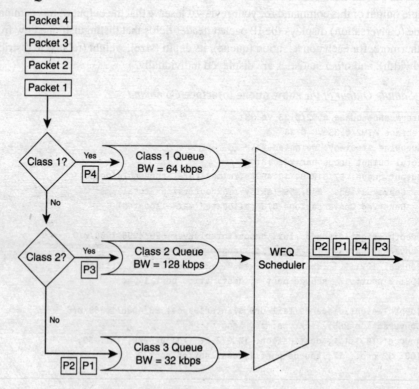

CBWFQ can create up to 64 queues, one for each user-defined class. Each queue is a FIFO queue with a defined bandwidth guarantee and a maximum packet limit. If a queue reaches its maximum packet limit, it incurs tail drop. To avoid tail drop, you can apply WRED to a queue. WRED is discussed in the "Congestion Avoidance" section of Chapter 5, "Congestion Avoidance, Policing, Shaping, and Link Efficiency Mechanisms." Note that if you apply WRED to one (or more) of the queues in CBWFQ, you cannot apply WRED directly to the interface, too. In addition to the 64 queues mentioned, a queue called class-default is always present. Packets that do not match any of the defined classes are assigned to this queue. The 64 queues and the class-default queue are all FIFO queues, but you can configure the class-default queue (but not the others) to be a WFQ. In 7500 series routers (and maybe others, by the time you read this book), you can configure all queues to be WFQ. Just as you can apply WRED to any of the queues, you can apply WRED to the class-default queue. The class-default queue, if you do not specify a reserved bandwidth for it, uses any remaining bandwidth of the interface.

Classification, Scheduling, and Bandwidth Guarantee

Classification of traffic for the purpose of CBWFQ is done using Cisco IOS modular command-line interface (MQC), specifically, using class maps. The options available for classification are based on the IOS version. Furthermore, relevance of certain match criteria depends on the interface, its encapsulation type, and any other options that might have been implemented on that interface. For example, you can match the Frame Relay DE (discard eligible) bit only on a Frame Relay interface. You should match MPLS EXP bits only if MPLS-IP packets are received; matching CoS bits only makes sense on 802.1Q trunk connections.

Scheduling and the bandwidth guarantee offered to each queue within a CBWFQ system is based on a weight that is assigned to it. The weight, in turn, is computed by the IOS based on the value you enter for bandwidth, bandwidth percent, or bandwidth remaining percent on the class that is assigned to the queue:

- **Bandwidth**—Using the **bandwidth** command, you allocate (reserve) a certain amount of bandwidth (Kbps) to the queue of a class. This bandwidth amount is subtracted (taken) from the available/unreserved portion of the maximum reserved bandwidth of the interface. The maximum reserved bandwidth of an interface is by default equal to 75 percent of the total bandwidth of that interface, but it is modifiable. Maximum reserved bandwidth is set/modified using the **max-reserved-bandwidth** command in the interface configuration mode.

- **Bandwidth percent**—Using the **bandwidth percent** command, you allocate/reserve an amount of bandwidth equal to a certain percentage of the interface bandwidth, to the queue of a class. Whatever this amount of bandwidth turns out to be, it is subtracted from the available/unreserved portion of the maximum reserved bandwidth of the interface. The Cisco IOS determines the bandwidth of the serial interfaces based on the configured value using the **bandwidth** statement.

■ **Bandwidth remaining percent**—Using the **bandwidth remaining percent** command, you allocate a certain percentage of the remaining available bandwidth of the interface to the queue of a class. Whatever this amount of bandwidth turns out to be, you subtract it from the available/unreserved portion of the maximum reserved bandwidth of the interface.

> **NOTE** When you configure the reserved bandwidth for each traffic class in a policy map, you cannot use the **bandwidth** command for one class and the **bandwidth percent** command on another class. In other words, for all classes within a policy map, you must use either the **bandwidth** command or the **bandwidth percent** command, but not a mix of the two commands.

From the total bandwidth of an interface, a certain percentage is available for reservation; this percentage is dictated by the value of a parameter called **max-reserved-bandwidth** on that interface. The default value of maximum reserved bandwidth is 75, meaning that 75 percent of the interface bandwidth can be reserved. However, as bandwidth reservation is made for different queues (and possibly flows or tunnels), the amount of bandwidth remaining for new reservations naturally diminishes. You can calculate the available bandwidth (available for reservation) based on this formula:

Available bandwidth = (interface bandwidth x maximum reserved bandwidth) – (sum of all existing reservations)

Note that the default value of 75 for maximum reserved bandwidth leaves 25 percent of interface bandwidth for network overhead, including Layer 2 overhead such as CDP. You can modify the default value for maximum reserved bandwidth, but you are cautioned to do so only if you are aware of the consequences.

Benefits and Drawbacks of CBWFQ

The main benefits of CBWFQ are as follows:

■ It allows creation of user-defined traffic classes. These classes can be defined conveniently using MQC class maps.

■ It allows allocation/reservation of bandwidth for each traffic class based on user policies and preferences.

■ Defining a few (up to 64) fixed classes based on the existing network applications and user policies, rather than relying on automatic and dynamic creation of flow-based queues (as WFQ does), provides for finer granularity and scalability.

The drawback of CBWFQ is that it does not offer a queue suitable for real-time applications such as voice or video over other IP applications. Real-time applications expect low-delay guarantee in addition to bandwidth guarantee, which CBWFQ does not offer.

Configuring and Monitoring CBWFQ

The first step in configuring CBWFQ is defining traffic classes, which is done using class maps. Example 4-3 shows two traffic classes: transaction-based and business-application. Any packet that matches access list 100 is classified as transaction-based, and any packet that matches access list 101 is classified as business-application.

Example 4-3   *Class Maps Define Traffic Classes*

```
!
class-map Transaction-Based
 match access-group 100
!
class-map Business-Application
 match access-group 101
!
```

Example 4-4 shows a policy map called Enterprise-Policy. This policy creates a queue with a bandwidth guarantee of 128 Kbps and a maximum packet limit (queue limit) of 50 for the traffic classified as transaction-based. Enterprise-Policy creates a second queue with a bandwidth guarantee of 256 Kbps and a maximum packet limit (queue limit) of 90 for the traffic classified as business-application. The default value for the **queue-limit** command is 64. Any traffic that does not belong to transaction-based or business-application classes is assigned to the queue created for the class-default class. The **fair-queue 16** command applied to the class-default class changes its queue discipline from FIFO to WFQ, and it sets the maximum number of dynamic queues for WFQ to 16. You can set the number of dynamic queues from 16 to 4096 (inclusive), but the number has to be a power of 2. Class-default has no bandwidth guarantees in this example.

Example 4-4   *Policy Map*

```
!
policy-map Enterprise-Policy
 class Transaction-Based
  Bandwidth 128
  queue-limit 50
 class Business-Application
  bandwidth 256
  queue-limit 90
 class class-default
  fair-queue 16
!
```

Example 4-5 shows the three alternative commands to reserve bandwidth for the queues of a CBWFQ. Remember that within a policy map, one or the other option can be used, but you cannot mix them within a single policy map.

Example 4-5 *Three Alternative Ways to Reserve Bandwidth for CBWFQ Queues*

```
!
policy-map Example-1
 class A
  Bandwidth 128
 class B
  bandwidth 64
!
policy-map Example-2
 class C
  bandwidth percent 30
 class D
  bandwidth percent 20
!
policy-map Example-3
 class E
  bandwidth remaining percent 20
 class F
  bandwidth remaining percent 20
!
```

Example 4-6 shows sample output of the **show policy-map interface** *interface* command. This command displays information about the policy map applied to an interface using the **service-policy** command. You can see the classes, bandwidth reservations, queuing disciplines, and traffic statistics for each class, on the output.

Example 4-6 *Sample Output of the* **show policy-map interface** *Command*

```
Router# show policy-map interface e1/1
 Ethernet1/1 output : po1
 Weighted Fair Queueing
    Class class1
      Output Queue: Conversation 264
        Bandwidth 937 (kbps) Max Threshold 64 (packets)
        (total/discards/tail drops) 11548/0/0
    Class class2
      Output Queue: Conversation 265
        Bandwidth 937 (kbps) Max Threshold 64 (packets)
        (total/discards/tail drops) 11546/0/0
    Class class3
      Output Queue: Conversation 266
        Bandwidth 937 (kbps) Max Threshold 64 (packets)
        (total/discards/tail drops) 11546/0/0
```

Low-Latency Queuing

Neither WFQ nor CBWFQ can provide guaranteed bandwidth and low-delay guarantee to selected applications such as VoIP; that is because those queuing models have no priority queue. Certain applications such as VoIP have a small end-to-end delay budget and little tolerance to *jitter* (delay variation among packets of a flow).

LLQ includes a strict-priority queue that is given priority over other queues, which makes it ideal for delay and jitter-sensitive applications. Unlike the plain old PQ, whereby the higher-priority queues might not give a chance to the lower-priority queues and effectively starve them, the LLQ strict-priority queue is policed. This means that the LLQ strict-priority queue is a priority queue with a minimum bandwidth guarantee, but at the time of congestion, it cannot transmit more data than its bandwidth permits. If more traffic arrives than the strict-priority queue can transmit (due to its strict bandwidth limit), it is dropped. Hence, at times of congestion, other queues do not starve, and get their share of the interface bandwidth to transmit their traffic.

Figure 4-6 shows an LLQ. As you can observe, LLQ is effectively a CBWFQ with one or more strict-priority queues added. Please note that it is possible to have more than one strict priority queue. This is usually done so that the traffic assigned to the two queues—voice and video traffic, for example—can be separately policed. However, after policing is applied, the traffic from the two classes is not separated; it is sent to the hardware queue based on its arrival order (FIFO).

Figure 4-6 *LLQ*

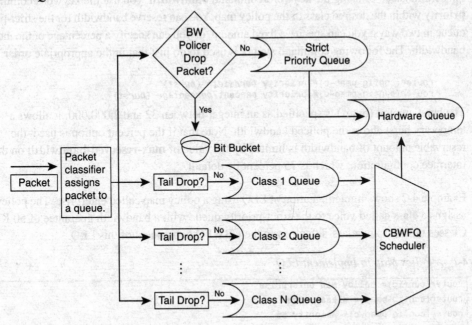

As long as the traffic that is assigned to the strict-priority class does not exceed its bandwidth limit and is not policed and dropped, it gets through the LLQ with minimal delay. This is the benefit of LLQ over CBWFQ.

Benefits of LLQ

LLQ offers all the benefits of CBWFQ, including the ability of the user to define classes and guarantee each class an appropriate amount of bandwidth and to apply WRED to each of the classes (except to the strict-priority queue) if needed. In the case of LLQ and CBWFQ, the traffic that is not explicitly classified is considered to belong to the class-default class. You can make the queue that services the class-default class a WFQ instead of FIFO, and if needed, you can apply WRED to it.

The benefit of LLQ over CBWFQ is the existence of one or more strict-priority queues with bandwidth guarantees for delay- and jitter-sensitive traffic. The advantage of LLQ over the traditional PQ is that the LLQ strict-priority queue is policed. That eliminates the chance of starvation of other queues, which can happen if PQ is used. As opposed to the old RTP priority queue, the LLQ strict-priority is not limited to accepting RTP traffic only. You can decide and assign any traffic you want to the LLQ strict-riority queue using special IOS keywords, using access lists, or using Network Based Application Recognition (NBAR) options. Finally, like many other queuing mechanisms, LLQ is not restricted to certain platforms or media types.

Configuring and Monitoring LLQ

Configuring LLQ is almost identical to configuring CBWFQ, except that for the strict-priority queue(s), instead of using the keyword/command **bandwidth**, you use the keyword/command **priority** within the desired class of the policy map. You can reserve bandwidth for the strict-priority queue in two ways: you can specify a fixed amount, or you can specify a percentage of the interface bandwidth. The following command syntax is used to do just that in the appropriate order:

```
router(config-pmap-c)# priority bandwidth {burst}
router(config-pmap-c)# priority percent percentage {burst}
```

The burst amount (bytes) is specified as an integer between 32 and 2,000,000; it allows a temporary burst above the policed bandwidth. Note that if the percent option is used, the reservable amount of bandwidth is limited by the value of **max-reserved-bandwidth** on the interface configuration, which is 75 percent by default.

Example 4-7 shows implementation of LLQ using a policy map called enterprise. The policy map assigns a class called voice to the strict-priority queue with a bandwidth guarantee of 50 Kbps. Classes business and class-default form the CBWFQ component of this LLQ.

Example 4-7 *A Policy Map to Implement LLQ*

```
router(config)# policy-map enterprise
router(config-pmap)# class voice
router(config-pmap-c)# priority 50
router(config-pmap)# class business
router(config-pmap-c)# bandwidth 200
router(config-pmap)# class class-default
router(config-pmap-c)# fair-queue
!
```

You can use the **show policy-map interface** *interface* command to see the packet statistics for all classes used within a policy map that is applied to an interface using the **service-policy** command. Example 4-8 shows (partial) output of this command for the serial 1/0 interface of a router.

Example 4-8   *Sample Output of the* **show policy-map interface** *Command*

```
router# show policy-map interface serial 1/0
Serial1/0
Service-policy output: AVVID (2022)
Class-map: platinum (match-all) (2035/5)
4253851 packets, 306277272 bytes
1 minute offered rate 499000 bps, drop rate 0 bps
Match: ip dscp 46 (2037)
Strict Priority
Output Queue: Conversation 264
Bandwidth 500 (kbps)
(pkts matched/bytes matched) 4248148/305866656
(total drops/bytes drops) 5/360
Class-map: silver (match-all) (2023/2)
251162 packets, 375236028 bytes
1 minute offered rate 612000 bps, drop rate 0 bps
Match: ip dscp 18 20 22 (2025)
Weighted Fair Queueing
Output Queue: Conversation 265
Bandwidth 25 (%)
(pkts matched/bytes matched) 3/4482
(depth/total drops/no-buffer drops) 0/0/0
mean queue depth: 0
Dscp Random drop Tail drop Minimum Maximum Mark
(Prec) pkts/bytes pkts/bytes threshold threshold probability
0(0) 0/0 0/0 20 40 1/10
1 0/0 0/0 22 40 1/10
2 0/0 0/0 24 40 1/10
3 0/0 0/0 26 40 1/10
4 0/0 0/0 28 40 1/10
(...up to DSCP 63......)
      61 0/0 0/0 30 40 1/10
62 0/0 0/0 32 40 1/10
63 0/0 0/0 34 40 1/10
rsvp 0/0 0/0 36 40 1/10
.
<OUTPUT DELETED>
.
Class-map: class-default (match-any) (2039/0)
4719109 packets, 1000522466 bytes
1 minute offered rate 1625000 bps, drop rate 0 bps
Match: any (2041)
4719109 packets, 1000522466 bytes
1 minute rate 1625000 bps
!
```

Foundation Summary

The "Foundation Summary" is a collection of information that provides a convenient review of many key concepts in this chapter. If you are already comfortable with the topics in this chapter, this summary can help you recall a few details. If you just read this chapter, this review should help solidify some key facts. If you are doing your final preparation before the exam, the information in this section is a convenient way to review the day before the exam.

Congestion happens when the rate of input (incoming traffic switched) to an interface exceeds the rate of output (outgoing traffic) from an interface. Aggregation, speed mismatch, and confluence are three common causes of congestion. Queuing is a congestion management technique that entails creating a few queues, assigning packets to those queues, and scheduling departure of packets from those queues. Table 4-2 provides a comparative summary for the queuing disciplines discussed in this chapter.

Table 4-2 *Comparison of FIFO, PQ, WRR (CQ), WFQ, CBWFQ, and LLQ*

Queuing Discipline	Default on Some Router Interfaces	Number of Queues	Allows User-Defined Classes	Allows User-Definable Interface Bandwidth Allocation	Provides a High-Priority Queue for Delay-Sensitive Traffic	Adequate for Both Delay-Sensitive and Mission-Critical Traffic	Configured Using MQC
FIFO	Yes	1	No	No	No	No	No
PQ	No	4	Yes	No	Yes	No	No
WRR (CQ)	No	User defined	Yes	Yes	No	No	No
WFQ	Yes	Number of active flows	No	No	No	No	No
CBWFQ	No	User defined	Yes	Yes	No	No	Yes
LLQ	No	User defined	Yes	Yes	Yes	Yes	Yes

Q&A

Some of the questions that follow challenge you more than the exam by using an open-ended question format. By reviewing now with this more difficult question format, you can exercise your memory better and prove your conceptual and factual knowledge of this chapter. The answers to these questions appear in Appendix A.

1. Why does congestion occur?
2. Define queuing.
3. What are three main tasks that congestion management/queuing mechanisms might perform?
4. What is the default queuing algorithm on Cisco router interfaces?
5. In what situation might FIFO be appropriate?
6. Describe priority queuing.
7. Cisco custom queuing is based on which queuing mechanism?
8. What are the Cisco router queuing components?
9. List the steps that a packet takes when it goes through an interface queuing system.
10. Describe WRR queuing.
11. Describe WFQ and its objectives.
12. How does WFQ define traffic flows?
13. Describe WFQ early dropping and aggressive dropping.
14. What are the benefits and drawbacks of WFQ?
15. What are the default values for CDT, dynamic queues, and reservable queues?
16. How do you adjust the hold queue size?
17. List at least two problems associated with PQ/CQ/WFQ.
18. Describe CBWFQ.
19. What are the three options for bandwidth reservation within CBWFQ?
20. How is available bandwidth calculated?
21. What are the benefits and drawbacks of CBWFQ?
22. How is CBWFQ configured?
23. Describe low-latency queuing.
24. What are the benefits of LLQ?
25. How do you configure LLQ?

This chapter covers the following subjects:

- Congestion Avoidance

- Traffic Shaping and Policing

- Link Efficiency Mechanisms

CHAPTER 5

Congestion Avoidance, Policing, Shaping, and Link Efficiency Mechanisms

This chapter intends to give you an overview of three main quality of service (QoS) concepts: congestion avoidance, traffic shaping and policing, and link efficiency mechanisms. Each concept is presented in its own section. WRED and class-based WRED are the main mechanisms covered in the "Congestion Avoidance" section. Traffic shaping and policing concepts are explained in the second section; you will learn the purpose of these mechanisms and where it is appropriate to use them. Different compression techniques, plus the concept of link fragmentation and interleaving, are the topics of discussion in the third and final section of this chapter.

"Do I Know This Already?" Quiz

The purpose of the "Do I Know This Already?" quiz is to help you decide whether you really need to read this entire chapter. The 12-question quiz, derived from the major sections of this chapter, helps you determine how to spend your limited study time.

Table 5-1 outlines the major topics discussed in this chapter and the "Do I Know This Already?" quiz questions that correspond to those topics. You can keep track of your score here, too.

Table 5-1 *"Do I Know This Already?" Foundation Topics Section-to-Question Mapping*

Foundation Topics Section Covering These Questions	Questions	Score
"Congestion Avoidance"	1–4	
"Traffic Shaping and Policing"	5–8	
"Link Efficiency Mechanisms"	9–12	
Total Score	**(12 possible)**	

CAUTION The goal of self-assessment is to gauge your mastery of the topics in this chapter. If you do not know the answer to a question or are only partially sure of the answer, mark this question wrong for purposes of the self-assessment. Giving yourself credit for an answer you correctly guess skews your self-assessment results and might provide you with a false sense of security.

You can find the answers to the "Do I Know This Already?" quiz in Appendix A, "Answers to the 'Do I Know This Already?' Quizzes and Q&A Sections." The suggested choices for your next step are as follows:

- **8 or less overall score**—Read the entire chapter. This includes the "Foundation Topics," "Foundation Summary," and "Q&A" sections.

- **9–10 overall score**—Begin with the "Foundation Summary" section and then follow up with the "Q&A" section at the end of the chapter.

- **11 or more overall score**—If you want more review on this topic, skip to the "Foundation Summary" section and then go to the "Q&A" section. Otherwise, proceed to the next chapter.

1. Which of the following is not a tail drop flaw?

   a. TCP synchronization

   b. TCP starvation

   c. TCP slow start

   d. No differentiated drop

2. Which of the following statements is not true about RED?

   a. RED randomly drops packets before the queue becomes full.

   b. RED increases the drop rate as the average queue size increases.

   c. RED has no per-flow intelligence.

   d. RED is always useful, without dependency on flow (traffic) types.

3. Which of the following is *not* a main parameter of a RED profile?

   a. Mark probability denominator

   b. Average transmission rate

   c. Maximum threshold

   d. Minimum threshold

4. Which of the following is *not* true about WRED?

   a. You cannot apply WRED to the same interface as CQ, PQ, and WFQ.

   b. WRED treats non-IP traffic as precedence 0.

   c. You normally use WRED in the core routers of a network.

   d. You should apply WRED to the voice queue.

5. Which of the following is *not* true about traffic shaping?

    a. It is applied in the outgoing direction only.

    b. Shaping can re-mark excess packets.

    c. Shaping buffers excess packets.

    d. It supports interaction with Frame Relay congestion indication.

6. Which of the following is *not* true about traffic policing?

    a. You apply it in the outgoing direction only.

    b. It can re-mark excess traffic.

    c. It can drop excess traffic.

    d. You can apply it in the incoming direction.

7. Which command is used for traffic policing in a class within a policy map?

    a. police

    b. drop

    c. remark

    d. maximum-rate

8. Which of the following does not apply to class-based shaping?

    a. It does not support FRF.12.

    b. It classifies per DLCI or subinterface.

    c. It understands FECN and BECN.

    d. It is supported via MQC.

9. Which of the following is not a valid statement about compression?

    a. Many compression techniques remove as much redundancy in data as possible.

    b. A single algorithm might yield different compression ratios for different data types.

    c. If available, compression is always recommended.

    d. Compression can be hardware based, hardware assisted, or software based.

10. Which of the following is not true about Layer 2 payload compression?

    a. It reduces the size of the frame payload.

    b. It reduces serialization delay.

    c. Software-based compression might yield better throughput than hardware-based compression.

    d. Layer 2 payload compression is recommended on all WAN links.

11. Which of the following is the only true statement about header compression?

    a. RTP header compression is not a type of header compression.

    b. Header compression compresses the header and payload.

    c. Header compression may be class based.

    d. Header compression is performed on a session-by-session (end-to-end) basis.

12. Which of the following is not true about fragmentation and interleaving?

    a. Fragmentation and interleaving is recommended when small delay-sensitive packets are present.

    b. Fragmentation result is not dependent on interleaving.

    c. Fragmentation and interleaving might be necessary, even if LLQ is configured on the interface.

    d. Fragmentation and interleaving is recommended on slow WAN links.

Foundation Topics

Congestion Avoidance

Congestion avoidance is used to avoid tail drop, which has several drawbacks. RED and its variations, namely WRED and CBWRED, are commonly used congestion-avoidance techniques used on Cisco router interfaces. Congestion avoidance is one of the main pieces of a QoS solution.

Tail Drop and Its Limitations

When the hardware queue (transmit queue, TxQ) is full, outgoing packets are queued in the interface software queue. If the software queue becomes full, new arriving packets are tail-dropped by default. The packets that are tail-dropped have high or low priorities and belong to different conversations (flows). Tail drop continues until the software queue has room. Tail drop has some limitations and drawbacks, including TCP global synchronization, TCP starvation, and lack of differentiated (or preferential) dropping.

When tail drop happens, TCP-based traffic flows simultaneously slow down (go into slow start) by reducing their TCP send window size. At this point, the bandwidth utilization drops significantly (assuming that there are many active TCP flows), interface queues become less congested, and TCP flows start to increase their window sizes. Eventually, interfaces become congested again, tail drops happen, and the cycle repeats. This situation is called *TCP global synchronization*. Figure 5-1 shows a diagram that is often used to display the effect of TCP global synchronization.

Figure 5-1 *TCP Global Synchronization*

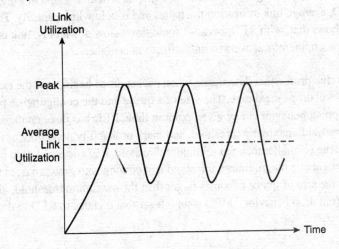

The symptom of TCP global synchronization, as shown in Figure 5-1, is waves of congestion followed by troughs during which time links are underutilized. Both overutilization, causing packet drops, and underutilization are undesirable. Applications suffer, and resources are wasted.

Queues become full when traffic is excessive and has no remedy, tail drop happens, and aggressive flows are not selectively punished. After tail drops begin, TCP flows slow down simultaneously, but other flows (non-TCP), such as User Datagram Protocol (UDP) and non-IP traffic, do not. Consequently, non-TCP traffic starts filling up the queues and leaves little or no room for TCP packets. This situation is called *TCP starvation*. In addition to global synchronization and TCP starvation, tail drop has one more flaw: it does not take packet priority or loss sensitivity into account. All arriving packets are dropped when the queue is full. This lack of differentiated dropping makes tail drop more devastating for loss-sensitive applications such as VoIP.

Random Early Detection

RED was invented as a mechanism to prevent tail drop. RED drops randomly selected packets before the queue becomes full. The rate of drops increases as the size of queue grows; better said, as the size of the queue grows, so does the probability of dropping incoming packets. RED does not differentiate among flows; it is not flow oriented. Basically, because RED selects the packets to be dropped randomly, it is (statistically) expected that packets belonging to aggressive (high volume) flows are dropped more than packets from the less aggressive flows.

Because RED ends up dropping packets from some but not all flows (expectedly more aggressive ones), all flows do not slow down and speed up at the same time, causing global synchronization. This means that during busy moments, link utilization does not constantly go too high and too low (as is the case with tail drop), causing inefficient use of bandwidth. In addition, average queue size stays smaller. You must recognize that RED is primarily effective when the bulk of flows are TCP flows; non-TCP flows do not slow down in response to RED drops. To demonstrate the effect of RED on link utilization, Figure 5-2 shows two graphs. The first graph in Figure 5-2 shows how, without RED, average link utilization fluctuates and is below link capacity. The second graph in Figure 5-2 shows that, with RED, because some flows slow down only, link utilization does not fluctuate as much; therefore, average link utilization is higher.

RED has a traffic profile that determines when packet drops begin, how the rate of drops change, and when packet drops maximize. The size of a queue and the configuration parameters of RED guide its dropping behavior at any given point in time. RED has three configuration parameters: minimum threshold, maximum threshold, and mark probability denominator (MPD). When the size of the queue is smaller than the minimum threshold, RED does not drop packets. As the size of queue grows above the minimum threshold and continues to grow, so does the rate of packet drops. When the size of queue becomes larger than the maximum threshold, all arriving packets are dropped (tail drop behavior). MPD is an integer that dictates to RED to drop 1 of MPD (as many packets as the value of mark probability denominator), while the size of queue is between the values of minimum and maximum thresholds.

Figure 5-2 *Comparison of Link Utilization with and Without RED*

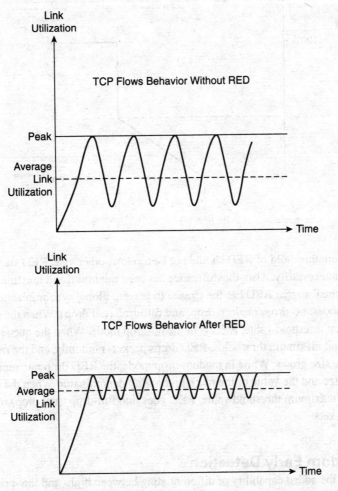

For example, if the MPD value is set to 10 and the queue size is between minimum and maximum threshold, RED drops one out of ten packets. This means that the probability of an arriving packet being dropped is 10 percent. Figure 5-3 is a graph that shows a packet drop probability of 0 when the queue size is below the minimum threshold. It also shows that the drop probability increases as the queue size grows. When the queue size reaches and exceeds the value of the maximum threshold, the probability of packet drop equals 1, which means that packet drop will happen with 100 percent certainty.

Figure 5-3 *RED Profile Demonstration*

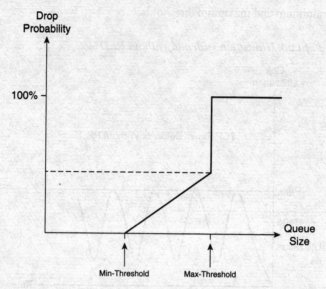

The minimum threshold of RED should not be too low; otherwise, RED starts dropping packets too early, unnecessarily. Also, the difference between minimum and maximum thresholds should not be too small so that RED has the chance to prevent global synchronization. RED essentially has three modes: no-drop, random-drop, and full-drop (tail drop). When the queue size is below the minimum threshold value, RED is in the no-drop mode. When the queue size is between the minimum and maximum thresholds, RED drops packets randomly, and the rate increases linearly as the queue size grows. While in random-drop mode, the RED drop rate remains proportional to the queue size and the value of the mark probability denominator. When the queue size grows beyond the maximum threshold value, RED goes into full-drop (tail drop) mode and drops all arriving packets.

Weighted Random Early Detection

WRED has the added capability of differentiating between high- and low-priority traffic, compared to RED. With WRED, you can set up a different profile (with a minimum threshold, maximum threshold, and mark probability denominator) for each traffic priority. Traffic priority is based on IP precedence or DSCP values. Figure 5-4 shows an example in which the minimum threshold for traffic with IP precedence values 0, 1, and 2 is set to 20; the minimum threshold for traffic with IP precedence values 3, 4, and 5 is set to 26; and the minimum threshold for traffic with IP precedence values 6 and 7 is set to 32. In Figure 5-4, the minimum threshold for RSVP traffic is set to 38, the maximum threshold for all traffic is 40, and the MPD is set to 10 for all traffic.

Figure 5-4 *Weighted RED Profiles*

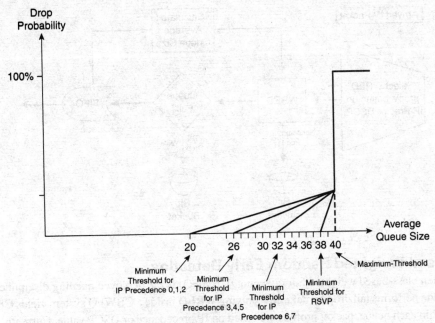

WRED considers RSVP traffic as drop sensitive, so traffic from non-RSVP flows are dropped before RSVP flows. On the other hand, non-IP traffic flows are considered least important and are dropped earlier than traffic from other flows. WRED is a complementary technique to congestion management, and it is expected to be applied to core devices. However, you should not apply WRED to voice queues. Voice traffic is extremely drop sensitive and is UDP based. Therefore, you must classify VoIP as the highest priority traffic class so that the probability of dropping VoIP becomes very low.

WRED is constantly calculating the current average queue length based on the current queue length and the last average queue length. When a packet arrives, first based on its IP precedence or DSCP value, its profile is recognized. Next, based on the packet profile and the current average queue length, the packet can become subject to random drop. If the packet is not random-dropped, it might still be tail-dropped. An undropped packet is queued (FIFO), and the current queue size is updated. Figure 5-5 shows this process.

Figure 5-5 *WRED Operation*

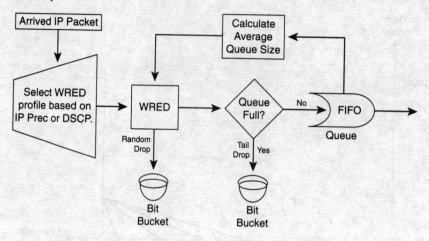

Class-Based Weighted Random Early Detection

When class-based weighted fair queueing (CBWFQ) is the deployed queuing discipline, each queue performs tail drop by default. Applying WRED inside a CBWFQ system yields CBWRED; within each queue, packet profiles are based on IP precedence or DSCP value. Currently, the only way to enforce assured forwarding (AF) per-hop behavior (PHB) on a Cisco router is by applying WRED to the queues within a CBWFQ system. Note that low-latency queuing (LLQ) is composed of a strict-priority queue (policed) and a CBWFQ system. Therefore, applying WRED to the CBWFQ component of the LLQ yields AF behavior, too. The strict-priority queue of an LLQ enforces expedited forwarding (EF) PHB.

Configuring CBWRED

WRED is enabled on an interface by entering the **random-detect** command in the IOS interface configuration mode. By default, WRED is based on IP precedence; therefore, eight profiles exist, one for each IP precedence value. If WRED is DSCP based, there are 64 possible profiles. Non-IP traffic is treated equivalent to IP traffic with IP precedence equal to 0. WRED cannot be configured on an interface simultaneously with custom queuing (CQ), priority queuing (PQ), or weighted fair queuing (WFQ). Because WRED is usually applied to network core routers, this does not impose a problem. WRED has little performance impact on core routers.

To perform CBWRED, you must enter the **random-detect** command for each class within the policy map. WRED is precedence-based by default, but you can configure it to be DSCP-based if desired. Each traffic profile (IP precedence or DSCP based) has default values, but you can modify those values based on administrative needs. For each IP precedence value or DSCP value, you can set a profile by specifying a min-threshold, max-threshold, and a mark-probability-denominator. With the default hold-queue size within the range 0 to 4096, the min-threshold minimum value is

1 and the max-threshold maximum value is 4096. The default value for the mark probability denominator is 10. The commands for enabling DSCP-based WRED and for configuring the minimum-threshold, maximum-threshold, and mark-probability denominator for each DSCP value and for each IP precedence value within a policy-map class are as follows:

```
Router(router-policy-c)# random-detect dscp-based
Router(router-policy-c)# random-detect dscp dscp-value min-threshold
    max-threshold mark-prob-denominator
Router(router-policy-c)# random-detect precedence precedence-value
    min-threshold max-threshold mark-prob-denominator
```

Applying WRED to each queue within a CBWFQ system changes the default tail-dropping behavior of that queue. Furthermore, within each queue, WRED can have a different profile for each precedence or DSCP value. Example 5-1 shows two class maps (Business and Bulk) and a policy map called Enterprise that references those class maps. Class Business is composed of packets with IP precedence values 3 and 4, and 30 percent of the interface bandwidth is dedicated to it. The packets with precedence 4 are considered low drop packets compared to the packets with a precedence value of 3 (high drop packets). Class Bulk is composed of packets with IP precedence values of 1 and 2 and is given 20 percent of the interface bandwidth. The packets with a precedence value of 2 are considered low drop packets compared to the packets with a precedence value of 1 (high drop packets). The policy map shown in Example 5-1 applies fair-queue and random-detect to the class class-default and provides it with the remainder of interface bandwidth. Note that you can apply fair-queue and random-detect simultaneously to the class-default only.

Example 5-1 *CBWRED: IP Precedence Based*

```
class-map Business
 match ip precedence 3 4
class-map Bulk
 match ip precedence 1 2
!
policy-map Enterprise
 class Business
  bandwidth percent 30
  random-detect
  random-detect precedence 3 26 40 10
  random-detect precedence 4 28 40 10
 class Bulk
  bandwidth percent 20
  random-detect
  random-detect precedence 1 22 36 10
  random-detect precedence 2 24 36 10
 class class-default
  fair-queue
  random-detect
!
```

Please remember that you cannot simultaneously apply WRED and WFQ to a class policy. (WRED **random-detect** and WFQ **queue-limit** commands are mutually exclusive.) Whereas WRED has its own method of dropping packets based on max-threshold values per profile, WFQ effectively tail-drops packets based on the queue-limit value. Recall that you cannot apply WRED and PQ, CQ, or WFQ to an interface simultaneously either.

Example 5-2 shows a CBWRED case that is similar to the one given in Example 5-1; however, Example 5-2 is DSCP based. All AF2s plus CS2 form the class Business, and all AF1s plus CS1 form the class Bulk. Within the policy map Enterprise, class Business is given 30 percent of the interface bandwidth, and DSCP-based random-detect is applied to its queue. For each AF and CS value, the min-threshold, max-threshold, and mark-probability-denominator are configured to form four profiles within the queue. Class Bulk, on the other hand, is given 20 percent of the interface bandwidth, and DSCP-based random-detect is applied to its queue. For each AF and CS value, the min-threshold, max-threshold, and mark-probability-denominator are configured to form four profiles within that queue.

Example 5-2   *CBWRED: DSCP Based*

```
class-map Business
 match ip dscp af21 af22 af23 cs2
class-map Bulk
 match ip dscp af11 af12 af13 cs1
!
policy-map Enterprise
 class Business
  bandwidth percent 30
  random-detect dscp-based
  random-detect dscp af21 32 40 10
  random-detect dscp af22 28 40 10
  random-detect dscp af23 24 40 10
  random-detect dscp cs2  22 40 10
 class Bulk
  bandwidth percent 20
  random-detect dscp-based
  random-detect dscp af11 32 36 10
  random-detect dscp af12 28 36 10
  random-detect dscp af13 24 36 10
  random-detect dscp cs1  22 36 10
 class class-default
  fair-queue
  random-detect dscp-based
!
```

In Example 5-2, similar to Example 5-1, the **fair-queue** and **random-detect** commands are applied to the class-default class. In Example 5-2 however, random-detect is DSCP-based as opposed to Example 5-1, where the class-default random-detect is based on IP precedence by default.

Use the **show policy-map interface** *interface* command to see the packet statistics for classes on the specified interface or PVC. (Service policy must be attached to the interface or the PVC.) The counters that are displayed in the output of this command are updated only if congestion is present on the interface. Note that the **show policy-map interface** command displays policy information about Frame Relay PVCs only if Frame Relay traffic shaping (FRTS) is enabled on the interface; moreover, ECN marking information is displayed only if ECN is enabled on the interface. Example 5-3 shows a policy map called sample-policy that forms an LLQ. This policy assigns voice class to the strict priority queue with 128 kbps reserved bandwidth, assigns gold class to a queue from the CBWFQ system with 100 kbps bandwidth reserved, and assigns the silver class to another queue from the CBWFQ system with 80 kbps bandwidth reserved and RED applied to it.

Example 5-3 *A Sample Policy Map Implementing LLQ*

```
policy-map sample-policy
  class voice
    priority 128
  class gold
  bandwidth 100
  class silver
  bandwidth 80
  random-detect
```

Example 5-4 shows sample output of the **show policy-map interface** command for the serial 3/1 interface with the sample-policy (shown in Example 5-3) applied to it.

Example 5-4 *Monitoring CBWFQ*

```
Router# show policy-map interface serial3/1

 Serial3/1

  Service-policy output: sample-policy

    Class-map: voice (match-all)
      0 packets, 0 bytes
      5 minute offered rate 0 bps, drop rate 0 bps
      Match: ip precedence 5
      Weighted Fair Queueing
        Strict Priority
        Output Queue: Conversation 264
        Bandwidth 128 (kbps) Burst 3200 (Bytes)
        (pkts matched/bytes matched) 0/0
        (total drops/bytes drops) 0/0
```

continues

Example 5-4 *Monitoring CBWFQ (Continued)*

```
Class-map: gold (match-all)
  0 packets, 0 bytes
  5 minute offered rate 0 bps, drop rate 0 bps
  Match: ip precedence 2
  Weighted Fair Queueing
    Output Queue: Conversation 265
    Bandwidth 100 (kbps) Max Threshold 64 (packets)
    (pkts matched/bytes matched) 0/0
    (depth/total drops/no-buffer drops) 0/0/0

Class-map: silver (match-all)
  0 packets, 0 bytes
  5 minute offered rate 0 bps, drop rate 0 bps
  Match: ip precedence 1
  Weighted Fair Queueing
    Output Queue: Conversation 266
    Bandwidth 80 (kbps)
    (pkts matched/bytes matched) 0/0
    (depth/total drops/no-buffer drops) 0/0/0
    exponential weight: 9
    mean queue depth: 0
```

class	Transmitted pkts/bytes	Random drop pkts/bytes	Tail drop pkts/bytes	Minimum thresh	Maximum thresh	Mark prob
0	0/0	0/0	0/0	20	40	1/10
1	0/0	0/0	0/0	22	40	1/10
2	0/0	0/0	0/0	24	40	1/10
3	0/0	0/0	0/0	26	40	1/10
4	0/0	0/0	0/0	28	40	1/10
5	0/0	0/0	0/0	30	40	1/10
6	0/0	0/0	0/0	32	40	1/10
7	0/0	0/0	0/0	34	40	1/10
rsvp	0/0	0/0	0/0	36	40	1/10

```
Class-map: class-default (match-any)
  0 packets, 0 bytes
  5 minute offered rate 0 bps, drop rate 0 bps
  Match: any
!
```

In Example 5-4, WRED is applied only to the silver class, and WRED is IP precedence-based by default. On the output of the **show** command for the silver class, you can observe the statistics for nine profiles: eight precedence levels plus RSVP flow.

Traffic Shaping and Policing

Traffic shaping and policing are two different mechanisms for traffic conditioning. Both mechanisms measure the rate of different traffic classes against a policy or SLA. SLA stands for service level agreement, and it is usually set up between an enterprise and a service provider with regard to bandwidth, traffic rates, reliability, availability, QoS, and billing matters. Traffic shaping usually buffers the traffic that is in excess of the policy/agreement. Policing either drops the excess traffic or changes its marking to a lower level (re-marking). Therefore, traffic shaping is applied on an interface in the outbound direction, but traffic policing can be applied in either the inbound or outbound direction. These traffic-conditioning mechanisms are often deployed at network edge.

Because traffic policing merely drops or re-marks excess traffic, it does not impose delay to the conforming (non-excess) traffic. If the excess traffic is dropped, it has to be retransmitted. Traffic policing can re-mark and transmit excess traffic instead of dropping it. Traffic shaping buffers excess traffic and releases it steadily based on the policy specifications. Traffic shaping comes in many variations, including class-based traffic shaping, FRTS, generic traffic shaping (GTS). Cisco IOS traffic-shaping tools do not provide the means for re-marking traffic.

The main purposes for traffic policing are as follows:

- **To limit the traffic rate to a value less than the physical access rate**—This is called enforcing subrate access. When the customer pays for an access rate (for example, 1.544 Mbps) that is less than the physical access rate (for example, 155.52 Mbps) between customer and service provider facilities, the provider uses rate limiting (policing) to enforce the subrate value.

- **To limit the traffic rate for each traffic class**—When an enterprise and service provider have an SLA that states the maximum rate for each traffic class (or marking), the provider uses traffic policing to enforce that SLA (at the edge).

- **To re-mark traffic**—Traffic is usually re-marked if it exceeds the rate specified in the SLA. Cisco IOS traffic policing allows you to mark and re-mark Layer 2 and Layer 3 protocol data units (PDU) such as IP precedence, IP DiffServ Codepoint (DSCP), Ethernet 802.1Q/p class of service (CoS), Frame Relay DE, and so on.

Following are the main purposes for traffic shaping:

- **To slow down the rate of traffic being sent to another site through a WAN service such as Frame Relay or ATM**—If the remote site or the carrier network becomes congested, the sending device is usually notified (such as by Frame Relay backward explicit congestion notification, or BECN), and it can buffer the traffic and drop its sending rate until the network condition improves. Different access rates at two sites connected via a wide area service is a common situation called *asymmetric circuit end access bandwidth*. However, sometimes the receiving end becomes congested and the senders have to slow down through shaping not due to asymmetric bandwidths, but because many sites send traffic to a single site at once; this is called *aggregation*.

■ **To comply with the subscribed rate**—A customer must apply traffic shaping to the traffic being sent to the service provider WAN (FR or ATM) or Metro Ethernet networks.

■ **To send different traffic classes at different rates**—If an SLA specifies a particular maximum rate for each traffic class (with specific markings), the sender must perform class-based traffic shaping to prevent traffic from being dropped or re-marked.

Figure 5-6 shows an enterprise that has a central site and three remote sites connected using Frame Relay virtual circuits. All the access rates at these sites are different. If the central site sends traffic at 1.544 Mbps (T1) to site A, then site A, which has a 512-Kbps access rate, will have congestion and possibly drops. To avoid that, the central site can shape the traffic being sent to site A. The rate mismatch between the central site and site A is an example of an asymmetric bandwidth situation. What will happen if sites A, B, and C simultaneously send traffic to the central site? In that case, if all remote sites send traffic at their maximum access rates, congestion will result, this time at the central site; that is because the aggregate traffic from the remote sites exceeds the access rate at the central site.

Figure 5-6 *Speed Mismatch and Aggregation Require Traffic Shaping*

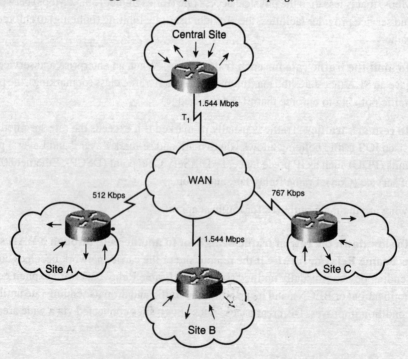

Where does traffic shaping and traffic policing usually take place? The CE devices can perform policing on the interfaces facing inside their site and enforce traffic rates. For instance, bulk traffic such as file-transfer over the WAN can be limited to a specific rate. Service providers usually perform policing on the edge device of their network on the interface receiving or sending traffic to the customer devices. Traffic shaping is often performed on the customer edge (CE) device, outbound on the interface sending traffic to remote sites over the provider backbone.

Traffic shaping and policing similarities and differences are as follows:

- Both traffic shaping and traffic policing measure traffic; sometimes, different traffic classes are measured separately.

- Policing can be applied to the inbound and outbound traffic (with respect to an interface), but traffic shaping applies only to outbound traffic.

- Shaping buffers excess traffic and sends it according to a preconfigured rate, whereas policing drops or re-marks excess traffic.

- Shaping requires memory for buffering excess traffic, which creates variable delay and jitter. Policing does not require extra memory, and it does not impose variable delay.

- If policing drops packets, certain flow types such as TCP-based flows will resend dropped traffic. Non-TCP traffic might resend a lot more traffic than just the dropped ones.

- Policing can re-mark traffic, but traffic shaping does not re-mark traffic.

- Traffic shaping can be configured based on network conditions and signals, but policing does not respond to network conditions and signals.

Measuring Traffic Rates

The operating systems on Cisco devices measure traffic rates using a bucket and token scheme. The token and bucket scheme has a few variations: single bucket with single rate, dual bucket with single rate, and dual bucket with dual rates. The Cisco ONT course covers only the single bucket with single rate model. To transmit one byte of data, the bucket must have one token. Tokens are put into the bucket at the rate equivalent to the SLA rate; for example, for a Frame Relay virtual circuit, the committed information rate (CIR) is used as the guide to replenish tokens in the bucket. If the size of data to be transmitted (in bytes) is smaller than the number of tokens, the traffic is called *conforming*; when traffic conforms, as many tokens as the size of data are removed from the bucket, and the conform action, which is usually forward data, is performed. If the size of data to be transmitted (in bytes) is larger than the number of tokens, the traffic is called *exceeding*. In the exceed situation, tokens are not removed from the bucket, but the action performed (exceed action) is either buffer and send data later (in the case of shaping) or drop or mark data (in the case of policing).

Figure 5-7 shows that tokens are dropped into the bucket based on an SLA rate; it also shows that if the bucket becomes full, excess tokens spill and are wasted in the single bucket model. Furthermore, Figure 5-7 shows that when traffic is forwarded one token is needed for each byte of data.

Figure 5-7   *Single Bucket, Single Rate Token Bucket Scheme*

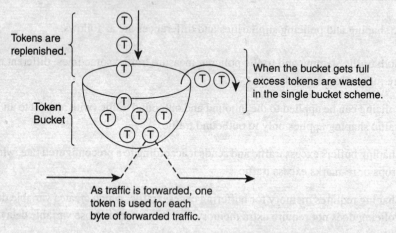

It is important to know the definitions and relationships between the parameters within the token bucket scheme. CIR stands for committed information rate, B_c stands for committed burst, and T_c stands for committed time interval. The relationship between these parameters is as follows:

$$CIR \text{ (bits per second)} = B_c \text{ (bits)} / T_c \text{ (seconds)}$$

Instead of continuously dropping tokens into the bucket, and when the bucket is full, discarding the just-added tokens, the operating system adds tokens to the buckets only when there is traffic activity. Every time a packet arrives, the operating system computes the time difference between the arrival time of the new packet and the arrival time of the last packet, and for the time difference computed, it adds the appropriate number of tokens according to this formula:

$$\text{Number of tokens added} = \text{time difference (sec)} \times CIR / 8$$

The time difference between the current packet arrival time and the previous packet arrival time is computed in seconds and then multiplied by CIR (which is expressed in bits per seconds) to compute the number of bits. Then the result is divided by eight to compute the number of bytes. The number of bytes computed indicates the number of tokens that should have been added to the token bucket during the time between the arrival of the last packet and the arrival of the current packet. The computed number of tokens is added to the bucket right away. The total number of tokens (bytes) in the bucket cannot exceed the B_c value. Any extra tokens are discarded and therefore wasted. Administrators usually specify the CIR and B_c values and let the system compute the T_c value automatically. The larger the B_c value, the larger burst of data that is possible; with a large B_c value, the bucket saves more tokens.

Cisco IOS Policing and Shaping Mechanisms

Cisco IOS offers class-based traffic policing. Using modular QoS command-line interface (MQC), class-based traffic policing is applied to a class within a policy map with the **police** command. As stated in the previous section, Cisco IOS offers different Token Bucket schemes for policing: single bucket/single rate, dual bucket/single rate, and dual bucket/dual rate. Furthermore, multiaction policing—meaning taking multiple actions when traffic conforms, exceeds, or violates—is also supported by class-based traffic policing. In addition to Cisco routers, class-based traffic policing is available on some Cisco Catalyst switches.

Cisco IOS also offers class-based traffic shaping. Using MQC, class-based traffic shaping is applied to a class within a policy map. When used in combination with CBWFQ, class-based traffic shaping controls the upper limit of the outgoing traffic rate for a class, while the bandwidth statement guarantees the minimum bandwidth or rate for that class.

Frame Relay traffic shaping controls Frame Relay traffic only and can be applied to a Frame Relay subinterface or Frame Relay DLCI. Whereas Frame relay traffic shaping supports Frame Relay fragmentation and interleaving (FRF.12), class-based traffic shaping does not. On the other hand, both class-based traffic shaping and Frame Relay traffic shaping interact with and support Frame Relay network congestion signals such as BECN and forward explicit congestion notification (FECN). A router that is receiving BECNs shapes its outgoing Frame Relay traffic to a lower rate. If it receives FECNs, even if it has no traffic for the other end, it sends test frames with the BECN bit set to inform the other end to slow down.

Enterprises apply traffic policing at the access and distribution layers to control traffic entering the core or leaving the campus toward the WAN circuits. Most enterprises apply traffic shaping on the interfaces of the edge devices connected to WAN service. Traffic shaping is useful when speed mismatch or aggregation occurs and you want to avoid congestion and drops. Service providers apply traffic policing on the interfaces of the edge devices receiving traffic from customers; this helps them meter different traffic class rates against the SLA rates. Service providers also apply traffic shaping on the edge devices, sending traffic to customer sites.

Link Efficiency Mechanisms

The main link efficiency mechanisms deployed today are compression- and fragmentation-based. There are several types of compression: link compression, layer 2 payload compression, RTP header compression, and TCP header compression. Fragmentation is usually combined with interleaving. Compression makes link utilization more efficient, and it is a QoS technique that actually makes more bandwidth available. Fragmentation aims at reducing the expected delay of packets by reducing the maximum packet size over a circuit or connection. Compression is a technique used in many of the link efficiency mechanisms. Compression reduces the size of data to be transferred; therefore, it increases throughput and reduces overall delay. Many compression algorithms have been developed over time. An example for a compression algorithm is Lempel-Ziv (LZ) used by Stacker compression. Most compression algorithms take advantage of and remove the repeated patterns and redundancy in data. One main difference between compression algorithms is the type of data the algorithm has been optimized for. For example, MPEG has been developed for and works well for compressing video, whereas the Huffman algorithm compresses text-based data well.

The success of compression algorithms is measured and expressed by the ratio of raw data to compressed data; a ratio of 2:1 is common. According to Shannon's theorem, compression has a theoretical limit; it is believed that algorithms of today that run on high-end CPUs can reach the highest possible compression levels. If compression is hardware based, the main CPU cycles are not used; on the other hand, if compression is software based, the main CPU is interrupted and its cycles are used for performing compression. For that reason, when possible, hardware compression is recommended over software compression. Some compression options are Layer 2 payload compression and upper layer (Layer 3 and 4) header compression.

Layer 2 Payload Compression

Layer 2 payload compression, as the name implies, compresses the entire payload of a Layer 2 frame. For example, if a Layer 2 frame encapsulates an IP packet, the entire IP packet is compressed. Layer 2 payload compression is performed on a link-by-link basis; it can be performed on WAN connections such as PPP, Frame Relay, high-level data link control (HDLC), X.25, and Link Access Procedure, Balanced (LAPB). Cisco IOS supports Stacker, Predictor, and Microsoft Point-to-Point Compression (MPPC) as Layer 2 compression methods. The primary difference between these methods is their overhead and utilization of CPU and memory.

Because Layer 2 payload compression reduces the size of the frame, serialization delay is reduced. Increase in available bandwidth (hence throughput) depends on the algorithm efficiency. Depending on the complexity of the compression algorithm and whether the compression is software based or hardware based (or hardware assisted), compression introduces some amount of delay. However, overall delay (latency) is reduced, especially on low-speed links, whenever Layer 2 compression is used. Layer 2 payload compression is useful over circuits or connections that require the Layer 2 headers to remain in tact. For example, over a Frame Relay or ATM circuit you can use Layer 2 payload compression. Link compression, on the other hand, compresses the entire Layer 2 data unit including its header, which won't work over Frame Relay and ATM, but would work well over PPP or HDLC connections.

Figure 5-8 shows three cases, the first of which makes no use of payload compression. The second and third scenarios in Figure 5-8 use software-based and hardware-based Layer 2 payload compression, respectively. Hardware compression and hardware-assisted compression are recommended, because they are more CPU efficient than software-based compression. The throughput gain that a Layer 2 payload compression algorithm yields depends on the algorithm itself and has no dependency on whether it is software or hardware based. In Figure 5-8, hardware compression resulted in the least overall delay, but its software compression counterpart yielded better throughput results.

Figure 5-8 *Layer 2 Payload Compression Options and Results*

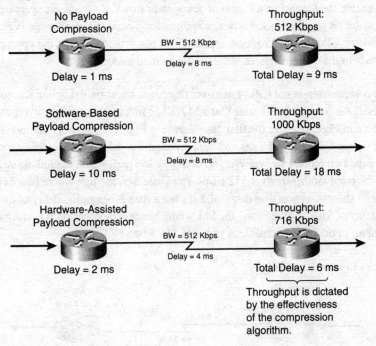

Header Compression

Header compression reduces serialization delay and results in less bandwidth usage, yielding more throughput and more available bandwidth. As the name implies, header compression compresses headers only; for example, RTP header compression compresses Real-time Transport Protocol (RTP), User Datagram Protocol (UDP), and IP headers, but it does not compress the application data. This makes header compression especially useful for cases in which application payload size is small. Without header compression, the header (overhead)-to-payload (data) ratio is large, but with header compression, the overhead-to-data ratio reduces significantly.

Common header compression options such as TCP header compression and RTP header compression use a simple yet effective technique. Because the headers of the packets in a single flow are identical (some exceptions may apply), instead of sending the identical (and relatively large) header with every packet, a number or index that refers to that entire header is sent instead. This technique is based on a dictionary style of compression algorithms, in which phrases or blocks of data are replaced with a short reference to that phrase or block of data. The receiving end, based on the reference number or index, places the real header back on the packet and forwards it.

When you enable TCP or RTP header compression on a link, all TCP or RTP flows are header-compressed as a result. First, note that this is done on a link-by-link basis. Second, note that you cannot enable the feature on a subset of sessions or flows. If you plan to perform header compression on specific packet types or applications, what you need to do is class-based header compression. Class-based header compression is performed by applying appropriate IOS commands to the desired classes within a policy map using MQC.

Header compression is not CPU-intensive; therefore, the extra delay introduced due to header compression is negligible. Assume that a 512-Kbps link exists between two routers, similar to the one shown in Figure 5-9. In the first case shown in Figure 5-9, header compression is not used, and the forwarding delay of 1 ms and data propagation delay of 8 ms yield a total delay of 9 ms between the two routers shown. With no compression performed, the link throughput is the same as the link bandwidth, which is 512 Kbps. In Figure 5-9, the link where header compression is performed shows a processing delay of 2 ms but a data propagation delay of only 4 ms, yielding a total delay of 6 ms. Furthermore, the link where header compression is performed provides more throughput, in this case a total throughput of 716 Kbps.

Figure 5-9 *Header Compression Results*

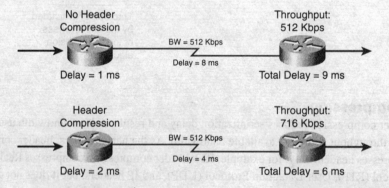

If the links shown in Figure 5-9 are configured as PPP links and RTP packets carry 20-byte voice payloads through them, the header (overhead) to payload (data) ratio can be reduced significantly with RTP header compression. Since a PPP header is 6 bytes long and RTP/UDP/IP headers add up to 40 bytes, the header to payload ratio is (40 + 6) / 20, which equals 230 percent without RTP header compression. On the other hand, with RTP header compression, if the no checksum option is used, the RTP/UDP/IP header is reduced to 2 bytes only; the header (overhead)-to-payload (data) ratio in this case reduces to (2 + 6) / 20, which equals 40 percent.

Link Fragmentation and Interleaving

When an interface is congested, packets first go through the software queue and then are forwarded to the hardware queue; when the interface has no congestion, packets skip the software queue and go straight to the hardware queue. You can use advanced queuing methods such as LLQ to minimize the software queuing delay that delay-sensitive packets such as VoIP experience.

Packets must always go through the hardware queue, which is FIFO based. If a VoIP packet ends up behind one or more large packets in the hardware queue, it might experience too much delay in that area and end up going over its total end-to-end delay budget. The goal for the end-to-end delay budget of a VoIP packet (one-way) is 150 ms to 200 ms.

Imagine that a VoIP packet ends up in a Tx (HW) queue behind a 1500-byte frame that has to be transmitted by the interface hardware out of a 256-Kbps link. The amount of time that the VoIP packet has to wait for transmission of the 1500-byte frame ahead of it is 47 ms (1500 (bytes) × 8 (bits/byte) / 256000 (bits/sec)). Typically, during the design phase, a 10- to 15-ms delay budget is allocated to serialization on slow links. This example clearly demonstrates that with the presence of large data units, the delay will go much beyond the normally expected value.

It is possible to mitigate the delay imposed by the large data units ahead of VoIP (or other delay-sensitive packets) in the hardware (Tx) queue. The solution is fragmentation and interleaving (LFI). You must enable fragmentation on a link and specify the maximum data unit size (called *fragment size*). Fragmentation must be accompanied by interleaving; otherwise, fragmentation will have no effect. Interleaving allows packets of different flows to get between fragments of large data units in the queue.

Applying Link Efficiency Mechanisms

Link efficiency mechanisms discussed in this section might not be necessary on all interfaces and links. It is important that you identify network bottlenecks and work on the problem spots. On fast links, many link efficiency mechanisms are not supported, and if they are, they might have negative results. On slow links and where bottlenecks are recognized, you must calculate the overhead-to-data ratios and consider all compression options. On some links, you can perform full link compression. On some, you can perform Layer 2 payload compression, and on others, you will probably perform header compression such as RTP or TCP header compression only. Link fragmentation and interleaving is always a good option to consider on slow links. It is noteworthy that compounding compression methods usually has an adverse affect and slows down throughput.

At the WAN edge on WAN links with equal or less bandwidth than T1/E1, it is recommended to enable both TCP/RTP header compression and LFI. These improve WAN link utilization and reduce the serialization delay. Because Layer 2 payload compression is CPU-intensive, it is recommended only if it can be hardware-based or hardware-assisted.

Foundation Summary

The "Foundation Summary" is a collection of information that provides a convenient review of many key concepts in this chapter. If you are already comfortable with the topics in this chapter, this summary can help you recall a few details. If you just read this chapter, this review should help solidify some key facts. If you are doing your final preparation before the exam, the information in this section is a convenient way to review the day before the exam.

Tail drop is the default queuing response to congestion. It has three significant drawbacks:

■ **TCP synchronization**—Packet drops from many sessions at the same time cause TCP sessions to slow down (decrease send windows size) and speed up (increase send window) at the same time, causing inefficient link utilization.

■ **TCP starvation**—Aggressive and non-TCP flows might fill up the queues, leaving little or no room for other less aggressive applications and TCP packets (specially after slowdown).

■ **No differentiated drop**—Tail drop does not punish aggressive flows in particular, and it does not differentiate between high- and low-priority packets.

RED avoids tail drop by randomly dropping packets when the queue size is above a min-threshold value, and it increases drop rate as the average queue size increases. RED has the following benefits:

■ Only the TCP sessions whose packets are dropped slow down.

■ The average queue size is kept small, reducing the chances of tail drop.

■ Link utilization becomes higher and more efficient.

RED, or RED profile, is configured using three parameters: minimum threshold, maximum threshold, and mark probability denominator. When the average queue size is below the minimum threshold, RED is in the no-drop mode. When the average queue size is between the minimum threshold and the maximum threshold, RED is in random-drop mode. When the average queue size is above the maximum threshold, RED is in full-drop mode.

WRED can use multiple profiles based on IP precedence (up to 8 profiles) or DSCP (up to 64 profiles). Using profiles, WRED can drop less important packets more aggressively than more important packets. You can apply WRED to an interface, a virtual circuit (VC), or a class within a policy map. The last case is called WRED, or CBWRED. CBWRED is configured in combination with CBWFQ.

Traffic-shaping and policing are traffic-conditioning tools. These mechanisms classify packets and measure traffic rates. Shaping queues excess packets to stay within a desired rate, whereas policing either re-marks or drops excess packets to keep them within a rate limit.

Policing is used to do the following:

- Limit access to resources when high-speed access is used but not desired (subrate access)

- Limit the traffic rate of certain applications or traffic classes

- Mark down (recolor) exceeding traffic at Layer 2 or Layer 3

Shaping is used to do the following:

- Prevent and manage congestion in ATM, Frame Relay, and Metro Ethernet networks, where asymmetric bandwidths are used along the traffic path.

- Regulate the sending traffic rate to match the subscribed (committed) rate in ATM, Frame Relay, or Metro Ethernet networks.

Following are the similarities and differences between policing and shaping:

- Both traffic shaping and traffic policing measure traffic. (Sometimes, different traffic classes are measured separately.)

- Policing can be applied to the inbound and outbound traffic (with respect to an interface), but traffic shaping applies only to outbound traffic.

- Shaping buffers excess traffic and sends it according to a preconfigured rate, whereas policing drops or re-marks excess traffic.

- Shaping requires memory for buffering excess traffic, which creates variable delay and jitter; policing does not require extra memory, and it does not impose variable delay.

- Policing can re-mark traffic, but traffic shaping does not re-mark traffic.

- Traffic shaping can be configured to shape traffic based on network conditions and signals, but policing does not respond to network conditions and signals.

The operating systems on Cisco devices measure traffic rates using a bucket and token scheme. The important points to remember about a token bucket scheme are these:

- To be able to transmit 1 byte of data, the bucket must have one token.

- If the size of data to be transmitted (in bytes) is smaller than the number of tokens, the traffic is called *conforming*. When traffic conforms, as many tokens as the size of data are removed from the bucket, and the conform action, which is usually forward data, is performed.

■ If the size of data to be transmitted (in bytes) is larger than the number of tokens, the traffic is called *exceeding*. In the exceed situation, tokens are not removed from the bucket, but the action performed (exceed action) is either buffer and send data later (in case of shaping), or it is drop or mark data (in the case of policing).

Similarities and differences between class-based shaping and FRTS are as follows:

■ FRTS controls Frame Relay traffic only and can be applied to a Frame Relay subinterface or Frame Relay DLCI.

■ Whereas Frame Relay traffic shaping supports Frame Relay fragmentation and interleaving (FRF.12), class-based traffic shaping does not.

■ Both class-based traffic shaping and FRTS interact with and support Frame Relay network congestion signals such as BECN and FECN.

■ A router that is receiving BECNs shapes its outgoing Frame Relay traffic to a lower rate, and if it receives FECNs, even if it has no traffic for the other end, it sends test frames with the BECN bit set to inform the other end to slow down.

Compression identifies patterns in data and removes redundancy as much as possible. It increases throughput and decreases latency. Many compression algorithms exist for different types of data. Hardware compression (or hardware-assisted) is preferred over software compression because it does not use main CPU cycles. Payload compression reduces the size of the payload. Header compression reduces the header overhead.

Link efficiency mechanisms are often deployed on WAN links to increase the throughput and decrease the delay and jitter. Cisco IOS link efficiency mechanisms include the following:

■ Layer 2 payload compression (Stacker, Predictor, MPPC)

■ Header compression (TCP, RTP, and class-based)

■ Link Fragmentation and Interleaving (LFI)

Q&A

Some of the questions that follow challenge you more than the exam by using an open-ended question format. By reviewing now with this more difficult question format, you can exercise your memory better and prove your conceptual and factual knowledge of this chapter. The answers to these questions appear in Appendix A.

1. Name two of the limitations and drawbacks of tail drop.

2. Explain TCP global synchronization.

3. Explain TCP starvation.

4. Explain why RED does not cause TCP global synchronization.

5. What are the three configuration parameters for RED?

6. Briefly explain how WRED is different from RED.

7. Explain how class-based weighted random early detection is implemented.

8. Explain how assured forwarding per-hop behavior is implemented on Cisco routers.

9. List at least two of the main purposes of traffic policing.

10. List at least two of the main purposes of traffic shaping.

11. List at least four of the similarities and differences between traffic shaping and policing.

12. In the token bucket scheme, how many tokens are needed for each byte of data to be transmitted?

13. Explain in the single bucket, single rate model when conform action and exceed action take place.

14. What is the formula showing the relationship between CIR, B_c, and T_c?

15. Compare and contrast Frame Relay traffic shaping and class-based traffic shaping.

16. Briefly explain compression.

17. Briefly explain Layer 2 payload compression.

18. Provide a brief explanation for header compression.

19. Is it possible to mitigate the delay imposed by the large data units ahead of delay-sensitive packets in the hardware (Tx) queue?

20. Where should link efficiency mechanisms be applied?

This chapter covers the following subjects:

- Implementing QoS Pre-Classify

- Deploying End-to-End QoS

CHAPTER 6

Implementing QoS Pre-Classify and Deploying End-to-End QoS

This brief chapter is composed of two sections. The first section is focused on the concept of QoS pre-classify and how it is used to ensure that IOS QoS features work in conjunction with tunneling and encryption. The second section deals with the topics related to deploying end-to-end QoS. The concept of control plane policing is discussed last.

"Do I Know This Already?" Quiz

The purpose of the "Do I Know This Already?" quiz is to help you decide whether you really need to read the entire chapter. The 10-question quiz, derived from the major sections of this chapter, helps you determine how to spend your limited study time.

Table 6-1 outlines the major topics discussed in this chapter and the "Do I Know This Already?" quiz questions that correspond to those topics.

Table 6-1 *"Do I Know This Already?" Foundation Topics Section-to-Question Mapping*

Foundation Topics Section Covering These Questions	Questions	Score
"Implementing QoS Pre-Classify"	1–5	
"Deploying End-to-End QoS"	6–10	
Total Score	**(10 possible)**	

CAUTION   The goal of self-assessment is to gauge your mastery of the topics in this chapter. If you do not know the answer to a question or are only partially sure of the answer, mark this question wrong for purposes of the self-assessment. Giving yourself credit for an answer you correctly guess skews your self-assessment results and might provide you with a false sense of security.

You can find the answers to the "Do I Know This Already?" quiz in Appendix A, "Answers to the "Do I Know This Already?" Quizzes and Q&A Sections." The suggested choices for your next step are as follows:

- **6 or less overall score**—Read the entire chapter. This includes the "Foundation Topics," "Foundation Summary," and "Q&A" sections.

- **7–8 overall score**—Begin with the "Foundation Summary" section and then follow up with the "Q&A" section at the end of the chapter.

- **9 or more overall score**—If you want more review on this topic, skip to the "Foundation Summary" section and then go to the "Q&A" section. Otherwise, proceed to the next chapter.

1. Which of the following is not a critical function of VPNs?

   a. Confidentiality

   b. Data integrity

   c. Authentication

   d. Accounting

2. Which of the following is not a VPN type?

   a. Client-initiated remote access

   b. Internet

   c. NAS-initiated remote access

   d. Intranet

3. Which type of interface is QoS pre-classify for?

   a. Tunnel interface

   b. Loopback interface

   c. VRF interface

   d. Logical interface

4. Which of these QoS pre-classify deployment options is invalid?

   a. Apply the policy to the tunnel interface without QoS pre-classify when you want to classify packets based on the pre-tunnel header.

   b. Apply the policy to the physical interface without QoS pre-classify when you want to classify packets based on the post-tunnel header.

   c. Apply the policy to the tunnel interface without QoS pre-classify when you want to classify packets based on the post-tunnel header.

   d. Apply the policy to the physical interface and enable QoS pre-classify when you want to classify packets based on the pre-tunnel header.

5. Which of the following Cisco IOS commands enables QoS pre-classify on an interface?

   a. qos classify

   b. preclassify

   c. preclassify qos

   d. qos pre-classify

6. Which of the following is not a typical IP QoS SLA parameter?

   a. Delay

   b. Jitter

   c. CLP

   d. Loss

7. Which of the following is an invalid campus QoS guideline?

   a. Mark traffic at the distribution layer device.

   b. Use multiple queues on the transmit interfaces.

   c. Perform QoS in hardware when possible.

   d. Police unwanted traffic as close to the source as possible.

8. Which of the following is not a Cisco router functional plane?

   a. Data plane

   b. Process plane

   c. Management plane

   d. Control plane

9. Which of the following is not a CoPP deployment step?

   a. Define a packet classification criteria.

   b. Define a service policy.

   c. Enter global configuration mode and apply a QoS policy.

   d. Enter control plane configuration mode and apply QoS policy.

10. Which of the following is not a typical customer edge-to-provider edge WAN link required QoS feature?

   a. Queuing

   b. Shaping

   c. LFI or cRTP

   d. CoPP

Foundation Topics

Implementing QoS Pre-Classify

QoS pre-classify was designed so that tunneled interfaces could classify packets on the output interface before data was encrypted and tunneled. Considering the growth of VPN popularity, the ability to classify traffic within a tunnel for QoS purposes is increasingly in demand. QoS pre-classify allows Cisco IOS QoS features and services to remain effective even on tunnel interfaces and when encryption is used. Therefore, service providers and customers can continue to provide appropriate service levels to voice, video, and mission-critical traffic while they use VPN for secure transport.

Virtual Private Networks (VPN)

Virtual private network (VPN) is a private connectivity path between two end points, built on a public or shared infrastructure. Traditional ATM and Frame Relay circuits are referred to as Layer 2 VPNs, whereas IPsec tunnels over the Internet are called Layer 3 VPNs. A Layer 3 VPN can use tunneling, encryption, or both. The three main functions that VPNs can provide are as follows:

- **Confidentiality**—This is usually accomplished by encryption, using methods such as DES or 3DES. The intention is that eavesdroppers should not be able to decrypt/decipher and read the encrypted data (within a reasonable period).

- **Authentication**—This provides proof of origin to the receiver. Through authentication, origin of information is certified and guaranteed by the receiver. Certificates are often exchanged to facilitate the authentication process.

- **Data integrity**—The receiver of packets and data is often interested in making sure that the data has not been altered or corrupted during transit. A data integrity check using hashing algorithms such as SHA and MD5 helps do just that.

You can implement confidentiality using encryption at different layers of the OSI model: at the application layer, transport layer, Internet layer, or network interface (data link) layer. Secure Shell (SSH) and Secure Multipurpose Internet Mail Extensions (S/MIME) are examples of protocols that provide encryption or authentication services to applications. Secure Socket Layer (SSL) can provide authenticity, privacy, and integrity to TCP-based applications. When these services are offered at the application or transport layer, they only work for one or a few concurrent applications; therefore, they are not considered application-independent and flexible. On the other hand, security services at the data link layer are nonscalable and expensive because they must be configured on a link/circuit-by-link/circuit basis. As a result, providing security services at Layer 3

(Internet layer), which means providing protection for as many applications as desired without having to do multiple configurations, has become the most popular.

The end points of a VPN are either end systems or networks; based on that, VPNs are divided into two categories:

■ Remote access VPNs

■ Site-to-site VPNs

The first category of VPN, remote access VPN, is either client-initiated or network access server (NAS)-initiated. When a person uses a VPN client application to establish a secure tunnel across an Internet service provider (ISP) (shared) network directly to an enterprise network, the VPN is referred to as client-initiated. In the network access server (NAS)-initiated case, however, the user dials in to the ISP, and the ISP NAS in turn establishes a secure tunnel to the enterprise private network.

The second category of VPN, site-to-site VPN, has two main types: intranet VPN and extranet VPN. The intranet VPN connects offices of an enterprise, such as the headquarters, branch offices, and remote offices, over a public network. The extranet VPN, on the other hand, provides private connectivity between offices of different companies and enterprises over a public infrastructure. These companies and enterprises, due to their business relationship, have connectivity requirements; suppliers, partners, or communities of interest often have such requirements.

QoS Pre-Classify Applications

Two commonly used tunneling protocols that are relevant to VPNs, discussed in the ONT course, are GRE and IPsec. Because these tunneling protocols, at the tunnel end points, encapsulate the original IP packet and use a new IP header, the original IP header is no longer available to the QoS mechanisms on the outbound (egress) interface. The good news is that the original ToS byte of an IP packet is copied to a ToS byte of the new IP header. Therefore, if the QoS mechanisms on the egress interface only consider the ToS byte (DSCP and ECN, or IP Precedence), it is unnecessary to perform any extra configurations, such as using the **qos pre-classify** command (on the router where the tunnel emanates). However, if other fields—such as the source or destination IP address, protocol number, or source port or destination port numbers—need to be processed, QoS pre-classify configuration is necessary on the tunnel head router. When packets from different flows and applications are transported through a tunnel interface, they are encapsulated with the same new IP header with identical source and destination IP addresses (tunnel ends) and protocol numbers (tunnel protocol number). The only difference between those packets might be the ToS byte, which is directly copied from the ToS byte of the original IP packet header.

GRE can encapsulate different protocol packet types inside IP tunnels, creating a virtual point-to-point link to remote Cisco routers over an IP internetwork. GRE, however, does not provide data confidentiality using encryption. The main strength of GRE tunnel is that, in addition to transporting IP unicast packets, it can transport packets of IP routing protocols, multicast packets, and non-IP traffic.

Secure VPNs use IPsec because it can provide data confidentiality, data integrity, and data authentication between the tunnel end points/peers. Two mechanisms protect data sent over an IPsec tunnel:

- Authentication Header (AH)

- Encapsulating Security Payload (ESP)

Using Secure Hash Algorithm (SHA) or Message Digest 5 (MD5), IPsec AH provides partial integrity and authentication for IP datagrams. IP protocol number assigned to AH is 51. IPsec AH can operate in either transport mode or tunnel mode. In transport mode the AH header is inserted after the original IP packet's header. In tunnel mode however, the original IP packet is entirely encapsulated in another IP packet (new/outer) and the AH header in inserted after the encapsulating/outer IP packet's header. Figure 6-1 illustrates this. Tunnel mode is often used to provide connectivity between networks that use private addressing; the outer IP packet's address is routable and allows delivery of the inner IP packet from one private site to another. Figure 6-1 shows two IPsec packets with AH headers: one in transport mode, and the other in tunnel mode. IPsec AH alone does not provide data confidentiality through encryption.

Figure 6-1 *IPsec AH in Tunnel Mode and in Transport Mode*

IPsec AH in Tunnel Mode:

Payload	IP Header	AH Header	New IP Header Protocol: 51 (AH) ToS = Inner ToS

IPsec AH in Transport Mode:

Payload	AH Header	Original IP Header Protocol: 51 (AH) Inner ToS

IPsec ESP provides data confidentiality (through encryption) and data authentication. If only the payload of the IP packet needs to be protected, the ESP header is inserted between the IP header and the IP payload, and only the IP payload is encrypted. This is ESP in transport mode. The IP protocol number 50 identifies ESP. If the entire IP packet including its header needs to be protected, the original IP packet is encrypted and encapsulated in another IP packet, with the ESP header between the new IP header and the encapsulated and encrypted (original) IP header. This is called *ESP tunnel mode*. Figure 6-2 shows two IPsec packets with ESP headers: one in transport mode, and the other in tunnel mode.

Figure 6-2 *IPsec ESP in Transport Mode and in Tunnel Mode*

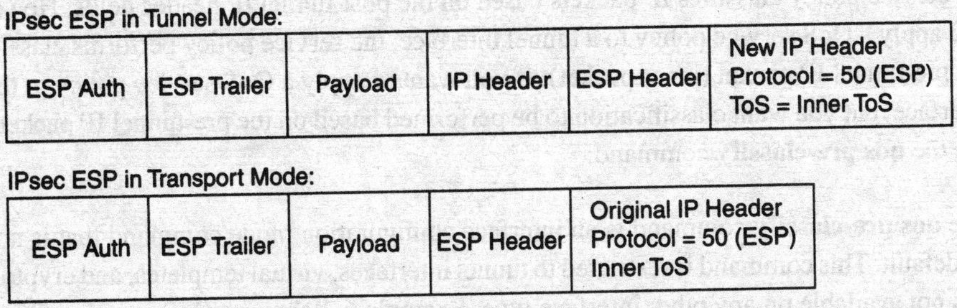

IPsec ESP in Tunnel Mode:

ESP Auth	ESP Trailer	Payload	IP Header	ESP Header	New IP Header Protocol = 50 (ESP) ToS = Inner ToS

IPsec ESP in Transport Mode:

ESP Auth	ESP Trailer	Payload	ESP Header	Original IP Header Protocol = 50 (ESP) Inner ToS

Please note that in tunnel mode, with both IPsec AH and ESP, the original packet header ToS byte is copied to the encapsulating IP packet header ToS byte; therefore, it is available for QoS purposes. In transport mode, the entire original IP header is available for QoS processing.

QoS Pre-Classification Deployment Options

Many QoS features that are supported on physical interfaces are also supported on, and are often required on, tunnel interfaces. A QoS service policy that is normally applied to a physical interface can also be applied to a tunnel interface. In that situation, you must answer two questions:

1. Does the QoS policy classify an IP packet merely based on the ToS byte?

2. If the QoS policy classifies traffic based on fields other than or in addition to the ToS byte, should the classification be done based on the values of those fields in the pre-tunnel IP packet header or based on the values of those fields in the post-tunnel IP packet header?

With GRE tunnel, IPsec AH (transport and tunnel mode), and IPsec ESP (transport and tunnel mode), if packet classification is ToS based only, no extra configuration is necessary. That is because the IOS by default copies the ToS byte from the inner IP packet to the ToS byte of the encapsulating IP packet when tunneling. Of course, when IPsec AH and IPsec ESP are in transport mode, the original ToS byte is already present and available for examination. Therefore, the challenge is presented when packet classification is based on fields other than or in addition to the ToS byte on the pre-tunnel IP packet. A pre-tunnel IP packet means that, in addition to being encapsulated, the inner IP packet of a tunnel may be encrypted.

The **qos pre-classify** command configures the IOS to make a temporary copy of the IP packet before it is encapsulated or encrypted so that the service policy on the (egress) interface can do its classification based on the original (inner) IP packet fields rather than the encapsulating (outer) IP packet header. If the classification is merely based on ToS byte, though, **qos pre-classify** is not necessary. A QoS service policy can be applied to the physical interface or to the tunnel interface. Applying a service policy to a physical interface causes that policy to affect all tunnel interfaces on that physical interface. Applying a service policy to a tunnel interface affects that particular tunnel only and does not affect other tunnel interfaces on the same physical interface.

When you apply a QoS service policy to a physical interface where one or more tunnels emanate, the service policy classifies IP packets based on the post-tunnel IP header fields. However, when you apply a QoS service policy to a tunnel interface, the service policy performs classification on the pre-tunnel IP packet (inner packet). If you want to apply a QoS service policy to the physical interface, but you want classification to be performed based on the pre-tunnel IP packet, you must use the **qos pre-classify** command.

The **qos pre-classify** command is an interface configuration mode command that is not enabled by default. This command is restricted to tunnel interfaces, virtual templates, and crypto maps, and it is not available on any other interface type. Example 6-1 shows a QoS service policy called to-remote-branch is applied to the serial1/1 interface of a router. A GRE tunnel with IPsec emanates from this serial interface. Because in this example it is required that the QoS service policy classifies pre-tunnel IP packets, the **qos pre-classify** command is applied to the tunnel1 interface and to the crypto map named vpn.

Example 6-1 *QoS Pre-Classification Example*

```
interface serial1/1
  ip address 10.1.1.1 255.255.255.252
  service-policy output to-remote-branch
  crypto map vpn

interface tunnel1
  ip address 192.168.1.1 255.255.255.252
  tunnel source serial1/1
  tunnel destination 10.1.1.2
  crypto map vpn
  qos pre-classify

crypto map vpn 10 ipsec-isakmp
  set peer 10.1.1.2
  set transform-set remote-branch-vpn
  match ip address 100
  qos pre-classify
```

You might wonder why the service policy applied to the serial1/1 interface in Example 6-1 was not applied to the tunnel1 interface instead. It is because, this way the service policy applies not to just one, but to all the tunnels that emanate from that physical interface. Also, please notice that the **qos pre-classify** command, in Example 6-1, is applied to both the tunnel1 and to the crypto map called vpn. If the **qos pre-classify** command were not applied to the crypto map, the router would see only one flow: the GRE tunnel (protocol 47).

Deploying End-to-End QoS

End-to-end QoS means that all the network components between the end points of a network communication dialogue need to implement appropriate QoS mechanisms consistently. If, for example, an enterprise (customer) uses the services and facilities of a service provider for connectivity between its headquarters and branch offices, both the enterprise and the service provider must implement the proper IP QoS mechanisms. This ensures end-to-end QoS for the packets going from one enterprise location to the other, traversing through the core network of the service provider.

At each customer location where traffic originates, traffic classification and marking need to be performed. The connection between the customer premises equipment and the provider equipment must have proper QoS mechanisms in place, respecting the packet markings. The service provider might trust customer marking, re-mark customer traffic, or encapsulate/tag customer traffic with other markings such as the EXP bits on the MPLS label. In any case, over the provider core, the QoS levels promised in the SLA must be delivered. SLA is defined and described in the next section. In general, customer traffic must arrive at the destination site with the same markings that were set at the site of origin. The QoS mechanisms at the customer destination site, all the way to the destination device, complete the requirements for end-to-end QoS.

Figure 6-3 shows several key locations within customer and provider premises where various QoS mechanisms must be deployed. As the figure points out, end-to-end QoS is accomplished by deploying proper QoS mechanisms and policies on both the customer (enterprise) devices and the service provider (core) devices.

Figure 6-3 *End-to-End QoS: Features and Related Implementation Points*

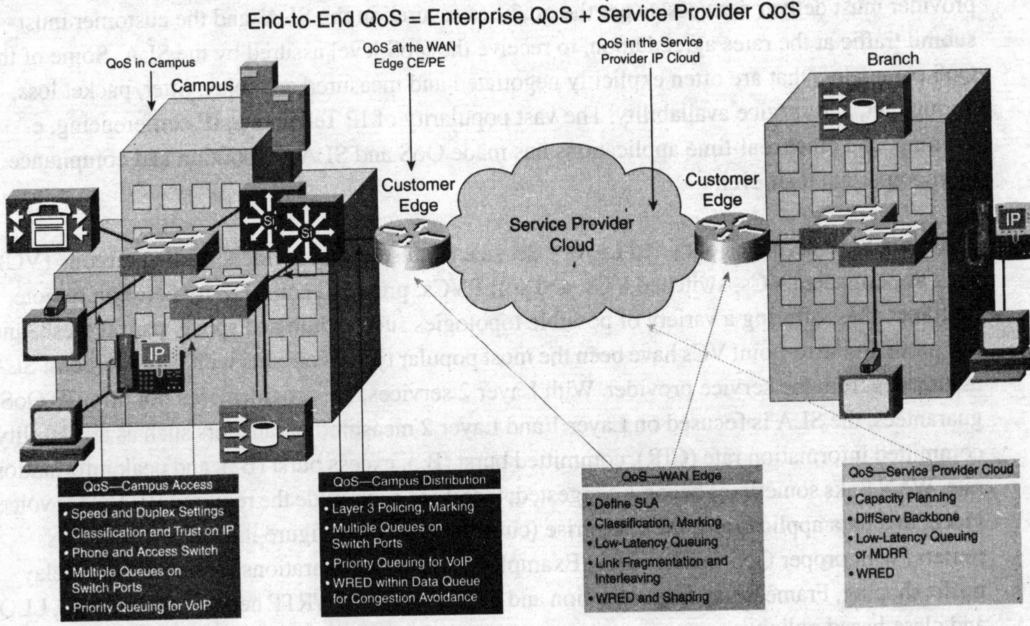

End-to-End QoS = Enterprise QoS + Service Provider QoS

QoS in Campus
Campus

QoS at the WAN Edge CE/PE

QoS in the Service Provider IP Cloud

Branch

Customer Edge

Service Provider Cloud

Customer Edge

IP

QoS—Campus Access
- Speed and Duplex Settings
- Classification and Trust on IP
- Phone and Access Switch
- Multiple Queues on Switch Ports
- Priority Queuing for VoIP

QoS—Campus Distribution
- Layer 3 Policing, Marking
- Multiple Queues on Switch Ports
- Priority Queuing for VoIP
- WRED within Data Queue for Congestion Avoidance

QoS—WAN Edge
- Define SLA
- Classification, Marking
- Low-Latency Queuing
- Link Fragmentation and Interleaving
- WRED and Shaping

QoS—Service Provider Cloud
- Capacity Planning
- DiffServ Backbone
- Low-Latency Queuing or MDRR
- WRED

Correct end-to-end per-hop behavior (PHB) for each traffic class requires proper implementation of QoS mechanisms in both the enterprise and the service provider networks. In the past, IP QoS was not given much attention in enterprise campus networks because of abundant available bandwidth. Today, however, with the emergence of applications such as IP Telephony, videoconferencing, e-learning, and mission-critical data applications in the customer campus networks, many factors such as packet drop management, buffer management, queue management, and so on, in addition to bandwidth management, are required within the campus to minimize loss, delay, and jitter.

Figure 6-3 displays some of the main requirements within the campus and provider building blocks constituting the end-to-end QoS. Proper hardware, software, and configurations such as buffer settings and queuing are the focus of the access layer QoS. Policing, marking, and congestion avoidance are implemented at the campus distribution layer. At the WAN edge, it is often required to make some complex QoS configurations related to the subscribed WAN service. Finally, in the service provider IP core, congestion-management and congestion-avoidance are the main mechanisms in operation; the key QoS mechanisms used within the service provider core IP network are low-latency queuing (LLQ) and weighted random early detection (WRED).

QoS Service Level Agreements (SLAs)

An SLA is a contractual agreement between an enterprise (customer) and a service provider regarding data, voice, and other service or a group of services. Internet access, leased line, Frame Relay, and ATM are examples of such services. After the SLA is negotiated, it is important that it is monitored for compliance of the parties involved with the terms of the agreement. The service provider must deliver services as per the qualities assured in the SLA, and the customer must submit traffic at the rates agreed upon, to receive the QoS level assured by the SLA. Some of the QoS parameters that are often explicitly negotiated and measured are delay, jitter, packet loss, throughput, and service availability. The vast popularity of IP Telephony, IP conferencing, e-learning, and other real-time applications has made QoS and SLA negotiation and compliance more important than ever.

Traditionally, enterprises obtained Layer 2 service from service providers. Virtual circuits (VC), such as permanent VCs, switched VCs, and soft PVCs, provided connectivity between remote customer sites, offering a variety of possible topologies such as hub and spoke, partial mesh, and full mesh. Point-to-point VCs have been the most popular type of circuits with point-to-point SLA assurances from the service provider. With Layer 2 services, the provider does not offer IP QoS guarantees; the SLA is focused on Layer 1 and Layer 2 measured parameters such as availability, committed information rate (CIR), committed burst (B_c), excess burst (B_e), and peak information rate. WAN links sometimes become congested; therefore, to provide the required IP QoS for voice, video, and data applications, the enterprise (customer) must configure its equipment (WAN routers) with proper QoS mechanisms. Examples of such configurations include Frame Relay traffic shaping, Frame Relay fragmentation and interleaving, TCP/RTP header compression, LLQ, and class-based policing.

In recent years, especially due to the invention of technologies such as IPsec VPN and MPLS VPN, most providers have been offering Layer 3 services instead of, or at least in addition to, the traditional Layer 2 services (circuits). In summary, the advantages of Layer 3 services are scalability, ease of provisioning, and service flexibility. Unlike Layer 2 services where each circuit has a single QoS specification and assurance, Layer 3 services offer a variety of QoS service levels on a common circuit/connection based on type or class of data (marking). For example, the provider and the enterprise customer might have an SLA based on three traffic classes called controlled latency, controlled load, and best effort. For each class (except best effort) the SLA states that if it is submitted at or below a certain rate, the amount of data drop/loss, delay, and jitter will be within a certain limit; if the traffic exceeds the rate, it will be either dropped or re-marked (lower).

It is important that the SLA offered by the service provider is understood. Typical service provider IP QoS SLAs include three to five traffic classes: one class for real-time, one class for mission-critical, one or two data traffic classes, and a best-effort traffic class. The real-time traffic is treated as a high-priority class with a minimum, but policed, bandwidth guarantee. Other data classes are also provided a minimum bandwidth guarantee. The bandwidth guarantee is typically specified as a percentage of the link bandwidth (at the local loop). Other parameters specified by the SLA for each traffic class are average delay, jitter, and packet loss. If the interface on the PE device serves a single customer only, it is usually a high-speed interface, but a subrate configuration offers the customer only the bandwidth (peak rate) that is subscribed to. If the interface on a PE device serves multiple customers, multiple VLANs or VCs are configured, each serving a different customer. In that case, the VC or subinterface that is dedicated to each customer is provisioned with the subrate configuration based on the SLA.

Figure 6-4 displays a service provider core network in the middle offering Layer 3 services with IP QoS SLA to its customer with an enterprise campus headquarters and an enterprise remote branch. The customer in this example runs IP Telephony applications such as VoIP calls between those sites.

To meet the QoS requirements of the typical telephony (VoIP) applications, the enterprise must not only negotiate an adequate SLA with the provider, but it also must make proper QoS configurations on its own premise devices so that the end-to-end QoS becomes appropriate for the applications. In the example depicted in Figure 6-4, the SLA guaranteed a delay (latency) <= 60 ms, jitter <= 20 ms, and packet loss <= 0.5 percent. Because the typical end-to-end objectives for delay, jitter, and packet loss for VoIP are <= 150 ms, <= 30 ms, and <= 1 percent, respectively, the enterprise must make sure that the delay, jitter, and loss within its premises will not exceed 90 ms, 10 ms, and 0.5 percent, respectively.

Figure 6-4 *Example for IP QoS SLA for VoIP*

Maximum One-Way End-to-End QoS Budget for Delay (Latency), Jitter, and Packet Loss:
Latency <= 150 ms/Jitter <= 30 ms/Loss <= 1%

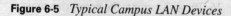

Maximum One-Way
Service Provider Service Levels
Latency <= 60 ms
Jitter <= 20 ms
Loss <= 0.5%

Enterprise Campus QoS Implementations

Provisioning QoS functions and features within campus networks on access, distribution, and core switches is a part of end-to-end QoS. This is in large part due to the growth of IP Telephony, video conferencing, e-learning, and mission-critical applications within enterprise networks. Certain efforts are spent on access devices, whereas others are spent on distribution and core equipment to minimize packet loss, delay, and jitter. Figure 6-5 shows the series of devices—all the way from end-user workstation (PC) to the core campus LAN switch and WAN edge router—that exist in a typical campus LAN environment.

Figure 6-5 *Typical Campus LAN Devices*

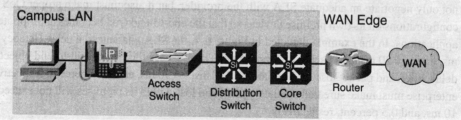

Important guidelines for implementing QoS in campus networks are as follows:

- **Classify and mark traffic as close to the source as possible**—Classifying and marking packets as close to the source as possible, and not necessarily by the source, eliminates the need for classification and marking efforts to be repeated and duplicated at various network locations. However, marking of all end devices cannot be trusted either, because it opens the door to abuse.

- **Police traffic as close to the source as possible**—Policing unwanted traffic as close to the source as possible is the most efficient way of handling excessive and possibly invasive and malicious traffic. Unwanted traffic, such as denial of service (DoS) attacks and worm attacks, can cause network outage by overwhelming network resources, device CPUs, and memories.

- **Establish proper trust boundaries**—Trust Cisco IP phones marking, but not the markings of user workstations (PCs).

- **Classify and mark real-time voice and video as high-priority traffic**— Higher priority marking for voice and video traffic gives them queue assignment, delay, jitter, and drop advantage over other types of traffic.

- **Use multiple queues on transmit interfaces**—This minimizes transmit queue congestion and packet drops and delays due to transmit buffer congestion.

- **When possible, perform hardware-based rather than software-based QoS**—Contrary to Cisco IOS routers, Cisco Catalyst switches perform QoS functions in special hardware (application-specific integrated circuits, or ASICs). Use of ASICs rather than software-based QoS is not taxing on the main processor and allows complex QoS functions to be performed at high speeds.

Congestion is a rare event within campus networks; if it happens, it is usually instantaneous and does not sustain. However, critical and real-time applications (such as Telephony) still need the protection and service guarantees for those rare moments. QoS features such as policing, queuing, and congestion avoidance (WRED) must be enabled on all campus network devices where possible. Within campus networks, link aggregation, oversubscription on uplinks, and speed mismatches are common causes of congestion. Enabling QoS within the campus is even more critical under abnormal network conditions such as during DoS and worm attacks. During such attacks, network traffic increases and links become overutilized. Enabling QoS features within the campus network not only provides service-level guarantees for specific application types, but it also provides network availability assurance, especially during network attacks.

In campus networks, access switches require these QoS policies:

- Appropriate trust, classification, and marking policies

- Policing and markdown policies

- Queuing policies

The distribution switches, on the other hand, need the following:

- DSCP trust policies

- Queuing policies

- Optional per-user micro-flow policies (if supported)

WAN Edge QoS Implementations

WAN edge QoS configurations are performed on CE and PE devices that terminate WAN circuits. Commonly used WAN technologies are Frame Relay and ATM. Important QoS features implemented on the CE and PE devices are LLQ, compression, fragmentation and interleaving, policing, and shaping. Figure 6-6 shows a customer site connected to a provider IP network through a Frame Relay connection between a CE device and a PE device. Note that a similar connection between the CE and the PE devices exists at the remote site.

Figure 6-6   *WAN Edge QoS Implementation Points*

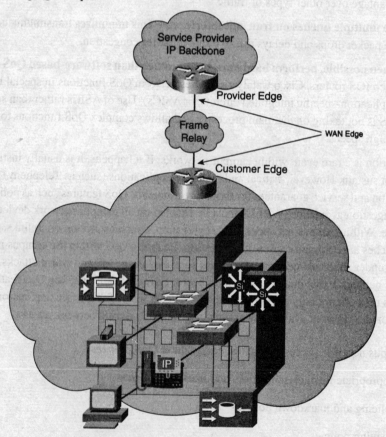

For the traffic that is leaving a local customer site through a CE device going toward the provider network and entering it through a PE device, output QoS mechanisms on the CE device and input QoS mechanisms on the PE device must be implemented. The implementation will vary somewhat, depending on whether the CE device is provider managed—in other words, if it is under the control of the provider. Table 6-2 shows the QoS requirements on the CE and the PE devices in both cases: when the CE device is provider managed, and when the CE device is not provider managed. When the CE device is provider managed, the service provider manages and performs the QoS policies and configurations. Otherwise, the customer enterprise controls the QoS policies and configures the CE device.

Table 6-2 *QoS Mechanisms Necessary for Traffic Leaving a Customer Site*

Managed CE	Unmanaged CE
The service provider controls the output QoS policy on the CE.	The service provider does not control the output QoS policy on the CE.
The service provider enforces SLA using the output QoS policy on the CE.	The service provider enforces SLA using the input QoS policy on the PE.
The output policy uses queuing, dropping, and shaping.	The input policy uses policing and marking.
Elaborate traffic classification or mapping of existing markings takes place on the CE.	Elaborate traffic classification or mapping of existing markings takes place on the PE.
LFI* and compressed RTP might be necessary. * LFI = link fragmentation and interleaving	

When the CE device is provider managed, the provider can enforce the SLA by applying an outbound QoS service policy on the CE device. For example, an LLQ or class-based weighted fair queueing (CBWFQ) can be applied to the egress interface of the CE device to provide a policed bandwidth guarantee to voice and video applications and a minimum bandwidth guarantee to mission-critical applications. You can use class-based shaping to rate-limit data applications. You can apply congestion avoidance (WRED), shaping, compression (cRTP), and LFI outbound on the managed CE device. When the CE device is not provider managed, the provider enforces the SLA on the ingress interface of the PE device using tools such as class-based policing. Policed traffic can be dropped, re-marked, or mapped (for example, DSCP to MPLS EXP).

At the remote site, where the traffic leaves the provider network through the PE router and enters the enterprise customer network through the CE device, most of the QoS configurations are configured on the PE device (outbound), regardless of whether the CE device is managed. The service provider enforces the SLA using output QoS policy on the PE device. Output policy performs congestion management (queuing), dropping, and possibly shaping. Other QoS techniques such as LFI or cRTP can also be performed in the PE device. CE input policy is usually not necessary; of course, the configuration of the CE device that is not provider managed is at the discretion of the enterprise customer.

Control Plane Policing (CoPP)

Control plane attacks are growing, so protecting the network infrastructure against these types of attacks is imminently required. Control plane policing (CoPP), a Cisco IOS feature that has been available since IOS release 12.2(18)S, allows you to configure a QoS filter that manages the traffic flow of control plane packets. Using CoPP, you can protect the control plane of Cisco IOS routers and switches against DoS and reconnaissance attacks and ensure network stability (router/switch stability in particular) during an attack. Deploying CoPP is a recommended best practice and a key protection mechanism.

The route processor routes and forwards the majority of the traffic that enters a router; the destination of this type of traffic, called *data plane traffic*, is elsewhere other than the router itself. On the other hand, some traffic—such as routing updates, management traffic, keepalives, and so on—is indeed for the router; this type of traffic is called *control and management plane traffic*. Formally, the Cisco router functional planes are enlisted as data plane, management plane, control plane, and service plane. Excessive and malicious traffic in the form of control and management traffic aimed at the route processor can have the following devastating results:

■ High or close to 100 percent utilization of CPU or other resources such as memory and buffers

■ Loss of routing updates and keepalives, resulting in route flaps and erroneous NLRI (network layer reachability information) withdrawals and updates

■ Slow response times and interactive sessions, including command-line interface (CLI) through virtual terminal lines

■ Queue buildups, resulting in excessive delays and tail drops, or drops due to lack of buffer space

CoPP mitigates control plane attacks and ensures stability and availability of the routers and switches. CoPP is configured by applying a policy map to the control plane from the control plane configuration mode. In other words, CoPP is applied using modular QoS command-line interface (MQC), providing filtering and rate-limiting for control plane packets. Those devices with route processors on line card modules can be protected by distributed CoPP or control plane configuration mode on the particular slot number. The four steps to configure CoPP are as follows:

Step 1   Define a packet classification criteria. (Use MQC **class-map**.)

Step 2   Define a service policy. (Use MQC **policy-map**.)

Step 3   Enter control plane configuration mode.

Step 4   Apply a QoS policy.

Example 6-2 shows a configuration that allows two trusted hosts with source addresses 10.1.1.1 and 10.1.1.2 to forward Telnet packets to the control plane without constraint, while policing all remaining Telnet packets to the control plane at the specified rate. The access list matches all Telnet traffic except that from hosts 10.1.1.1 and 10.1.1.2. The class map telnet-class is defined for all traffic matching access list 100. The policy map telnet-policy applies the **police** command to the traffic matching class telnet-class. Finally, the telnet-policy is applied to the control plane using the **service-policy** command. The QoS policy shown in Example 6-2 is applied for aggregate CP services to all packets that are entering the control plane from all line cards in the router.

Example 6-2   *CoPP Example: QoS Policy Applied for Aggregate CP Services*

```
!
class-map telnet-class
  match access-group 100
!
policy-map telnet-policy
  class telnet-class
    police 80000 conform transmit exceed drop
!
control-plane
  service-policy input telnet-policy
!
access-list 100 deny tcp host 10.1.1.1 any eq telnet
access-list 100 deny tcp host 10.1.1.2 any eq telnet
access-list 100 permit tcp any any eq telnet
!
```

Example 6-3 shows a similar example, but for distributed CP services, allowing two trusted hosts with source addresses 10.1.1.1 and 10.1.1.2 to forward Telnet packets to the control plane without constraint, while policing all remaining Telnet packets that enter through slot 1 at the specified rate.

Example 6-3   *CoPP Example: QoS Policy Applied for Distributed CP Services*

```
!
class-map telnet-class
  match access-group 100
!
policy-map telnet-policy
  class telnet-class
    police 80000 conform transmit exceed drop
!
control-plane slot 1
  service-policy input telnet-policy
!
access-list 100 deny tcp host 10.1.1.1 any eq telnet
access-list 100 deny tcp host 10.1.1.2 any eq telnet
access-list 100 permit tcp any any eq telnet
!
```

Foundation Summary

The "Foundation Summary" is a collection of information that provides a convenient review of many key concepts in this chapter. If you are already comfortable with the topics in this chapter, this summary can help you recall a few details. If you just read this chapter, this review should help solidify some key facts. If you are doing your final preparation before the exam, the information in this section is a convenient way to review the day before the exam.

A virtual private network (VPN) carries private traffic over a public network. It is established between end systems or between networks. VPNs provide three functions:

- Confidentiality

- Data integrity

- Origin authentication

Two general types of VPN exist, each with its own variations:

- Remote access

    — Client initiated

    — Network access server (NAS) initiated

- Site-to-site

    — Intranet

    — Extranet

The most common Layer 3 tunneling protocols are as follows:

- Generic routing encapsulation (GRE)

- Internet Protocol security (IPsec)

QoS pre-classify is a Cisco IOS feature that allows packets to be classified before tunneling and encryption occur. The need to classify traffic within a traffic tunnel is growing side by side with the growth in VPN popularity.

The QoS pre-classify feature provides access to the original (encapsulated) IP packet header fields. If IP QoS classification needs access to those fields, using the QoS pre-classify feature will be necessary. You can use one of three approaches to apply the QoS policy and the QoS pre-classify features:

■ To classify packets based on the pre-tunnel header, apply the QoS policy to the tunnel interface without QoS pre-classify.

■ To classify packets based on the post-tunnel header, apply the QoS policy to the physical interface without QoS pre-classify.

■ To classify packets based on the pre-tunnel header, apply the QoS policy to the physical interface and enable QoS pre-classify.

With the growth of multimedia and real-time applications such as IP Telephony, conferencing, and e-learning, QoS service level agreements (SLAs) have become more important than before. The QoS SLAs provide contractual assurance for parameters such as availability, throughput, delay, jitter, and packet loss.

To meet the QoS requirements of customer applications, the service provider and customer both must implement proper QoS mechanisms. This means that you must implement QoS in the customer campus, at the customer WAN edge device outbound toward the provider network, on the PE device inbound from the customer edge, on the provider network, on the PE device at the remote site outbound toward the remote customer site, and on the remote customer site (remote campus). Generally, deploying end-to-end QoS is specified to be necessary at three locations:

■ On campus

■ On the WAN edge (CE/PE)

■ On the service provider cloud

Table 6-3 provides a short list of important QoS-related tasks that might be necessary at different locations on the customer and provider premises. Implementing these and possibly other tasks on both the customer and provider devices supports the effort to provide end-to-end QoS.

Table 6-3 *Necessary QoS Tasks (at Different Spots) for End-to-End QoS*

Campus Access	Campus Distribution	WAN Edge	Service Provider Cloud
Speed and duplex settings	Layer 3 policing and marking	SLA definitions	Capacity planning
Classification and trust settings	Multiple queues on switch ports	Classification and marking	DiffServ implementation (PHB)
Phone and access switch configurations	Priority queuing for VoIP	Low-latency queuing	Low-latency queuing
Multiple queues on switch ports	WRED within data queues for congestion avoidance	Link fragmentation and interleaving	Modified deficit round robin
Priority queuing for VoIP	-	WRED and traffic shaping	WRED

Following are the general guidelines for enterprise campus QoS implementations:

- Implement multiple queues on all interfaces to prevent transmit queue congestion and packet drops.

- Assign voice (and video) traffic to the highest priority queue.

- Establish proper trust boundaries. (Trust the Cisco IP phone CoS setting, not the PCs.)

- Classify and mark traffic as close to the source as possible.

- Use class-based policing to rate-limit certain unwanted excess traffic.

- Try to perform QoS in hardware rather than software when possible.

WAN edge QoS implementation has two facets: features applied to the traffic leaving the enterprise network (toward the provider network), and features applied to the traffic leaving the provider network toward the customer network. In both cases, note whether the CE device is provider managed.

For the traffic leaving the enterprise network (via CE) moving toward the provider network, if the CE device is provider managed, these are the QoS requirements:

- The service provider controls output of the QoS policy on the CE.

- The service provider should enforce SLA using the output QoS policy on the CE.

- The output policy uses queuing, dropping, and shaping.

- Elaborate traffic classification or mapping of existing markings takes place on the CE.

- Link fragmentation and interleaving and compressed RTP might be necessary.

If the CE device is not provider managed, these are the QoS requirements:

- The service provider controls output of the QoS policy on the CE.

- The service provider should enforce SLA using the input QoS policy on the PE.

- The input policy should use policing and marking.

- Elaborate traffic classification or mapping of existing markings takes place on the PE.

For traffic leaving the service provider network (via PE) moving toward the enterprise customer network, these are the QoS requirements (for both managed and unmanaged-CE cases):

- The service provider should enforce SLA using the output QoS policy on the PE.

- The output policy should use queuing, dropping, and optionally shaping.

- LFI or cRTP might be required.

- The input QoS policy on the CE is not implemented if the CE is provider managed, but the customer might implement certain QoS features on the customer-managed CE to meet the end-to-end QoS budgets.

The functional planes of Cisco routers are data plane, management plane, control plane, and service plane. Control plane policing (CoPP) is a Cisco IOS feature that allows you to build QoS filters to manage the flow of control plane packets to protect the control plane against DoS attacks. Because infrastructure attacks are becoming increasingly common, protecting the control plane of the routers and switches using CoPP against reconnaissance and DoS attacks is crucial. The four steps required to deploy CoPP (using MQC) are as follows:

Step 1   Define the packet classification criteria.

Step 2   Define a service policy.

Step 3   Enter the control plane configuration mode.

Step 4   Apply a QoS policy.

Q&A

Some of the questions that follow challenge you more than the exam by using an open-ended question format. By reviewing now with this more difficult question format, you can exercise your memory better and prove your conceptual and factual knowledge of this chapter. The answers to these questions appear in Appendix A.

1. Provide a definition for VPN.

2. What types of interfaces is QoS pre-classify designed for?

3. What Cisco IOS command enables QoS pre-classify on an interface?

4. What are the QoS pre-classification deployment options?

5. Provide a definition for QoS SLA.

6. What are the typical maximum end-to-end (one-way) QoS SLA requirements (delay, jitter, loss) for voice?

7. Provide at least two of the guidelines for implementing QoS in campus networks.

8. Provide at least two QoS policies to be implemented on campus network access or distributed switches.

9. Provide a definition for CoPP.

10. How is CoPP deployed?

This chapter covers the following subjects:

- Introducing AutoQoS

- Implementing and Verifying AutoQoS

- AutoQoS Shortcomings and Remedies

CHAPTER 7

Implementing AutoQoS

This chapter is focused on Cisco AutoQoS. AutoQoS is a QoS deployment automation tool that is suitable for midsize enterprise networks. It has evolved from its limited Voice over IP (VoIP)-focused version to an enterprise version (for Cisco routers) with protocol discovery and more general and sophisticated configuration results. This chapter provides a description for AutoQoS and its benefits followed by a lesson on implementing AutoQoS enterprise on routers and AutoQoS VoIP on Cisco LAN switches. Next, the chapter discusses verifying and monitoring results of enabling AutoQoS on Cisco devices. Finally, it presents the shortcomings of AutoQoS along with recommendations to address and resolve those issues.

"Do I Know This Already?" Quiz

The purpose of the "Do I Know This Already?" quiz is to help you decide whether you really need to read the entire chapter. The 10-question quiz, derived from the major sections of this chapter, helps you determine how to spend your limited study time.

Table 7-1 outlines the major topics discussed in this chapter and the "Do I Know This Already?" quiz questions that correspond to those topics. You can keep track of your score here, too.

Table 7-1 *"Do I Know This Already?" Foundation Topics Section-to-Question Mapping*

Foundation Topics Section Covering These Questions	Questions	Score
"Introducing AutoQoS"	1–4	
"Implementing and Verifying AutoQoS"	5–7	
"AutoQoS Shortcomings and Remedies"	8–10	
Total Score	**(10 possible)**	

CAUTION The goal of self-assessment is to gauge your mastery of the topics in this chapter. If you do not know the answer to a question or are only partially sure of the answer, mark this question wrong for purposes of the self-assessment. Giving yourself credit for an answer you correctly guess skews your self-assessment results and might provide you with a false sense of security.

You can find the answers to the "Do I Know This Already?" quiz in Appendix A, "Answers to the 'Do I Know This Already?' Quizzes and Q&A Sections." The suggested choices for your next step are as follows:

- **6 or less overall score**—Read the entire chapter. This includes the "Foundation Topics," "Foundation Summary," and "Q&A" sections.

- **7–8 overall score**—Begin with the "Foundation Summary" section and then follow up with the "Q&A" section at the end of the chapter.

- **9 or more overall score**—If you want more review on this topic, skip to the "Foundation Summary" section and then go to the "Q&A" section. Otherwise, proceed to the next chapter.

1. Which of the following is *not* a key benefit of Cisco AutoQoS?

   a. It automates and simplifies QoS deployment and provisioning.

   b. AutoQoS results are maintenance free and can't be tuned.

   c. It reduces configuration errors.

   d. It allows customers to retain complete control over their QoS configuration.

2. Which of the following statements is true about the evolution of Cisco AutoQoS?

   a. Cisco AutoQoS has evolved from AutoQoS VoIP to AutoQoS for Enterprise. AutoQoS for Enterprise extends the AutoQoS capabilities beyond VoIP, but it is only supported on Catalyst Switches.

   b. Cisco AutoQoS has evolved from AutoQoS VoIP to AutoQoS for Enterprise. AutoQoS for Enterprise extends the AutoQoS capabilities beyond VoIP, and it has an autodiscovery step.

   c. Cisco AutoQoS has evolved from basic AutoQoS to AutoQoS VoIP. AutoQoS VoIP extends the AutoQoS capabilities to support Voice over IP.

   d. Cisco AutoQoS has evolved from basic AutoQoS to AutoQoS VoIP. AutoQoS VoIP extends the AutoQoS capabilities to support Voice over IP, but it is supported only on Cisco routers.

3. Which of the following is *not* one of the five key elements of QoS deployment?

   a. Intrusion detection

   b. Application classification and policy generation

   c. Configuration and monitoring (reporting)

   d. Consistency

4. Which of the following is *not* true about NBAR protocol discovery?

   a. NBAR protocol discovery is able to identify and classify static port applications.

   b. NBAR protocol discovery is able to identify and classify dynamic port applications.

   c. NBAR protocol discovery is able to identify and classify HTTP applications based on URL, MIME type, or host name.

   d. NBAR protocol discovery is able to identify and classify IP applications only.

5. Which of the following is a Cisco AutoQoS router configuration prerequisite?

   a. No QoS policy (service) policy can be applied to the interface.

   b. CEF must be enabled on the interface.

   c. Correct bandwidth must be configured on the interface.

   d. All of the above.

6. In deploying Cisco AutoQoS for Enterprise on routers, what is Step 1 (or Phase 1) of the two-step (2-phase) approach?

   a. Profiling the data using autodiscovery

   b. Assigning the appropriate bandwidth and scheduling parameters

   c. Mapping applications to their corresponding DiffServ classes

   d. Enabling CEF

7. Which of the following is *not* a Cisco LAN switch AutoQoS verification command?

   a. **show auto qos**

   b. **show auto qos interface** *interface*

   c. **show auto discovery qos**

   d. **show mls qos maps** [**cos-dscp** l **dscp-cos**]

8. Which of the following is *not* one of the three most common Cisco AutoQoS issues that can arise?

   a. Too many traffic classes are generated; classification is overengineered.

   b. The configuration that AutoQoS generates does not adapt to changing network traffic conditions automatically.

   c. The configuration that AutoQoS generates is not modifiable.

   d. The configuration that AutoQoS generates fits common network scenarios but does not fit some circumstances, even after extensive autodiscovery.

9. Which of the following is a possible way to tune and modify the class maps or policy maps that AutoQoS generates?

    a. Do it directly at the router command-line interface (CLI) using MQC

    b. Use Cisco QoS Policy Manager (QPM)

    c. Copy the class maps or policy maps into a text editor, and modify the configuration offline

    d. All of the above

10. Besides NBAR and ACLs, which of the MQC classification options can you use to tune an AutoQoS-generated configuration?

    a. **match input interface, match ip dscp, match ip precedence, match ip cos**

    b. **match input interface, match ip dscp, match ip precedence, match ip rtp**

    c. **match ip dscp, match ip precedence, match ip rtp, match ip cos**

    d. **match input interface, match ip dscp, match ip cos, match ip rtp**

Foundation Topics

Introducing AutoQoS

With the growth of bandwidth requirements by today's applications and convergence of voice, video, and data applications over common IP infrastructures (networks), deploying QoS technologies and services is a necessity within modern networks. Although you must manage delay, jitter, available bandwidth, and packet loss, the solution must remain scalable and manageable with respect to both simplicity and cost. Following are some of the challenges that enterprises face:

- The voice quality of IP Telephony applications must be high.

- The required bandwidth for mission-critical applications must be guaranteed.

- QoS must be simple enough to reduce errors, the deployment period, and costs.

Cisco AutoQoS is a QoS deployment automation tool that is suitable for midsize enterprises and branches. Following are the main benefits of Cisco AutoQoS:

- The built-in intelligence of AutoQoS makes its auto-generated configuration code suitable for most common enterprise QoS requirements.

- AutoQoS protects mission-critical applications against otherwise less-important applications, providing guaranteed resources and preferential treatments.

- Using AutoQoS does not require in-depth knowledge of QoS, Cisco IOS commands, or the varied networking technologies involved.

- AutoQoS-generated configurations are based on modular QoS command-line interface (MQC) and follow the Cisco recommendations for best practices and the DiffServ model.

- You can examine the results of AutoQoS-generated commands, and modify them if necessary, to suit each particular need.

The first phase or release of AutoQoS, referred to as AutoQoS VoIP, was developed to automate generation of QoS configurations for those who had or planned to deploy IP Telephony in their enterprise but lacked the expertise to do so properly. AutoQoS VoIP operates both on Cisco routers and Catalyst switches. It generates the required access lists, class maps, policy maps, interface configurations, and so on to provide adequate configuration supporting IP Telephony applications. AutoQoS VoIP uses Network Based Application Recognition (NBAR) for classification and marking of packet DiffServ Codepoint (DSCP) fields. It can also trust markings of the packets and not re-mark them.

The second phase or release of AutoQoS, referred to as AutoQoS for Enterprise (or AutoQoS Enterprise for brevity), is available only for routers. AutoQoS Enterprise has added capabilities for voice, video, and data, plus another feature called protocol discovery. AutoQoS Enterprise has two deployment stages:

1. Discovering types and volumes of traffic types using NBAR protocol discovery and generating appropriate policies accordingly

2. Implementing the generated policies

You can review the application types discovered during the auto-discovery stage and the QoS policies generated (suggested) by AutoQoS Enterprise first. After that review, you can implement the AutoQoS-generated policies completely, modify them, or not implement them at all. However, it is noteworthy that AutoQoS Enterprise addresses all of the following five key elements of QoS deployment:

- **Application classification**—Utilizing NBAR, AutoQoS Enterprise can perform intelligent classification based on deep packet inspection; using CDP (version 2), an IP phone is recognized as an attached device whose packets will be classified accordingly.

- **Policy generation**—AutoQoS Enterprise generates policies based on device and interface settings and the traffic observed in the discovery stage. These policies can be tuned further if desired. For example, on WAN interfaces, auto-generated policies take into account the need for techniques such as fragmentation and compression.

- **Configuration**—AutoQoS Enterprise is easily enabled on router interfaces. It automates detection of connected IP phones, which in turn affects the QoS configuration of the interface.

- **Monitoring and reporting**—AutoQoS can automate generation of alerts, SNMP traps, system loggings, and summary reports. You can use QPM to monitor, view, and evaluate the statistics and the information (QoS feedback) gathered.

- **Consistency**—AutoQoS generates consistent policies and configurations on the Cisco devices on which it is deployed. A user can inspect generated policies, filters, and so on, plus the gathered statistics from the discovery stage.

The discovery stage of AutoQoS Enterprise uses NBAR protocol discovery. NBAR protocol discovery first collects and analyzes packets that are going through the interface of a router; then it generates statistics on the types and numbers of the packets processed. All traffic types that NBAR supports (close to 100 applications and protocols) that go through an interface in either direction (input or output) are discovered and analyzed in real-time. The statistics reported per-interface and per-protocol include 5-minute bit rates (bps), packet counts, and byte counts. NBAR protocol discovery can identify and classify all of the following application types:

- Applications that target a session to a well-known (UDP/TCP) destination port number, referred to as *static port applications*

- Applications that start a control session using a well-known port number but negotiate another port number for the session, referred to as *dynamic port applications*

- Some non-IP applications

- HTTP applications based on URL, MIME type, or host name

Implementing and Verifying AutoQoS

Before you implement AutoQoS and enable it on router interfaces, it is useful to know the router AutoQoS deployment restrictions. Some design considerations are also worth learning with regard to deploying AutoQoS on routers. Finally, you must know the prerequisites for configuring AutoQoS on Cisco routers.

You can enable Cisco AutoQoS Enterprise on certain types of interfaces and permanent virtual circuits (PVCs) only. These are the interface and PVC types on which you can enable AutoQoS enterprise for a Cisco router:

- Serial interfaces with PPP or high-level data link control (HDLC) encapsulation.

- Frame Relay point-to-point subinterfaces. (Multipoint is not supported.)

- ATM point-to-point subinterfaces (PVCs) on both slow (<=768 kbps) and fast serial (>768 kbps) interfaces.

- Frame Relay-to-ATM interworking links.

On low-speed serial links, you must enable AutoQoS Enterprise on both ends, and the configured bandwidths must be consistent. For PPP encapsulations, Multilink PPP (MLP) is enabled automatically, and the IP address of the serial interface is removed and put on the virtual template (MLP bundle). Frame Relay data-link connection identifier (DLCI) and ATM PVCs have some similar restrictions with respect to enabling AutoQoS. Table 7-2 shows those restrictions side by side.

Table 7-2 *AutoQoS Restrictions on Frame Relay DLCIs and ATM PVCs*

Frame Relay DLCI Restrictions	ATM PVC Restrictions
You cannot configure AutoQoS on a Frame Relay DLCI if a map class is attached to the DLCI.	—
You cannot configure AutoQoS on a low-speed Frame Relay DLCI if a virtual template is already configured for the DLCI.	You cannot configure AutoQoS on a low-speed PVC if a virtual template is already configured for the ATM PVC.
For low-speed Frame Relay DLCI configured with Frame Relay-to-ATM interworking, MLP over Frame Relay is configured automatically; the subinterface must have an IP address.	For low-speed ATM PVCs, MLP over ATM is configured automatically; the subinterface must have an IP address.
When MLP over Frame Relay is configured, the IP address is removed and placed on the MLP bundle.	When MLP over ATM is configured, the IP address is removed and put on the MLP bundle.

Based on the interface type, interface bandwidth, and encapsulation, AutoQoS might enable different features on the router interfaces. The bandwidth that is configured on a router interface at the time AutoQoS is enabled on that interface plays a significant role toward the configuration that AutoQoS generates for that interface. AutoQoS will not respond and alter the generated configuration if the interface bandwidth is changed afterward. Following are examples of the features that AutoQoS can enable on router interfaces:

■ **LLQ**—Low-latency queuing reserves a priority queue for VoIP (RTP) traffic, providing a guaranteed but policed bandwidth. Other queues (class-based weighted fair queueing, or CBWFQ) serve traffic such as mission-critical, transactional, and signaling traffic and give them bandwidth guarantees.

■ **cRTP**—Compressed RTP reduces the IP/UDP/RTP header from 40 bytes to 2/4 bytes (without/with CRC). This feature is enabled on low-speed serial interfaces. The reduced header overhead significantly improves link efficiency.

■ **LFI**—The link fragmentation and interleaving feature fragments large data packets on slow interfaces. Therefore, on shared outbound queues (such as the hardware queues) of slow interfaces, VoIP packets are not stuck behind large packets, experiencing jitter and long delays.

On Frame Relay interfaces, fragmentation is configured based on the assumption that the G.729 codec is used and that a voice packet should not experience more than 10-ms delay due to being stuck behind another packet on the hardware queue. If G.729 is the assumed codec, an IP packet that is encapsulating two 10-ms digitized voice samples ends up being 60 bytes long ((8000 bps × 20/1000 sec / 8)+ 40 bytes). Because a VoIP packet should not be fragmented, the minimum fragment size is set to 60 bytes. The maximum fragment size, on the other hand, is calculated based on the 10-ms maximum delay and the configured bandwidth. For example, if the bandwidth is configured as 64 kbps, the maximum fragment size is calculated as 80 bytes (64,000 bps × 10/ 1000 sec / 8 bits/byte). If a codec such as G.711 is used instead of G.729, or if the bandwidth of an interface changes, you might have to modify the fragmentation size or disable and enable AutoQoS so that the changes affect the generated configuration.

Some prerequisites must be satisfied before AutoQoS is enabled on a router. Those prerequisites are as follows:

- You must enable Cisco Express Forwarding (CEF) on the interface where AutoQoS is intended to be enabled, because AutoQoS relies on NBAR for discovery, and NBAR needs CEF.

- You cannot apply a QoS policy (service policy) to the interface prior to enabling AutoQoS on that interface.

- On all interfaces and subinterfaces, you must properly configure the bandwidth. On slow interfaces or subinterfaces, you must configure an IP address. AutoQoS enables MLP on slow interfaces and moves the IP address to the MLP virtual template.

- For AutoQoS SNMP traps to work, you must enable SNMP on the router and specify the server address for SNMP traps destination. This address must be reachable from the router. The SNMP community string "AutoQoS" must have write permission.

Two-Step Deployment of AutoQoS Enterprise on Routers

Deploying AutoQoS for the Enterprise on Cisco routers is a two-step (or two-phase) process. Step 1 is the auto-discovery step. Step 2 is generation and deployment of MQC-based QoS policies based on the discovery step.

AutoQoS discovery uses NBAR protocol discovery. The type and volume of traffic on the network is discovered and analyzed in real-time to be able to generate realistic policies in Step 2. Generally speaking, the longer the auto-discovery runs, the more accurate the results will be. The default period is 3 days, but the administrator can certainly decide if 3 days is sufficient, or if it is too long or too short. Depending on the variety of applications and how often they run (once a day, week, or month), the length of time for running auto-discovery must be determined. The auto-discovery step is/was missing in AutoQoS VoIP; it goes straight to policy generation.

In Step 2, AutoQoS for Enterprise uses the results from the auto-discovery step to generate templates and install them on router interface(s). Templates are the basis for generation of MQC class maps and policy maps. After the policy maps are generated, AutoQoS applies them to the intended interfaces (using service-policy).

In Step 1, auto-discovery is enabled from the interface configuration mode by entering the **auto discovery qos** command:

```
Router(config-if)# auto discovery qos [trust]
```

The optional keyword **trust** allows packets to be classified and receive appropriate QoS treatments based on preset QoS (DSCP) markings. Without the optional **trust** keyword, packets are classified based on the NBAR classification scheme, not based on the preset packet markings. The interface in which you enable auto-discovery must have CEF enabled and have its bandwidth configured (serial interface). Also, if it is a slow interface (<=768 kbps), it must have an IP address. The **auto discovery qos** command is not supported on a subinterface, and it is not supported on an interface that has a policy attached to it already. The configured bandwidth of the interface should not be changed after the command has been applied. Typing **no auto discovery qos** will stop auto-discovery (data collection), and it will remove any reports that have been generated. If you want to view the auto-discovery results, even before they are completed, you can do so by typing this command:

```
Router# show auto discovery qos
```

The second step of implementing AutoQoS for Enterprise is enabling AutoQoS on the interface upon completion of the discovery step. The **auto qos** command causes generation of QoS templates that are used to create MQC class maps and policy maps and application of the policies to the interface. This command is also entered from the interface configuration mode:

```
Router(config-if)# auto qos [voip [trust] [fr-atm]]
```

You use the keyword **voip** if you are enabling AutoQoS VoIP rather than AutoQoS Enterprise. On an earlier Cisco IOS release, this might be your only option. AutoQos for Enterprise was introduced in IOS release 12.3(7)T. Remember that AutoQoS VoIP does not require the discovery step. The **trust** keyword, again, is about respecting the preset marking of the entering packets rather than ignoring their marking and classifying them using NBAR. The keyword **fr-atm** enables AutoQoS VoIP for Frame Relay-to-ATM interworking.

Deploying AutoQoS VoIP on IOS-Based Catalyst Switches

Cisco Catalyst (LAN) switches support only AutoQoS VoIP. Catalyst switches with Cisco IOS are configured differently from Catalyst switches with Cisco Catalyst operating systems. The ONT course and exam focus on the Cisco IOS-based configuration and commands. More specifically, the emphasis is put on 2950(EI), 3550, and 4500 switches, with a few references made to 6500 switches. Please note that the 2950 switches require the Enhanced Image (EI) software and not the Standard Image (SI) for AutoQoS VoIP.

To enable AutoQoS VoIP on Catalyst switches, you need to be aware of two commands. The first one is meant for an access port where either a workstation or an IP phone is connected. The second command you need is meant for ports that are connected to other trusted devices such as routers and switches. A trusted device is a device whose marked traffic (QoS marking) is honored by the local device. Please note that AutoQoS VoIP support for IP softphone is only available on Catalyst 6500 switches (up to the time the Cisco ONT course was first released).

NOTE   An IP phone has a built-in 3-port Ethernet switch. One port is connected to the IP phone and is not visible from outside the IP phone case. The two other Ethernet ports are accessible and located under the IP phone case. One port is meant to be connected to a LAN switch and the other is for a user workstation to plug into it and get connectivity to the LAN switch.

From the following two AutoQoS VoIP commands, the first command is for the IP phone connections, and the other is for trusted connections to other network devices:

```
switch(config-if)# auto qos voip cisco-phone
switch(config-if)# auto qos voip trust
```

The command **auto qos voip trust** is applied to an interface that is assumed to be connected to a trusted device; the interface is usually an uplink trunk connection to another switch or router. This command also reconfigures the egress queues on the interface where it is applied.

On the interface where you apply the **auto qos voip cisco-phone** command, you must have CDP version 2 enabled. Using CDP version 2, the switch determines whether a Cisco IP phone is attached to the port. If CDP is not enabled or if it is CDP version 1, a syslog warning message is displayed. When a Cisco IP phone is detected on a port where the **auto qos voip cisco-phone** command is entered, the port classification trusts the QOS marking of the incoming packets. The command is said to extend the trust boundary to the Cisco IP phone when it is detected. The command also reconfigures the egress queues on the interface. The **mls qos** global configuration command is automatically enabled when you enter the **auto qos voip** command on the first interface. The **mls qos** command enables the QoS feature on the Catalyst switch.

The AutoQoS VoIP commands should not be applied to an interface where QoS commands have previously been configured. However, after you enable AutoQoS on an interface, you can fine-tune and modify the AutoQoS-generated configuration commands if necessary. The QoS markings of the incoming traffic are honored (trusted) on an interface in two cases. The first case is when the **auto qos voip trust** command is applied to an interface. The second case is when a Cisco IP phone is attached to the switch port, and the **auto qos voip cisco-phone** is applied to the interface. If a Cisco IP phone is disconnected from such a port and a workstation is connected to the port directly, the switch discovers the departure of the Cisco IP phone (using CDP version 2), and it changes its behavior to no trust on that port. The egress queuing and buffer allocation on a port are determined automatically based on the interface type; AutoQoS VoIP generates optimal priority queuing (PQ) and weighted round-robin (WRR) configurations for all port types, including static, dynamic access, voice VLAN (VVLAN), and trunk ports. As for mapping of the QoS markings, AutoQoS VoIP maps class of service (CoS) to DSCP as it forwards traffic toward the egress interface queue.

Verifying AutoQoS on Cisco Routers and IOS-Based Catalyst Switches

Monitoring and verifying AutoQoS on routers and switches have similarities and differences. Recall that AutoQoS Enterprise, which includes an initial protocol discovery phase, is not supported on Catalyst switches yet. On the other hand, Cisco Catalyst switches have a unique behavior of mapping the CoS setting of the incoming frames to DSCP, using a CoS-to-DSCP mapping scheme; this is useful for egress interface queuing purposes.

On both Cisco routers and Cisco IOS-based Catalyst switches, the **show auto qos** command displays the AutoQoS templates and initial configuration, whereas the **show policy-map interface** command displays the autogenerated policies and QoS parameters for each interface. The **show auto discovery qos** command, which relates to the discovery phase of the AutoQoS for enterprise and is therefore applicable only to routers, displays autodiscovery results for you to review. On Cisco IOS-based catalyst switches, the CoS-to-DSCP mapping can be displayed using the **show mls qos maps** command. Table 7-3 shows some important QoS verification commands for routers and Cisco IOS-based Catalyst switches.

Table 7-3 *AutoQoS Verification Commands*

Command Type	Command Syntax
Router	**show auto discovery qos** [**interface** *interface*]
Router	**show auto qos** [**interface** *interface*]
Router	**show policy-map interface** *interface*
Switch	**show auto qos** [**interface** *interface*]
Switch	**show mls qos interface** [*interface* | **vlan** *vlan-id* | **buffers** | **policers** | **queuing** | **statistics**]
Switch	**show mls qos maps** [**cos-dscp** | **dscp-cos**]

Sample (and partial) output of the router commands included in Table 7-3 is shown in Example 7-1. As displayed, the output of the **show auto discovery qos interface** command on a router displays the results of the collected data during the autodiscovery phase on the specified interface. It is recommended that you run the discovery phase for at least three days for more accurate results.

Example 7-1 *Sample Output of AutoQoS Monitoring Commands*

```
router# show auto discovery qos interface serial 3/1.1
Serial3/1.1
 AutoQoS Discovery enabled for applications
 Discovery up time: 3 hours, 53 minutes
```

Example 7-1   *Sample Output of AutoQoS Monitoring Commands (Continued)*

```
AutoQoS Class information:
Class Voice:
 Recommended Minimum Bandwidth: 512 Kbps/50% (PeakRate).
 Detected applications and data:
 Application/          AverageRate         PeakRate            Total
 Protocol              (kbps/%)            (kbps/%)            (bytes)
 ---------             ----------          ---------           --------
 rtp audio             3/<1                512/50              841512
...
router# show auto qos
!
policy-map AutoQoS-Policy-Se3/1.1
   class AutoQoS-Voice-Se3/1.1
    priority percent 70
    set dscp ef
   class AutoQoS-Inter-Video-Se3/1.1
    bandwidth remaining percent 10
    set dscp af41
   class AutoQoS-Stream-Video-Se3/1.1
    bandwidth remaining percent 5
    set dscp cs4
   class AutoQoS-Transactional-Se3/1.1
    bandwidth remaining percent 5
...
router# show policy-map interface FastEthernet0/0.1
FastEthernet0/0.1
Service-policy output: voice_traffic
Class-map: dscp46 (match-any)
0 packets, 0 bytes
5 minute offered rate 0 bps, drop rate 0 bps
Match: ip dscp 46
0 packets, 0 bytes
5 minute rate 0 bps
Traffic Shaping
  Target    Byte    Sustain    Excess    Interval  Increment  Adapt
  Rate      Limit   bits/int   bits/int  (ms)      (bytes)    Active
  2500      10000   10000      333       1250
...
```

As shown on the sample output display, the **show auto qos interface** command on a router displays the MQC-based policy maps, class maps, and access lists generated by AutoQoS for the specified interface. The **show policy-map interface** command displays the packet statistics for all classes that are configured and referenced by the policy that is applied to the specified interface. Please note that for brevity, only small portions of the outputs are displayed.

In Example 7-2, you can see sample (and partial) output of the switch commands included in Table 7-3. The **show auto qos** command on a Catalyst switch displays the commands that the AutoQoS VoIP has initially generated for the switch (prior to any modifications that might have been applied). The sample output shows that 20 percent of the bandwidth is allocated to queue 1, 1 percent to queue 2, and 80 percent to queue 3. Because a value of 0 percent is assigned to queue number 4, this queue is the designated priority queue. CoS values of 0, 1, 2, and 4 are directed to queue 1, whereas CoS values 3, 6, and 7 are mapped to queue 3. CoS value 5 is mapped to queue 4. Queue 2 is not used at all. Finally, the CoS-to-DSCP mappings are shown (CoS 0 to DSCP 0, CoS 1 to DSCP 8, and so on).

Example 7-2 *Sample (and Partial) Output of the Switch Commands Included in Table 7-3*

```
switch# show auto qos
Initial configuration applied by AutoQoS:
wrr-queue bandwidth 20 1 80 0
no wrr-queue cos-map
wrr-queue cos 1 0 1 2 4
wrr-queue cos 3 3 6 7
wrr-queue cos 4 5
mls qos map cos-dscp 0 8 16 26 32 46 48 56
!
interface FastEthernet0/3
mls qos trust device cisco-phone
mls qos trust cos
…
switch# show mls qos interface gigabitethernet0/1 statistics
Ingress
    dscp: incoming  no_change   classified   policed   dropped (in bytes)
      1 : 0         0           0            0         0
    Others: 203216935 24234242  178982693    0         0

Egress
    dscp: incoming  no_change   classified   policed   dropped (in bytes)
      1 : 0         n/a         n/a          0         0

WRED drop counts:
    qid thresh1   thresh2  FreeQ
     1 : 0        0        1024
     2 : 0        0        1024
…
switch# show mls qos maps dscp-cos
Dscp-cos map:
    dscp: 0 8 10 16 18 24 26 32 34 40 46 48 56
         ---------------------------------------------
     cos: 0 1  1  2  2  3  7  4  4  5  5  7  7
...
```

The output of the **show mls qos interface** *interface* command has various optional keywords available. A sample output in which the **statistics** keyword is used is shown in Example 7-2. The output of the **show mls qos maps dscp-cos** is shown last; it is obvious that the output displays the way DSCP is mapped to the CoS value for the egress packets. Please note that you can modify the default CoS-to-DSCP and DSCP-to-CoS mappings using the global configuration mode **mls qos map** command.

AutoQoS Shortcomings and Remedies

The policy maps and class maps that AutoQoS generates do not always suit the needs of a network completely. In that case, you can modify the policy maps and class maps to meet the specific network requirements. Therefore, it is important to know how to fine-tune the configuration that Cisco AutoQoS generates. Some Cisco IOS **show** commands are specifically helpful for determining which parts of the configuration need modification.

Automation with Cisco AutoQoS

Cisco AutoQoS is capable of performing the following tasks and might generate appropriate configurations to accomplish them:

- Defining the trust boundaries (or extended trust boundaries) and re-marking incoming traffic on trusted and untrusted links

- Defining traffic classes based on the applications and protocols discovered in the network

- Creating queuing mechanisms with proper configurations such as bandwidth guarantee for each traffic type, based on the DiffServ model

- Enabling interface-specific transport features, such as LFI, Multilink PPP (MLP), cRTP, TCP Header compression, traffic shaping, and Frame Relay traffic shaping (FRTS), when necessary based on link bandwidth and encapsulation

- Defining alarms and event logging settings for monitoring purposes

- Defining CoS-to-DSCP mappings (or other required mappings), DSCP-to-egress queue mappings, and the proper queue sizes and WRR weights on Cisco Catalyst LAN switches

Based on Cisco best-practices recommendations and the discovered application and protocol types, AutoQoS can enable six QoS mechanisms using DiffServ technology. Table 7-4 shows the six DiffServ functions and the corresponding Cisco IOS features that AutoQoS can enable for that function.

Table 7-4 *DiffServ Functions and Cisco IOS Features That AutoQoS Enables*

DiffServ Function	Cisco IOS QoS Feature That AutoQoS Uses
Classification	Using NBAR (on untrusted links) Using IP precedence, DSCP, or CoS (trusted)
Marking	Class-based marking
Congestion management	LLQ (Strict PQ + CBWFQ) using percentage BW WRR (on Catalyst LAN switches)
Shaping	CBTS[1] FRTS[2]
Congestion avoidance	WRED[3]
Link efficiency	LFI MLP cRTP

[1] CBTS = class-based traffic shaping
[2] FRTS = Frame Relay traffic shaping
[3] WRED = weighted random early detection

Using MQC, AutoQoS defines up to 10 traffic classes based on packet marking on trusted links or using NBAR on untrusted links. Classified packets are marked at trust boundary spots (as close to the traffic source as possible), preferably in the wiring closet switches and IP phones. Table 7-5 shows the ten classes of traffic that AutoQoS can define along with the DSCP and CoS values that AutoQoS assigns to them. The number of traffic classes defined depends on the results of the discovery phase.

Table 7-5 *Traffic Classes That AutoQoS Defines*

Class Name	Traffic Type	DSCP Value	CoS Value
IP Routing	Network control traffic such as routing protocols	CS6	6
Interactive Voice	Interactive voice bearer traffic	EF	5
Interactive Video	Interactive video data traffic	AF41	4

Table 7-5 *Traffic Classes That AutoQoS Defines (Continued)*

Class Name	Traffic Type	DSCP Value	CoS Value
Streaming Video	Streaming media traffic	CS4	4
Telephony Signaling	Telephony signaling and control traffic	CS3	3
Transactional and Interactive	Database applications that are transactional in nature	AF21	2
Network Management	Network management traffic	CS2	2
Bulk Data	Bulk data transfers, web traffic, general data service	AF11	1
Scavenger	Entertainment, rogue traffic, and less than best-effort traffic	CS1	1
Best Effort	All noncritical and miscellaneous traffic	BE	0

To ensure predictable network behavior and good voice (and video) quality while providing the appropriate amount of bandwidth to Enterprise applications, especially during congestion, AutoQoS enables the most modern queuing mechanisms—LLQ and WRR—where they are needed. Voice traffic is treated as DiffServ EF with highest priority and placed in a strict priority queue with a guaranteed but policed bandwidth. Signaling and enterprise data traffic are treated as DiffServ AF classes, and CBWFQ is utilized for those classes, giving each class a separate queue with minimum bandwidth guarantees. Unclassified traffic is treated as DiffServ BE and is assigned to the default class. The bandwidth allocations are done using a percentage of the link bandwidth for better scalability and manageability reasons. On LAN switches, WRR is utilized with a priority queue for real-time traffic. Also, AutoQoS uses modifiable CoS-to-DSCP and DSCP-to-CoS mappings within Cisco LAN switches.

AutoQoS enables FRTS where it is needed. FRTS is especially important for two reasons:

■ The interface clock rate (physical speed) is usually higher than the committed information rate (CIR). As stated before, correct bandwidth configuration on serial interfaces and sub-interfaces is necessary before activation of AutoQos on those interfaces.

■ Enterprise sites are usually connected in a hub-and-spoke topology, and traffic flows from one or many sites to another site can cause congestion and data loss at the destination site.

WRED is the congestion avoidance technique that AutoQoS deploys to avoid tail drop and congestion at network bottleneck areas. Global synchronization and dropping of high-priority packets are the mitigation targets of congestion avoidance using WRED. AutoQoS deploys link-efficiency mechanisms to address insufficient bandwidth and long delays on slow links. The link-efficiency mechanisms that AutoQoS deploys include LFI, MLP, Frame Relay fragmentation, and cRTP.

Common AutoQoS Problems

AutoQoS was developed to automate QoS configuration for common enterprise network scenarios. Therefore, the configuration that AutoQoS yields does not necessarily suit and satisfy the requirements of every network. Following are the three most common Cisco AutoQoS issues that might arise:

- Too many traffic classes are generated; classification is overengineered.

- The configuration that AutoQoS generates does not adapt automatically to changing network traffic conditions.

- The configuration that AutoQoS generates fits common network scenarios but does not fit some circumstances, even after extensive autodiscovery.

Based on the traffic and protocol types discovered during the autodiscovery phase, AutoQoS can generate up to ten traffic classes. Most enterprises, to keep the configurations simple and manageable, deploy only three to six traffic classes. Currently, AutoQoS does not have a knob to let you configure the maximum number of classes to be generated. However, it is recommended that if the number of generated traffic classes is too many for your needs, you should modify the AutoQoS-generated configuration and reduce the number of traffic classes. You can consolidate two or more similar traffic classes into a common class.

AutoQoS generates QoS templates and policies based on the device configuration at the time AutoQoS was enabled and based on the network applications and protocols detected at the time autodiscovery was run. Therefore, it is recommended that configurations such as interface band-width be done carefully, and before the AutoQoS discovery is allowed to run for as long as possible (preferably several days). If the device configuration changes, or if network traffic conditions change, AutoQoS-generated configuration will not adapt to the changes. However, if you disable AutoQoS, rerun the AutoQoS discovery, and enable AutoQoS again, the AutoQoS will generate its templates and policies based on the new network conditions.

If AutoQoS-generated configuration does not suit your network needs and circumstances, you might have to give the autodiscovery phase more time for a more thorough discovery and classification. However, letting the autodiscovery run for a long time does not always solve this problem. This is because the AutoQoS was developed for most common Enterprise networks and based on Cisco best-practice recommendations, but it does not necessarily meet the special requirements of all networks. To solve this problem, you can modify the configuration that AutoQoS generates. The AutoQoS-generated configuration is MQC compliant, and you can use MQC to enhance the configuration to meet your specific needs.

Interpreting and Modifying AutoQoS Configurations

The **show auto qos** command displays all the QoS mechanisms (and the corresponding configurations) that Cisco AutoQoS has enabled on a router, with or without autodiscovery. Therefore, you can inspect all the QoS templates that were generated as a result of applying Cisco AutoQoS. You can gather several particular facts from the output of the **show auto qos** command, the most important of which are these:

- The number of traffic classes.

- The classification options used.

- The traffic markings performed.

- The queuing mechanisms generated and the options used.

- Other QoS mechanisms, such as traffic shaping, applied per traffic class.

- Other traffic parameters, such as CIR, suggested for a Frame Relay connection.

- The interface, subinterface, or virtual circuit where the policies are applied.

The number of traffic classes that AutoQoS identifies is recognized based on the number of class maps that have been generated. The **match** and **set** statements within each class map reveal the classification options used and the class-based markings performed. From within the policy maps, you can observe the queue types generated and the corresponding parameters; the **priority** and **bandwidth** commands reveal the queue type and the amount of bandwidth guarantee for each queue. From within the policy maps, you can also observe other QoS mechanisms, such as class-based shaping, congestion avoidance (WRED), or link efficiency mechanisms (LFI or cRTP) applied to each traffic class. You can discover traffic parameters such as the CIR or committed burst applied to a Frame Relay map class—in other words, suggested by AutoQoS—by inspecting the **show auto qos** command output. The output of this command also shows the actual interface, subinterface, or virtual circuit where the policies that AutoQoS generates are applied. Finally, the Remote Monitoring (RMON) traps that are logged for voice packet drops are displayed in the output of the **show auto qos** command.

Using Cisco IOS command-line interface (CLI), you can modify the class maps, policy maps, and traffic parameters that AutoQoS generates. You might have to do this for two major reasons:

- The AutoQoS-generated commands do not completely satisfy the specific requirements of the Enterprise network.

- The network condition, policies, traffic volume and patterns, and so on might change over time, rendering the AutoQoS-generated configuration dissatisfying.

If the network engineers (or administrators) have the ability and the expertise to modify and adapt the AutoQoS-generated configuration, they will not need to redeploy the whole AutoQoS procedure again. You can modify and tune the AutoQoS-generated class maps and policy maps by doing the following:

- Using Cisco QoS Policy Manager (QPM).

- Directly entering the commands one at the time at the router CLI using MQC.

- Copying the existing configuration, a class map for example, into a text editor and modifying the configuration using the text editor, offline. Next, using CLI, remove the old undesirable configuration and then add the new configuration by copying and pasting the text from the text editor. This is probably the easiest way to modify and tune the AutoQoS-generated class maps and policy maps.

For classification purposes, in addition to using NBAR and ACLs, MQC offers more classification options that you can use for tuning. Some of those classification options and their corresponding **match** statements are as follows:

- Based on the specific ingress interface where the traffic comes from:

  `match input interface interface`

- Based on the Layer 2 CoS value of the traffic:

  `match cos cos-value [cos-value ...]`

- Based on the Layer 3 IP precedence value:

  `match ip precedence ip-prec-value [ip-prec-value ...]`

- Based on the Layer 3 IP DSCP value:

  `match ip dscp ip-dscp-value [ip-dscp-value ...]`

- Based on the RTP port value range:

  `match ip rtp starting-port-number port-range`

The modifying and tuning of the configuration that AutoQoS generates will probably take a few rounds of modification and testing before it fully satisfies your requirements. Figure 7-1 shows a flowchart about using AutoQoS, verifying its auto-generated commands, and modifying the auto-generated commands if necessary.

Figure 7-1   *Verifying and Modifying AutoQoS-Generated Configurations*

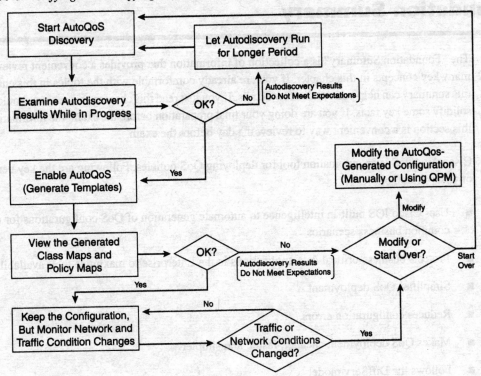

The procedure for modifying an existing, active classification or policy that AutoQoS generates can be summarized into a three-step process:

Step 1   Review the existing QoS policy, identify the new requirements, and outline the configuration modifications necessary.

Step 2   Modify the AutoQoS-generated configuration according to the new requirements.

Step 3   Review the new (modified) configuration.

Please note that if you modify the AutoQoS-generated configuration, the AutoQoS generated commands will not be removed properly when you enter the **no auto qos** command. The **no auto qos** command only removes the original (unmodified) commands that AutoQoS generated.

Foundation Summary

The "Foundation Summary" is a collection of information that provides a convenient review of many key concepts in this chapter. If you are already comfortable with the topics in this chapter, this summary can help you recall a few details. If you just read this chapter, this review should help solidify some key facts. If you are doing your final preparation before the exam, the information in this section is a convenient way to review the day before the exam.

Cisco AutoQoS is an automation tool for deploying QoS policies. Following are the key benefits of Cisco AutoQoS:

- Uses Cisco IOS built-in intelligence to automate generation of QoS configurations for most common business scenarios

- Protects business-critical data applications in the Enterprise to maximize their availability

- Simplifies QoS deployment

- Reduces configuration errors

- Makes QoS deployment cheaper, faster, and simpler

- Follows the DiffServ model

- Allows customers to have complete control over their QoS configuration

- Enables customers to modify and tune the configurations that Cisco AutoQoS automatically generates to meet their specific needs or changes in the network conditions

The two phases of Cisco AutoQoS evolution are as follows:

1. AutoQoS VoIP

   This was the first phase of AutoQoS.

   One command provisions the basic required QoS commands.

   It is supported across a broad range of router and switch platforms.

2. AutoQoS for Enterprise

   This is the second phase of AutoQoS.

   It extends the AutoQoS capabilities for data, voice, and video.

   It is, however, supported only on routers.

It is deployed in a two-step process. In the first step, called autodiscovery, it discovers the traffic types and loads using NBAR protocol discovery. In the second step, it generates and implements QoS policies.

Cisco AutoQoS addresses five key elements of QoS deployment:

- Application classification

- Policy generation

- Configuration

- Monitoring and reporting

- Consistency

AutoQoS for Enterprise uses NBAR protocol discovery. NBAR protocol discovery analyzes traffic in real-time, identifies approximately 100 Layer 4 through 7 applications and protocols using stateful and deep packet inspection, and provides bidirectional, per-interface, and per-protocol statistics. NBAR protocol discovery is able to identify and classify all of the following application types:

- Applications that target a session to a well-known (UDP/TCP) destination port number, referred to as static port applications

- Applications that start a control session using a well-known port number but negotiate another port number for the session, referred to as dynamic port applications

- Some non-IP applications

- HTTP applications based on URL, MIME type, or host name

You can enable Cisco AutoQoS Enterprise on certain types of interfaces and permanent virtual circuits (PVCs) only. These are the interface and PVC types that you can enable AutoQoS Enterprise for on a Cisco router:

- Serial interfaces with PPP or HDLC encapsulation.

- Frame Relay point-to-point subinterfaces. (Multipoint is not supported.)

- ATM point-to-point subinterfaces (PVCs) on both slow (<=768 kbps) and fast serial (>768 kbps) interfaces.

- Frame Relay-to-ATM interworking links.

Following are the router prerequisites for configuring Cisco AutoQoS:

■ The router cannot have a QoS policy attached to the interface.

■ You must enable CEF on the router interface (or PVC).

■ You must specify the correct bandwidth on the interface or subinterface.

■ You must configure a low-speed interface (<= 768 Kbps) and an IP address.

You deploy AutoQoS for Enterprise on Cisco routers in two steps (or two phases):

Step 1   Traffic is profiled using autodiscovery.

You do this by entering the **auto qos discovery** command in the interface configuration mode.

Step 2   MQC-based QoS policies are generated and deployed.

You do this by entering the **auto qos** command in interface configuration mode.

On Cisco LAN switches, AutoQoS VoIP is enabled on each interface using the **auto qos voip** [**trust** | **cisco-phone**] command. The **trust** keyword is used for trusted connections such as an uplink to a trusted switch or router so that the ingress VoIP packet marking is trusted. You use the **cisco-phone** keyword for Cisco IP phone connections and to enable the trusted boundary feature. You use CDP to detect the presence or absence of a Cisco IP phone.

The commands for verifying Cisco AutoQoS on routers are as follows:

■ **show auto discovery qos**

Allows you to examine autodiscovery results

■ **show auto qos**

Allows you to examine Cisco AutoQoS templates and initial configuration

■ **show policy-map interface**

Allows you to explore interface statistics for autogenerated policy

The commands for verifying Cisco AutoQoS on Cisco LAN switches are as follows:

■ **show auto qos**

Allows you to examine Cisco AutoQoS templates and initial configuration

- **show policy-map interface**

  Allows you to explore interface statistics for autogenerated policy

- **show mls qos maps**

  Allows you to examine CoS-to-DSCP maps

The three most common Cisco AutoQoS issues that might arise, and their corresponding solutions, are as follows:

- Too many traffic classes are generated; classification is overengineered.

  Solution: Manually consolidate similar classes to produce the number of classes needed.

- The configuration that AutoQoS generates does not automatically adapt to changing network traffic conditions.

  Solution: Run Cisco AutoQoS discovery on a periodic basis, followed by re-enabling of Cisco AutoQoS.

- The configuration that AutoQoS generates fits common network scenarios but does not fit some circumstances, even after extensive autodiscovery

  Solution: Manually fine-tune the AutoQoS-generated configuration.

You examine the AutoQoS-generated configuration using the **show auto qos** command, which provides the following information:

- Number of traffic classes identified (class maps)

- Traffic classification options selected (within class maps)

- Traffic marking options selected (within policy maps)

- Queuing mechanisms deployed and their corresponding parameters (within policy maps)

- Other QoS mechanisms deployed (within policy maps)

- Where the autogenerated policies are applied: on the interface, subinterface, or PVC

You might have to modify the configuration that AutoQoS generates for two reasons:

- The AutoQoS-generated commands do not completely satisfy the specific requirements of the Enterprise network.

- The network condition, policies, traffic volume and patterns, and so on might change over time, rendering the AutoQoS-generated configuration dissatisfying.

You can modify and tune the AutoQoS-generated class maps and policy maps by doing the following:

- Using Cisco QoS Policy Manager (QPM).

- Directly entering the commands one at a time at the router command-line interface using MQC.

- Copying the existing configuration, a class map for example, into a text editor and modifying the configuration using the text editor offline. Next, using CLI, remove the old undesirable configuration and then add the new configuration by copying and pasting the text from the text editor. This is probably the easiest way.

For classification purposes, in addition to using NBAR and ACLs, you can use the following classification options that MQC offers for tuning:

- Based on the specific ingress interface where the traffic comes from:

  `match input interface` *interface*

- Based on the Layer 2 CoS value of the traffic:

  `match cos` *cos-value* `[`*cos-value* `...]`

- Based on the Layer 3 IP precedence value:

  `match ip precedence` *ip-prec-value* `[`*ip-prec-value* `...]`

- Based on the Layer 3 IP DSCP value:

  `match ip dscp` *ip-dscp-value* `[`*ip-dscp-value* `...]`

- Based on the RTP port value range:

  `match ip rtp` *starting-port-number port-range*

Q&A

Some of the questions that follow challenge you more than the exam by using an open-ended question format. By reviewing now with this more difficult question format, you can exercise your memory better and prove your conceptual and factual knowledge of this chapter. The answers to these questions appear in Appendix A.

1. List at least three key benefits of Cisco AutoQoS.

2. What are the two phases of AutoQoS evolution?

3. What are the five key elements of QoS deployment that Cisco AutoQoS addresses?

4. Which application types is NBAR protocol discovery able to identify and classify?

5. On what types of router interfaces or PVCs can you enable Cisco AutoQoS?

6. What are the router prerequisites for configuring AutoQoS?

7. What are the two steps (or phases) of AutoQoS for Enterprise?

8. List at least two commands for verifying AutoQoS on Cisco routers.

9. List at least two commands for verifying AutoQoS on Cisco LAN switches.

10. What are the three most common Cisco AutoQoS issues that can arise, and their corresponding solutions?

11. List at least three pieces of information that can be obtained from the output of the **show auto qos** command.

12. What are the two major reasons for modifying the configuration that AutoQoS generates?

13. Specify two methods for modifying and tuning the AutoQoS-generated class maps and policy maps.

14. In addition to using NBAR and ACLs, what classification options does MQC offer?

This part covers the following ONT exam topics. (To view the ONT exam overview, visit http://www.cisco.com/web/learning/le3/current_exams/642-845.html.)

- Describe and configure WLAN QoS.

- Describe and configure wireless security on Cisco Clients and APs (e.g., SSID, WEP, LEAP, etc.).

- Describe basic wireless management (e.g., WLSE and WCS). Configure and verify basic WCS configuration (i.e., login, add/review controller/AP status, security, and import/review maps).

Part III: Wireless LAN

This chapter covers the following subjects:

- **The Need for Wireless LAN QoS**

- **Current Wireless LAN QoS Implementation**

- **Configuring Wireless LAN QoS**

CHAPTER 8

Wireless LAN QoS Implementation

This chapter first describes WLAN QoS and why it is needed. Next, it covers the current implementation of WLAN QoS. The last section describes how to configure WLAN QoS for different QoS profiles using the Cisco WCS web user interface.

"Do I Know This Already?" Quiz

The purpose of the "Do I Know This Already?" quiz is to help you decide whether you really need to read the entire chapter. The 10-question quiz, derived from the major sections of this chapter, helps you determine how to spend your limited study time.

Table 8-1 outlines the major topics discussed in this chapter and the "Do I Know This Already?" quiz questions that correspond to those topics. You can keep track of your score here, too.

Table 8-1 *"Do I Know This Already?" Foundation Topics Section-to-Question Mapping*

Foundation Topics Section Covering These Questions	Questions	Score
"The Need for Wireless LAN QoS"	1–6	
"Current Wireless LAN QoS Implementation"	7–8	
"Configuring Wireless LAN QoS"	9–10	
Total Score	**(10 possible)**	

CAUTION The goal of self-assessment is to gauge your mastery of the topics in this chapter. If you do not know the answer to a question or are only partially sure of the answer, mark this question wrong for purposes of the self-assessment. Giving yourself credit for an answer you correctly guess skews your self-assessment results and might provide you with a false sense of security.

You can find the answers to the "Do I Know This Already?" quiz in Appendix A, "Answers to the 'Do I Know This Already?' Quizzes and Q&A Sections." The suggested choices for your next step are as follows:

- **6 or less overall score**—Read the entire chapter. This includes the "Foundation Topics," "Foundation Summary," and "Q&A" sections.

- **7–8 overall score**—Begin with the "Foundation Summary" section and then follow up with the "Q&A" section at the end of the chapter.

- **9 or more overall score**—If you want more review on this topic, skip to the "Foundation Summary" section and then go to the "Q&A" section. Otherwise, proceed to the next chapter.

1. Select the correct statement about wireless LANs.

   a. WLANs are mostly implemented as extensions to wired LANS.

   b. WLANs are occasionally implemented as overlays to wired LANs.

   c. WLANs are sometimes implemented as substitutes for wired LANs.

   d. All of the above.

2. Which statement is true about 802.11 wireless media access control?

   a. It uses CSMA/CD.

   b. It uses token passing.

   c. It uses CSMA/CA.

   d. All of the above.

3. Distributed coordinated function (DCF) performs collision avoidance using which of these?

   a. Radio frequency (RF) carrier sense

   b. Interframe spacing (IFS)

   c. Random back-off/contention windows (CW)

   d. All of the above

4. IEEE provides QoS extensions to wireless LANs by which of the following drafts/standards?

   a. 802.11g

   b. 802.11e

   c. 802.11d

   d. 802.11a

5. Select the item that is *not* a real-time function performed by the access point in the Split-MAC architecture.

   a. Key management

   b. Beacon generation

   c. Probe transmission

   d. Encryption/decryption

6. Which of the following shows the correct mapping of 802.11e priority levels to WMM access categories?

   a. Voice(Platinum)=6/7, Video(Gold)=4/5, Best-Effort(Silver)=1/2, Background(Bronze)=0/3

   b. Voice(Platinum)=6/7, Video(Gold)=4/5, Best-Effort(Silver)=3/2, Background(Bronze)=0/1

   c. Voice(Platinum)=6/7, Video(Gold)=4/5, Best-Effort(Silver)=0/3, Background(Bronze)=1/2

   d. None of the above

7. Select the correct statement about how wireless LAN controller copies/maps QoS fields in the Split-MAC architecture.

   a. Wireless LAN controller copies the IP DSCP field (inner) to the DSCP field (outer) of the LWAPP data unit.

   b. Wireless LAN controller maps the IP DSCP field (inner) to the 802.1p field (outer) of the LWAPP data unit.

   c. Wireless LAN controller maps the DSCP field from the LWAPP data unit to the 802.1p field on the 802.1Q frame.

   d. All of the above.

8. Which priority (802.1p) value is used/reserved for LWAPP control messages?

   a. 6

   b. 7

   c. 0

   d. 1

9.   Which of the following is *not* a parameter set in the Edit QoS Profile page of the Web User Interface for Wireless LAN Controller, as a part of Per-User Bandwidth Contract?

   a.   Average voice rate

   b.   Average data rate

   c.   Burst data rate

   d.   Burst real-time rate

10.   On the **WLANs > Edit** page of the web user interface of the wireless LAN controller, what does it mean if the general WMM or 802.11e policy for the interaction between the wireless client and the access point is set to **Required**?

   a.   This setting means that WMM or 802.11e QoS requests are ignored.

   b.   This setting means that QoS is offered to WMM or 802.11e-capable clients.

   c.   This setting means that all clients must be WMM/802.11e compliant to use this WLAN ID.

   d.   None of the above is correct.

Foundation Topics

The Need for Wireless LAN QoS

WLANs are growing in popularity. They are mostly implemented as extensions to, but are occasionally deployed as overlays to, wired LANs, or replacements for wired LANs. The difference between wired and wireless LANs is in the physical layer and in the MAC layer. Please note that Logical Link Control (LLC) and MAC are considered upper and lower sublayers of the OSI Layer 2 Data Link Control (DLC) layer, respectively. Upper-layer protocols and applications such as IP, TCP, and FTP run identically on both wired and wireless platforms. Figure 8-1 shows two access switches (Layer 2) connected to a distribution (multilayer) switch. The access switch on the right side has wired devices plugged into its access ports. The access switch on the left side, however, is connected to a wireless LAN controller (WLC), which in turn is connected to and controls two wireless LAN APs. Each wireless client on the left side of Figure 8-1 communicates with an AP by sending and receiving frames over the radio frequency (RF) link, and it gains access to the network.

Figure 8-1 *Wireless LAN Extending the Wired LAN*

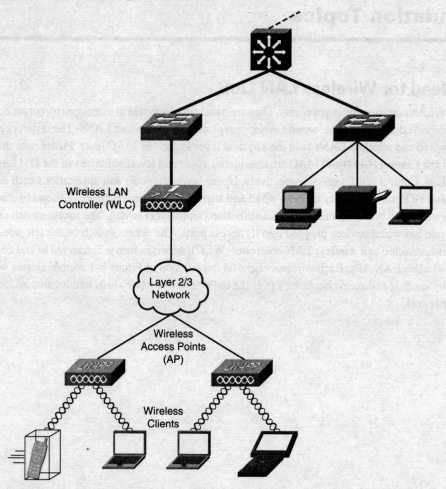

Wired Ethernet uses carrier sense multiple access with collision detection (CSMA/CD) as its MAC mechanism. Wireless LAN (802.11), on the other hand, lacks the ability to read and send data at the same time; therefore, it cannot detect collision like its wired counterpart can. Hence, WLAN uses carrier sense multiple access with collision avoidance (CSMA/CA) as the MAC mechanism. Collision avoidance is accomplished by distributed coordinated function (DCF). DCF uses RF carrier sense, inter-frame spacing (IFS), and random back-off/CWs. Please note that random back-off/CWs are sometimes casually referred to as *random wait timers*.

To be able to offer end-to-end QoS, the wireless portion and components of a network must comply with and satisfy the QoS needs of the applications. Following are some of the main QoS needs of applications, such as voice and video:

■ Dedicated bandwidth

■ Controlled jitter and delay (*latency*)

■ Managed congestion

■ Shaped traffic (rate limited)

■ Prioritized traffic (with drop preference)

WLAN QoS Description

IEEE has provided the QoS extensions to WLANs in the 802.11e specifications. The ONT courseware refers to 802.11e as a draft for standardization, but at the time of this writing, 802.11e is already approved and is considered a new standard. IEEE defines 802.11e as the first wireless standard, adding QoS features to the existing IEEE 802.11b and IEEE 802.11a (and other) wireless standards, while maintaining full backward compatibility with them. While 802.11e was in the standardization process, Wi-Fi Alliance released a specification called the Wi-Fi Multimedia (WMM) for the interim period.

WMM is a subset of 802.11e; for instance, WMM reduces the eight priority levels of 802.11e to four access categories. Note that access category has the same meaning as priority level. Using the basic CSMA/CA-based DCF, each client generates a random back-off number between 0 and a minimum contention window (CW_{min}) and waits until the RF channel is free for an interval called distributed coordinated function inter-frame space (DCF IFS or DIFS). From that moment on, the channel is continuously checked; if it is free, the random back-off number is decremented by 1 until it becomes 0. At that time, the client sends the frame. If the channel becomes busy, the client has to wait until the channel is free, wait for a DIFS interval, and start decrementing the random back-off interval all over again.

The CSMA/CA-based DCF gives all devices the same priority, so it is considered a best-effort mechanism. WMM, on the other hand, provides traffic prioritization (or RF prioritization) by using four access categories: Platinum (or voice), Gold (or video), Silver (best-effort), and Bronze (background), in descending priority order. The four access categories are in effect four queues, each of which gets a higher probability of transmitting than the access priority (or queue) below it. If a specific type of traffic is not assigned to an access category, it is categorized as best-effort (Silver). The eight 802.11e priority levels are mapped to four WMM access categories, as shown in Table 8-2.

Table 8-2 *Mapping of 802.11e Priority Levels to WMM Access Categories*

WMM Access Category	802.11e Priority Level
Voice (Platinum)	6 or 7
Video (Gold)	4 or 5
Best-Effort (Silver)	0 or 3
Background (Bronze)	1 or 2

802.11e (and its subset WMM) uses Enhanced Distributed Coordination Function (EDCF) by employing different CW/back-off timer values for different priorities (access categories). If a client finds the RF channel available, it waits for a DIFS period, and then it has to wait for a random back-off period based on the CW_{min} associated with the priority of the traffic being submitted (more accurately, the queue that the traffic is submitted from). If the traffic is high priority, its CW_{min} is smaller, giving it a shorter back-off timer value; if the traffic is lower priority, its CW_{min} is larger, giving it a longer back-off timer value. Note that with EDCF, even though high-priority traffic such as voice is statistically expected to be transmitted before lower-priority traffic, it is not guaranteed to do so at all times; therefore, technically EDCF cannot be equated to a strict priority system. With EDCF, IFS (Inter Frame Space) is referred to as AIFS (Arbitrated IFS).

> **NOTE** In the original ONT student course material, on the page titled "WLAN QoS RF Back-Off Timing," SIFS is mistakenly used instead of DIFS. Short inter-frame space (SIFS) is used only before transmitting important frames such as acknowledgements, and it has no random back-off. SIFS is not used to transmit regular data frames. Data frames, on the other hand, must wait for a DIFS and then begin the random back-off procedure.

Split MAC Architecture and Light Weight Access Point

To centralize the security, deployment, management, and control aspects of WLANs, Split MAC Architecture (a part of Cisco Unified Wireless Network Architecture) shifts some of the functions traditionally performed on the autonomous AP to a central location (device). The main functions performed on legacy autonomous APs are shown in Table 8-3 categorized under two columns: real-time 802.11/MAC functionality, and non-real-time 802.11/MAC functionality.

Table 8-3 *Real-Time and Non-Real-Time 802.11 MAC Functions*

802.11/MAC Real-Time Functions	802.11/MAC Non-Real-Time Functions
Beacon generation	Association/disassociation/reassociation
Probe transmission and response	802.11e/WMM resource reservation
Power management	802.1x EAP

Table 8-3 *Real-Time and Non-Real-Time 802.11 MAC Functions (Continued)*

802.11/MAC Real-Time Functions	802.11/MAC Non-Real-Time Functions
802.11e/WMM scheduling and queuing	Key management
MAC layer data encryption/decryption	Authentication
Control frame/message processing	Fragmentation
Packet buffering	Bridging between Ethernet and WLAN

To address the centralized RF management needs of the enterprises, Cisco designed a centralized lightweight AP (LAP or LWAP) wireless architecture with Split-MAC architecture as its core. Split-MAC architecture divides the 802.11 data and management protocols and AP capabilities between a lightweight AP and a centralized WLAN controller. The real-time MAC functions, such as those listed in the left column of Table 8-3, including handshake with wireless clients, MAC layer encryption, and beacon handling, are assigned to the LWAP. The non-real-time functions such as those listed in the right column of Table 8-3, including frame translation and bridging, plus user mobility, security, QoS, and RF management, are assigned to the wireless LAN controller.

Current Wireless LAN QoS Implementation

Wireless RF is an OSI Layer 2 technology, and its QoS is currently based on 802.11e or WMM specifications. With the addition of WLANs, to maintain end-to-end QoS in a network, it is necessary to perform mapping between Layer 2 (802.1p) priority or Layer 3 DSCP (or IP precedence) and 802.11e priority (or WMM access category). If a wireless AP connects to an access port (non-trunk port, lacking 801.1p marking) of a LAN switch, the Layer 2 802.11e (or WMM) marking of data coming from the wireless client is lost because the data is forwarded from the AP to the LAN switch. This is also true for the traffic arriving at the LAN switch (with Layer 2 801.1p marking), which then has to forward the traffic through an access port to the wireless AP. In the absence of Layer 2 QoS information, such as on a non-trunk connection, it will be necessary to utilize the Layer 3 QoS information such as the DSCP marking.

In the Cisco centralized LWAP wireless architecture (with Split-MAC architecture as its core), WLAN controller ensures that traffic traversing between it and the LWAP maintains its QoS information. The WLAN data coming from the wireless clients to the LWAP is tunneled to the WLAN controller using Lightweight Access Point Protocol (LWAPP). In the opposite direction, the traffic coming from the wired LAN to the WLAN controller is also tunneled to the LWAP using LWAPP.

Figure 8-2 shows a WLAN controller with a wired 802.1Q trunk connection to a multilayer LAN switch. The WLAN controller has two LWAPs associated to it. The WLAN controller has an LWAPP tunnel set up with each of the LWAPs. The LWAPP tunnel can be set up over a Layer 2 or a Layer 3 network. In Layer 2 mode, the LWAPP data unit is in an Ethernet frame. Furthermore, the WLAN controller and the AP must be in the same broadcast domain and IP subnet. In Layer 3 mode, however, the 3 LWAPP data unit is in a User Datagram Protocol (UDP/IP frame). Moreover, the WLAN controller and AP can be in the same or different broadcast domains and IP subnets. Examples for the supported wireless LAN controllers are Cisco 2000, 4100, 4400 Series wireless LAN controllers, Cisco WiSM, Cisco WLCM for integrated services routers, Airespace 3500, 4000, and 4100 Series wireless LAN controllers. Examples for the supported APs are Cisco Aironet 1000, 1130, 1230, 1240, and 1500 series LWAPs.

Figure 8-2 *LWAPP Tunnel in the Split-MAC Architecture*

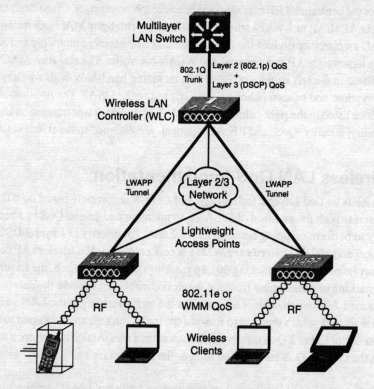

To maintain continuous (end-to-end) QoS, the WLAN controller on one end of the LWAPP tunnel and the LWAP at the other end of the LWAPP tunnel must do some mapping between the QoS marking of the received data units and the QoS markings/fields of the data unit they send forward. The wireless LAN controller sends and receives 802.1Q frames to and from the wired multilayer LAN switch. 802.1Q frames have the CoS (priority/802.1p) field for QoS marking purposes. The wireless LAN controller and the LWAP send and receive LWAPP data units to each other. The LWAPP data unit has an 802.1p (CoS) equivalent field and a DSCP equivalent field. (The LWAP does not understand the 802.1p field of the LWAPP data unit.) The LWAP and the wireless clients exchange RF, with 802.11e (or WMM) providing the QoS marking field. Table 8-4 shows the mapping between IP DSCP value and 802.1p and 802.11e values.

Table 8-4 *QoS Markings Mapping Table*

Cisco 802.1Q/P Priority-Based Traffic Type	IP DSCP	802.1p Priority	802.11e Priority
Network control/reserved	56–62	7	7
Inter-network control/IP routing	48	6	7
Voice	46 (EF)	5	6
Video	34 (AF41)	4	5
Voice control	26 (AF31)	3	4
Background (Gold)	18 (AF21)	2	2
Background (Silver)	10 (AF11)	1	1
Best effort	0 (BE)	0	0 or 3

Figure 8-3 is a comprehensive depiction of data moving from a multilayer LAN switch to a wireless client through a wireless LAN controller and an LWAP, and data moving in the opposite direction from the wireless client to the multilayer LAN switch through an LWAP and a wireless LAN controller. This process involves four steps, accordingly marked in Figure 8-3, which will be addressed next.

Step 1 in Figure 8-3 shows that when the WLAN controller receives an 802.1Q frame (encapsulating an IP packet) from the multilayer LAN switch, it forwards the IP packet toward the LWAP, encapsulating it in an LWAPP data unit. For QoS continuity purposes, the WLAN controller copies the IP DSCP field (inner) to the LWAPP data unit DSCP field (outer). The WLAN controller also maps the IP DSCP field (inner) to the LWAPP data unit's 802.1p field (outer). The mapping of DSCP to 802.1p is done according to Table 8-4. Please note that the LWAPP control packets exchanged between the WLAN controller and the LWAP are always tagged with the 802.1p value of 7. Indeed, LWAPP reserves the 802.1p value of 7 for the LWAPP control packets.

Step 2 in Figure 8-3 shows that when the LWAP receives a LWAPP data unit (encapsulating an IP packet) from the WLAN controller, it forwards the IP packet toward the wireless client using RF, and it uses 802.11e/WMM for Layer 2 QoS marking. The LAWP maps the DSCP field from the LWAPP data unit to the 802.11e/WMM field based on Table 8-4.

Figure 8-3 *Mapping of Inner QoS Fields to LWAPP Tunnel QoS Fields*

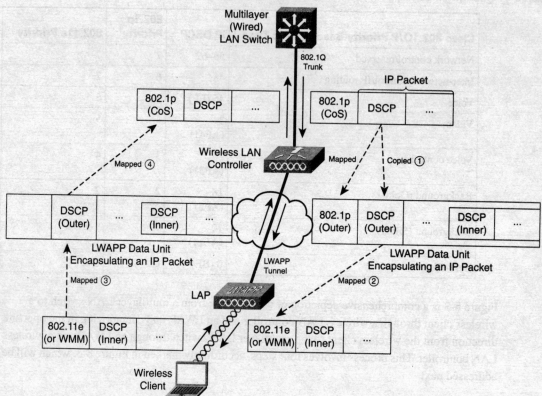

In Step 3, shown in Figure 8-3, the LWAP receives RF from the wireless client transporting an IP packet with the Layer 2 QoS marking in the 802.11e/WMM field. The LWAP forwards the IP packet toward the WLAN controller, encapsulating it in an LWAPP data unit. For QoS continuity purposes, the LWAP maps the 802.11e value to the DSCP field on the LWAPP data unit based on Table 8-4. Note that because the LWAP does not understand 802.1p, it does not mark that field on the LWAPP data unit.

Finally, in Step 4, shown in Figure 8-3, the WLAN controller receives an LWAPP data unit from the LWAP encapsulating an IP packet. The WLAN controller forwards the IP packet toward the multilayer LAN switch, encapsulating it in an 801.1Q frame (over the trunk connection). For QoS continuity purposes, the WLAN controller maps the DSCP field from the LWAPP data unit to the 802.1p field on the 802.1Q frame based on Table 8-4. Please note that packets with no QoS markings received from the WLAN will be categorized as best-effort (default Silver) when the WLAN controller transmits them toward the LAN.

Configuring Wireless LAN QoS

Cisco WLAN controllers have a built-in web user interface. Figure 8-4 shows a typical web user interface.

Figure 8-4 *A Typical Web User Interface for Cisco WLAN Controllers*

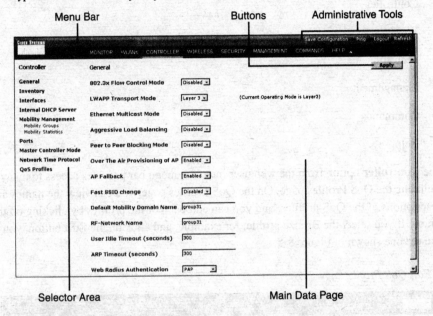

The web user interface has five main areas:

- Administrative tools

- Menu bar

- Buttons

- Selector area

- Main data page

The menu bar has the following selections available:

- Monitor

- WLANs

- Controller

- Wireless

- Security

- Management

- Commands

- Help

The **Controller** option from the web user interface menu bar provides access to many pages, including the QoS Profiles page. On the QoS Profiles page, you can view the names and descriptions of the QoS profiles, and you can edit each of the profiles by clicking on the **Edit** button. If you select the Bronze profile, for example, and click on the **Edit** button, you see a page like the one shown in Figure 8-5.

Figure 8-5 *Edit QoS Profile Page*

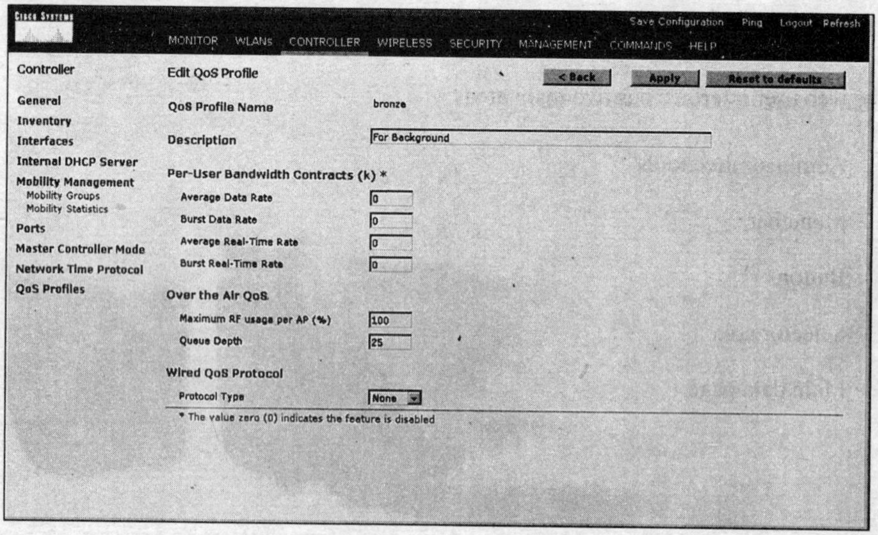

Even though the EDCF sets the priority or access category for each profile, in the Edit QoS Profile page (shown in Figure 8-5), you can set the average data rate, burst data rate, average real-time rate, and burst real-time rate, as parts of per-user bandwidth contract. You can set these fields to 0 up to 60,000 bits per second; their default value is 0, which means that the feature is off.

You can configure two Over the Air QoS fields on the Edit QoS Profile Page for the profile you are editing: **Maximum RF Usage Per AP (%)**, and **Queue Depth**. The maximum RF usage per AP for each profile is set to 100 (%) by default. If the queue depth for a profile is reached, packets of that profile are dropped at the AP. The default queue depth values can vary from one controller model to another. The controller example used in the ONT courseware has these queue depth default values: 100 for Platinum, 75 for Gold, 50 for Silver, and 25 for Bronze.

On the Edit QoS Profile page, under the Wired QoS Protocol heading, you can select the protocol type as either **802.1P** or **None**. Selecting **802.1P** activates 802.1P Priority Tags, and selecting **None** deactivates 802.1P Priority Tags (default). If you select **802.1P** for protocol type, you can then set **802.1P Tag** for the wired connection to a number from 0 to 7. The default mappings for the four access categories are 6 for Platinum, 5 for Gold, 3 for Silver, and 1 for Bronze.

WLANs is another option from the web user interface menu bar (see Figure 8-4). It allows you to create, configure, and delete WLANs on your controller. The WLANs menu bar provides you with these selections:

- WLANs

- WLANs > New

- WLANs > Edit

- WLANs > Mobility Anchors

- AP Groups VLAN

To configure existing WLANs, you must click on **Edit**. A page similar to the one shown in Figure 8-6 is displayed.

Figure 8-6 *WLANs > Edit Page*

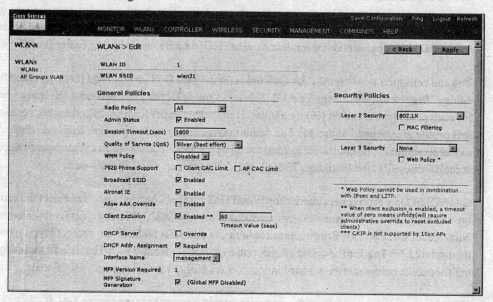

On the **WLANs > Edit** page, for each WLAN ID, you can set the **Quality of Service** field to one of **Platinum (voice)**, **Gold (video)**, **Silver (best effort)**, or **Bronze (background)**. On the same page, you can set the general WMM or 802.11e policy for the interaction between wireless client and the AP to **Disabled**, **Allowed**, or **Required**:

- **Disabled**—This setting means that WMM or 802.11e QoS requests are ignored.

- **Allowed**—This setting means that QoS is offered to WMM or 802.11e-capable clients. Default QoS is offered to non-WMM/802.11e-capable clients.

- **Required**—This setting means that all clients must be WMM/802.11e compliant to use this WLAN ID.

Foundation Summary

The "Foundation Summary" is a collection of information that provides a convenient review of many key concepts in this chapter. If you are already comfortable with the topics in this chapter, this summary can help you recall a few details. If you just read this chapter, this review should help solidify some key facts. If you are doing your final preparation before the exam, the information in this section is a convenient way to review the day before the exam.

Wireless LANs (WLANs) are extensions to wired LANs; the same protocols and applications can run on both. The media access method of WLAN is carrier sense multiple access collision avoid (CSMA/CA). Wireless (802.11) uses distributed coordinated function (DCF) to avoid collision. DCF is based on RF carrier sense, inter-frame spacing (IFS), and random wait timers.

To continue to support real-time applications such as voice and video that have specific requirements such as minimum dedicated bandwidth, maximum delay, maximum jitter, maximum packet loss, and so on, the wireless components of a network must also offer QoS capabilities and features. 802.11e, which was in draft but is now a standard, provides QoS extensions to 802.11 wireless. Wi-Fi Alliance released a Wi-Fi Multimedia (WMM) standard while the 802.11e was in the process of being approved as a standard. WMM has four access categories compared to the eight priority levels of 802.11e. Table 8-5 shows the mapping between 802.11e priorities and the WMM access categories.

Table 8-5   *Mapping of 802.11e Priority Levels to WMM Access Categories*

WMM Access Category	802.11e Priority Level
Voice (Platinum)	6 or 7
Video (Gold)	4 or 5
Best-Effort (Silver)	0 or 3
Background (Bronze)	1 or 2

802.11e and WMM replace DCF with Enhanced DCF (EDCF). In addition to prioritizing/categorizing the data (see Table 8-5), 802.11e/WMM uses different minimum wait times and random back-off times for traffic with different priorities (access categories). Figure 8-7 provides a pictorial representation of this method.

Figure 8-7 *WLANs QoS RF Back-Off Timings*

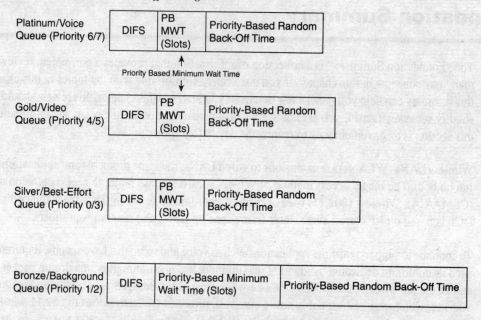

The Cisco Split-MAC architecture separates the real-time aspects of the 802.11 protocol from its non-real-time/management aspects. Instead of an autonomous access point (AP), the Split-MAC architecture uses lightweight access points (LWAPs), which will handle real-time functions, and WLAN controllers, which will handle the non-real-time functions. A WLAN controller can have one or more LAPs associated with it. The wireless LAN controller and LWAP communicate using Lightweight Access Point Protocol (LWAPP) over a Layer 2 (Ethernet) or a Layer 3 (UDP/IP) network. Table 8-6 shows the main real-time tasks assigned to the LWAP and the main non-real-time tasks assigned to the wireless LAN controller within the Cisco Split-MAC model.

Table 8-6 *Division of Functions Between Wireless LAN Controller and LWAP*

802.11/MAC Real-Time Functions Performed at the LWAP	802.11/MAC Non-Real-Time Functions Performed at the WLAN Controller
Beacon generation	Association/disassociation/reassociation
Probe transmission and response	802.11e/WMM resource reservation
Power management	802.1x EAP
802.11e/WMM scheduling and queuing	Key management
MAC layer data encryption/decryption	Authentication
Control frame/message processing	Fragmentation
Packet buffering	Bridging between Ethernet and WLAN

To provide end-to-end QoS within a network that includes wireless subsets, the LWAPP data units moving between the wireless LAN controller and the lightweight access point (LWAP) have Layer 2 (802.1p) or Layer 3 (DSCP) fields. Figure 8-8 shows how the WLAN controllers and LWAPs accomplish the mapping of QoS markings (within the Split-MAC architecture).

Figure 8-8 *Mapping of QoS Fields by LAPs and WLAN Controllers*

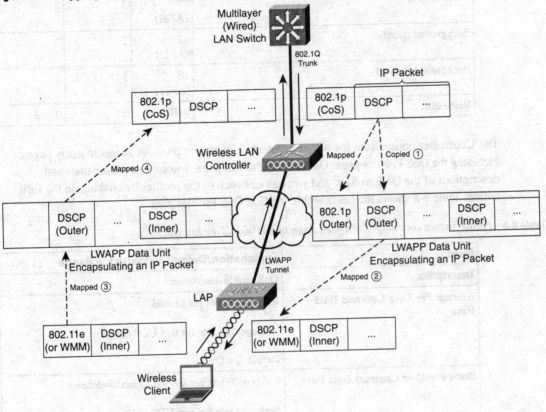

Packet marking translations among DSCP, 802.1p, and 802.11e priorities performed at wireless LAN controller and LWAP are based on Table 8-7.

Table 8-7 *QoS Markings Mapping Table*

Cisco 802.1Q/P Priority-Based Traffic Type	IP DSCP	802.1p Priority	802.11e Priority
Network control/reserved	56–62	7	7
Inter-network control/IP routing	48	6	7
Voice	46 (EF)	5	6

continues

Table 8-7 *QoS Markings Mapping Table (Continued)*

Cisco 802.1Q/P Priority-Based Traffic Type	IP DSCP	802.1p Priority	802.11e Priority
Video	34 (AF41)	4	5
Voice control	26 (AF31)	3	4
Background (Gold)	18 (AF21)	2	2
Background (Silver)	10 (AF11)	1	1
Best-effort	0 (BE)	0	0 or 3

The **Controller** option from the web user interface menu bar provides access to many pages, including the QoS Profiles page. On the QoS Profiles page, you can view the names and descriptions of the QoS profiles, and you can edit each of the profiles by clicking on the **Edit** button. Table 8-8 shows the fields within the Edit QoS Profiles page.

Table 8-8 *Fields Shown on the QoS Profiles Page of the Web User Interface*

Field	Explanation/Default Value/Value Range
Description	QoS profile description.
Average Per-User Contract Data Rate	0 to 60,000 bits per second. Average data rate for non-UDP traffic. Default 0 = OFF.
Burst Per-User Contract Data Rate	0 to 60,000 bits per second. Operator-defined. Peak data rate for non-UDP traffic. Default 0 = OFF.
Average Per-User Contract Real-Time Rate	0 to 60,000 bits per second. Average data rate for UDP traffic. Default 0 = OFF.
Burst Per-User Contract Real-Time Rate	0 to 60,000 bits per second. Peak data rate for UDP traffic. Default 0 = OFF.

Table 8-8 *Fields Shown on the QoS Profiles Page of the Web User Interface (Continued)*

Field	Explanation/Default Value/Value Range
Maximum QoS RF Usage per AP	1 to 100%. Maximum air bandwidth available to a class of clients. Default = 100%.
QoS Queue Depth	Depth of queue for a class of client. Causes packets with a greater value to be dropped at the access point. (25 for Bronze, 50 for Silver, 75 for Gold, and 100 for Platinum on some controllers.)
Wired QoS Protocol	**802.1P** activates 802.1P priority tags, and **None** deactivates 802.1P priority tags (default).
802.1P Tag	802.1P priority tag for the wired connection. 0 to 7. Used for traffic and LWAPP packets. 1 for Bronze, 3 for Silver, 4/5 for Gold, and 6 for Platinum.

Q&A

Some of the questions that follow challenge you more than the exam by using an open-ended question format. By reviewing now with this more difficult question format, you can exercise your memory better and prove your conceptual and factual knowledge of this chapter. The answers to these questions appear in Appendix A.

1. How does distributed coordinated function (DCF) accomplish collision avoidance?

2. What is the standard (or draft name) for the wireless QoS of IEEE?

3. What is the Wi-Fi Alliance specification for wireless QoS?

4. Describe the relationship between 802.11e priorities and WMM access categories.

5. What contention mechanism does 802.11e use to provide prioritized RF access?

6. Describe the Split-MAC architecture.

7. List at least three of the real-time MAC functions that are assigned to the LWAP in the Split-MAC architecture.

8. List at least three of the non-real-time MAC functions that are assigned to the wireless LAN controller in the Split-MAC architecture.

9. Which protocol is used between the wireless LAN controller and the lightweight access point in the Split-MAC architecture?

10. From which page of the web user interface of the wireless LAN controller can you examine and modify QoS profiles?

This chapter covers the following subjects:

- Overview of WLAN Security

- 802.1x and EAP Authentication Protocols

- Configuring Encryption and Authentication on Lightweight Access Points

Introducing 802.1x and Configuring Encryption and Authentication on Lightweight Access Points

This chapter is composed of three sections. In the first section, you are provided with an introduction to wireless security, its issues, and how it has evolved. In the next section, the 802.1 extensible authentication protocol (EAP) and some of its popular variants are presented. Wireless protected access (WPA and WPA2) and 802.11i security standards are also presented in this section. The final section of this chapter shows how you can navigate through the graphic user interface of a wireless LAN controller (WLC) using a web browser to set up various authentication and encryption options on lightweight access points (LWAP).

"Do I Know This Already?" Quiz

The purpose of the "Do I Know This Already?" quiz is to help you decide whether you really need to read the entire chapter. The 10-question quiz, derived from the major sections of this chapter, helps you determine how to spend your limited study time.

Table 9-1 outlines the major topics discussed in this chapter and the "Do I Know This Already?" quiz questions that correspond to those topics.

Table 9-1 *"Do I Know This Already?" Foundation Topics Section-to-Question Mapping*

Foundation Topics Section Covering These Questions	Questions	Score
"Overview of WLAN Security"	1–4	
"802.1x and EAP Authentication Protocols"	5–9	
"Configuring Encryption and Authentication on Lightweight Access Points"	10	
Total Score	**(10 possible)**	

CAUTION The goal of self-assessment is to gauge your mastery of the topics in this chapter. If you do not know the answer to a question or are only partially sure of the answer, mark this question wrong for purposes of the self-assessment. Giving yourself credit for an answer you correctly guess skews your self-assessment results and might provide you with a false sense of security.

You can find the answers to the "Do I Know This Already?" quiz in Appendix A, "Answers to the 'Do I Know This Already?' Quizzes and Q&A Sections." The suggested choices for your next step are as follows:

- **6 or less overall score**—Read the entire chapter. This includes the "Foundation Topics," "Foundation Summary," and "Q&A" sections.

- **7–8 overall score**—Begin with the "Foundation Summary" section and then follow up with the "Q&A" section at the end of the chapter.

- **9 or more overall score**—If you want more review on this topic, skip to the "Foundation Summary" section and then go to the "Q&A" section. Otherwise, proceed to the next chapter.

1. Which of the following is *not* an issue or a weakness of initial WLAN security approaches?

   a. Relying on SSID as a security measure

   b. Relying on MAC filters

   c. Overhead of mutual authentication between wireless clients and access control/authentication servers

   d. Usage of static WEP

2. Which of the following is *not* considered a weakness of WEP?

   a. With enough data captured, even with initialization vector used, the WEP key can be deducted.

   b. WEP is vulnerable to dictionary attacks.

   c. Because with basic WEP the wireless client does not authenticate the access point, the client can be victimized by rogue access points.

   d. The WEP usage of certificates is not convenient for some customers.

3. Which of the following organizations developed LEAP to address the shortcomings of WEP?

   a. Wi-Fi Alliance Group

   b. Cisco

   c. IEEE

   d. Microsoft

4. Which of the following organizations developed WPA?

   a. Wi-Fi Alliance Group

   b. Cisco

   c. IEEE

   d. Microsoft

5. Which of the following is *not* a required component for 802.1x authentication?

   a. External user database

   b. Supplicant (EAP-capable client)

   c. Authenticator (802.1x-capable access point)

   d. Authentication server (EAP-capable RADIUS server)

6. Which of the following is *not* a LEAP feature?

   a. Usage of PKI

   b. Fast, secure roaming with Cisco or Cisco-compatible clients

   c. True single login with an existing username and password using Windows NT/2000 Active Directory (or Domain)

   d. Support for a wide range of operating systems (such as Microsoft, Macintosh, Linux, and DOS)

7. Which of the following is *not* an EAP-FAST feature?

   a. Provides full support for 802.11i, 802.1x, TKIP, and AES

   b. Supports Windows single sign-on for Cisco Aironet clients and Cisco-compatible clients

   c. Uses certificates (PKI)

   d. Supports password expiration or change (Microsoft password change)

8. Which of the following is an EAP-TLS feature?

   a. It uses PKI.

   b. Its supported clients include Microsoft Windows 2000, XP, and CE, plus non-Windows platforms with third-party supplicants such as Meetinghouse.

   c. It permits a single logon to a Microsoft domain.

   d. All of the above.

9. Which of the following is *not* true about PEAP?

   a. It builds an encrypted tunnel in Phase 1.

   b. Only the server authentication is performed using PKI certificate.

   c. All PEAP varieties support single login.

   d. Cisco Systems, Microsoft, and RSA Security developed PEAP.

10. When you use a web browser to access a WLC GUI to modify or configure the encryption and authentication settings of a wireless LAN, which item of the main toolbar should you click on first?

   a. **Security**

   b. **Configure**

   c. **WLAN**

   d. **Management**

Foundation Topics

Overview of WLAN Security

Affordability, ease of use, and convenience of wireless devices, wireless local-area networks (WLAN), and related technologies have caused a substantial increase in their usage over recent years. At the same time, the number of reported attacks on wireless devices and networks has surged. Hackers have access to affordable wireless devices, wireless sniffers, and other tools. Unfortunately, the default wireless security settings are usually open and vulnerable to intrusion and attacks. For example, if encryption is not enabled, sensitive and private information sent over a wireless LAN can easily be sniffed (captured). One of the common methods that hackers use is called war driving. *War driving* refers to the process whereby someone drives around with a laptop equipped with a wireless network interface card (NIC), looking for vulnerable wireless devices and networks. Best practices require that authentication and encryption be used to protect wireless client data from security and privacy breaches. User authentication allows the network devices to check and ensure legitimacy of a user and protect the network from unauthorized users trying to gain access to the network and all the confidential data/files. Encryption is used so that, if someone captures data during transit through sniffing, for example, he cannot read it. The illegitimate capturer of data needs to know the key and the algorithm used to encrypt the data to decrypt it.

WLAN Security Issues

The main security problem with wireless LANs is and has been that the available security features are not enabled and used. However, for those who have been interested and keen to secure their wireless networks, the available features have not always been as sophisticated as they are today.

Service Set Identifier (SSID) is the method for naming a wireless network. The SSID configuration of a client must match the SSID of the wireless access point (AP) for the client to communicate with that AP. However, if the client has a null SSID, it can request and acquire the SSID from the AP. Unless the AP is configured not to broadcast its SSID, the AP responds to the wireless client request and supplies the SSID to the client; the client can then associate to that AP and access the wireless network. Some people mistakenly think that if the AP is configured not to broadcast its SSID, they have a secure wireless LAN; that is not true. When a legitimate wireless client with the correct SSID attempts to associate with its AP, the SSID is exchanged over the air unencrypted; that means that an illegitimate user can easily capture and use the SSID. The conclusion is that SSID should not be considered a wireless security tool. SSID is used to logically segment wireless clients and APs into groups.

Rogue APs impose threats to wireless LANs. A rogue AP is illegitimate; it has been installed without authorization. If an attacker installs a rogue AP and clients associate with it, he can easily collect sensitive information such as keys, usernames, passwords, and MAC addresses. Unless the client has a way of authenticating the AP, a wireless LAN should have a method to detect rogue APs so that they can be removed. Furthermore, attackers sometimes install rogue APs intending to interfere with the normal operations and effectively launch denial of service (DoS) attacks.

Some wireless LANs use MAC filters. Using MAC filters, the wireless LANS check the wireless MAC address of a client against a list of legitimate MAC addresses before granting the client access to the network. Unfortunately, MAC addresses can be easily spoofed, rendering this technique a weak security feature.

The 802.11 Wired Equivalent Privacy (WEP), or basic 802.11 security, was designed as one of the first real wireless security features. WEP has several weaknesses; therefore, it is not recommended for use unless it is the only option available. For example, with enough data captured, hacking software can deduct the WEP key. Because of this weakness, usage of initialization vector (IV) with WEP has become popular. The initialization vector is sent to the client, and the client uses it to change the WEP key, for example, after every packet sent. However, based on the size of the IV, after so much data is sent, the cycle begins with the initial key again. Because the IV is sent to the client in clear text and the keys are reused after each cycle, with enough data captured, the hacker can deduct the WEP key. WEP has two other weaknesses. First, it is vulnerable to dictionary attacks because, using dictionary words, the hackers keep trying different WEP keys and might succeed in guessing the correct WEP key. Second, using WEP, the wireless client does not authenticate the AP; therefore, rogue APs can victimize the client.

Evolution of WLAN Security Solutions

802.11 WEP using 40-bit keys shared between the wireless AP (AP) and the wireless client was the first-generation security solution to wireless authentication and encryption that IEEE offered. WEP is based on the RC4 encryption algorithm (a stream cipher) and supports encryption up to 128 bits. Some vendors, such as Cisco Systems, supported both 40-bit and 128-bit keys on their wireless devices; an example would be Cisco Aironet 128-bit devices. RC4 vulnerabilities, plus the WEP usage of static keys, its weak authentication, and its nonscalable method of manually configuring WEP keys on clients, soon proved to be unacceptable, and other solutions were recommended.

To address the shortcomings of WEP, from 2001 to 2002, Cisco Systems offered a wireless authentication and encryption solution that was initially called Lightweight Extensible Authentication Protocol (LEAP). LEAP had negative connotations for some people; therefore,

Cisco Systems decided to rename it Cisco Wireless EAP. In brief, this solution offered the following improvements over WEP:

- Server-based authentication (leveraging 802.1x) using passwords, one-time tokens, Public Key Infrastructure (PKI) certificates, or machine IDs

- Usage of dynamic WEP keys (also called session keys) by reauthenticating the user periodically and negotiating a new WEP key each time (Cisco Key Integrity Protocol, or CKIP)

- Mutual authentication between the wireless client and the RADIUS server

- Usage of Cisco Message Integrity Check (CMIC) to protect against inductive WEP attacks and replays

In late 2003, the Wi-Fi Alliance Group provided WPA as an interim wireless security solution until the IEEE 802.11i standard becomes ready. WPA requires user authentication through preshared key (PSK) or 802.1x (EAP) server-based authentication prior to authentication of the keys used. WPA uses Temporal Key Integrity Protocol (TKIP) or per-packet keying, and message integrity check (MIC) against man-in-the-middle and replay attacks. WPA uses expanded IV space of 48 bits rather than the traditional 24-bits IV. WPA did not require hardware upgrades and was designed to be implemented with only a firmware or software upgrade.

In mid-2004, IEEE 802.11i/WPA2 became ready. The main improvements to WPA were usage of Advanced Encryption Standard (AES) for encryption and usage of Intrusion Detection System (IDS) to identify and protect against attacks. WPA2 is more CPU-intensive than WPA mostly because of the usage of AES; therefore, it usually requires a hardware upgrade.

802.1x and EAP Authentication Protocols

IEEE developed the 802.1x standard, called Extensible Authentication Protocol (EAP), so that LAN bridges/switches can perform port-based network access control. 802.1x was therefore considered a supplement to the IEEE 802.1d standard. The 802.1x (EAP) standard was quickly discovered and adopted for wireless LAN access control. Cisco Systems has supported the 802.1x authentication since December 2000.

Cisco Systems, Microsoft, and other vendors have developed several variations of EAP; different clients support one or more of those EAP varieties. 802.1x leverages many of the existing standards. Following are a few of the important EAP features and benefits:

- The RADIUS protocol with a RADIUS server can be used for AAA centralized authentication. Users are authenticated based on usernames and passwords stored in an active directory available in the network (based on RFC 2284). The RADIUS server or Cisco Access Control Server (ACS) can use this directory. See Figure 9-1 in this chapter.

- Authentication is mutual between the client and the authentication server (RADIUS Server). The client software, which is required by the authentication protocols to participate in the authentication process, is commonly referred to as a supplicant.

- 802.1x can be used with multiple encryption algorithms, such as AES, WPA TKIP, and WEP.

- Without user intervention, 802.1x uses dynamic (instead of static) WEP keys. These WEP encryption keys are derived after authentication.

- One-time password (OTP) can be used to encrypt plaintext passwords so that unencrypted passwords do not have to be sent over insecure connections/applications such as Telnet and FTP.

- 802.1x supports roaming in public areas and is compatible with existing roaming technologies.

- Policy control is centralized, as is management of the user database.

The components that are required for 802.1x authentication are an EAP-capable client (the supplicant), 802.1x-capable AP (the authenticator), and EAP-capable RADIUS server (the authentication server). Optionally, the authentication server may use an external user database. Figure 9-1 shows these components.

Figure 9-1 *801.2x (EAP) Authentication Components*

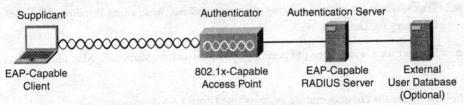

The EAP-capable client requires an 802.1x-capable driver and an EAP supplicant. The supplicant may be provided with the client card, be native in the client operating system, or be obtained from the third-party software vendor. The EAP-capable wireless client (with the supplicant) sends authentication credentials to the authenticator. The authenticator is usually located at the enterprise edge, between the enterprise network and the public or semipublic devices. The authenticator sends the received authentication credentials to the authentication server. The authentication server refers to a user database to check the validity of the authentication credentials and to determine the network access level of a valid user. Some examples of authentication servers are Cisco Secure ACS, Microsoft IAS, and Meetinghouse Aegis. The local RADIUS database or an external database such as Microsoft Active Directory can be used for authentication. Authentication does not always use a RADIUS database or an external database; for example, Cisco IOS can perform local authentication based on the usernames and passwords stored in a device configuration (running-config). Please note however that local authentication is neither a scalable nor a secure authentication option.

EAP Authentication Protocols

802.1x does not provide LAN access to a client that is attempting access through a LAN switch port or a wireless AP until the client has been authenticated. Many authentication protocols are variations of EAP and work within the framework of 802.1x. The most popular protocols used in Cisco wireless networking environments are briefly discussed in the following sections.

Cisco LEAP

Cisco LEAP is one of the 802.1x authentication types for WLANs and, like the other EAP types, it is supported by Wi-Fi WPA and WPA2. Cisco LEAP supports strong mutual authentication between the client and a RADIUS server using a logon password as the shared secret, and it provides dynamic per-user, per-session encryption keys. Cisco LEAP is included with all Cisco wireless products, Cisco Aironet products, and Cisco-compatible client devices.

Following are the important capabilities that LEAP provides, making it somewhat unique compared to the other EAP variations:

- Fast, secure roaming (Layer 2 and Layer 3) with Cisco or Cisco-compatible clients

- True single login with an existing username and password using Windows NT/2000 Active Directory (or Domain)

- Support for a wide range of operating systems (such as Microsoft, Macintosh, Linux, and DOS)

Following are the client operating systems that Cisco LEAP supports:

- Microsoft Windows 98, XP, and CE

- Mac OS (9.X or 10.X)

- Linux (Kernel 2.2 or 2.4)

- DOS

Following are the RADIUS servers and user databases that Cisco LEAP supports:

- Cisco Secure ACS and Cisco Network (Access) Registrar

- Meetinghouse Aegis

- Interlink Merit

- Funk Odyssey Server and Funk Steel-Belted

- Products that use the Interlink Networks server code (such as LeapPoint appliances)

Following are the Cisco wireless devices that Cisco LEAP supports:

- Cisco Aironet autonomous APs and LWAPs

- Cisco WLAN controllers

- Cisco Unified Wireless IP Phone 7920 handset

- Workgroup bridges, wireless bridges, and repeaters

- Many Cisco and Cisco-compatible WLAN client devices

Figure 9-2 displays the Cisco LEAP authentication process. A wireless client can only transmit EAP traffic (no other traffic type) until a RADIUS server authenticates it. The authentication can be initiated by the client Start message or by the AP Request/Identity message. Either way, the client responds to the AP with a username. When the AP receives the username, it encapsulates it in the Access Request message (a RADIUS message type) and sends it to the RADIUS server. In the next two steps, the RADIUS server authenticates the client, and then the client authenticates the RADIUS server through a challenge/response process (through the AP).

Figure 9-2 *Cisco LEAP*

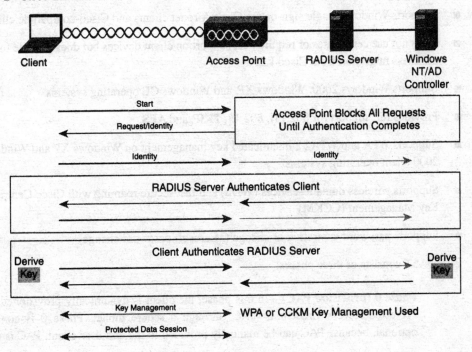

In the challenge/response process, one party sends a challenge (a randomly generated bit sequence) to the other, and the other party sends a response back. The response is generated using an algorithm such as MD5, which takes the challenge, plus a password that both parties share, and perhaps other input such as a session ID. The benefit of the challenge/response process is that the shared password is not sent from one party to the other.

When the RADIUS server and the client successfully authenticate each other, they submit a Success (RADIUS) message to each other (through AP). Next, the RADIUS server and the client generate a pairwise master key (PMK). The RADIUS server sends its PMK to the AP so that the AP stores it locally for this particular client. Finally, the client and the AP, using the PMKs each hold, perform a four-way handshake that allows them to exchange encrypted traffic and have a protected data session.

EAP-FAST

Extensible Authentication Protocol-Flexible Authentication via Secure Tunneling (EAP-FAST) was developed by Cisco Systems and submitted to the Internet Engineering Task Force (IETF) in 2004. Cisco LEAP requires use of strong passwords; for a customer who cannot enforce a strong password policy and does not want to use certificates, migrating to EAP-FAST is a good solution because it provides safety from dictionary attacks. EAP-FAST is standards based (nonproprietary) and is considered flexible and easy to deploy and manage. Some of the main features and benefits of EAP-FAST are as follows:

- Supports Windows single sign-on for Cisco Aironet clients and Cisco-compatible clients

- Does not use certificates or require PKI support on client devices but does provide for a seamless migration from Cisco LEAP

- Supports Windows 2000, Windows XP, and Windows CE operating systems

- Provides full support for 802.11i, 802.1x, TKIP, and AES

- Supports WPA and WPA2 authenticated key management on Windows XP and Windows 2000 client operating systems

- Supports wireless domain services (WDS) and fast secure roaming with Cisco Centralized Key Management (CCKM)

- Supports password expiration or change (Microsoft password change)

EAP-FAST consists of three phases:

> **Phase 0 (provision PAC)**—In this phase, the client is dynamically provisioned with a Protected Access Credential (PAC) through a secure tunnel. Phase 0 is considered optional, because PAC can be manually provided to the end-user client. PAC is used in

Phase 1 of EAP-FAST authentication. PAC consists of a secret part and an opaque part. It has a specific user ID and an authority ID associated with it.

Phase 1 (establish secure tunnel)—In this phase, the Authentication, Authorization, and Accounting (AAA) server (such as the Cisco Secure ACS v. 3.2.3) and the client use PAC to authenticate each other and establish a secure tunnel.

Phase 2 (client authentication)—In this phase, the client sends its credentials to the RADIUS server through the secure tunnel, and the RADIUS server authenticates the client and establishes a client authorization policy.

Figure 9-3 displays the EAP-FAST authentication process. A wireless client can transmit only EAP traffic (no other) until a RADIUS server authenticates it. First, the client sends an EAP over LAN (EAPOL) start frame to the AP, and the AP returns a request/identity to the client.

Figure 9-3 *EAP-FAST*

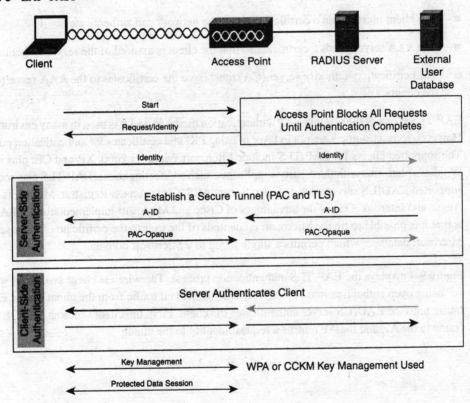

Next, the client sends its network access identifier (NAI) address to the AP, which in turn sends it to the RADIUS server. The client and the server then perform mutual authentication using Phase 1 and Phase 2 of EAP-FAST process, and the RADIUS server sends a session key to the AP in a Success packet.

After that, the client and the RADIUS server negotiate and derive a session key. (This process varies depending whether the client is using WEP or 802.11i.) The client and the AP use these keys during this session.

At the end of the session, the client sends an EAPOL-logoff packet to the AP, returning it to the preauthentication state (filtering all but EAPOL traffic).

EAP-TLS

Extensible Authentication Protocol-Transport Layer Security (EAP-TLS) uses the Transport Layer Security (TLS) protocol. TLS is an IETF standard protocol that has replaced the Secure Socket Layer (SSL) protocol. TLS provides secure communications and data transfers over public domains such as the Internet, and it provides protection against eavesdropping and message tampering. EAP-TLS uses PKI; therefore, the following three requirements must be satisfied:

- The client must obtain a certificate so that the network can authenticate it.

- The AAA server needs a certificate so that the client is assured of the server authenticity.

- The certification authority server (CA) must issue the certificates to the AAA server(s) and the clients.

EAP-TLS is one of the original EAP authentication methods, and it is used in many environments. However, some customers are not in favor of using PKI and certificates for authentication purposes. The supported clients for EAP-TLS include Microsoft Windows 2000, XP, and CE, plus non-Windows platforms with third-party supplicants, such as Meetinghouse. EAP-TLS also requires a supported RADIUS server such as Cisco Secure ACS, Cisco Access Registrar, Microsoft IAS, Aegis, and Interlink. One of the advantages of Cisco and Microsoft implementation of EAP-TLS is that it is possible to tie the Microsoft credentials of the user to the certificate of that user in a Microsoft database, which permits a single logon to a Microsoft domain.

Figure 9-4 displays the EAP-TLS authentication process. The wireless client associates with the AP using open authentication. The AP restricts (denies) all traffic from the client except EAP traffic until the RADIUS server authenticates the client. First, the client sends an EAPOL start frame to the AP, and the AP returns a request/identity to the client.

Figure 9-4 *EAP-TLS*

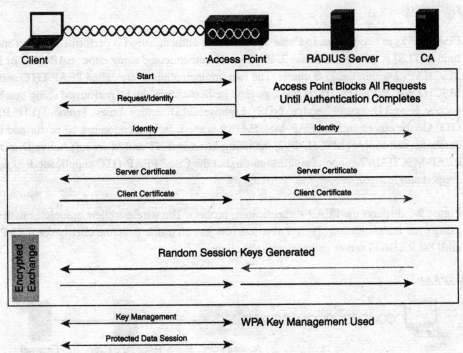

Second, the client sends its NAI address to the AP, which in turn sends it to the RADIUS server. The client and the server then perform mutual authentication using an exchange of digital certificates, and the RADIUS server sends a session key to the AP in a Success packet.

Third, the RADIUS server and the client negotiate and derive the session encryption; this process varies depending on whether the client is using WEP or 802.11i. The client and the AP use these keys during this session.

At the end of the session, the client sends an EAPOL-logoff packet to the AP, returning it to the preauthentication state (filtering all but EAPOL traffic).

PEAP

Protected Extensible Authentication Protocol (PEAP) is yet another 802.1x authentication type for WLANs, submitted by Cisco Systems, Microsoft, and RSA Security to the IETF as an Internet Draft. With PEAP, only the server authentication is performed using PKI certificate; therefore, installing digital certificates on every client machine (as is required by EAP-TLS) is not necessary. The RADIUS server must have self-issuing certificate capability, you must purchase a server certificate per server from a PKI entity, or you must set up a simple PKI server to issue server certificates.

PEAP works in two phases. In Phase 1, server-side authentication is performed, and an encrypted tunnel (TLS) is created. In Phase 2, the client is authenticated using either EAP-GTC or EAP-MSCHAPv2 within the TLS tunnel. The two implementations are called PEAP-GTC and PEAP-MSCHAPv2. If PEAP-GTC is used, generic authentication can be performed using databases such as Novell Directory Service (NDS), Lightweight Directory Access Protocol (LDAP), and OTP. On the other hand, if PEAP-MSCHAPv2 is used, authentication can be performed using databases that support MSCHAPv2, including Microsoft NT and Microsoft Active Directory. PEAP-MSCHAPv2 supports single sign-on, but the Cisco PEAP-GTC supplicant does not support single logon.

Figure 9-5 displays the PEAP authentication process. The wireless client associates with the AP using open authentication. The AP restricts (denies) all traffic from the client except EAP traffic until the RADIUS server authenticates the client.

Figure 9-5 *PEAP*

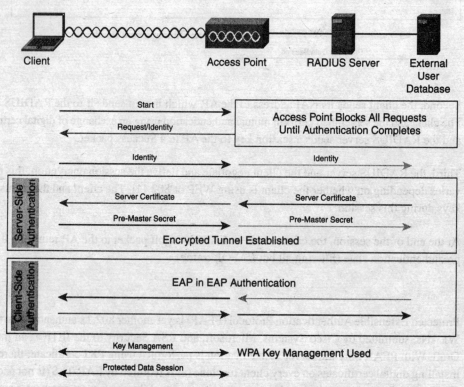

As stated earlier, PEAP goes through two phases. As shown in Figure 9-5, in Phase 1, or the server-side authentication phase, the client authenticates the server using a CA to verify the digital certificate of the server. Then the client and server establish an encrypted tunnel. In Phase 2, or the client-side authentication phase, the client submits its credentials to the server inside the TLS tunnel using either EAP-GTC or EAP-MSCHAPv2.

Next, the RADIUS server sends the session key to the AP in a Success packet, and the RADIUS server and client negotiate and derive a session encryption key. (This process varies depending whether the client is using WEP or 80211i.) The client and the AP use the session key during this session.

At the end of the session, the client sends an EAPOL-logoff packet to the AP, returning it to the preauthentication state (filtering all but EAPOL traffic).

WPA, 802.11i, and WPA2

WPA is a standards-based security solution introduced by Wi-Fi Alliance in late 2003 to address the vulnerabilities of the original 802.11 security implementations (WEP). The IEEE standard for security, IEEE 802.11i was ratified in 2004.

The most important features/components of WPA that you need to know and remember are as follows:

- **Authenticated key management**—WPA performs authentication using either IEEE 802.1x or PSK prior to the key management phase.

- **Unicast and broadcast key management**—After successful user authentication, message integrity and encryption keys are derived, distributed, validated, and stored on the client and the AP.

- **Utilization of TKIP and MIC**— Temporal Key Integrity Protocol (TKIP) and Message Integrity Check (MIC) are both elements of the WPA standard, and they secure a system against WEP vulnerabilities such as intrusive attacks.

- **Initialization Vector Space Expansion**—WPA provides per-packet keying (PPK) via IV hashing and broadcast key rotation. The IV is expanded from 24 bits (as in 802.11 WEP) to 48 bits.

Figure 9-6 displays the WPA (and 802.11i) authentication process. First, the client and the AP exchange the initial association request (probe request) and agree to a specific security capability. Next, the client and the authentication server (RADIUS server) perform the standard 802.1x authentication. Upon successful authentication, the authentication server generates and sends a master key to the AP; the client generates the same master key. These are called the PMK, which can be generated as a result of an 802.1x authentication process between the client and the server. The PMK can also be generated based on a 64-HEX character PSK.

Figure 9-6 *WPA and 802.11i Authentication and Key Management*

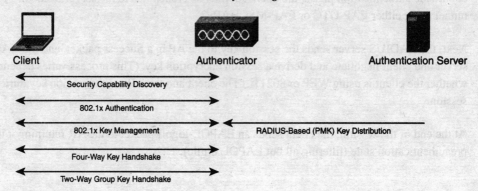

After completion of 802.1x authentication and 802.1x key management, the client and the AP perform a Four-Way Key Handshake and exchange a nonce, a WPA information element, a pairwise transient key (PTK), and MIC key information. This ensures validity of the AP and creates a trusted session between the client and the AP.

The final step is the two-way key handshake that the client and the AP exchange. The purpose of this handshake is to derive a group transient key (GTK), which provides a group key plus MIC keys (used for checking data integrity).

Following are the main shortcomings and issues of WPA:

■ Even though WPA uses TKIP, which is an enhancement to 802.11 WEP, it relies on the RC4 encryption. (RC4 has known shortcomings.)

■ WPA requires AP firmware support, software driver support for wireless cards, and operating system support (or a supplicant client). There is no guarantee that the manufacturers of all these components that you own will release upgrades to support WPA. Furthermore, because some vendors do not support mixing WEP and WPA (Wi-Fi Alliance does not support mixing WEP and WPA either), an organization wanting to deploy WPA has to replace a significant number of wireless infrastructure components.

■ WPA is susceptible to a specific DoS attack; if an AP receives two successive packets with bad MICs, the AP shuts down the entire basic service set (wireless service) for one minute. Furthermore, if small and noncomplex PSKs are used instead of 802.11i or EAP, an attacker who performs dictionary attacks on captured traffic can discover them.

Less than a year after the release of WPA by Wi-Fi Alliance, IEEE ratified the 802.11i standard (June 2004). 802.11i provides stronger encryption, authentication, and key management strategies for wireless data and system security than its predecessor, 802.11 WEP. Following are the three main components added by 802.11i:

- 802.1x authentication

- AES encryption algorithm

- Key management (similar to WPA)

WPA2, the next generation or supplement to WPA, was developed by Wi-Fi Alliance and is interoperable with IEEE 802.11i. WPA2 implements AES as per the National Institute of Standards and Technology (NIST) recommendation, using Counter Mode with Cipher Block Chaining Message Authentication Code Protocol (CCMP). Following are the key facts about WPA2:

- It uses 802.1x for authentication. (It also supports PSKs.)

- It uses a similar method of key distribution and key renewal to WPA.

- It supports Proactive Key Caching (PKC).

- It uses Intrusion Detection System (IDS).

Because of the nature of RF medium, the wireless standards mandate that IDS works at physical and data link layers. Wireless IDS addresses wireless and standards-based vulnerabilities with the following capabilities:

- Detect, locate, and mitigate rogue devices.

- Detect and manage RF interference.

- Detect reconnaissance.

- Detect management frames and hijacking attacks.

- Enforce security configuration policies.

- Perform forensic analysis and compliance reporting as complementary functions.

WPA and WPA2 have two modes: Enterprise mode and Personal mode. Within each mode is an encryption support and user authentication. Products that support both the PSK and the 802.1x authentication methods are given the term Enterprise mode. Note that for 802.1x authentication, an AAA/RADIUS server is required. Enterprise mode is targeted at medium to large medium to large environments, such as education and government departments. Products that only support PSK for authentication and require manual configuration of a PSK on the AP and clients are given the term Personal mode. (No authentication server is required.) Personal mode is targeted at small business environments such as small office, home office (SOHO). Table 9-2 displays the authentication and encryption methods that WPA and WPA2 use in Enterprise and Personal modes.

Table 9-2 *WPA/WPA2 Enterprise and Personal Modes*

Mode	WPA	WPA2
Enterprise mode	Authentication: IEEE 802.1x/EAP Encryption: TKIP/MIC	Authentication: IEEE 802.1x/EAP Encryption: AES-CCMP
Personal mode	Authentication: PSK Encryption: TKIP/MIC	Authentication: PSK Encryption: AES-CCMP

Even though WPA2 addresses the security shortcomings of WPA, an enterprise must consider the following WPA2 issues while evaluating and deciding to migrate to WPA2:

- The wireless client (supplicant) must have a WPA2 driver that is EAP compatible.

- The RADIUS server must support EAP.

- Because WPA2 is more CPU-intensive than WPA (mostly due to usage of AES encryption), hardware upgrades are often required (rather than just firmware upgrades).

- Some older devices cannot be upgraded, so they might need to be replaced.

Configuring Encryption and Authentication on Lightweight Access Points

In this section, you will learn how to navigate through the GUI of a WLC (Cisco WLC2006, specifically) to configure encryption and authentication on a lightweight AP (Cisco AP1020, specifically). The specific tasks shown are configuring open authentication, static WEP authentication, WPA with PSK, web authentication, and 802.1x authentication.

Open Authentication

Open authentication means that you are interested neither in authenticating the client/user nor in encrypting the data exchanged between the wireless client and the network. This type of setting is often used in public places or hotspots such as airports, hotels, and lobbies for guest wireless access (to the Internet, for example). To set up open authentication, open a web browser page to your WLAN controller (using its name or IP address), log on, and click on the WLAN option on the main toolbar.

After you are on the WLAN page, you can set up a new wireless LAN by clicking on **New** or change the settings on an existing WLAN by clicking on **Edit** beside the name of an existing WLAN. The default method for authentication is 802.1x. This protects your WLAN against accidentally setting it up with open authentication. Figure 9-7 shows the page that you will see if you choose to modify an existing WLAN by clicking on **Edit**.

Figure 9-7 *Configuring Open Authentication*

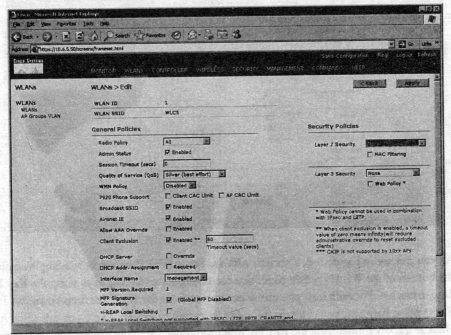

As you can see in Figure 9-7, on the right side of the WLAN > Edit page is a drop-down list with the title **Layer 2 Security** under the Security Policies section. To set up for open authentication, you must select **None** from the drop-down list. (Remember that the default is 802.1x.)

Static WEP Authentication

To set up a WLAN for static WEP authentication, you must go to the WLAN > Edit page. On the right side of this page, in the Security Policies section, select **Static WEP** from the **Layer 2 Security** drop-down list. After you select this option, the Static WEP options are displayed on the bottom of this page. (See Figure 9-8.)

Figure 9-8 *Configuring Static WEP Authentication*

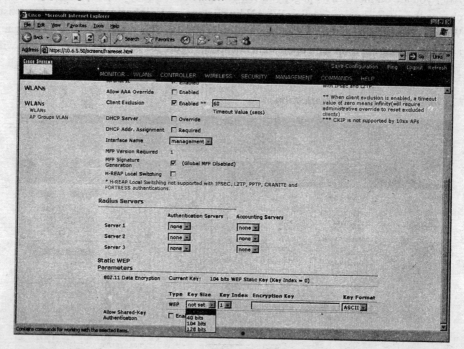

As you can see in Figure 9-8, a section with the Static WEP Parameters heading is displayed on the bottom of the WLAN > Edit page. You can configure up to four keys using the **Key Index** drop-down list. For each key, you can select its size from the **Key Size** drop-down list. In the **Encryption Key** box, you can type the value for each key. For each key, you can select **ASCII** or **HEX** as the key format from the **Key Format** drop-down list. Note that each WLAN is associated to only one key index; therefore, with a maximum of four key indexes available from the drop-down list, you can set up a maximum of four wireless LANs with the Static WEP option.

WPA Preshared Key

WPA PSK authentication is also configured on the WLAN > Edit page. From the **Layer 2 Security** drop-down list under the Security Policies section, you must select **WPA** (or **WPA1 + WPA2** depending on your software version). If you select the **WPA1 + WPA2** (or **WPA**) option, the appropriate fields for setting up the WPA parameters are displayed on the bottom of the WLAN > Edit page, as shown in Figure 9-9.

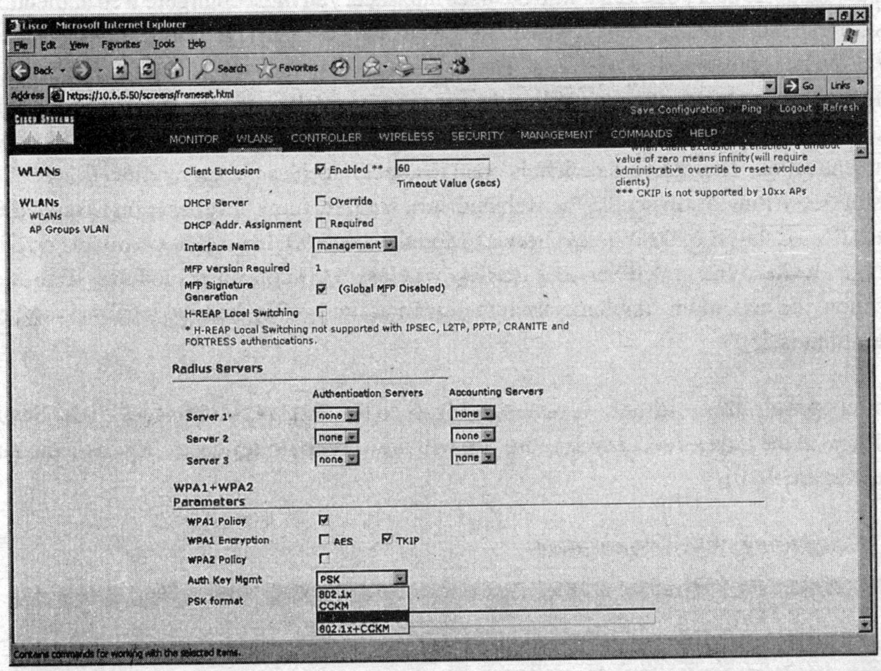

Figure 9-9 *Configuring WPA PSK*

> **NOTE**   Please note that in the figure that is in the ONT courseware, WPA is chosen from the **Layer 2 Security** drop-down list, and the bottom of the page has a WPA Parameters section instead. The reason for the discrepancy between Figure 9-9 of this book and the figure that is in the ONT courseware is the software version difference on the wireless controller.

To set up for WPA PSK, under the WPA1 + WPA2 Parameters section, you must select the **WPA1 Policy** check box. For WPA1 encryption, you can choose either the **AES** or **TKIP** check box. Next, from the **Auth Key Mgmt** drop-down list, you must select **PSK**. Finally, on the last line in the WPA1 + WPA2 Parameters section, you must type the PSK in the long text box provided. Note the **PSK format** drop-down list allows you to specify the format of the PSK as either **ASCII** or **HEX**.

> **NOTE**   Again, the figure in the ONT courseware shows that after you select **WPA** from the **Layer 2 Security** drop-down list, a WPA Parameters section displays on the bottom of the WLAN > Edit page. Within that section, you are asked to click and enable a **Pre-Shared Key** check box and then type a PSK in the long text box provided.

Web Authentication

To authenticate users through a web browser interface, you must configure web authentication and its corresponding parameters. If a user has a web browser open (HTTP) and attempts to access the WLAN, he is presented a login page. The login page is customizable; you can configure the logos and the text on the login page. Web authentication is usually used for guest access; the data exchanged between the wireless client and the AP is not encrypted, nor is there MIC or per-packet authentication. Therefore, the client is open to attacks such as packet modification and hijacking. As of the writing of this book, the web authentication feature is available on Cisco 4400 WLCs and Cisco Catalyst 6500 Wireless Service Modules (WiSM), but it is not available on Cisco 2000 WLCs or Cisco Integrated Services Routers wireless LAN controller modules. With web authentication, the maximum simultaneous authentication limit is 21; the total local web authentication user limit is 2500.

To set up web authentication, you must navigate to the WLAN > Edit page. Under Security Policies in the Layer 3 security section, you will find a **Web Policy** check box that you must enable (see Figure 9-10).

Figure 9-10 *Configuring Web Authentication*

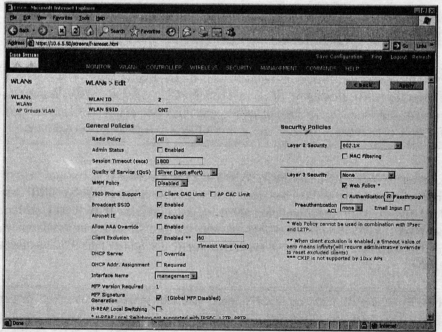

Below the **Web Policy** check box, you must choose between **Authentication** or **Passthrough** options. If you select **Authentication**, the users are prompted for a username and password when they attempt to access the network. The username and password are verified against the internal user database of WLC; if no match is found, the username and password are verified from an external RADIUS server if one is configured. If **Passthrough** is selected, the user is not prompted for a username and password; however, if the **Email Input** check box (which is beneath the **Passthrough** option) is enabled, the users are prompted for their e-mail address. The last option you have under Layer 3 security is selecting an access list from the **Preauthentication ACL** drop-down list to be used against the traffic exchanged between the wireless client and the WLC.

To customize the login page for web authentication, you must click the **Security** option in the main toolbar. From the security options listed on the left side of this page, click the **Web Login Page** option. You are then presented with a page similar to the one shown in Figure 9-11.

> **NOTE**   In the ONT courseware, either because of a WLC hardware/software difference or because of typing error, you are asked to go to Management > Web Login Page instead of Security > Web Login Page.

Figure 9-11   *Customizing the Web Login Page*

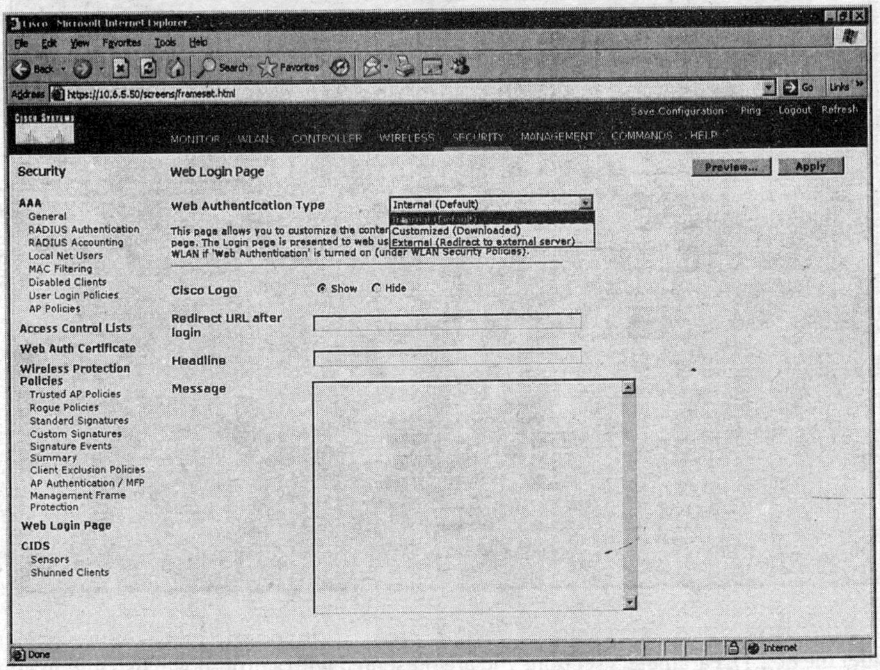

As shown in Figure 9-11, on the Web Login Page, you have three choices for **Web Authentication Type**: **Internal (Default), Customized (Downloaded),** and **External (Redirect to external server)**. If you choose the external or customized types, you must then enter a URL in the

Redirect URL after login box below. Otherwise, if you want the default authentication page of the WLC, select the **Internal (Default)** option. The other options you have are selecting to show or hide the Cisco logo, and entering a headline and a message. These options are only available if you select external or customized web authentication types. An example for the headline would be "AMIRACAN Inc. Wireless Network," and an example for the message would be "Access is only offered to authorized users. Please enter your username and password."

802.1x Authentication

802.1x authentication is the default setting. To change the setting from other options back to 802.1x, you must navigate to the WLAN > Edit page and select **802.1x** from the **Layer 2 Security** drop-down list under the Security Policies section. After you select this option, on the bottom of the WLAN > Edit page, a section with the 802.1x Parameters heading is displayed (see Figure 9-12).

Figure 9-12 *802.1x Authentication*

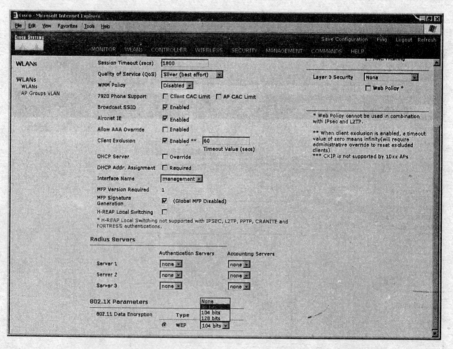

Under the 802.1x Parameters section, you are presented with a drop-down list, giving you a choice of **None**, **40 bits**, **104 bits**, and **128 bits** WEP encryption for 802.11 data encryption. Note that 802.11 standards only support 40/64-bit and 104/128-bit keys; 128/152-bit keys are only supported by 802.11i, WPA, and WPA2-compliant clients. It is also important to note that Microsoft Windows XP clients only support 40-bit and 104-bit WEP keys.

From the **Layer 2 Security** drop-down list under the Security Policies section, you can also select **WPA1 + WPA2**. As stated earlier, on some hardware/software, **WPA** and **WPA2** might be presented as separate options. If you intend to use WPA with 802.1x, select the **WPA1 + WPA2** (or **WPA**) option. In response, the WLAN > Edit page displays the WPA1 + WPA2 Parameters section on the bottom, as shown in Figure 9-13.

Figure 9-13 *WPA with 802.1x*

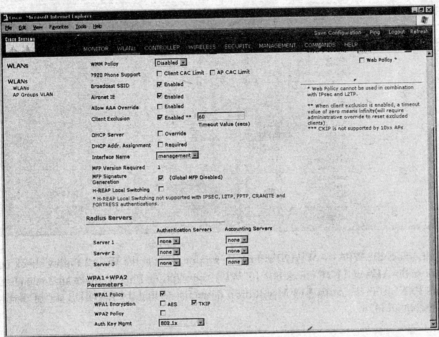

Next, under the WPA1 + WPA2 Parameters section, enable the **WPA1 Policy** check box and choose the **AES** or **TKIP** check box for WPA1 encryption. Finally, make sure you choose **802.1x** (not **PSK**) from the **Auth Key Mgmt** drop-down list so that the RADIUS server performs authentication.

To configure a WLAN for WPA2 security with dynamic keys, from the **Layer 2 Security** drop-down list under the Security Policies section, select **WPA1 + WPA2**. (On some hardware/software, **WPA** and **WPA2** might be presented as separate options.) In response, the WLAN > Edit page displays the WPA1 + WPA2 Parameters section on the bottom, as shown in Figure 9-14.

Figure 9-14 *WPA2 with Dynamic Keys*

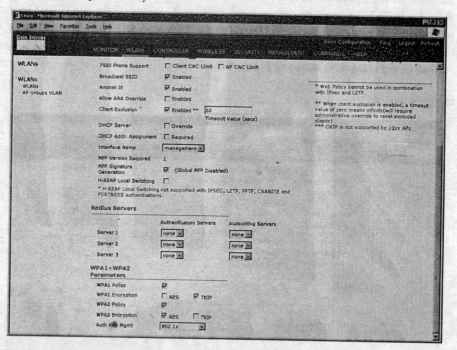

Next, under the WPA1 + WPA2 Parameters section, enable the **WPA2 Policy** check box and choose the **AES** or **TKIP** check box for WPA2 encryption. Finally, make sure you choose **802.1x** (not **PSK**) from the **Auth Key Mgmt** drop-down list so that the RADIUS server performs authentication.

If you enable both the **WPA1 Policy** and the **WPA2 Policy** check boxes, you are effectively setting up your WLAN for WPA compatibility mode. WPA compatibility mode supports both WPA and WPA2 clients and allows them to use the same SSID. Selecting both **AES** and **TKIP** for **WPA2 Encryption** allows support of legacy hardware that does support WPA2 but not AES.

NOTE   In the ONT courseware, it shows that you can select **WPA2** from the **Layer 2 Security** drop-down list under the Security Policies section (instead of **WPA1 + WPA2**); this is because of a hardware/software difference. Next, the ONT courseware states that a section titled WPA2 Parameters appears on the bottom of the WLAN > Edit page. In the WPA2 Parameters section, you are then presented with the choice of enabling any of the following three options:

- WPA2 Compatibility Mode

- Allow WPA2 TKIP Clients

- Pre-Shared Key

This note has been added so that you are prepared for a possible question in the certification exam, should it be based on software/hardware variances.

Foundation Summary

The "Foundation Summary" is a collection of information that provides a convenient review of many key concepts in this chapter. If you are already comfortable with the topics in this chapter, this summary can help you recall a few details. If you just read this chapter, this review should help solidify some key facts. If you are doing your final preparation before the exam, the information in this section is a convenient way to review the day before the exam.

Following are the traditional wireless local-area network (WLAN) security issues:

- Reliance on Service Set Identifier (SSID) as a security feature

- Vulnerability to rogue access points (AP)

- Reliance on MAC filters as a security feature

- Usage of Wired Equivalent Privacy (WEP)

Following are the shortcomings of WEP:

- The distribution of WEP keys to clients is not scalable.

- WEP keys can be deducted if enough data is captured (even with IV).

- WEP is vulnerable to dictionary attacks.

- WEP does not provide protection against rogue APs.

The main features and benefits of 802.1x/EAP are as follows:

- Usage of RADIUS server for AAA centralized authentication

- Mutual authentication between the client and the authentication server

- Ability to use 802.1x with multiple encryption algorithms, such as Advanced Encryption Standard (AES), wireless protected access (WPA), Temporal Key Integrity Protocol (TKIP), and WEP

- Without user intervention, the ability to use dynamic (instead of static) WEP keys

- Support of roaming

Following are the required components for 802.1x authentication:

- EAP-capable client (the supplicant)

- 802.1x-capable AP (the authenticator)

- EAP-capable RADIUS server (the authentication server)

Table 9-3 displays important features of the main EAP variants discussed in this chapter.

Table 9-3 *Comparison of Main EAP Variants*

Feature	Cisco LEAP	EAP-FAST	EAP-TLS	PEAP-GTC	PEAP-MSCHAPv2
User authentication database and server	Windows NT domains, Active Directory	Windows NT domains, Active Directory, LDAP (limited)	OTP, LDAP, Novell NDS, Windows NT domains, Active Directory	OTP, LDAP, Novell NDS, Windows NT domains, Active Directory	Windows NT domains, Active Directory
Requires server certificates	No	No	Yes	Yes	Yes
Requires client certificates	No	No	Yes	No	No
Able to use single sign-on using Windows login	Yes	Yes	Yes	No	Yes
Works with fast secure roaming	Yes	Yes	No	No	No
Works with WPA and WPA2	Yes	Yes	Yes	Yes	Yes

Following are the most important features/components of WPA:

- **Authenticated key management**—WPA performs authentication using either IEEE 802.1x or preshared key (PSK) prior to the key management phase.

- **Unicast and broadcast key management**—After successful user authentication, message integrity and encryption keys are derived, distributed, validated, and stored on the client and the AP.

- **Utilization of TKIP and MIC**— Temporal Key Integrity Protocol (TKIP) and Message Integrity Check (MIC) are both elements of the WPA standard and they secure a system against WEP vulnerabilities such as intrusive attacks.

- **Initialization vector space expansion**—WPA provides per-packet keying (PPK) via initialization vector (IV) hashing and broadcast key rotation. The IV is expanded from 24 bits (as in 802.11 WEP) to 48 bits.

The main shortcomings and issues of WPA are as follows:

- Even though WPA uses TKIP, which is an enhancement to 802.11 WEP, it relies on the RC4 encryption. (RC4 has known shortcomings.)

- WPA requires AP firmware support, software driver support for wireless cards, and operating system support (or a supplicant client). It is not guaranteed that the manufacturers of all these components that you own will release upgrades to support WPA.

- WPA is susceptible to a specific denial of service (DoS attack); if an AP receives two successive packets with bad MICs, the AP shuts down the basic service set for one minute.

- If small and noncomplex PSKs are used instead of 802.11i or EAP, an attacker who performs dictionary attacks on captured traffic can discover them.

Following are the key features of WPA2:

- It uses 802.1x for authentication. (It also supports PSKs.)

- It uses a similar method of key distribution and key renewal to WPA.

- It supports Proactive Key Caching (PKC).

- It uses Intrusion Detection System (IDS).

WPA and WPA2 have two modes: Enterprise mode and Personal mode. Each mode has encryption support and user authentication. Table 9-4 displays the authentication and encryption methods that WPA and WPA2 use in Enterprise and Personal modes.

Table 9-4 *WPA/WPA2 Enterprise and Personal Modes*

Mode	WPA	WPA2
Enterprise mode	Authentication: IEEE 802.1x/EAP Encryption: TKIP/MIC	Authentication: IEEE 802.1x/EAP Encryption: AES-CCMP
Personal mode	Authentication: PSK Encryption: TKIP/MIC	Authentication: PSK Encryption: AES-CCMP

Following are some of the issues that an enterprise must consider while evaluating and deciding to migrate to WPA2:

- The wireless client (supplicant) must have a WPA2 driver that is EAP compatible.

- The RADIUS server must support EAP.

- Because WPA2 is more CPU-intensive than WPA (mostly due to usage of AES encryption), hardware upgrades are often required (rather than just a firmware upgrade).

- Some older devices cannot be upgraded, so they might need to be replaced.

To set up or change the authentication and encryption settings for your WLANS (LWAPs), open a web browser page to your WLAN controller (using its name or IP address), log on, and click on the **WLAN** option on the main toolbar. Next, click on **Edit** for an existing WLAN; the WLAN > Edit page appears. The Security Policies section on the WLAN > Edit page allows you to set up Layer 2 and Layer 3 security settings.

Q&A

Some of the questions that follow challenge you more than the exam by using an open-ended question format. By reviewing now with this more difficult question format, you can exercise your memory better and prove your conceptual and factual knowledge of this chapter. The answers to these questions appear in Appendix A.

1. What is a rogue access point, and what are its dangers?

2. Specify at least two weaknesses of basic 802.11 (WEP) security.

3. Specify at least two benefits of LEAP over the basic 802.11 (WEP).

4. Specify at least one benefit and one drawback of WPA2 over WPA.

5. Provide at least three important features and benefits of 802.1x/EAP.

6. What are the required components for 802.1x authentication?

7. What is the role of EAP client supplicant?

8. Specify at least three of the main features and benefits of EAP-FAST.

9. What are the three phases of EAP-FAST?

10. Provide at least two important features or facts about EAP-TLS.

11. Provide at least two important features or facts about PEAP.

12. Specify at least two important features of WPA.

13. What are the three key security features that the 802.11i standard has offered?

14. Provide at least two important features/facts about WPA2.

15. List at least three services that wireless IDS provides to address RF and standards-based vulnerabilities.

16. What are the two modes of WPA and WPA2?

This chapter covers the following subjects:

- The Need for WLAN Management

- CiscoWorks Wireless LAN Solution Engine

- Cisco Wireless Control System

CHAPTER 10

WLAN Management

This chapter provides an understanding of the network manager's tools to discover, configure, and monitor the various components in a WLAN solution. Cisco offers autonomous and lightweight access points (LWAP), which can both be centrally managed. Centralization simplifies WLAN management and improves scalability. Lightweight access points and their associated controllers can be managed using the Cisco Wireless Control System (WCS). Autonomous access points can be managed using the CiscoWorks Wireless LAN Solution Engine (WLSE).

Additional capabilities are available when centrally managing lightweight access points, for example, when WCS brings real-time device location tracking to life using the Cisco RF Fingerprinting technology. This is one of the many benefits customers can experience using WCS.

"Do I Know This Already?" Quiz

The purpose of the "Do I Know This Already?" quiz is to help you decide whether you really need to read the entire chapter. The 10-question quiz, derived from the major sections of this chapter, helps you determine how to spend your limited study time.

Table 10-1 outlines the major topics discussed in this chapter and the "Do I Know This Already?" quiz questions that correspond to those topics.

Table 10-1 *"Do I Know This Already?" Foundation Topics Section-to-Question Mapping*

Foundation Topics Section Covering These Questions	Questions	Score
"The Need for WLAN Management"	1–4	
"CiscoWorks Wireless LAN Solution Engine"	5–8	
"Cisco Wireless Control System"	9–13	
Total Score	**(13 possible)**	

> **CAUTION** The goal of self-assessment is to gauge your mastery of the topics in this chapter. If you do not know the answer to a question or are only partially sure of the answer, mark this question wrong for purposes of the self-assessment. Giving yourself credit for an answer you correctly guess skews your self-assessment results and might provide you with a false sense of security.

You can find the answers to the "Do I Know This Already?" quiz in Appendix A, "Answers to the 'Do I Know This Already?' Quizzes and Q&A Sections." The suggested choices for your next step are as follows:

- **9 or less overall score**—Read the entire chapter. This includes the "Foundation Topics," "Foundation Summary," and "Q&A" sections.

- **10–11 overall score**—Begin with the "Foundation Summary" section and then follow up with the "Q&A" section at the end of the chapter.

- **12 or more overall score**—If you want more review on this topic, skip to the "Foundation Summary" section and then go to the "Q&A" section. Otherwise, proceed to the next chapter.

1. The Cisco Unified Wireless Network unique approach addresses all layers of the WLAN network through what five interconnected elements?

   a. Access points, mobility platform, network unification, world-class network management, and unified advanced services

   b. Client devices, access points, mobility platform, network unification, and unified advanced services

   c. Client devices, access points, network unification, world-class network management, and unified advanced services

   d. Client devices, mobility platform, network unification, world-class network management, and unified advanced services

2. What are the two Cisco WLAN implementations?

   a. Centralized and decentralized

   b. Thick and thin

   c. Autonomous and lightweight

   d. None of the above

3. Control and radio monitoring is accomplished based on which of the following?

    a. The controller providing power mitigation

    b. The end solution being autonomous or lightweight

    c. Both A and B

    d. Neither A nor B

4. Centralized WLAN management is performed by using which of the following?

    a. CiscoWorks WLSE for both lightweight and autonomous implementations

    b. Cisco WCS for both lightweight and autonomous implementations

    c. CiscoWorks WLSE for autonomous implementations and Cisco WCS for lightweight implementations

    d. Cisco WCS for autonomous implementations and CiscoWorks WLSE for lightweight implementations

5. CiscoWorks WLSE discovery process requires routers, switches, and access points to be properly configured with what protocol(s)?

    a. SNMP and LWAPP

    b. CDP and LWAPP

    c. CDP and SNMP

    d. LWAPP only

6. CiscoWorks WLSE Express supports what modes of setup?

    a. Manual only

    b. Manual and Automatic

    c. Automatic only

    d. Manual, Automatic, and Assisted

7. What are the two features of WLSE that enforce optimization and high availability?

    a. Auto Re-Site Survey and Assisted Site Survey

    b. ACLs and QoS

    c. ACLs and MTU

    d. Assisted Site Survey and QoS

8. What are the two versions of CiscoWorks for WLANs?

    a. Demo and Registered

    b. Registered and WLSE Express

    c. WLSE and WLSE Express

    d. WLSE and Demo

9. How many Cisco wireless LAN controllers and access points is the Cisco WCS designed to handle?

   a. 50 Cisco wireless LAN controllers and 1500 access points

   b. 1 Cisco wireless LAN controller and 50 access points

   c. 0 Cisco wireless LAN controllers and 500 access points

   d. 50 Cisco wireless LAN controllers and 500 access points

10. How many versions of the Cisco WCS exist?

    a. 1

    b. 2

    c. 3

    d. Depends on license purchased

11. True or False: Some Cisco WCS features might not function properly if you use a web browser other than Internet Explorer 7.0 on a Windows workstation.

    a. True

    b. False

12. What is the most secure way to configure controller management?

    a. Through the controller-dedicated service port

    b. Through the console cable

    c. Through SNMP v3

    d. Through SSH

13. When Cisco wireless LAN controller detects a rogue access point, what does it immediately do?

    a. Sends an SNMP trap

    b. Sends an e-mail notification to the recipient entered in the controller

    c. Notifies Cisco WCS, which creates a rogue access point alarm

    d. Both A and B

Foundation Topics

The Need for WLAN Management

WLAN management is one piece of a puzzle for network managers to understand. WLANs address the business drivers such as mobile users, Wi-Fi enabled notebooks, and anytime, anywhere access. WLAN management helps Network Managers plan for scalable WLANs that are both centralized and secure.

WLAN management within the Cisco Unified Wireless Network is composed of five elements. Those elements are fundamental to building successful enterprise-class WLANs that are scalable, centralized, and secure.

Cisco Unified Wireless Networks

The Cisco Unified Wireless Network is a total-enterprise solution composed of five comprehensive elements. The Cisco Unified Wireless Network enables the use of advanced wireless services and addresses security concerns. It also addresses deployment, control, and the management of WLAN components and RF.

Following are the five elements of Cisco Unified Wireless Network:

- **Client devices**—Use the Cisco Compatible Extensions program to help ensure interoperability. The Cisco Compatible Extensions program delivers services such as wireless mobility, QoS, network management, and enhanced security.

- **Mobility platform**—Provides ubiquitous access in any environment indoors or out. The LWAPs are dynamically configured and managed by wireless LAN controllers (WLC) through LightWeight Access Point Protocol (LWAPP).

- **Network unification**—Creates seamless integration into the routing and switching infrastructure. The WLCs are responsible for functions such as RF management, n+1 deployment, and Intrusion Prevention System (IPS).

- **World-class network management**—Enables WLANs to have the equivalent LAN security, scalability, reliability, ease of deployment, and management via Cisco Wireless Control System (WCS). Cisco WCS provides features for design, control, and monitoring.

■ **Unified advanced services**—Support new mobility applications, emerging Wi-Fi technologies, and advanced threat detection and prevention capabilities such as wireless VoIP, future unified cellular, location services, Network Admission Control (NAC), the Self-Defending Network, Identity Based Networking Services (IBNS), Intrusion Detection Systems (IDS), and guest access.

Following are Cisco WLAN products supporting the Cisco Unified Wireless Network:

■ **Client devices**—These include the Cisco 7920 IP Phone, PDAs, and client cards for notebooks. Cisco client device compatibility is higher than 90 percent, reducing conflicts or issues.

■ **Mobility platform**—Lightweight access points (AP) include the 1500, 1300, 1240AG, 1230AG, 1130AG, and 1000. Bridges include the 1400 and 1300.

■ **Network unification**—WLCs include the 4400 and 2000. Catalyst devices include the 6500 WiSM, ISR, and 3750 integration.

■ **World-class network management**—Cisco WCS provides features for design, control, and monitoring.

■ **Unified advanced services**—Cisco Wireless Location Appliance, WCS, Self-Defending Network (SDN), NAC, Wi-Fi phones, and RF firewalls.

Cisco WLAN Implementation

Cisco offers two WLAN implementations. The first is the autonomous WLAN solution based on autonomous APs, and the second is the lightweight WLAN solution based on LWAPs and WLCs. Table 10-2 compares the two WLAN solutions.

Table 10-2   *Comparison of WLAN Implementation Solutions*

Category	Autonomous WLAN Solution	Lightweight WLAN Solution
Access Point	Autonomous APs	LWAPs
Control	Individual configuration on each AP	Configuration via Cisco WLC
Dependency	Independent operation	Dependent on Cisco WLC
WLAN Management	Management via CiscoWorks WLSE and Wireless Domain Services (WDS)	Management via Cisco WCS
Redundancy	AP redundancy	Cisco WLC redundancy

The two WLAN solutions have different characteristics and advantages:

- **Autonomous APs**— Configuration is accomplished on each AP. Each AP places RF control, security, and mobility functions within the local configuration. Individual configuration is required because each AP operates independently. However, centralized configuration, monitoring, and management can be done through CiscoWorks WLSE. WDS provides the radio monitoring and management communication between the autonomous APs and CiscoWorks WLSE.

- **LWAPs**—Configuration, monitoring, and security are accomplished via the WLAN controller. The LWAPs depend on the controller for control and data transmission. However, Remote-Edge Access Point (REAP) mode does not need the controller for data transmission. Cisco WCS can centralize configuration, monitoring, and management. Cisco WLAN controllers can be implemented with redundancy within the WLC groups.

Without centralized WLAN management both implementations eventually have scalability issues. However, LWAPs and their associated WLAN Controllers provide a more scalable solution for WLANs than autonomous APs. In fact, the growth and management of autonomous APs becomes an important concern since independently managing APs increases operational costs and staffing requirements. Moreover, correlating and forecasting across the enterprise WLAN becomes more difficult due to the lack of visibility and/or personnel time. Client handoff times decrease between APs and real-time applications such as voice and video start to suffer.

Security starts to lose effectiveness because of the growth and no centralized management. Detection and mitigation of denial of service (DoS) attacks across an entire WLAN are not possible. Interferences cannot be viewed on a systemwide basis because of the lack of centralized management. Each autonomous AP is a single point of enforcement for security policies across Layer 1, Layer 2, and Layer 3. Security is at risk when an AP is stolen or compromised because the passwords, keys, and community strings all reside within the local configuration.

Regardless of which implementation is chosen, Cisco provides a centralized WLAN management solution.

WLAN Components

Figure 10-1 provides a clear hierarchy of the components that are required to build a WLAN.

Figure 10-1   *WLAN Components*

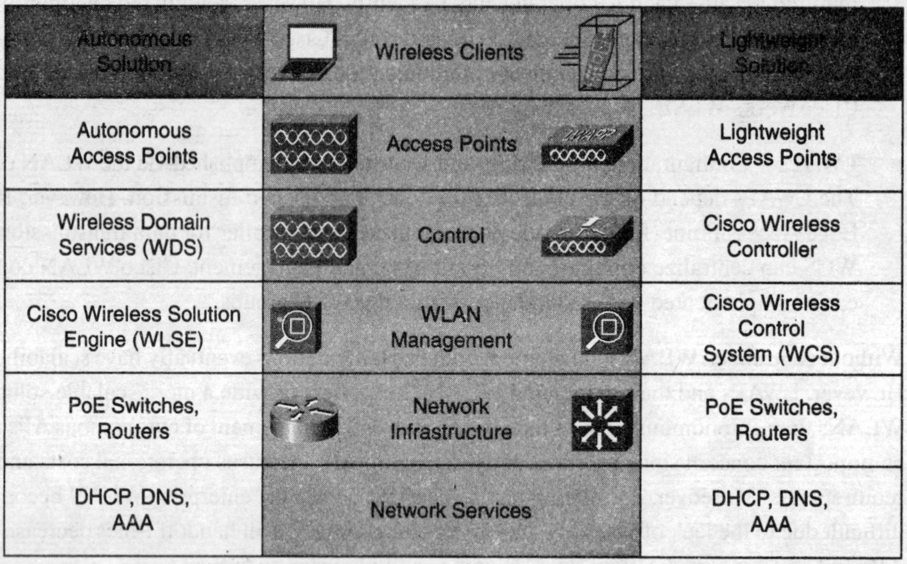

Autonomous Solution	Wireless Clients	Lightweight Solution
Autonomous Access Points	Access Points	Lightweight Access Points
Wireless Domain Services (WDS)	Control	Cisco Wireless Controller
Cisco Wireless Solution Engine (WLSE)	WLAN Management	Cisco Wireless Control System (WCS)
PoE Switches, Routers	Network Infrastructure	PoE Switches, Routers
DHCP, DNS, AAA	Network Services	DHCP, DNS, AAA

Client devices are the most obvious of the WLAN components. Client devices come in many forms such as PDAs, IP phones, notebooks, and bar-code scanners.

Access Points are another obvious WLAN component—either autonomous or lightweight. The APs are used to build the WLAN infrastructure. Configuration is performed independently on the autonomous APs. Lightweight APs are configured through their associated LAN controller.

Control is the WLAN component that provides device control and radio monitoring. Control and radio monitoring are specific to the end solution implementation. The autonomous AP solution uses Wireless Domain Services (WDS). All WDS configured APs aggregate their information through WDS which sends it to the WLSE. The lightweight APs use their associated LAN controllers via LWAPP.

WLAN management is the WLAN component that addresses how large-scale deployments are centrally managed. Autonomous APs use CiscoWorks WLSE and lightweight APs use Cisco WCS management.

The network infrastructure WLAN component includes the routers and switches that interconnect all the APs, controllers, management, and servers together.

Network services is the last WLAN component in Figure 10-1. Network services function to provide services such as Dynamic Host Configuration Protocol (DHCP), Domain Name System (DNS), and Authentication, Authorization and Accounting (AAA)—DHCP, DNS, and AAA.

> **NOTE** Cisco Aironet bridges operate at the MAC address layer (data link layer).

CiscoWorks Wireless LAN Solution Engine

CiscoWorks WLSE is part of the CiscoWorks network management products. CiscoWorks WLSE provides centralized management for autonomous APs. WLANs benefit from the WLSE major features such as configuration, fault and policy monitoring, reporting, firmware, and radio management. In addition, the RF and device-management features help reduce operating expenses and deployment. CiscoWorks WLSE covers fault, configuration, and performance management, which are three of the FCAPS (Fault, Configuration, Accounting, Performance, and Security) management tools. Proper Cisco Discovery Protocol (CDP) and Simple Network Management Protocol (SNMP) configuration on all switches, routers, WDS, and APs is required for the CiscoWorks WLSE discovery process to work. After the devices are discovered, a decision is required on whether to manage them through CiscoWorks WLSE.

WLSE Software Features

Network management of system-wide autonomous APs through CiscoWorks WLSE has these major software features:

- **Configuration**—One CiscoWorks WLSE console supports up to 2500 APs. Configuration changes can be performed in mass, individually, or in defined groups as desired or on a schedule time. All Cisco Aironet APs are supported.

- **Fault and policy monitoring**—WLSE monitors device faults and performance threshold conditions such as memory, CPU, associations, Lightweight Extensible Authentication Protocol (LEAP) server responses, and policy configuration errors.

- **Reporting**—WLSE provides the capability to e-mail, print, and export reports. Client, device, and security information can all be tracked and reported.

- **Firmware**—WLSE performs centralized firmware upgrades. Upgrades can be done in mass, individually, or in defined groups as desired or on a scheduled time.

- **Radio management**—WLSE assists in management of the WLAN radio environment. Radio management features include parameter generation, network status, and reports.

- **CiscoWorks WLSE administration**—WLSE administration includes status by means of WLSE log files, software (WLSE system software), security (authentication modules, SSH, Telnet access), backup and restore (WLSE data), diagnostics (WLSE test and reports), connectivity tools, and redundancy (managment of redundant WLSEs.) Two WLSE devices can create a highly available WLAN management solution. CiscoWorks WLSE supports warm-standby redundancy.

- **Deployment wizard**—WLSE provides a deployment wizard that discovers, uploads configurations, and manages all deployed APs.

> **NOTE** You can configure a CiscoWorks WLSE backup server to take over wireless management if there is a primary CiscoWorks WLSE failure.

WLSE Key Benefits

Managing autonomous APs and bridges through CiscoWorks WLSE provides centralized management and RF visibility for the WLAN. This provides many key benefits, such as the following:

- **Improved WLAN security**—Wireless IDS with rogue AP detection handles security threats such as malicious intruders, ad hoc networks, excess 802.11 management frames that signal denial-of-service (DoS) attacks, and man-in-the-middle attacks.

- **Simplified AP deployment**—Deployment Wizards automatically apply configuration policies to new APs.

- **RF visibility**—WLSE provides information and displays to show RF coverage, received signal strength indicator (RSSI) displays, rogue AP location, and roaming boundaries of the WLAN.

- **Dynamic RF management**—WLSE offers self-healing, assisted site survey, automatic re-site survey, and interference detection capabilities within the WLAN.

- **Simplified operations**—Threshold-based monitoring, reporting, template-based configuration, and image updates are all features designed to simplify operations.

CiscoWorks WLSE and WLSE Express

Two versions of CiscoWorks WLSE are available based on the network sizes: WLSE and WLSE Express.

WLSE is for medium to large enterprise WLAN solutions with up to 2500 managed devices. WLSE requires an external AAA server such as a Cisco ACS server since the WLSE does not include one.

CiscoWorks WLSE Express includes AAA providing security services that support 802.1x LEAP, Protected Extensible Authentication Protocol (PEAP), Extensible Authentication Protocol-Flexible Authentication via Secure Tunneling (EAP-FAST), and Extensible Authentication Protocol-Transport Layer Security (EAP-TLS). The user directory supports Lightweight Directory Access Protocol (LDAP), Microsoft Active Directory, and a local user database. In addition, user authentication mechanisms are supported for both wired and wireless. WLAN IDS features are also supported.

WLSE Express is designed for small to medium businesses with up to 100 WLAN devices. In addition, service providers with public WLAN (PWLAN) hot spot management would use WLSE Express because of the smaller number of devices.

CiscoWorks WLSE and CiscoWorks WLSE Express both support the following WLAN devices:

- Cisco Aironet autonomous APs and bridges

- AP- and Cisco Catalyst Series Wireless LAN Services Module (WLSM)-based WDS

CiscoWorks WLSE and CiscoWorks WLSE Express both support the following protocols:

- Secure Shell (SSH)

- HTTP

- Cisco Discovery Protocol (CDP)

- Simple Network Management Protocol (SNMP)

- CiscoWorks WLSE and CiscoWorks WLSE Express both integrate with CiscoWorks wired management tools and third-party NMSs. Fault notification and forwarding can be integrated via SNMP traps and syslog messages. In addition, CiscoWorks WLSE and CiscoWorks WLSE Express both provide the ability to export data via Simple Object Access Protocol (SOAP) Extensible Markup Language (XML) application programming interface (API).

Simplified WLSE Express Setup

CiscoWorks WLSE Express supports two modes of setup:

- **Automatic**—DHCP is enabled by default. DHCP options 66 and 67 provide the TFTP IP address and filename. A special configuration file can be downloaded automatically, making the WLSE Express ready for use.

- **Manual**—CiscoWorks WLSE Express can be manually configured with setup scripts and by entering CLI commands.

WLSE Configuration Templates

CiscoWorks WLSE supports performance optimization and high availability beyond the basic configuration and monitoring. The configuration is performed through a browser or web-based GUI. Templates ease the configuration and deployment of the WLAN environment. Several templates exist, such as these:

- Plug-and-play deployment

- Automatic configuration of APs added to CiscoWorks WLSE

- Automatic RF configuration of APs

- Calculation of optimal RF configurations by APs

WLSE IDS Features

CiscoWorks WLSE includes intrusion detection features, such as these:

- Rogue APs are automatically shut down when they are detected and located by disabling the switch ports.

- Ad hoc network devices are detected in addition to rogue APs.

- Man-in-the-middle attacks are detected via Message Integrity Check (MIC) failures.

- AP configuration monitoring ensures that security policies are always enforced.

- Sensor-mode APs can add enhanced features to the WLAN.

WLSE Summary

All the features CiscoWorks WLSE offers help improve the day-to-day WLAN management. CiscoWorks WLSE is a solution providing performance optimization and high availability for autonomous WLAN networks. Following are two features of WLSE that enforce optimization and high availability:

- **Auto re-site survey**—This feature can optimize the WLAN environment by selecting a more effective channel and adjusting the power levels. The most effective results come from performing a client walkabout during the assisted site survey. The assisted site survey is highly recommended but not required.

- **Self-healing**—This feature allows CiscoWorks WLSE to detect AP failures and compensate by automatically increasing the power and cell coverage of the others nearby. Moreover, when the AP comes back, it recalculates the power and channel selections. This minimizes the client impact and maintains availability.

CiscoWorks WLSE supports centralized configuration, firmware, and radio management. These can save time and resources normally required to operate large deployments of APs not centrally managed. Moreover, CiscoWorks WLSE pulls all the configurations, images, and management information into one location. The templates simplify large-scale implementations by auto-configuration of new APs. The security policies minimize the security vulnerabilities due to rogue APs and misconfigurations. Upon detection, CiscoWorks WLSE sends out an alert. CiscoWorks WLSE is capable of monitoring AP utilization and client association and reporting the information to help in capacity planning and troubleshooting. CiscoWorks WLSE proactively monitors APs, bridges, and 802.1x EAP servers and provides improved WLAN uptime. Table 10-3 briefly summarizes this information.

Table 10-3 *CiscoWorks WLSE Features and Benefits*

Feature	Benefit
Centralized configuration, firmware, and radio management	Reduces WLAN total cost of ownership by saving time and resources required to manage large numbers of APs
Autoconfiguration of new APs	Simplifies large-scale deployments
Security policy misconfiguration alerts and rogue AP detection	Minimizes security vulnerabilities
AP utilization and client association reports	Helps in capacity planning and troubleshooting
Proactive monitoring of APs, bridges, and 802.1x EAP servers	Improves WLAN uptime

Cisco Wireless Control System

Cisco WCS is an advanced centralized WLAN solution for LWAPs. It provides configuration, firmware, radio management, and IDS for LWAP and their associated controllers. The same configuration, performance monitoring, security, fault management, and accounting options found on the individual controllers also exist on the WCS. It is designed to support 50 Cisco WLCs and 1500 APs.

Administrators can define operator permissions within the administration menu where accounts and maintenance tasks are located. Features like autodiscovery help simplify configuration and reduce data entry errors. WCS administration is accessible via HTTPS and supports SNMPv1, SNMPv2, and SNMPv3. Cisco WCS uses SNMP for controller communications.

WCS runs on both Microsoft Windows and Linux platforms. The WCS implementation can either be run as a normal application or as a service that is always running even after reboot.

Cisco WCS has three versions:

- WCS Base

- WCS Location

- WCS Location + 2700 Series Wireless Location Appliance

WCS Location Tracking Options

The three WCS tracking options are increasingly enhanced with features. *Tracking* refers to the management of wireless assets and how each version can help improve on that task.

The simplest version of Cisco WCS, WCS Base, informs managers which AP a device is associated with. This allows managers to have an approximation of the device location. The optional version, called WCS Location, is the second level of WCS. It provides users with the RF fingerprinting technology and can provide location accuracy to within a few meters (less than 10 meters 90 percent of the time; less than 5 meters 50 percent of the time). The third and final option, the one with the most capabilities, is called WCS Location + 2700 Series Wireless Location Appliance. The WCS Location + 2700 Series Wireless Location Appliance provides the capability to track thousands of wireless clients in real time.

With these advanced location-tracking capabilities, the Cisco Unified Wireless Network is an ideal platform for helping to enable key business applications that take advantage of wireless mobility, such as asset tracking, inventory management, and enhanced 911 (e911) services for voice. By incorporating indoor location tracking into the wireless LAN infrastructure itself, Cisco reduces the complexities of wireless LAN deployment and minimizes total cost of ownership.

WCS Base Software Features

Cisco WCS Base is a full-featured software product for WLAN monitoring and control. Wireless client data access, rogue AP detection to the nearest Cisco AP, and containment are examples that are offered in Cisco WCS Base.

Cisco WCS graphical views provide the following:

- Autodiscovery of APs as they associate with controllers

- Autodiscovery and containment or notification of rogue APs

- Map-based organization of AP coverage areas

- User-supplied campus, building, and floor plan graphics that provide locations and status of managed APs, RF coverage maps as well as location to the nearest AP, and coverage hole alarms

Cisco WCS Base also provides system-wide control of the following:

- Configuration for controllers and managed APs using customer-defined templates

- Status and alarm monitoring of all managed devices with automated and manual client monitoring and control functions

- Automated monitoring of rogue APs, coverage holes, security violations, controllers, and APs

- Event log information for data clients, rogue APs, coverage holes, security violations, controllers, and APs

- Automatic channel and power level assignment using radio resource management (RRM)

- User-defined audit status, missed trap polling, configuration backups, and policy cleanups

WCS Location Software Features

Cisco WCS Location includes the WCS Base features with some enhancements. WCS Location has the ability to use the historical location data management of the location appliance. WCS Location also features the on-demand monitoring of any single device using RF fingerprinting technology, providing high location accuracy. Any rogue AP, client, or device tracking can be performed on-demand within 10 meters or 33 feet using RF fingerprinting.

WCS Location + 2700 Series Wireless Location Appliance Features

Cisco Wireless Location Appliance scales on-demand location tracking to a new level, significantly improving the functionality of Cisco WCS Location. Whereas WCS Location could track one on-demand device, the Cisco Wireless Location Appliance can track up to 1500 devices simultaneously. It can record historical information that can be used in capacity management and trending.

WCS System Features

The Cisco WCS operating system manages all data client, communications, and system administration functions and performs radio resource management (RRM) functions. Moreover, WCS manages systemwide mobility policies using the operating systems security solution and coordinates all security functions using the operating system security framework.

Cisco WCS User Interface

Three user interfaces exist for Cisco WCS. The first is a full featured CLI that can be used to configure and monitor individual controllers. The second interface is the industry standard SNMP Cisco WCS supports SNMPv1, SNMP 2c, and SNMPv3. The third interface is a full featured HTTPS web browser interface. It is hosted by Cisco controllers and can be used to configure and monitor individual controllers and their associated access pointAPs.

The Cisco WCS user interface is where the administrator can create, modify, and delete user accounts; change passwords; assign permissions; and schedule periodic maintenance tasks. The administrator creates usernames and passwords, assigning them to predefined permissions groups.

In addition, the administrator can configure operating system parameters, monitor real-time operations, create and configure coverage area layouts, and perform troubleshooting tasks via HTTPS.

The user interface has four menus on each screen. A general description of each menu function follows:

- **Monitor**—See a top-level description of all devices

- **Configure**—Configure APs, controllers, and templates

- **Administration**—Schedule tasks such as backups, device status, network audits, and location server synchronization

- **Location**—Configure the Cisco Wireless Location Appliances

Cisco WCS System Requirements

Cisco WCS is supported under Microsoft Windows 2000, Windows 2003, and Red Hat Enterprise Linux ES v.3 servers as either a normal application or a service.

Minimum server requirements are as follows:

- Windows 2000 Service Pack 4 (SP4) or greater, Windows 2003 SP1 or greater, or Red Hat Enterprise Linux ES v.3

- Up to 500 APs: 2.4-GHz Pentium with 1-GB RAM

- More than 500 APs: dual processors (at least 2.4 GHz each) with minimum 2-GB RAM

- 20-GB hard drive

NOTE   The minimum client requirement is Internet Explorer 6.0 with SP1 or later.

WCS Summary Pages

The WCS Network Summary (Network Dashboard) page is displayed after logging in success-fully. It is a top-level overview of the network with information about controllers, coverage areas, APs, and clients. Systems configuration and devices can be added from this page. Access the Network Summary page from other areas by choosing **Monitor > Network Summary**. Figure 10-2 shows a sample WCS Network Summary page.

Figure 10-2 *WCS Network Summary Page*

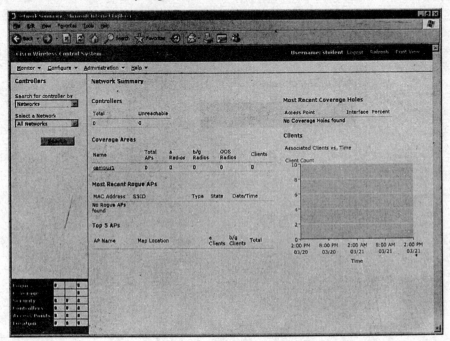

The Network Summary page is an at-a-glance view that is ideal for an operational monitoring environment. In the lower-left portion of the page is the Alarm Monitor, which shows the received alarms from all the controllers. The Alarm Monitor reflects the current state of alarms needing attention. They are usually generated by one or more events. Alarms can be cleared, but the event remains. The alarm color codes are given in Table 10-4.

Table 10-4 *WCS Alarm Color Codes*

Color Code	Type of Alarm
Clear	No alarm
Red	Critical alarm
Orange	Major alarm
Yellow	Minor alarm

The WCS Controller Summary page provides visibility for the supported 50 Cisco WLCs and 1500 APs. To access this page, select **Monitor > Devices > Controllers**. (The Monitor Controllers > Search Results page is the default.) The WCS Controller Summary page provides detailed information about the specific controller, such as the IP address, controller name, location, mobility group name, and reachability. Figure 10-3 shows a sample WCS Controller Summary page.

Figure 10-3 *WCS Controller Summary Page*

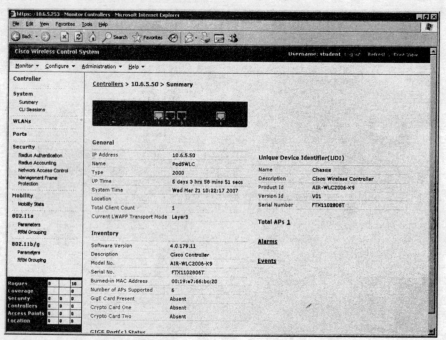

Wireless Location Appliance

The Cisco Wireless Location Appliance is part of the Cisco Unified Wireless Network using LAN Controllers and LWAPs that can track the location of devices to within a few meters. The Cisco Wireless Location Appliance solution uses an advanced technology called RF fingerprinting to track thousands of devices, increasing visibility and control of the airspace. The RF fingerprinting technology performs location computations using the site survey results and the RSSI information to improve the location accuracy over other location methods.

The appliance can provide location-based alerts for business policy enforcement as well as location trending, rapid problem resolution, and RF capacity management using its stored location data. Cisco Wireless Location Appliances are servers that compute, collect, and store historical location data for up to 1500 devices, including laptops, Voice over IP (VoIP) telephone clients, radio frequency identification (RFID) asset tags, rogue APs, and rogue clients.

The centralized management of WCS is extended via the capabilities and easy-to-use GUI of the Cisco Wireless Location Appliance, which makes setup fast and easy. This is after an initial configuration using the CLI console. After the Location Appliance configuration is complete, the location server communicates directly with the LAN Controllers.

The Cisco Wireless Location Appliance will collect the assigned operator-defined location data. The collected information is used for tracking up to 1500 devices for a 30-day period.

Wireless Location Appliance Architecture

The Cisco Wireless Location Appliance architecture is designed so it can interact with WCS as a client. This allows WCS to centrally control and provide visualization services. The Cisco Wireless Location Appliance utilizes the same LWAPs as wireless client and Wi-Fi tag location "readers." The readers or Cisco LWAPs collect the RSSI information and send it to the Cisco WLCs. The aggregate RSSI information is then sent to the associated Cisco Wireless Location Appliance via SNMP. The Cisco Wireless Location Appliance uses the aggregated RSSI information and performs location computations.

An RF prediction and heat map can be generated once the network maps and APs are added. The site floor plans can then graphically display all the wireless devices. The WCS visualization provides immediate asset location application for many administrators.

Wireless Location Appliance Applications

All enterprises could benefit from RF capacity planning and location-based security as well as maintaining asset visibility. The location information can be made available to third-party applications via SOAP XML APIs on the appliance. A multitude of specialized wireless applications can be created based on such features as these:

- **Visibility and tracking of mobile devices by using Wi-Fi tags**—Anything you can put a Wi-Fi tag on is manageable, such as computer equipment, office furniture, business phones, and trade tools. Any asset can be quickly located within the WLAN.

- **Workflow automation and people tracking**—This involves automating awareness of inbound or outbound deliveries or shoppers coming to the register. Police, firefighters, security personnel, and children can all be tracked at any time.

■ **Telemetry**—This involves delivering information in a serialized format containing variable information, such as car and truck mileage or inventory changes.

■ **WLAN security and network control**—This involves containing information and awareness by locating rogue APs, rogue clients, and secure network control.

■ **RF capacity management and visibility**—Integrating and reviewing location-based trend reports for RF traffic patterns allows for an improvement to capacity management.

WCS Configuration Examples

The WCS configuration first requires an authorized login. Several configuration steps must take place after the initial authorized login, such as adding devices and site maps.

WCS Login Steps

The Cisco WCS Server login involves three major steps:

Step 1 Start Microsoft Internet Explorer version 6.0 or later.

Step 2 Enter **https://localhost** in the address bar when the Cisco WCS user interface is on a Cisco WCS server. Enter **https://wcs-ip-address** when the Cisco WCS interface is on any other workstation.

Step 3 Enter your username and password on the login page. The default username is **root**, and the default password is **public**.

> **NOTE** Some Cisco WCS features might not function properly if you use a web browser other than Internet Explorer 6.0 or later.

Changing the Root Password

The following are the steps to change the root password:

Step 1 Log in as **root**.

Step 2 Select **Administration > Accounts**.

Step 3 From the User Name column, click **root**.

Step 4 Enter a new password in the **New Password** text box, and retype the new password in the **Confirm New Password** text box.

Step 5 Click **Submit**.

Adding a Wireless LAN Controller

The first step when adding a WLC is gathering the IP address of the controller service port. Use the following steps to add the controller:

Step 1   Log into Cisco WCS.

Step 2   Choose **Configure > Controllers** from the All Controllers page.

Step 3   Click the **Select a Command** drop-down menu, choose **Add Controller**, and click **GO**.

Step 4   Enter the controller IP address, network mask, and required SNMP settings in the Add Controller fields (see Figure 10-4).

Figure 10-4   *Adding a WLC*

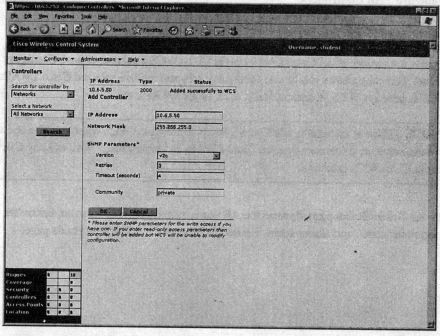

Step 5   Click **OK**.

> **NOTE**   Cisco WCS displays the Please Wait dialog box during the initial contact and while it is being added to the Cisco WCS database. Control is returned to the Add Controller page again upon success.

Controller management through the dedicated service port of the controller improves security. Some controllers do not have dedicated service ports, such as the Cisco 2000 Series WLC, which must use the controller management interface. Moreover, if a controller service port is disabled, the management interface of the controller must be used.

An issue might arise in which the WCS cannot communicate with the controller. A Discovery Status dialog box appears with a message "No response from device, check SNMP." A few checks can verify the correct settings:

■ A bad IP address on the controller service port

■ A blocked network path can be verified by pinging the controller from the WCS server

■ SNMP mismatch between the controller and Cisco WCS

You can continue to add or return additional controllers to the All Controllers page by choosing **Configure > All Controllers**.

Configuring Access Points

To view a summary of all Cisco LWAPs in the Cisco WCS database, choose **Configure > Access Points**. This page allows you to add third-party APs and remove selected Cisco LWAPs. When a WLC is added to WCS, it automatically adds all the LWAPs, too.

NOTE There is no need to add Cisco LWAPs to the Cisco WCS database. The operating system software automatically adds Cisco LWAPs as they associate with existing Cisco WLCs in the Cisco WCS database.

The All Access Points page displays the AP name, radio type, map location, controller, port, operational status, and alarm status. Figure 10-5 shows the All Access Points page.

Figure 10-5 *All Access Points Page*

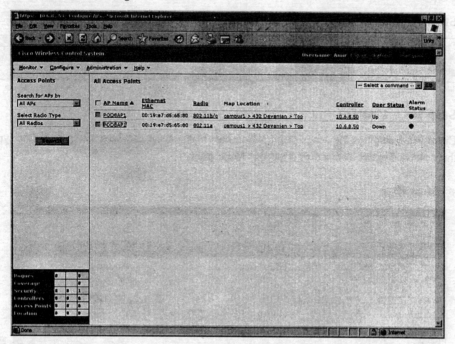

WCS Map

Cisco WCS can use real floor, building, and campus plans to view the physical and RF environments together. This section discusses adding a campus map and a new building.

Adding a Campus Map

Use the following steps to add a campus map:

Step 1   Save the map in a format such as .png, .jpg, .jpeg, or .gif. Do not worry about the size, because WCS will manage it.

Step 2   Browse to the map and import it from anywhere in the file system.

Step 3   Choose the **Monitor** tab.

Step 4   Choose **Maps**.

Step 5   From the **Select a Command** drop-down menu, choose **New Campus** and click **Go**.

Step 6   On the New Campus page, enter the campus name and contact.

Step 7   Choose **Browse**, and select the campus graphic name.

Step 8 Choose **Maintain Aspect Ratio** so that WCS does not distort the map.

Step 9 Enter the horizontal and vertical span size in feet.

NOTE The campus horizontal and vertical spans should be larger than any building or floor plan to be added to the campus.

Step 10 Click **OK**.

Cisco WCS displays the Maps page, which lists maps in the database along with map types and their status. Figure 10-6 shows a sample Maps page.

Figure 10-6 *Maps Page*

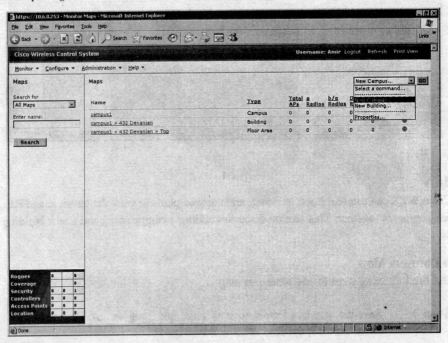

A WCS map can start out as either a building or a campus map. The building map can be a single entity or part of the campus map. Moreover, the campus map can have an outdoor coverage area.

Adding a New Building

Buildings can be added without maps. Use the following steps to add a building:

Step 1 Choose the **Monitor** tab.

Step 2   Choose **Maps**.

Step 3   When you choose the desired campus, WCS displays the Campus page (see
Figure 10-7).

Figure 10-7 *Campus Page*

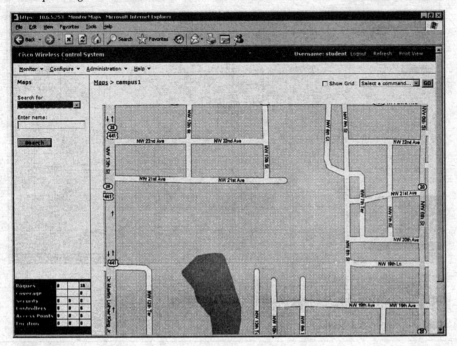

Step 4   From the **Select a Command** drop-down menu, choose **New Building** and
click **Go**.

Step 5   Create a virtual building to organize related floor plan maps by entering the
building name, contact, number of floors and basements, and the horizontal
and vertical span size in feet.

> **NOTE**   **Ctrl-Left-Select** is an alternative key stroke combination to resize the bounding area
> in the upper left corner of the campus map. When changing the bounding size, the building
> horizontal span and vertical span parameters automatically adjust to match your changes.

Step 6   Choose **Place** to put the scaled rectangular building on the campus map.
Figure 10-8 shows the placement of a new building.

Figure 10-8 *Adding a New Building*

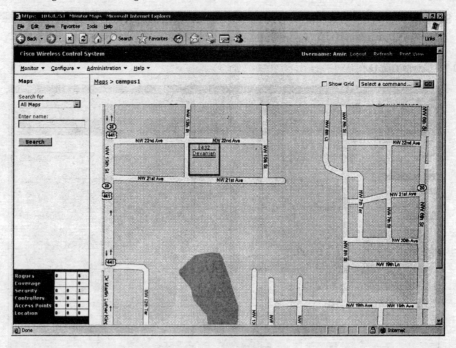

Step 7 Move the building to the desired location.

Step 8 Choose **Save**.

NOTE A hyperlink that is associated with the building links the corresponding **Maps page**.

Rogue Access Point Detection

The process flow of a rogue AP being detected in a WLAN environment is based on the LWAPs already being powered up and associated to their controllers. The WLC detects a rogue AP and immediately notifies WCS, which creates a rogue AP alarm that appears in the lower-left corner of the user interface pages. Simply selecting the indicator displays the Rogue AP Alarms page.

Rogue Access Point Alarms

The alarms for rogue APs are naturally listed on the Rogue Access Point Alarms page. This page details the severity, the rogue MAC address, the vendor, the radio type, the strongest AP RSSI, the date and time, the channel number, and the SSID. You can view further details by clicking the link in the Rogue MAC Address column. Then you see the associated Alarms > Rogue AP MAC Address page. To view rogue AP information using the menu bar, choose **Monitor > Alarms > Rogue AP Alarms**.

You can handle the alarms by checking a box to the left of the severity and manage them using the **Select a Command** drop-down menu. The choices available are **Assign to Me**, **Unassign**, **Delete**, **Clear**, or **Email Notification**.

Rogue Access Point Location

To see the rogue AP calculated location on a map, choose **Map** from the Rogue AP MAC Address page, or from the menu bar choose **Monitor > Maps > Building Name > Floor Name**. A small skull-and-crossbones indicator appears at the calculated location. The calculated location is to the nearest AP based on the strongest RSSI with WCS Base. WCS Location compares the RSSI signal strength from multiple APs to pinpoint the most probable location using RF fingerprinting technology.

Foundation Summary

The "Foundation Summary" is a collection of information that provides a convenient review of many key concepts in this chapter. If you are already comfortable with the topics in this chapter, this summary can help you recall a few details. If you just read this chapter, this review should help solidify some key facts. If you are doing your final preparation before the exam, the information in this section is a convenient way to review the day before the exam.

Following are the five elements of Cisco Unified Wireless Network:

- **Client devices**—Use the Cisco Compatible Extensions program helps ensure interoperability. The Cisco Compatible Extensions program delivers services such as wireless mobility, QoS, network management, and enhanced security.

- **Mobility platform**—Provides ubiquitous access in any environment indoors or out. The lightweight access points (LWAP) are dynamically configured and managed by wireless LAN controllers (WLC) through LightWeight Access Point Protocol (LWAPP).

- **Network unification**—Creates seamless integration into the routing and switching infrastructure. The WLCs are responsible for functions such as RF management, n+1 deployment, and Intrusion Prevention System (IPS).

- **World-class network management**—Enables wireless local-area network (WLANs) to have the equivalent LAN security, scalability, reliability, ease of deployment, and management via Cisco Wireless Control System (WCS). Cisco WCS provides features for design, control, and monitoring.

- **Unified advanced services**—Support new mobility applications, emerging Wi-Fi technologies, and advanced threat detection and prevention capabilities such as wireless VoIP, future unified cellular, location services, Network Admission Control (NAC), the Self-Defending Network, (Identity Based Network Services(IBNS), Intrusion Detection Systems (IDS), and guest access.

Cisco offers two WLAN implementations: autonomous and lightweight. Table 10-5 contrasts the two solutions.

Table 10-5 *Comparison of WLAN Implementation Solutions*

Category	Autonomous WLAN Solution	Lightweight WLAN Solution
Access Point	Autonomous APs	LWAPs
Control	Individual configuration on each AP	Configuration via Cisco WLC

Table 10-5   *Comparison of WLAN Implementation Solutions (Continued)*

Category	Autonomous WLAN Solution	Lightweight WLAN Solution
Dependency	Independent operation	Dependent on Cisco WLC
WLAN Management	Management via CiscoWorks WLSE and Wireless Domain Services (WDS)	Management via Cisco WCS
Redundancy	AP redundancy	Cisco WLC redundancy

CiscoWorks WLSE is a management tool for WLANs with autonomous APs. It is designed to centralize management, reduce total cost of ownership, minimize security vulnerabilities, and improve WLAN uptime. Features and benefits of Cisco WLSE are summarized in Table 10-6.

Table 10-6   *CiscoWorks WLSE Features and Benefits*

Feature	Benefit
Centralized configuration, firmware, and radio management	Reduces WLAN total cost of ownership by saving time and resources required to manage large numbers of APs
Autoconfiguration of new APs	Simplifies large-scale deployments
Security policy misconfiguration alerts and rogue AP detection	Minimizes security vulnerabilities
AP utilization and client association reports	Helps in capacity planning and troubleshooting
Proactive monitoring of APs, bridges, and 802.1x EAP[1] servers	Improves WLAN uptime

[1] EAP = extensible authentication protocol

CiscoWorks WLSE supports Secure Shell (SSH), HTTP, Cisco Discovery Protocol (CDP), and Simple Network Management Protocol (SNMP). CiscoWorks WLSE comes in two versions: CiscoWorks WLSE and WLSE Express. CiscoWorks WLSE supports up to 2500 WLAN devices. WLSE Express supports up to 100 WLAN devices. The WLSE Express setup option is either Automatic or Manual.

Cisco WCS is a Cisco WLAN solution network-management tool that is designed to support 50 Cisco WLCs and 1500 APs. Cisco WCS supports SNMPv1, SNMPv2, and SNMPv3.

Cisco WCS comes in three versions:

- **Cisco WCS Base**—The base version of Cisco WCS can determine which AP a wireless device is associated with.

- **Cisco WCS Location**—Cisco WCS Location is the base plus Cisco RF fingerprinting technology.

- **Cisco WCS Location + 2700 Series Wireless Location Appliance**—Cisco Wireless Location + 2700 Appliance tracks thousands of devices in real time, enabling key business applications such as asset tracking, inventory management, and e911.

The Cisco Wireless Location Appliance provides simultaneous device tracking and data collection for capacity management or location trending:

- The Cisco Wireless Location Appliance is an innovative, easy-to-deploy solution that uses advanced RF fingerprinting technology to simultaneously track thousands of 802.11 wireless devices from directly within a WLAN infrastructure.

- Cisco 2700 Series Wireless Location Appliances are servers that enhance the high-accuracy built-in Cisco WCS location abilities by computing, collecting, and storing historical location data for up to 1500 laptop clients, palmtop clients, Voice over IP (VoIP) telephone clients, radio frequency identification (RFID) asset tags, rogue APs, and rogue AP clients.

To access the Cisco WCS Network Summary page, choose **Monitor > Network Summary**.

To access the Cisco WCS Controller Summary details, choose **Monitor > Devices > Controllers**.

The default Cisco WCS username is **root**, and the default password is **public**.

The WLC detects rogue APs and immediately notifies the WCS, which in turn creates a rogue AP alarm in the lower-left corner of the user interface pages. To view rogue AP information using the menu bar, choose **Monitor > Alarms > Rogue AP Alarms**. The alarms choices available are **Assign to Me**, **Unassign**, **Delete**, **Clear**, or **Email Notification**. To see the location of a rogue AP, either choose **Map** from the Rogue AP MAC Address page, or choose **Monitor > Maps > Building Name > Floor Name** from the menu bar. A small skull-and-crossbones indicator appears at the calculated location.

Q&A

Some of the questions that follow challenge you more than the exam by using an open-ended question format. By reviewing now with this more difficult question format, you can exercise your memory better and prove your conceptual and factual knowledge of this chapter. The answers to these questions appear in Appendix A.

1. Discuss the different characteristics and advantages of the two WLAN solutions.

2. Does WLSE support both lightweight and autonomous access points?

3. When do you use CiscoWorks WLSE versus WLSE Express?

4. Discuss the platform support for Cisco WCS.

5. What are the three WCS versions for tracking wireless devices?

6. When does Cisco WCS listen for rogue access points?

7. How do you add lightweight access points to the WCS database?

8. Does Cisco WCS support SNMPv3?

9. What page is displayed upon a successful WCS login?

10. What is the Cisco WCS default username and password?

11. For the WLAN components, what are the WLAN Management solutions?

12. What happens to Rogue APs when they are detected?

13. What are the differences between WCS base, Location, and Location + Appliance (including how many clients can be tracked)?

Part IV: Appendix

Answers to the "Do I Know This Already?" Quizzes and Q&A Sections

Chapter 1

"Do I Know This Already?" Quiz

1. D
2. C
3. B
4. A
5. D
6. D
7. B
8. A
9. B
10. C
11. A
12. D
13. C
14. D
15. A
16. C
17. B
18. D
19. A
20. B

Q&A

1. The benefits of packet telephony networks include these:

   - More efficient use of bandwidth and equipment

   - Lower transmission costs

   - Consolidated network expenses

   - Improved employee productivity

   - Access to new communication devices

2. Following are the components of a packet telephony (VoIP) network:

   - Phones

   - Gateways

   - Multipoint control units

   - Application servers

   - Gatekeepers

   - Call agents

   - Video end points

3. The analog interfaces through which legacy analog devices can connect to a VoIP network include these:

   - FXS

   - FXO

   - E&M

4. The digital interface options to connect VoIP equipment to PBXs or the PSTN include the following:

   - BRI

   - T1/E1 CAS

   - T1/E1 CCS

5. The three stages of a phone call are:

   1. Call setup
   2. Call maintenance
   3. Call teardown

6. The two main models of call control are distributed call control and centralized call control. Examples of distributed call control include H.323 and SIP. An example of centralized call control is MGCP.

7. The steps for converting analog signals to digital signals include the following:

   1. Sampling
   2. Quantization
   3. Encoding
   4. Compression (optional)

8. Following are the steps for converting digital signals to analog signals:

   1. Decompression of the samples, if compressed
   2. Decoding
   3. Reconstruction of the analog signal from PAM signals

9. The sampling rate must be at least twice the maximum signal frequency. Because the maximum voice frequency over a telephone channel was considered 4000 Hz, based on the Nyquist theorem, a rate of 8000 samples per second is required.

10. The two main quantization techniques are linear quantization and logarithmic quantization.

11. μ-Law is used in the United States, Canada, and Japan. A-Law is used in other countries. Both methods are quasi-logarithmic; they use logarithmic segment sizes and linear step sizes within each segment. For communication between a μ-Law and an A-Law country, the μ-Law country must change its signaling to accommodate the A-Law country.

12. The main codec/compression standards and their bandwidth requirements are as follows:

   - G.711 (PCM)—64 Kbps

   - G.726 (ADPCM)—16, 24, or 32 Kbps

   - G.728 (LDCELP)—16 Kbps

   - G.729 (CS-ACELP)—8 Kbps

13. MOS stands for mean opinion score. It is a measurement of voice quality derived from the judgment of several subscribers. The range of MOS scores is 1 to 5, where 5 is the perfect score for direct conversation.

14. DSP stands for digital signal processor. It is a specialized processor used for the following telephony applications: voice termination, conferencing, and transcoding.

15. The TCP/IP protocols that are responsible for transporting voice are RTP (12 bytes), UDP (8 bytes), and IP (20 bytes).

16. RTP provides sequence numbering (reordering) and time-stamping to complement UDP.

17. cRTP stands for Compressed RTP. cRTP reduces the IP, UDP, and RTP headers from 40 to 2 bytes (without a checksum), and to 4 bytes (with a checksum). cRTP provides significant bandwidth savings, but it is only recommended for use on slow links (less than 2 Mbps).

18. Packet rate, packetization size, IP overhead, data link overhead, and tunneling overhead influence the bandwidth requirements of VoIP.

19. The packet rate and packetization period are reciprocal. For example, if the packetization period is 20 milliseconds (0.020 seconds), the packet rate is equal to 1 over 0.020, or 50 packets per second.

20. The sizes of Ethernet, 902.1Q, Frame Relay, and Multilink PPP (MLP) overheads are as follows:

- Ethernet—18 bytes

- 802.1Q+Ethernet—4 + 18 = 22 bytes

- Frame Relay—6 bytes

- MLP—6 bytes

21. Following are the tunneling and security protocols and their associated overheads:

- IPsec transport mode—30 to 53 bytes

- IPsec Tunnel mode—50 to 73 bytes

- L2TP—24 bytes

- GRE—24 bytes

- MPLS—4 bytes

- PPPoE—8 bytes

22. Following are the steps necessary to compute the total bandwidth for a VoIP call:

1. Determine the codec type and packetization period.
2. Gather the link information. Determine whether cRTP, any type of tunneling, or IPsec is used.
3. Calculate the packetization size or period.
4. Add all the headers to the packetization size.
5. Calculate the packet rate.
6. Calculate the total bandwidth.

23. VAD stands for voice activity detection. It suppresses the transmission of silence; therefore, it might result in up to 35 percent bandwidth savings. The success of VAD depends on the types of audio, the level of background noise, and other factors.

24. The components of the enterprise voice implementations include the following:

   ■ Gateways

   ■ Gatekeepers

   ■ IP phones

   ■ Cisco Unified CallManager

25. On a Cisco router, voice gateway functions include the following:

   ■ Connect traditional telephony devices

   ■ Convert analog signals to digital and vice versa

   ■ Encapsulate digital voice into IP packets

   ■ Perform voice compression

   ■ Provide DSP resources for conferencing and transcoding

   ■ Provide Cisco survivable remote site telephony (SRST)

   ■ Act as the call agent (Cisco Unified CallManager Express)

26. The main functions of Cisco Unified CallManager include the following:

   ■ Call processing

   ■ Dial plan administration

   ■ Signaling and device control

   ■ Phone feature administration

   ■ Directory and XML services

   ■ API for external applications

27. The main enterprise IP Telephony deployment models are as follows:

   ■ The single site

   ■ Multisite with centralized call processing

   ■ Multisite with distributed call processing

   ■ Clustering over WAN

28. CAC stands for call admission control. CAC artificially limits the number of concurrent voice calls to prevent oversubscription.

29. CAC complements QoS features, and it is necessary. If more than ten calls become concurrently active in this case, all calls experience packet loss and extra delays. Therefore, the quality of all calls will drop.

Chapter 2

"Do I Know This Already?" Quiz

1. D
2. B
3. C
4. B
5. C
6. D
7. A
8. A
9. B and C
10. D
11. C
12. B
13. C
14. C
15. D
16. A
17. A and C

CLI is the most time-consuming QoS implementation method, and AutoQoS is the least time-consuming QoS implementation method.

18. D
19. B and D
20. B

Q&A

1. The four key quality issues with converged networks include available bandwidth, end-to-end delay, variation of delay (jitter), and packet loss.

2. The maximum available bandwidth is equal to the bandwidth of the lowest link (from source to destination). The average bandwidth available per flow is the maximum available bandwidth divided by the number of flows.

3. Delay types include processing delay, queuing delay, serialization delay, propagation delay, compression/decompression delay, and encryption/decryption delay.

4. You can reduce delay by increasing the link bandwidth (capacity), prioritizing delay-sensitive packets, reprioritizing packets if necessary, performing payload compression, or performing header compression.

5. You can reduce or prevent loss of important packets by doing any of the following:

   ■ Increasing the (upgrade) link bandwidth (capacity)

   ■ Guaranteeing enough bandwidth to drop sensitive (important) packets

   ■ Preventing congestion by dropping less important packets before congestion occurs

6. The latest definition included in Cisco educational material defines QoS as the ability of the network to provide better or "special" service to a set of users or applications or both to the detriment of other users or applications or both.

7. The three key steps involved in implementing QoS on a network include the following:

   1. Identifying the network traffic and its requirements
   2. Defining traffic classes
   3. Defining a QoS policy for each traffic class

8. The three main QoS models are best-effort, IntServ, and DiffServ.

9. The best-effort model is the default; it does not differentiate among different traffic types.

10. The benefits of the best-effort model are that it is scalable, and it requires special mechanisms.

    The drawbacks of the best-effort model are that it does not provide service guarantee, and it does not provide Differentiated Service.

11. IntServ is a guaranteed QoS model that is often referred to as Hard QoS. It uses a signaling mechanism such as RSVP to make resource reservation and guarantee for each traffic flow before it becomes active. If resources are secured first, the flow is not admitted. IntServ can provide multiple service levels and uses intelligent queuing mechanisms to provide guaranteed rate and controlled load.

12. The IntServ model requires the following functions on the network routers and switches:

- Admission control

- Classification

- Policing

- Queuing

- Scheduling

13. The benefits of the IntServ model include explicit end-to-end resource admission control, per-request policy admission control, and signaling of dynamic port numbers.

The drawbacks of the IntServ model include continuous signaling because of stateful architecture and low scalability because of the flow-based nature of the model.

14. The DiffServ model was designed to overcome the limitations of the best-effort and the IntServ models. Within this model, the network traffic is classified and marked, differentiated treatment of traffic classes is enforced by network QoS policies, and different service levels are chosen for traffic classes based on business requirements.

15. The benefits of the DiffServ model include high scalability and the ability to provide many different service quality levels.

The drawbacks of the DiffServ model include lack of an absolute service guarantee and a requirement for implementation of complex mechanisms throughout the network.

16. The four QoS implementation methods are as follows:

- Legacy command-line interface (CLI) for basic QoS deployments

- Modular QoS command-line interface (MQC) for high-level deployment and fine-tuning of QoS

- AutoQoS for automatic (general) QoS configuration

- Cisco Router and Security Device Manager (SDM) QoS Wizard for web-based (GUI) and interactive QoS configuration

17. Of the four QoS implementation methods, legacy CLI is nonmodular and the most time consuming.

18. Modular QoS command-line interface (MQC) allows implementation of the most recent and modern QoS features and mechanisms in a modular fashion. It separates the concept and process of traffic classification from the definition and deployment of QoS policy. MQC is less error prone and promotes code reuse and consistency.

19. The main advantage of AutoQoS is that it simplifies the task of QoS configuration. Network administrators who lack in-depth knowledge of QoS commands and features can use AutoQoS to implement those features consistently and accurately.

20. Enabling CEF and configuring the correct bandwidth on the interface are the prerequisites for Auto QoS VoIP.

21. Enabling CEF and NBAR, plus configuring the correct bandwidth on the interface, are the prerequisites for Auto QoS on the enterprise.

22. AutoQoS is the fastest QoS implementation method.

23. The SDM QoS Wizard enables you to do three things:

    ■ Implement QoS

    ■ Monitor QoS

    ■ Troubleshoot QoS on the network

Chapter 3

"Do I Know This Already?" Quiz

1. B
2. C
3. D
4. A
5. D
6. D
7. D
8. C
9. B
10. A
11. D
12. D
13. C
14. A
15. B

Q&A

1. Classification is the process or mechanism that identifies traffic and categorizes it into classes.

2. Marking is the process of tagging or coloring traffic based on the category it falls into. You normally mark the traffic after it is classified.

3. The marker field on the 802.1Q/P frame is called PRI (priority) or CoS (class of service).

4. The names and definitions for CoS values 0 through 7 are as follows:

CoS (bits)	CoS (in Decimal)	Definition	Application
000	0	Routine	Best-effort data
001	1	Priority	Medium-priority data
010	2	Immediate	High-priority data
011	3	Flash	Call signaling
100	4	Flash-Override	Video conferencing
101	5	Critical	Voice bearer
110	6	Internet	Reserved (inter-network control)
111	7	Network	Reserved (network control)

5. The class selector (CS) PHB (CS1 through CS7) provides backward compatibility with ToS-based IP precedence. The three least-significant DSCP bits are set to 000 to identify the class selector (CS) PHB.

6. The four DiffServ (DSCP) PHBs are as follows:

   Default PHB—Used for best-effort service (000---)

   Class selector PHB—Used for backward compatibility with non-DiffServ-compliant devices (---000)

   Assured forwarding (AF) PHB—Used for guaranteed bandwidth services (001---, 010---, 011---, 100---)

   Expedited forwarding (EF) PHB—Used for low-delay service (101110)

7. Compatibility between MPLS and network layer QoS is achieved by mapping between MPLS EXP bits and IP precedence or DSCP bits. A service provider can map the customer network layer QoS marking or change it to meet an SLA.

8. A QoS service class is a logical grouping of packets that are to receive a similar level of applied quality.

9. A trust boundary is the point within the network in which markings such as CoS or DSCP begin to be accepted. For scalability reasons, classification and marking should be done as close to the ingress edge of the network as possible, depending on the capabilities of the edge devices, at the end system, access layer, or distribution layer.

10. Network Based Application Recognition (NBAR) is a classification and protocol discovery tool or feature. You can use NBAR to perform three tasks:

    ■ Protocol discovery

    ■ Traffic statistics collection

    ■ Traffic classification

11. NBAR has several limitations:

    ■ NBAR does not function on Fast EtherChannel and on interfaces that are configured to use encryption or tunneling.

    ■ NBAR can only handle up to 24 concurrent URLs, hosts, or MIME types.

    ■ NBAR analyzes only the first 400 bytes of the packet.

    ■ NBAR supports only CEF and does not work if another switching mode is used.

    ■ Multicast packets, fragmented packets, and packets that are associated with secure HTTP (URL, host, or MIME classification) are not supported.

    ■ NBAR does not analyze or recognize the traffic that is destined to or emanated from the router running NBAR.

12. You can use NBAR to recognize packets that belong to different types of applications: applications that use static (well-known) TCP or UDP port numbers, applications that use dynamic (negotiated during control session) port numbers, and some non-IP protocols. NBAR also can do deep-packet inspection and classify packets based on information stored beyond the IP, TCP, or UDP headers; for example, NBAR can classify HTTP sessions based on requested URL, MIME type, or hostname.

13. Packet Description Language Modules (PDLM) allow NBAR to recognize new protocols matching text patterns in data packets without requiring a new Cisco IOS software image or a router reload. PDLMs can also enhance an existing protocol recognition capability.

14. NBAR offers audio, video, and CODEC-type RTP payload classifications.

15. **match protocol fasttrack file-transfer** *regular-expression* allows you to identify FastTrack peer-to-peer protocols.

Chapter 4

"Do I Know This Already?" Quiz

1. D
2. C
3. B
4. B
5. A
6. D
7. D
8. A
9. B
10. D
11. C
12. C
13. D

Q&A

1. Congestion occurs when the rate of input (incoming traffic switched) to an interface exceeds the rate of output (outgoing traffic) from an interface. Aggregation, speed mismatch, and confluence are three common causes of congestion.

2. Queuing is a congestion management technique that entails creating a few queues, assigning packets to those queues, and scheduling departure of packets from those queues.

3. Congestion management/queuing mechanisms might create queues, assign packets to the queues, and schedule a departure of packets from the queues.

4. On fast interfaces (faster than E1 or 2.048 Mbps), the default queuing is FIFO, but on slow interfaces (E1 or less), the default queuing is WFQ.

5. FIFO might be appropriate on fast interfaces and when congestion does not occur.

6. PQ has four queues available: high-, medium-, normal-, and low-priority queues. You must assign packets to one of the queues, or the packets will be assigned to the normal queue. Access lists are often used to define which types of packets are assigned to the four queues. As long as the high-priority queue has packets, the PQ scheduler only forwards packets from

that queue. If the high-priority queue is empty, one packet from the medium-priority queue is processed. If both the high- and medium-priority queues are empty, one packet from the normal-priority queue is processed, and if high-, medium-, and normal-priority queues are empty, one packet from the low-priority queue is processed.

7. Cisco custom queuing is based on weighted round-robin (WRR).

8. The Cisco router queuing components are software queue and hardware queue (also called transmit queue).

9. The software queuing mechanism usually has several queues. Packets are assigned to one of those queues upon arrival. If the queue is full, the packet is dropped (tail drop). If the packet is not dropped, it joins its assigned queue, which is usually a FIFO queue. The scheduler dequeues and dispatches packets from different queues to the hardware queue based on the particular software queuing discipline that is deployed. After a packet is classified and assigned to one of the software queues, it might be dropped if a technique such as weighted random early detection (WRED) is applied to that queue.

10. A modified version of RR called weighted round-robin (WRR) allows you to assign a "weight" to each queue. Based on that weight, each queue effectively receives a portion of the interface bandwidth, not necessarily equal to the others.

11. WFQ has these important goals and objectives: divide traffic into flows, provide fair bandwidth allocation to the active flows, provide faster scheduling to low-volume interactive flows, and provide more bandwidth to the higher-priority flows.

12. WFQ identifies flows based on the following fields from IP and either TCP or UDP headers: Source IP Address, Destination IP Address, Protocol Number, Type of Service, Source TCP/UDP Port Number, Destination TCP/UDP Port Number.

13. WFQ has a hold queue for all the packets of all flows (queues within the WFQ system). If a packet arrives while the hold queue is full, it is dropped. This is called WFQ aggressive dropping.

   Each flow-based queue within WFQ has a congestive discard threshold (CDT). If a packet arrives and the hold queue is not full but the CDT of that packet flow queue is reached, the packet is dropped. This is called WFQ early dropping.

14. Benefits: Configuring WFQ is simple and requires no explicit classification, WFQ does not starve flows and guarantees throughput to all flows, and WFQ drops packets from most aggressive flows and provides faster service to nonaggressive flows.

   Drawbacks: WFQ classification and scheduling are not configurable and modifiable, WFQ does not offer guarantees such as bandwidth and delay guarantees to traffic flows, and multiple traffic flows might be assigned to the same queue within the WFQ system.

15. The default values for CDT, dynamic queues, and reservable-queues are 64, 256, and 0. The dynamic queue's default is 256 only if the interface's bandwidth is more than 512, but is based on the interface bandwidth.

16. You adjust the hold queue size by entering the following command in interface configuration mode:

    `hold-queue max-limit out`

17. To use PQ and CQ, you must define traffic classes using complex access lists. PQ might impose starvation on packets of lower-priority queues. WFQ does not allow creation of user-defined classes. WFQ and CQ do not address the low delay requirements of real-time applications.

18. CBWFQ allows the creation of user-defined classes, each of which is assigned to its own queue. Each queue receives a user-defined amount of (minimum) bandwidth guarantee, but it can use more bandwidth if it is available.

19. The three options for bandwidth reservation within CBWFQ are bandwidth, bandwidth percent, and bandwidth remaining percent.

20. Available bandwidth is calculated as follows:

    Available bandwidth = (interface bandwidth x maximum reserved bandwidth) × (sum of all existing reservations)

21. CBWFQ has a couple of benefits. First, it allows creation of user-defined traffic classes. You can define these classes conveniently using MQC class maps. Second, it allows allocation/reservation of bandwidth for each traffic class based on user policies and preferences. The drawback of CBWFQ is that it does not offer a queue that is suitable for real-time applications such as voice or video over IP applications.

22. CBWFQ is configured using Cisco modular QoS command-line interface (MQC) class map, policy map, and service policy.

23. Low-latency queuing (LLQ) adds a strict-priority queue to CBWFQ. The LLQ strict-priority queue is given priority over other queues, which makes it ideal for delay- and jitter-sensitive applications. The LLQ strict-priority queue is policed so that other queues do not starve.

24. Low-latency queuing offers all the benefits of CBWFQ, including the ability of the user to define classes and guarantee each class an appropriate amount of bandwidth and to apply WRED to each of the classes (except to the strict-priority queue) if needed. In both LLQ and CBWFQ, the traffic that is not explicitly classified is considered to belong to the class-default class. You can make the queue that services the class-default class a WFQ instead of FIFO, and if needed, you can apply WRED to it, too. The benefit of LLQ over CBWFQ is the existence of one or more strict-priority queues with bandwidth guarantees for delay- and jitter-sensitive traffic.

25. Configuring LLQ is almost identical to configuring CBWFQ, except that for the strict priority queue(s), instead of using the keyword/command **bandwidth**, you use the keyword/command **priority** within the desired class of the policy map.

Chapter 5

"Do I Know This Already?" Quiz

1. C
2. D
3. B
4. D
5. B
6. A
7. A
8. B
9. C
10. D
11. C
12. B

Q&A

1. The limitations and drawbacks of tail drop include TCP global synchronization, TCP starvation, and lack of differentiated (or preferential) dropping.

2. When tail drop happens, TCP-based traffic flows simultaneously slow down (go into slow start) by reducing their TCP send window size. At this point, the bandwidth utilization drops significantly (assuming there are many active TCP flows), interface queues become less congested, and TCP flows start to increase their window sizes. Eventually, interfaces become congested again, tail drops happen, and the cycle repeats. This situation is called TCP global synchronization.

3. Queues become full when traffic is excessive and has no remedy, tail drop happens, and aggressive flows are not selectively punished. After tail drops begin, TCP flows slow down simultaneously, but other flows (non-TCP), such as UDP and non-IP traffic, do not. Consequently, non-TCP traffic starts filling up the queues and leaves little or no room for TCP packets. This situation is called TCP starvation.

4. Because RED drops packets from some and not all flows (statistically, more aggressive ones), all flows do not slow down and speed up at the same time, causing global synchronization.

5. RED has three configuration parameters: minimum threshold, maximum threshold, and mark probability denominator (MPD). While the size of the queue is smaller than the minimum threshold, RED does not drop packets. As the queue size grows, so does the rate of packet drops. When the size of the queue becomes larger than the maximum threshold, all arriving packets are dropped (tail drop behavior). The mark probability denominator is an integer that dictates to RED to drop one of MPD (as many packets as the value of mark probability denominator); the size of the queue is between the values of minimum and maximum thresholds.

6. Weighted random early detection (WRED) has the added capability of differentiating between high- and low-priority traffic, compared to RED. With WRED, you can set up a different profile (with a minimum threshold, maximum threshold, and mark probability denominator) for each traffic priority. Traffic priority is based on IP precedence or DSCP values.

7. When CBWFQ is the deployed queuing discipline, each queue performs tail drop by default. Applying WRED inside a CBWFQ system yields CBWRED; within each queue, packet profiles are based on IP precedence or DSCP value.

8. Currently, the only way to enforce assured forwarding (AF) per hop-behavior (PHB) on a Cisco router is by applying WRED to the queues within a CBWFQ system. Note that LLQ is composed of a strict-priority queue (policed) and a CBWFQ system. Therefore, applying WRED to the CBWFQ component of the LLQ also yields AF behavior.

9. The purposes of traffic policing are to enforce subrate access, to limit the traffic rate for each traffic class, and to re-mark traffic.

10. The purposes of traffic shaping are to slow down the rate of traffic being sent to another site through a WAN service such as Frame Relay or ATM, to comply with the subscribed rate, and to send different traffic classes at different rates.

11. The similarities and differences between traffic shaping and policing include the following:

   ■ Both traffic shaping and traffic policing measure traffic. (Sometimes, different traffic classes are measured separately.)

   ■ Policing can be applied to the inbound and outbound traffic (with respect to an interface), but traffic shaping applies only to outbound traffic.

- Shaping buffers excess traffic and sends it according to a preconfigured rate, whereas policing drops or re-marks excess traffic.

- Shaping requires memory for buffering excess traffic, which creates variable delay and jitter; policing does not require extra memory, and it does not impose variable delay.

- Policing can re-mark traffic, but traffic shaping does not re-mark traffic.

- Traffic shaping can be configured to shape traffic based on network conditions and signals, but policing does not respond to network conditions and signals.

12. To transmit one byte of data, the bucket must have one token.

13. If the size of data to be transmitted (in bytes) is smaller than the number of tokens, the traffic is called conforming. When traffic conforms, as many tokens as the size of data are removed from the bucket, and the conform action, which is usually forward data, is performed. If the size of data to be transmitted (in bytes) is larger than the number of tokens, the traffic is called exceeding. In the exceed situation, tokens are not removed from the bucket, but the action performed (exceed action) is either buffer and send data later (in the case of shaping) or drop or mark data (in the case of policing).

14. The formula showing the relationship between CIR, B_c, and T_c is as follows:

   CIR (bits per second) = B_c (bits) / T_c (seconds)

15. Frame Relay traffic shaping controls Frame Relay traffic only and can be applied to a Frame Relay subinterface or Frame Relay DLCI. Whereas Frame Relay traffic shaping supports Frame Relay fragmentation and interleaving (FRF.12), class-based traffic shaping does not. On the other hand, both class-based traffic shaping and Frame Relay traffic shaping interact with and support Frame Relay network congestion signals such as BECN and FECN. A router that is receiving BECNs shapes its outgoing Frame Relay traffic to a lower rate. If it receives FECNs—even if it has no traffic for the other end—it sends test frames with the BECN bit set to inform the other end to slow down.

16. Compression is a technique used in many of the link efficiency mechanisms. It reduces the size of data to be transferred; therefore, it increases throughput and reduces overall delay. Many compression algorithms have been developed over time. One main difference between compression algorithms is often the type of data that the algorithm has been optimized for. The success of compression algorithms is measured and expressed by the ratio of raw data to compressed data. When possible, hardware compression is recommended over software compression.

17. Layer 2 payload compression, as the name implies, compresses the entire payload of a Layer 2 frame. For example, if a Layer 2 frame encapsulates an IP packet, the entire IP packet is compressed. Layer 2 payload compression is performed on a link-by-link basis; it can be performed on WAN connections such as PPP, Frame Relay, HDLC, X.25, and LAPB. Cisco IOS supports Stacker, Predictor, and Microsoft Point-to-Point Compression (MPPC) as Layer

2 compression methods. The primary difference between these methods is their overhead and utilization of CPU and memory. Because Layer 2 payload compression reduces the size of the frame, serialization delay is reduced. An increase in available bandwidth (hence throughput) depends on the algorithm efficiency.

18. Header compression reduces serialization delay and results in less bandwidth usage, yielding more throughput and more available bandwidth. As the name implies, header compression compresses headers only. For example, RTP compression compresses RTP, UDP, and IP headers, but it does not compress the application data. This makes header compression especially useful when application payload size is small. Without header compression, the header (overhead)-to-payload (data) ratio is large, but with header compression, the overhead-to-data ratio.

19. Yes, you must enable fragmentation on a link and specify the maximum data unit size (called fragment size). Fragmentation must be accompanied by interleaving; otherwise, it will not have an effect. Interleaving allows packets of different flows to get between fragments of large data units in the queue.

20. Link efficiency mechanisms might not be necessary on all interfaces and links. It is important that you identify network bottlenecks and work on the problem spots. On fast links, many link efficiency mechanisms are not supported, and if they are, they might have negative results. On slow links and where bottlenecks are recognized, you must calculate the overhead-to-data ratios, consider all compression options, and make a choice. On some links, you can perform full link compression. On some, you can perform Layer 2 payload compression, and on others, you will probably perform header compression such as RTP or TCP header compression only. Link fragmentation and interleaving is always a good option to consider on slow links.

Chapter 6

"Do I Know This Already?" Quiz

1. D
2. B
3. A
4. C
5. D
6. C
7. A
8. B

9. C

10. D

Q&A

1. A VPN provides private network connectivity over a public/shared infrastructure. The same policies and security as a private network are offered using encryption, data integrity, and origin authentication.

2. QoS pre-classify is designed for tunnel interfaces such as GRE and IPsec.

3. **qos pre-classify** enables QoS pre-classify on an interface.

4. You can apply a QoS service policy to the physical interface or the tunnel interface. Applying a service policy to a physical interface causes that policy to affect all tunnel interfaces on that physical interface. Applying a service policy to a tunnel interface affects that particular tunnel only and does not affect other tunnel interfaces on the same physical interface. When you apply a QoS service policy to a physical interface where one or more tunnels emanate, the service policy classifies IP packets based on the post-tunnel IP header fields. However, when you apply a QoS service policy to a tunnel interface, the service policy performs classification on the pre-tunnel IP packet (inner packet).

5. The QoS SLA provides contractual assurance for parameters such as availability, throughput, delay, jitter, and packet loss.

6. The typical maximum end-to-end (one-way) QoS SLA requirements for voice delay <= 150 ms, jitter <= 30 ms, and loss <= 1 percent.

7. The guidelines for implementing QoS in campus networks are as follows:

■ Classify and mark traffic as close to the source as possible.

■ Police traffic as close to the source as possible.

■ Establish proper trust boundaries.

■ Classify and mark real-time voice and video as high-priority traffic.

■ Use multiple queues on transmit interfaces.

■ When possible, perform hardware-based rather than software-based QoS.

8. In campus networks, access switches require these QoS policies:

■ Appropriate trust, classification, and marking policies

■ Policing and markdown policies

■ Queuing policies

The distribution switches, on the other hand, need the following:

- DSCP trust policies

- Queuing policies

- Optional per-user micro-flow policies (if supported)

9. Control plane policing (CoPP) is a Cisco IOS feature that allows you to configure a quality of service (QoS) filter that manages the traffic flow of control plane packets. Using CoPP, you can protect the control plane of Cisco IOS routers and switches against denial of service (DoS) and reconnaissance attacks and ensure network stability (router/switch stability in particular) during an attack.

10. The four steps required to deploy CoPP (using MQC) are as follows:

Step 1   Define a packet classification criteria.

Step 2   Define a service policy.

Step 3   Enter control plane configuration mode.

Step 4   Apply a QoS policy.

Chapter 7

"Do I Know This Already?" Quiz

1. B
2. B
3. A
4. D
5. D
6. A
7. C
8. C
9. D
10. B

Q&A

1. Cisco AutoQoS has many benefits, including the following:

- It uses Cisco IOS built-in intelligence to automate generation of QoS configurations for most common business scenarios.

- It protects business-critical data applications in the Enterprise to maximize their availability.

- It simplifies QoS deployment.

- It reduces configuration errors.

- It makes QoS deployment cheaper, faster, and simpler.

- It follows the DiffServ model.

- It allows customers to have complete control over their QoS configuration.

- It enables customers to modify and tune the configurations that Cisco AutoQoS automatically generates to meet their specific needs or changes to the network conditions.

2. The two phases of AutoQoS evolution are AutoQoS VoIP and AutoQoS for Enterprise.

3. Cisco AutoQoS addresses the following five key elements:

   - Application classification

   - Policy generation

   - Configuration

   - Monitoring and reporting

   - Consistency

4. NBAR protocol discovery is able to identify and classify the following:

   - Applications that target a session to a well-known (UDP/TCP) destination port number, referred to as static port applications

   - Applications that start a control session using a well-known port number but negotiate another port number for the session, referred to as dynamic port applications

   - Some non-IP applications

   - HTTP applications based on URL, MIME type, or host name

5. You can enable Cisco AutoQoS on the following types of router interfaces or PVCs:

   - Serial interfaces with PPP or HDLC encapsulation.

   - Frame Relay point-to-point subinterfaces. (Multipoint is not supported.)

   - ATM point-to-point subinterfaces (PVCs) on both slow (<=768 kbps) and fast serial (>768 kbps) interfaces.

   - Frame Relay-to-ATM interworking links.

6.   The router prerequisites for configuring AutoQoS are as follows:

■ The router cannot have a QoS policy attached to the interface.

■ You must enable CEF on the router interface (or PVC).

■ You must specify the correct bandwidth on the interface or subinterface.

■ You must configure a low-speed interface (<= 768 Kbps) and an IP address.

7.   Following are the two steps (or phases) of AutoQoS for Enterprise:

1. Traffic is profiled using autodiscovery. You do this by entering the **auto qos discovery** command in the interface configuration mode.
2. MQC-based QoS policies are generated and deployed. You do this by entering the **auto qos** command in interface configuration mode.

8.   Following are the commands for verifying AutoQoS on Cisco routers:

■ **show auto discovery qos** allows you to examine autodiscovery results.

■ **show auto qos** allows you to examine Cisco AutoQoS templates and initial configuration.

■ **show policy-map interface** allows you to explore interface statistics for autogenerated policy.

9.   The commands for verifying AutoQoS on Cisco LAN switches are as follows:

■ **show auto qos** allows you to examine Cisco AutoQoS templates and the initial configuration.

■ **show policy-map interface** allows you to explore interface statistics for autogenerated policy.

■ **show mls qos maps** allows you to examine CoS-to-DSCP maps.

10.   The three most common Cisco AutoQoS issues that can arise, and their corresponding solutions, are as follows:

■ Too many traffic classes are generated; classification is overengineered.

Solution: Manually consolidate similar classes to produce the number of classes needed.

■ The configuration that AutoQoS generates does not automatically adapt to changing network traffic conditions.

Solution: Run Cisco AutoQoS discovery on a periodic basis, followed by re-enabling of Cisco AutoQoS.

■ The configuration that AutoQoS generates fits common network scenarios but does not fit some circumstances, even after extensive autodiscovery.

Solution: Manually fine-tune the AutoQoS-generated configuration.

11. You can obtain the following information from the output of the **show auto qos** command:

■ Number of traffic classes identified (class maps)

■ Traffic classification options selected (within class maps)

■ Traffic marking options selected (within policy maps)

■ Queuing mechanisms deployed, and their corresponding parameters (within policy maps)

■ Other QoS mechanisms deployed (within policy maps)

■ Where the autogenerated policies are applied: on the interface, subinterface, or PVC

12. Following are the two major reasons for modifying the configuration that AutoQoS generates:

■ The AutoQoS-generated commands do not completely satisfy the specific requirements of the Enterprise network.

■ The network condition, policies, traffic volume and patterns, and so on might change over time, rendering the AutoQoS-generated configuration dissatisfying.

13. You can modify and tune the AutoQoS-generated class maps and policy maps by doing the following:

■ Using Cisco QoS Policy Manager (QPM).

■ Directly entering the commands one at a time at the router command-line interface using MQC.

■ Copying the existing configuration, a class map for example, into a text editor and modifying the configuration using the text editor, offline. Next, using CLI, remove the old undesirable configuration and then add the new configuration by copying and pasting the text from the text editor. This is probably the easiest way.

14. MQC offers the following classification options, in addition to using NBAR:

■ Based on the specific ingress interface where the traffic comes from:

```
match input interface interface
```

■ Based on the Layer 2 CoS value of the traffic:

```
match cos cos-value [cos-value ...]
```

■ Based on the Layer 3 IP precedence value:

```
match ip precedence ip-prec-value [ip-prec-value ...]
```

■ Based on the Layer 3 IP DSCP value:

```
match ip dscp ip-dscp-value [ip-dscp-value ...]
```

■ Based on the RTP port value range:

```
match ip rtp starting-port-number port-range
```

Chapter 8

"Do I Know This Already?" Quiz

1. D
2. C
3. D
4. B
5. A
6. C
7. D
8. B
9. A
10. C

Q&A

1. DCF uses radio frequency (RF) carrier sense, inter-frame spacing (IFS), and random back-off/contention windows (CW) to accomplish collision avoidance.

2. IEEE defines 802.11e as the first wireless standard, adding QoS features to the existing IEEE 802.11b and IEEE 802.11a (and other) wireless standards.

3. While 802.11e was in the standardization process, Wi-Fi Alliance released a wireless QoS specification called Wi-Fi Multimedia (WMM) for the interim period.

4. WMM reduces the eight priority levels of 802.11e to four access categories: Platinum, Gold, Silver, and Bronze. Platinum (voice) maps to priority 6/7, Gold (video) maps to priority 5/6, Silver (best-effort) maps to priority 0/3, and Bronze (background) maps to priority 1/2.

5. 802.11e (and its subset WMM) provides Enhanced Distributed Coordination Function (EDCF) by using different contention window (CW)/back-off timer values for different priorities (access categories).

6. To address the centralized RF management needs of the Enterprises, Cisco designed a centralized lightweight access point wireless architecture with Split-MAC architecture as its core. Split-MAC architecture divides the 802.11 data and management protocols and access point capabilities between a lightweight access point (LWAP) and a centralized WLAN controller. The real-time MAC functions, including handshake with wireless clients, MAC layer encryption, and beacon handling, are assigned to the LWAP. The non-real-time functions, including frame translation and bridging, plus user mobility, security, QoS, and RF management, are assigned to the wireless LAN controller.

7. The real-time MAC functions that are assigned to the LWAP in the Split-MAC architecture include beacon generation, probe transmission and response, power management, 802.11e/WMM scheduling and queuing, MAC layer data encryption/decryption, control frame/message processing, and packet buffering.

8. The non-real-time MAC functions that are assigned to the wireless LAN controller in the Split-MAC architecture include association/disassociation, 802.11e/WMM resource reservation, 802.1x EAP, key management, authentication, fragmentation, and bridging between Ethernet and wireless LAN.

9. Lightweight Access Point Protocol (LWAPP) is used between the wireless LAN (WLAN) controller and the lightweight access point (LWAP) in the Split-MAC architecture. In the Cisco centralized lightweight access point wireless architecture (with Split-MAC architecture as its core), the WLAN controller ensures that traffic traversing between it and the LWAP maintains its QoS information. The WLAN data coming from the wireless clients to the LWAP is tunneled to the WLAN controller using LWAPP. In the opposite direction, the traffic coming from the wired LAN to the WLAN controller is also tunneled to the LWAP using LWAPP. You can set up the LWAPP tunnel over a Layer 2 or a Layer 3 network. In Layer 2 mode, the LWAPP data unit is in an Ethernet frame. Furthermore, the WLAN controller and the access point must be in the same broadcast domain and IP subnet. In Layer 3 mode, however, the 3 LWAPP data unit is in a UDP/IP frame. Moreover, the WLAN controller and access point can be in the same or different broadcast domains and IP subnets.

10. The **Controller** option from the web user interface menu bar provides access to many pages, including the QoS Profiles page. On the QoS Profiles page, you can view the names and descriptions of the QoS profiles, and you can edit each of the profiles by clicking on the **Edit** button.

Chapter 9

"Do I Know This Already?" Quiz

1. C
2. D
3. B
4. A
5. A
6. A
7. C
8. D
9. C
10. C

Q&A

1. Rogue access points impose threats to wireless LANs. A rogue access point is illegitimate; it has been installed without authorization. If an attacker installs a rogue access point and clients associate with it, the attacker can easily collect sensitive information such as keys, usernames, passwords, and MAC addresses. Unless the client has a way of authenticating the access point, a wireless LAN should have a method to detect rogue access points so that they can be removed. Furthermore, rogue access points are sometimes installed by attackers intending to interfere with the normal operations and effectively launch denial of service attacks.

2. Following are the weaknesses of basic 802.11 (WEP) security:

   ■ A lack of mutual authentication makes WEP vulnerable to rogue access points.

   ■ Usage of static keys makes WEP vulnerable to dictionary attacks.

   ■ Even with use of initialization vector (IV), attackers can deduct WEP keys by capturing enough data.

   ■ Configuring clients with the static WEP keys is nonscalable.

3. Following are the benefits of LEAP over the basic 802.11 (WEP):

   ■ Server-based authentication (leveraging 802.1x) using passwords, one-time tokens, public key infrastructure (PKI) certificates, or machine IDs

- Usage of dynamic WEP keys (also called session keys) through reauthenticating the user periodically and negotiating a new WEP key each time (Cisco Key Integrity Protocol or CKIP)

- Mutual authentication between the wireless client and the RADIUS server

- Usage of Cisco Message Integrity Check (CMIC) to protect against inductive WEP attacks and replays

4. The main improvements of WPA2 to WPA are usage of Advanced Encryption Standard (AES) for encryption and usage of Intrusion Detection System (IDS). However, WPA2 is more CPU-intensive than WPA mostly because of the usage of AES; therefore, WPA2 usually requires a hardware upgrade.

5. The important features and benefits of 802.1x/EAP are as follows:

- Usage of RADIUS server for AAA centralized authentication

- Mutual authentication between the client and the authentication server

- Ability to use 802.1x with multiple encryption algorithms, such as AES, WPA TKIP, and WEP

- Without user intervention, the ability to use dynamic (instead of static) WEP keys

- Support of roaming

6. The required components for 802.1x authentication are as follows:

- EAP-capable client (the supplicant)

- 802.1x-capable access point (the authenticator)

- EAP-capable RADIUS server (the authentication server)

7. The EAP-capable client requires an 802.1x-capable driver and an EAP supplicant. The supplicant might be provided with the client card, be native in the client operating system, or be obtained from the third-party software vendor. The EAP-capable wireless client (with the supplicant) sends authentication credentials to the authenticator.

8. Following are the main features and benefits of EAP-FAST:

- Supports Windows single sign-on for Cisco Aironet clients and Cisco-compatible clients

- Does not use certificates or require Public Key Infrastructure (PKI) support on client devices

- Provides for a seamless migration from Cisco LEAP

- Supports Windows 2000, Windows XP, and Windows CE operating systems

- Provides full support for 802.11i, 802.1x, TKIP, and AES

- Supports password expiration or change (Microsoft password change)

9. EAP-FAST has three phases:

Phase 0: Provision PAC
Phase 1: Establish secure tunnel
Phase 2: Client authentication

10. The important features and facts about EAP-TLS are these:

- EAP-TLS uses the Transport Layer Security (TLS) protocol.

- EAP-TLS uses Public Key Infrastructure (PKI).

- EAP-TLS is one of the original EAP authentication methods, and it is used in many environments.

- The supported clients for EAP-TLS include Microsoft Windows 2000, XP, and CE, plus non-Windows platforms with third-party supplicants, such as Meetinghouse.

- One of the advantages of Cisco and Microsoft implementation of EAP-TLS is that it is possible to tie the Microsoft credentials of the user to the certificate of that user in a Microsoft database, which permits a single logon to a Microsoft domain.

11. The important features and facts about PEAP are as follows:

- PEAP was developed by Cisco Systems, Microsoft, and RSA Security to the IETF.

- With PEAP, only the server authentication is performed using PKI certificate.

- PEAP works in two phases. In Phase 1, server-side authentication is performed and an encrypted tunnel (TLS) is created. In Phase 2, the client is authenticated using either EAP-GTC or EAP-MSCHAPv2 within the TLS tunnel.

- PEAP-MSCHAPv2 supports single sign-on, but Cisco PEAP-GTC supplicant does not support single logon.

12. Following are the important features of WPA:

Authenticated key management—WPA performs authentication using either IEEE 802.1x or preshared key (PSK) prior to the key management phase.
Unicast and broadcast key management—After successful user authentication, message integrity and encryption keys are derived, distributed, validated, and stored on the client and the AP.

Utilization of TKIP and MIC—Temporal Key Integrity Protocol (TKIP) and Message Integrity Check (MIC) are both elements of the WPA standard and they secure a system against WEP vulnerabilities such as intrusive attacks.

Initialization vector space expansion—WPA provides per-packet keying (PPK) via initialization vector (IV) hashing and broadcast key rotation. The IV is expanded from 24 bits (as in 802.11 WEP) to 48 bits.

13. 802.11i has three key security features:

   ■ 802.1x authentication

   ■ Advanced Encryption Standard (AES) encryption algorithm

   ■ Key management (similar to WPA)

14. The important features/facts about WPA2 are as follows:

   ■ It uses 802.1x for authentication. (It also supports preshared keys.)

   ■ It uses a similar method of key distribution and key renewal to WPA.

   ■ It supports PKC.

   ■ It implements AES.

   ■ It uses IDS.

15. The services that wireless IDS provides to address RF and standards-based vulnerabilities are as follows:

   ■ Detect, locate, and mitigate rogue devices.

   ■ Detect and manage RF interference.

   ■ Detect reconnaissance.

   ■ Detect management frames and hijacking attacks.

   ■ Enforce security configuration policies.

   ■ Perform forensic analysis and compliance reporting as complementary functions.

16. WPA and WPA2 have two modes: Enterprise mode and Personal mode. Each mode has encryption support and user authentication. Products that support both the preshared key (PSK) and the 802.1x authentication methods are given the term Enterprise mode. Enterprise mode is targeted at medium to large environments such as education and government departments. Products that only support PSK for authentication and require manual

configuration of a preshared key on the access point and clients are given the term Personal mode. Personal mode is targeted at small business environments such as small office, home office (SOHO).

Chapter 10

"Do I Know This Already?" Quiz

1. D
2. C
3. B
4. C
5. C
6. B
7. A
8. C
9. A
10. C
11. B
12. A
13. C

Q&A

1. Autonomous access points are configured individually. They require individual configuration because each access point operates independently. However, centralized configuration, monitoring, and management can be done through CiscoWorks WLSE. WDS provides the radio monitoring and management communication between the autonomous access points and CiscoWorks WLSE.

A WLAN Controller configures and controls lightweight access points. The lightweight access points depend on the controller for control and data transmission. However, REAP modes do not need the controller for data transmission. Cisco WCS can centralize configuration, monitoring, and management. Cisco WLAN Controllers can be implemented with redundancy within the wireless LAN controller groups.

2. No, the WLSE is part of CiscoWorks. WLSE supports basic centralized configuration, firmware, and radio management of autonomous access points.

3. You use CiscoWorks WLSE for medium to large enterprises and wireless verticals (up to 2500 WLAN devices). You use CiscoWorks WLSE Express for SMBs (250 to 1500 employees) and commercial and branch offices (up to 100 WLAN devices) looking for a cost-effective solution with integrated WLAN management and security services.

4. Cisco WCS runs on the Microsoft Windows and Linux platforms. It can run as a normal application or as a service, which runs continuously and resumes running after a reboot. Cisco WCS is designed to support 50 Cisco wireless LAN controllers and 1500 access points.

5. The simplest version of Cisco WCS, WCS Base, informs managers which access point a device is associated with. This allows managers to have an approximation of the device location. The optional version called WCS Location, the second level of WCS, provides users with the RF fingerprinting technology. It can provide location accuracy to within a few meters (less than 10 meters 90 percent of the time; less than 5 meters 50 percent of the time). The third and final option, the one with the most capabilities, is called WCS Location + 2700 Series Wireless Location Appliance. The WCS Location + 2700 Series Wireless Location Appliance provides the capability to track thousands of wireless clients in real time.

6. When lightweight access points on the WLAN power up and associate with the controllers, Cisco WCS immediately starts listening for rogue access points. When Cisco wireless LAN controller detects a rogue access point, it immediately notifies Cisco WCS, which creates a rogue access point alarm. When Cisco WCS receives a rogue access point message from Cisco wireless LAN controller, an alarm indicator appears in the lower-left corner of all Cisco WCS user interface pages.

7. You do not need to add Cisco lightweight access points to the Cisco WCS database. The operating system software automatically adds Cisco lightweight access points as they associate with existing Cisco wireless LAN controllers in the Cisco WCS database.

8. Yes, Cisco WCS supports SNMPv1, SNMPv2, and SNMPv3.

9. The WCS Network Summary page or Network Dashboard is displayed after logging in successfully. It is a top-level overview of the network with information about controllers, coverage areas, access points, and clients. You can add systems configuration and devices from this page. Access the Network Summary page from other areas by choosing **Monitor > Network Summary**.

10. The default username is root, and the default password is public.

11. WLAN Management for autonomous APs is CiscoWorks Wireless LAN Solution Engine (WLSE). Lightweight APs use Cisco WCS for management. Both provide administrative and monitoring capabilities for large WLAN deployments.

CiscoWorks WLSE simplifies and automates the deployment and security of WLANs. CiscoWorks WLSE provides Intrusion Detection System (IDS) capabilities for detecting rogue access points, ad-hoc networks, and excess management frames on the air that typically signal a WLAN attacks.

Cisco Wireless Control System (WCS) can centrally manage all Cisco wireless LAN controllers and lightweight APs. Cisco WCS also provides advanced features such as location tracking and visual heat maps for better visibility into the RF environment.

12. WLSE automatically shuts down the rogue APs when they are detected and located by disabling the switch ports. This is called the automatic rogue AP suppression policy and it can be disabled.

   WCS can take appropriate steps toward containment if desired. Containment is when APs close to the rogue send deauthenticate and disassociate messages to the rogue's clients. To see a rogue AP located on the building or campus map, a small skull-and-crossbones indicator appears at the calculated location.

13. Cisco WCS Base is a full-featured software product for WLAN monitoring and control. Wireless client data access, rogue AP detection, and containment are examples of the services offered in Cisco WCS Base. A single device can be located to the nearest AP.

   WCS Location includes all base features plus more. It features the on-demand monitoring of any single device using RF fingerprinting technology, providing high location accuracy. Any rogue APs, client, or device tracking can be performed on-demand within 10 meters or 33 feet using RF fingerprinting.

   Cisco Wireless Location Appliance scales on-demand location tracking to a new level, significantly improving the functionality of Cisco WCS Location. The Cisco Wireless Location Appliance can track up to 1500 devices simultaneously.

Index

Numerics